Diaries of Mario M. Cuomo
THE CAMPAIGN FOR GOVERNOR

Diaries of
Mario M. Cuomo

THE CAMPAIGN FOR GOVERNOR

RANDOM HOUSE
New York

Book design by Charlotte Staub

Library of Congress Cataloging in Publication Data
Cuomo, Mario Matthew.
    Diaries of Mario M. Cuomo.
    Includes index.
    1. Cuomo, Mario Matthew. 2. New York (State)—Politics
and government—1951– . 3. Elections—New York
(State)—History—20th century. 4. New York (State)—
Governors—Biography. I. Title.
F125.C86A33 1984   974.7'043'0924   83-43200
ISBN 0-394-53695-9

To my family

Preface

The diary entries set out in the pages that follow were originally not intended for publication, nor even to be read except by
me. For some ten years I have kept a journal more or less regularly as a vehicle for adjusting my own perspective. I've found
it a convenient way of stepping back occasionally to see what
forms and shades my sometimes hectic activities were leaving on
the canvas of my life.

That the last decade is also the precise span of my public career
is not altogether coincidental. Leaving private life and moving
into a world that was dramatically different in so many ways
made me feel it was necessary to stay closer to my charts and
course. Making random notes about people, events and decisions
that were at the front of my mind helped me do that, and I
preferred the diary to imposing on my family the burden of
weighing occurrences and decisions that were basically my responsibility, especially since they were already being incon-
venienced so much by my decision to enter this difficult and
consuming profession.

I had no reservations about keeping my journal: indeed, I
continue to make regular entries. I did, however, have reservations about publishing these excerpts. My principal concern was
that someone other than myself might unnecessarily be embarrassed or offended. I have sought to avoid that result even at the
cost of not making available to the public every entry that appears in the original. If there are nevertheless individuals who
feel they have been dealt with less than fairly, then I regret it and

plead that the imperfection of my recollection and the inartfulness of my language are probably at fault.

Whatever this book is worth as a book, it would have been worth a lot less were it not for three people. Mary Tragale is responsible for the original manuscript. It was typed by her—for the most part, at home—from my handwritten pages. She was my first secretary in 1958 and, after taking time out to help raise her beautiful family, has returned in recent years to see that I am not too far misdirected by some of the distractions of the political life. Her opinions in general—and on this work in particular—have always been relentlessly candid and uniformly helpful.

Jason Epstein is responsible for the publication of both my books. He is bright, sensitive, interested and interesting, although occasionally politically errant as far as I'm concerned. His confidence and encouragement have been unremitting, as is my gratitude.

Not the least thing I'm grateful to him for is asking Corona Machemer to serve as my editor. Her guidance has been persistent and persuasive but never impatient. I'm sure she writes better than most whose writing she improves: surely that is true in my case. Most of all, I thank her for being nice.

And whatever the life and experience that are described in the book are worth, they would have been worth very much less if it weren't for Matilda and Margaret and Andrew and Maria and Madeline and Christopher Charles and the beautiful family that surrounds us. I try to describe many things in my private journal; I make no effort really to describe Matilda and the kids. I didn't have to. All I had to do was express over and over my love and my gratitude—and my regret at not being able to do more for them.

MARIO M. CUOMO
December 1983

Contents

Diaries of Mario M. Cuomo
THE CAMPAIGN FOR GOVERNOR

Introduction

These diaries are my account of the New York gubernatorial campaigns of 1982, from my decision to run—no spur-of-the-moment one, it took a year to make—through the primary campaign against New York City's Mayor Edward Koch, the general election and the inauguration. It was a "local" election on which the nation focused to a remarkable degree for a nonpresidential year, probably for two reasons. First, the campaigns set a record for money spent in such elections. The Republican candidate, Lewis Lehrman, spent $13.9 million, $9.6 million from his own personal fortune. All together the losing candidates spent a total of $17.5 million—and the winner $4.8 million.

Money, it thus turned out, wasn't everything—although it came very close to being so in the end. The second factor of national significance was the fact that both the primary and the general elections were perceived as clashes over fairly clear ideas and issues. A *New York Times Magazine* cover story on the general election called it the "New Conservatism versus the Old Liberalism," and although I found the legend annoyingly simplistic, like most political clichés it embodied a degree of truth. Both Ed Koch and Lew Lehrman argued that government was trying to do too much; that more should be left to market forces and volunteers. I argued that their view was reactive and sloganeering, and that it might have been computed from the latest popularity polls. I suggested that a kind of government-aided progressive pragmatism—what I was eventually to call a "family kind of politics"—would serve the public better. Frankly, I have always had doubts about how much of this ideological debate ever registered with the voters; nevertheless, the forces that create perceptions that become realities have left the opinion that, contrary to expectations aroused by the victory of conservative Republican Ronald Reagan in the 1980 presidential election, "traditional Democratic principles" prevailed in 1982 in New York.

Whatever one calls my political philosophy—whether traditional Democratic principles or a family kind of politics or progressive pragmatism—my commitment to it goes back a long way, well before I entered politics.

Some people become Democrats or Republicans the way they become Catholics or Jews or Protestants—they're born to it. I became a Catholic because at a stage in my life when I was too young to understand, my mother and father took me to church, had a priest pour holy water on my head and say words in Latin. I became a Democrat in about the same way. Although I was considerably older, the ritual was almost as automatic. I chose to register as a Democrat because all the people we knew in my neighborhood who had voted voted Democrat. And, why not? Poor, or struggling middle-class, immigrants and the children of immigrants, in the era of the Great Depression—one could hardly have been surprised at their choice.

But while affiliation was thrust on me in the one case and undertaken casually in the other, eventually both my religion and my politics became matters of conviction, and I have never felt that the two commitments were incompatible.

As I understand it, the so-called Christian ethic, while recognizing that we are too weak to do it perfectly, calls on us nevertheless to try to do good things for other people. Prudently; without ignoring our obligations to ourselves; realistically. But insistently. Trying always to arrange a package of justice, charity and mercy, proffering it beyond the walls of our own homes, our own churches, our own lives.

More than thirty years ago, when I registered to vote, it seemed to me that despite many failures to live up to them, the traditional principles of the Democratic party came closer to giving political content to this ideal than the tenets of the Republicans. It seems so to me now. The thrust of the "New Conservatism," as enunciated by Ronald Reagan in 1980 and Lew

Lehrman in 1982, was that government's principal role should be to help the strong flourish, in the hope that the force of their economic ambition—or charity—would take care of the rest of us. It is, it seems to me, a philosophy that is defensible only in the abstract. It depends on the cynical assumption that those who do well will accept the sacrifice of others as the necessary price offered up for the commonweal—and the effects on human beings of the policies derived from it are devastating. They were brought home to me with particular poignancy early in my first year as governor when I traveled with Lane Kirkland of the AFL-CIO and other union and government officials to Lackawanna, New York, where a steel mill had just been closed. In my diary for April 30, 1983, I wrote:

> All around us there are evidences that we have failed as a society to do the good things we could have done.
>
> New York State has within its borders some of the richest people and places in the world. Million-dollar condominiums used twice a month in Manhattan; baseball players who earn more than a million dollars and complain; Rolls-Royces parked behind Jaguars alongside Porsches in affluent suburban neighborhoods. Success, comfort, liberty—everywhere, from Clinton to Suffolk.
>
> And in the midst of affluence, children, unwashed and unwatched, frolic in streets, surrounded by drug addicts, prostitutes and every kind of social disorientation. The largest army of homeless people since the Great Depression now roams our streets, vacant, aimless, uncaring and uncared for.
>
> Still we politicians are able to claim success, almost always.
>
> But not today in Lackawanna. We looked down into the faces of steelworkers discharged by the Bethlehem Company, which had surrendered to foreign competition and obsolescence.
>
> They sat in the hall, refusing to stand when others did for the governor or the congressman or even the national leader of their own union, because to stand would be to approve of something. They don't feel like approval at the moment. They are 26 and 33 and 55. Uncomplicated. They want a family, a glass of beer on the weekend, a television on which to watch Ron Jaworski; a chance to vote if they feel like it.
>
> Everything they've ever wanted depended on their being able to earn their own bread with dignity, as steelworkers. They were raised taking for granted that they would have that opportunity. Through all

of their youth they remembered "Help Wanted" signs on the face of the Bethlehem plant. They knew nothing of protectionism or shifting technologies or even the effects of wars on economies. Life was an easy calculus: if you were willing to work hard, you could earn the simple pleasures. Since they were willing to work hard and wanted only the simple pleasures, their equations were balanced, their lives untroubled. Then their company failed them, and shocked them, by telling them that they would no longer be allowed to work because there would be no job for them.

Now their lives have become complicated and confused. Now they have become bitter and they will not stand to greet a governor or anyone else associated with a system that has failed them.

I stood on a stage with Lane Kirkland and all the local leaders, aching with frustration because I knew I had no answer that would satisfy them.

If I believed there *is* no answer, it would be bad enough. But I know with all my heart—and mind—that we can make it better than it is.

Surely it is wrong to say that twenty years ago we could not have foreseen the coming of obsolescence, the gathering of forces that would humble our outdated efforts. Surely it is even more wrong to say that it is too late now to reindustrialize. We can find ways to restore the old industries. Is it not foolish to suggest that a nation that has committed the largest part of its wealth to a defense establishment that depends on steel and the capacity to bend it can turn its back on its own ability to do that work?

It is not necessary to abandon our old industries in an exhaustive pursuit of new ones. Both can flourish.

What hurts most is knowing that it can be done but hasn't been.*

If I believed that nothing could be done, that there was no answer, I would not be in politics. But there is an answer, and it is not to turn our back as a nation on any region, or, as the economic wagon train moves on, to abandon those left behind. I agree that government should allow the strong, the wealthy, the so-called producers to stay strong, and even encourage them to grow stronger. But I also believe that there are two major groups that deserve more of government's attention than they are receiving at the moment. The first consists of those who work

---

*This entry was the basis for a piece that appeared on the Op-Ed page of the New York *Times* on May 21, 1983.

for a living—not because a psychiatrist suggested to them that it would be a good way to fill the tedious interval between birth and eternity, but because they have to work. People not poor enough to be on welfare but not rich enough to be worry-free. People who labor, live modestly, ask little and get less than they deserve: the so-called middle class. The second group is made up of those who want to be in the first but haven't been able to make it: those who want to work but can't because they're too old or too frail or because there just isn't a job for them.

These are things I have said a thousand times in a hundred different ways beginning with my first campaign in 1974. If such views are called "traditional Democratic principles," I find that perfectly acceptable.

In the campaigns of 1982, however, my opponents sought to make of this "traditionalism" a vice. It's not difficult. So few people are ever satisfied with the status quo that if a government or a political party, no matter what its principles, has been in power long enough to be perceived as having created the conditions that exist, it becomes vulnerable. In 1982, when I was campaigning for governor, I was also lieutenant governor in the Democratic administration of Hugh Carey, which had been in place for eight years. Hence, I needed a new way to describe my political philosophy—not a way to fool the people into "buying" the same old politics disguised as something new, but a way to make them listen to what I was saying without concluding that it was somehow out of date.

I found it in the most extraordinarily obvious place; I found it in the idea of "family." That concept described as well as it can be described by me the indispensable importance of sharing benefits and burdens, the notion of communal strength and of obligation to the whole. It became the theme of my campaign—"The Family of New York." I spent eight months proclaiming it as a platform, and, on January 1, 1983, I had the great honor and privilege of spending thirty minutes repeating it as a pledge.

It is a notion that owes less to the arguments of political philosophers than to my own experience—and I can think of no better way to explain what I mean by it than to describe my own family.

In 1975 the Romulus Club in Buffalo, New York, asked me

to tell a group of professionals about the lessons I had been taught by my "upbringing." This is part of what I said:

My mother and father are Neopolitan. Actually, they're from just outside Naples, in the Provincia di Salerno. They came to America, with hundreds of thousands of other Italians, in the late twenties, illiterate, without money or property and with only a few friends. My father worked awhile in New Jersey, cleaning what were euphemistically called trenches: they were in fact sewers. He was like most of the other immigrants: powerless but prideful; anguished by a lack of education but ambitious; frightened by a society he didn't know but forceful about making his way in. And always, cursed with that unrelenting Italian passion, the passion for the family; a driving desire to sacrifice a large part of his own life only to make something better for his children; that ultimate humility that gives up nearly everything to the next generation.

By the time he and my mother had their third child, it was clear to him that he would have to do something more than dig "trenches" to provide what he wanted for his family. He opened a grocery store with the few pennies they had saved. It was in South Jamaica, in Queens— an Italian-Black-German-Irish-Polish neighborhood, inhabited by the poor and the nearly poor who lived in close to miserable conditions but were free from real frustration, because they had never experienced much better.

The store was open twenty-four hours a day, and by the time I was born in 1932, during the Depression, my father was making a living from sandwiches he made in the early morning for the construction crews and quick midnight snacks he prepared for the night shift in the factory across the street. In between, his store was the neighborhood corner grocery.

Almost everything he did, he did for his children. The small bankbooks—each small deposit a new dream for his kids. Every dollar a little bit closer to a sit-down reception for my sister Marie's wedding. A little bit better for his children than he and my mother had for themselves. And of the little that was left, he and Momma sent money religiously to the parents they had left behind in Italy.

My father never had a man-to-man talk with me or my brother. My father never had time for long drives in the country, where he could teach us about life. He never had time to counsel us on school; he only had time to insist that we study and get A's and be good.

He never sermonized or lectured. But he taught us, and my mother taught us, every single day—just by being what they were. They taught us the simple values: respect for your family, respect for your obligation to your children and to the parents who made you and raised you.

They taught us all we needed to know about the importance of family to society, and they did this just by being what they were.

My father paid his taxes to the government of the great land that had given him opportunity. He sent his eldest son, my brother, Frank, off to war without complaining that he needed him to deliver the groceries, and he kept his star in the window of the store for the duration. He lived by the rules: the law. He wouldn't violate the rationing—sugar only with stamps—because that goes for everybody; that's the law.

Poppa had calluses on both hands. I saw him once literally bleed from the bottom of his feet. He had a heart attack when he was fifty years of age. One day he fell down an open stairwell at the produce market at three o'clock in the morning, carrying a sack of potatoes to his small truck, a sack that was almost as big as he was, because he was a very little man physically even then. But in so doing he taught us all about the dignity of work and man's instinct to survive by his own hand wherever possible. No monk bearing the inscription "to labor is to pray" could have taught us more.

And he taught us about God's delights for man. How his eyes gleamed on the occasion when he opened the new giant provolone just before Easter every year! The four-foot provolone that had been hanging in the window for months awaiting the ceremonial day. On that day the neighbors stood around for the annual ritual, and my father would pierce the provolone and slide out the sample cores. Everyone tasting. Everyone slapping him on the back and offering him compliments. "Andrea, this is your best provolone ever."

Oh, the Genoa salami and the prosciutto and the bread, hot from the ovens of Lanzone, the baker down the block! And the glory of the fresh fruit! Cherries, peaches, tart Italian prunes. I tell you, nothing Omar Khayyám ever wrote taught me more about the delights of the food God lets us eat than did my father's store.

And to have this food at the beach on Sunday mornings! Because, finally, my father decided he could afford the luxury of a single morning a week—on Sundays, of course—to take the family out. Imagine being nine or ten years old and having this food in the summer, at the ocean, sitting on the clean, white sand of the beautiful beaches of Long Island or on the sweet, clean grass of the beautiful parks of Queens County. My father would bite a piece of grass or splash us with a handful of the Atlantic Ocean and say to us, "You see, kids, the beautiful things that God has made."

I was young then and didn't appreciate these things the way I should have. But I grew older. And I did come to appreciate the beauty of

being an Italian American in this country and learn to cherish the
contributions those magnificent immigrants made, not in Roman sculpture or opera or law or philosophy . . . I inherited very little of that.
What they gave me and what they had to give our society was, I believe,
a lot more permanent and more valuable. For what indeed does our
society need more now than respect for family; the sense of obligation
to senior citizens; a shameless, bold patriotism; a respect for work; a
sense of law and order; a recognition of the overriding importance of
education; a gratitude for God's nature and a feeling of responsibility
for it? And most of all, simple love.

What I said about my parents in this speech I might have
written about the two people who eventually became my father-
and mother-in-law. Charles and Mary Raffa were extraordinarily
like Andrea and Immaculata Cuomo. Charles—Carmelo then—
also came from the Mezzogiorno, from Messina, in Sicily. Like
Andrea, he had arrived in the United States with little more than
courage and a desire to avail himself and his family of the opportunities afforded by the New World. He, too, was followed by
his wife about a year later, and their first son was also—by a
strange coincidence—named Frank. The Raffas' struggles, their
strengths, their eventual success differed from the Cuomos' only
in degree. Charlie Raffa became a highly successful and respected businessman in Brooklyn, a manufacturer of supermar-
ket equipment. He and Mary raised in comfort five children—
Frank, Sam, Matilda, who was to become my wife, Joe and
Nancy. They taught the same lessons my parents had taught, and
in the same way—silently, just by being what they were.
    For the last thirty years, most members of the two families,
Matilda's and mine, have continued to live within easy visiting
distance of one another in the Metropolitan New York City area.
Only Joey strayed any real distance; he lives now in San Diego
with his wife and their two girls. But Matilda and I still have our
home in Queens, a house not far from the furnished apartment
in which we began our married life, and our five children grew
up as part of an extended family, surrounded by grandparents,
aunts and uncles and cousins, a source of continuity and stability
even as our individual circumstances changed.
    Like all families, extended or otherwise, ours has had prob-

lems and successes, known joy and heartbreak. Margaret and Andrew Mark took the brunt of the early years of our marriage, years of financial insecurity when I was a law student and young lawyer, and Matilda taught school. Maria and Madeline grew up during another stage of our lives, in which success on behalf of one or two community groups entangled me in a whole series of cases on behalf of individuals and communities against governments, cases that precipitated my political career. And Christopher, our beautiful second son—a lefty and a first baseman—who was born in 1970, lost a part of his childhood to politics.

But through it all the extended family has remained close, supportive of one another. Similar in many ways, all of us are also different. Some stronger than others, some luckier than others, some gentler than others. One thing, however, has always been clear: our coming together and staying together as a family has been good for all of us. The sharing of benefits and burdens has given us all a strength none of us would have had alone.

Why shouldn't that be true for polities as well?

Though the idea of family is the bedrock on which my political philosophy rests, there are two other influences that are part of its foundation: ideas I formed early about religion and the law. As I read this diary, I find their effects everywhere—sometimes explicitly, more often implicitly, but pervasively.

For whatever combination of genetic, environmental and educational reasons, I have always found it easier to discern a challenge than to acknowledge success. Momma and Poppa, I suppose, had something to do with that. So did the six o'clock mass at St. Monica's Church across the street from the cemetery. There on dark winter mornings in cassock and surplice I would recite "*Ad Deum, qui laetificat*" to begin my prayers as an altar boy. Then I would struggle carefully, apprehensively, through the more difficult prayers—the *Confiteor* and the *Suscipiat*—and the many intricate moves that, if done perfectly, could earn a server the "big time," a solemn high mass on Sunday!

The whole religious experience of Catholics like myself in that time and place painted for us a world of moral pitfalls that needed to be avoided in order to earn an eternal peace. It was as though God had created the world as a kind of hard passage to eternity. It was the ultimate in the "carrot and stick" approach to religious philosophy, with the stick being a lot more ominous than the carrot was appealing.

Of course that's not the way it was supposed to be. Those who were learned enough or wise enough saw in our religion even forty years ago the kind of joy and hope and affirmation that is apparent now every Sunday morning at mass. But for the simple folk of South Jamaica, in Queens County, who came from behind the grocery stores and from the tenements and from the little houses on Liverpool Street, it was often a world of guilt and repentance and renewed effort to avoid the final defeat. Seen that way, the greatest danger was forming an attachment to the things of this world that would distract one from the long-range—indeed, from the eternal—view.

I see things a little differently today. So do the modern young altar boys who have been freed from having to stumble through the *Suscipiat.* But I am sure that I will never be totally free of the tentativeness, the concern—even, from time to time, the twinges of guilt—that accompany anything I might be tempted to regard as material success. Primary night, the general election, the inaugural, a thousand congratulations and embraces and even cheers: all of them create a little discomfort that, if detected, might even be mistaken for ingratitude.

So I am not surprised to find all through this diary self-interrogation about motive and direction and result. Anyone who went to Father Eugene Erny for confession, and prayed that the old German pastor wouldn't recognize the voice from the darkened cubicle on the other side of the screen, will understand this syndrome.

There was also a bright side to our old-fashioned religion, for those disposed to see it. It was the joy of giving, as compared to the joy of having. If you wanted to earn that carrot and avoid that stick, you could do it by sharing, contributing, helping. That's why they called them—those marvelous, inscrutable women, those faces surrounded in starched white linen and flowing black —the Sisters of Charity. Their whole mission at St. Monica's and elsewhere was to teach that while you were suffering the pains of denying yourself temporary and superficial delights, you could also earn yourself an occasional moment of warmth and even, my

God . . . self-satisfaction! You could do it by helping the sick, feeding the hungry, comforting the bereaved.

It is this part of my background that has always made it difficult for me to accept the so-called conservative idea that, when it comes to government's redistributive function, "God helps those whom God has helped, and if He's left you out, who are we to presume on His will?" And ten years of Vincentian training at St. John's Prep and St. John's University only reinforced my conviction that if St. Francis of Assisi were alive today, and was reckless enough to get involved in politics, he would be fighting for some kind of progressivism that sought to help people improve their lives. I just can't see him arguing for the kind of social Darwinism that has been thrust upon us in recent years. (That some of the current believers in "survival of the fittest" were altar boys with me nearly forty years ago, or were my schoolmates, never ceases to surprise me.)

I suppose that to some extent the patterns of conduct and concern that are formed early in life don't really change a great deal, at least not fundamentally. Surely, some refinement of manner, some flourish, the ability to deal in nuances, may come with a few gray hairs at the temple. But the instincts born in the incense and the Baltimore catechism, amidst the groceries piled high in the back of the store, or while sitting alone in the backyard in the summer's heat lost in a book—those instincts operate through every campaign, every legislative session, even every decision on what words to write down for other people to read.

I suspect they also had something to do with shortening my career as a professional baseball player.

Other than school and St. Monica's Church, my youth was spent in three activities: reading, playing ball and working in the store. Of these, what I liked best and did most was play ball. I loved being totally involved: every bit of energy and attention concentrated on grabbing a rebound or getting to the line drive headed for the gap between me and my right fielder. Left to read and think, I would spend my time analyzing, probing, trying to find short and simple answers to profound and complex questions. But to play ball was to suspend for a while the arduous and frustrating task of looking into every situation for some ultimate purpose. It was to use all of one's strength, all of one's being, in a single exciting episode—the game, which had a beginning, a middle and an end, all in one day—and for as long as it lasted, there was no need and little temptation to puzzle about deeper meanings.

A series of good games on baseball fields in Queens and Bridgeport, Connecticut, caught the attention of a Pittsburgh Pirate scout and, at nineteen, I wound up receiving a small bonus to become a professional baseball player. For a couple of months I was in heaven, playing center field seven days a week with a Pirate farm team in Georgia in towns called Brunswick, Way-cross, Thomasville and Valdosta, and I did well enough for the organization to schedule me to go up a few notches the next season to a team in a higher league, in Waco, Texas.

I never went. I spent the next winter thinking a great deal about playing ball and how much I enjoyed it. Perhaps because I enjoyed it so much, the old instincts made me uncomfortable. There had to be more to life than playing ball. I felt I had to do something else. I didn't know what, but I knew—I thought—that I had to look beyond center field for it.

And so I went to St. John's, and found and fell in love with Our Lady of the Law. The years of study at St. John's Law School and two years as a law clerk to the Honorable Adrian Paul Burke of New York State's highest court, the Court of Appeals, were the beginning of an affair that would last a lifetime. I found the beauty of the law's logic and power awesome. And when I learned to use it—as a practicing lawyer—to serve what I thought were good ends, the daily joy of the office and the courtroom became so absorbing that they threatened to eclipse the other parts of my life. I was particularly taken by my work as *pro bono* counsel to criminal defendants who could not afford an attorney. Twice I was assigned to handle appeals for men sentenced to the electric chair. After years of argument, both death sentences were commuted, but those two experiences—the visits to death row, the sight of the electric chair, the growing knowledge of the fragility and vulnerability of our system of justice—made indelible impressions on me.

The practice of law in America is often seen as productive of conflict, but such has not been my experience. For I have learned from it what is, I think, the essence of my political philosophy, something more basic than whatever is implied by "traditional Democratic principles" or even "a family kind of politics." And that is reasonableness. Not an addiction to ideology or pat phrases or canned solutions, but an intelligent application of general principles to specific situations. So viewed, the truth is often found at neither Scylla nor Charybdis but somewhere near the middle of the straits, and effective government—despite the competitive frenzies of campaigns—must be more a matter of compromise and mediation than confrontation.

It is evident, then, on reflection, that my approach to public life, in both content and style, is an extension of all that I had lived and learned before I entered politics "officially" in 1974. I have developed no new talents or strengths, or even, I am afraid, new basic points of view. In a way, it has been like trying another case: I have applied whatever skills I had to each new set of facts.

For the most part, the transition from private to public life was a smooth one, but it has produced one hard question arising out of the apparent paradox created by what seem to be the conflicting values of religious belief and governmental action. I have given a great deal of thought to the matter of where private morality ends and public policy begins, but still the question remains a delicate one.*

No doubt the basic strength of our democratic system lies in the fact that it allows us greater freedom than any other government on earth. So we are free to conduct our private affairs as we wish. We are also free to argue that our laws should be changed so that everyone would be required to lead his or her private life as we wish. At this moment, somewhere in this nation groups are marching up and down the sidewalk calling for "Nazism" or "pacifism." Others demand a nuclear freeze or insist that God be recognized in the public schools as he was at P.S. 50 in Queens half a century ago, when King David's psalm was read in the assembly to all the children whatever they or their

---

*At about the time this portion of the introduction was being written, I was asked to address the congregation at Sunday mass at the Episcopal church of St. John the Divine in New York. My homily, which dealt with this subject more extensively than is possible here—and with predictably mixed results—appears on pp. 462–68.

parents believed. Many demand that homosexuality be "legitimated"; still others that abortion be declared a crime under any circumstances . . . or almost any circumstances.

We revel in the fact that no policeman has the right to halt these expressions of opinion, no legislative body or governor the right to silence them.

But this practically absolute ability to advocate raises questions about how the ability should be used by a public official.

Am I, as a Catholic governor who was elected to serve Protestants, Jews, Moslems, Sikhs, deists, animists, agnostics and atheists, obliged to seek to legislate my particular morality, in all of its exquisite detail? And if I fail, am I then required to surrender stewardship rather than risk hypocrisy?

The question comes up frequently. The answer, I think, is found in the organic law on which our democracy is built, the Constitution. The geniuses who wrote that instrument had the chance to select a specific religion or formal morality and make it an article of civic duty. They chose not to because that was precisely the condition in other parts of the world from which many of their forebears had fled. Instead—as I read this wonderful instrument—it says that no group has the right to insist that the rest of the community follow its religious views. It provides simply that where matters of private morality are involved—that is, belief or actions that don't impinge on other people or deprive them of their rights—the state has no right to intervene. I like the principle.

As a result of it, while the relationship between my private philosophical commitment and the law we make and enforce for the commonweal remains difficult to articulate, I have for the most part felt comfortable living with both of them simultaneously. My Church allows me to participate in a government that does not enforce adherence to all my Church's mandates; and my government regards my religion as irrelevant and will not permit itself to enforce religious mandates for fear of having to choose among many conflicting ones.

All of this, however, is not to say that our Constitution is simply an invitation to selfishness. In it is also embodied a central truth of the Judeo-Christian tradition—that is, a sense of the common good. The Constitution says to me, as the Gospel says to me, that freedom isn't license; that liberty creates responsibility; that we have been given freedom in order to encourage us to pursue that common good. And if the Constitution restricts the powers of the state in order to save us from the temptation to judge and persecute others, it does not thereby deny the necessity of the shared commitment to help one another—a shared commitment that is the basis for justice and mercy and human dignity and, therefore, the basis of any religion that believes in a loving God.

Seen that way, there is a perfect consistency between everything I believe privately and everything I am free to do publicly.

PART I

Deciding to Run

It was by way of the law that I came to politics—or, rather, that politics came to me, for until 1974 I had never even considered the possibility of a political career. Now, however, looking back, I can see that the beginning was actually in 1960, when I was retained as counsel by a group of scrap dealers and junkyard owners from Willets Point in Queens whose land was scheduled for condemnation by the city of New York to accommodate the World's Fair of 1964.

A three-year battle ended successfully when the Court of Appeals agreed with my plea on behalf of the Willets Point people. That victory attracted the attention of some homeowners in Corona, Queens, mostly hard-working Italian families who were threatened by a city administration that wanted to bulldoze their entire community to build a high school. After six years of litigation and negotiation, in 1972 we won a compromise that saved most of the homes.

The victory in Corona was a memorable experience. Many of those who lived there had never known another home. When confronted by the power of a government they did not know and believed they could not affect, they felt nothing but fear and confusion. To have dealt with that power—indeed, fought with it, and survived—exhilarated them. It gave them a new sense of assurance and comfort with a system of laws and government that until then had been mostly a tax bill, a policeman and a summons to war. The experience had much the same effect on me.

Shortly after the Corona situation was resolved, I found myself in the midst of the so-called Forest Hills controversy, which erupted when the city tried to move some 840 poor families— mostly Black and on welfare—into an established middle-class white community in Queens, as part of the old "scatter-site" housing program. The attempt created what appeared to be an irreconcilable and bitterly hostile dispute between residents of Forest Hills and the city administration, a dispute that was to have the ugliest racial and religious implications. Unable to re- solve it, and pleased by the way I had managed the Corona problem, Mayor John Lindsay asked me to mediate the conflict.

It was an unusual assignment, perhaps even a unique one. I was not a public official. I was not a party to the controversy. I hadn't represented anyone in the dispute and I wasn't even a mediator. But despite the novelty and uncertainty, the opportu- nity to help was irresistible.

By the time I became involved, the two sides had driven themselves into intractable opposition. Those who favored the project, including most of what thought of itself as New York's liberal community, insisted that the entire project be built exactly as proposed: three twenty-four-story buildings, 840 units in all, occupying two square blocks in the heart of Forest Hills. Those who opposed it, the residents who felt it would bring crime, disorientation and reduced property values to their comfortable middle-class lives, wanted the entire project to go elsewhere.

In a dramatic way, the conflict revealed tensions that had been developing for a long time in New York and in the nation. A community that had previously seemed progressive was now being asked to demonstrate its commitment to its principles. The price was accepting the inconvenience and, as they saw it, the danger of having poor people as neighbors. Forest Hills taught a whole nation lessons about the difference between political theory and the reality of sacrifice.

Several weeks of discussion with hundreds of people on both sides of the issue led to proposal of a compromise that would permit the construction of a smaller project with a number of features—buildings only twelve stories high, a fixed percentage of the apartments for the elderly, apartment ownership rather than rental—designed to alleviate the concerns of the neighbors. After a difficult period of explanation and intense negotiation, the compromise was accepted, and the project was eventually built.*

Until Corona and Forest Hills, I was perfectly content with a professional career that had brought me satisfaction as a lawyer and an adjunct professor of law at St. John's. I felt I had been able to make my contribution to the community through efforts like Willets Point, Corona and Forest Hills and through constant activity with bar associations, civic groups and my church. Our family was by then living comfortably in a house in Queens, close to all those we loved most and free of real intrusion from the world outside our own. We wanted for very little that was important.

Corona and Forest Hills were heavily publicized, however, and the public recognition led almost naturally to opportunities for public service. Mayor Lindsay offered me a number of commissioner-level appointments; political leaders suggested I run for everything from borough president to governor, and some newspaper columnists invited me to enter the lists.

I was—understandably, I think—most reluctant to give up any part of a full and fulfilling life. But as our personal good fortune had increased, all of us in the family had also felt a growing obligation to try to give something more back to the wonderful system that had made our own lives so comfortable. And so, in 1974, I ran for office for the first time. With no political experience, I lost a three-way Democratic primary for lieutenant governor to Mary Ann Krupsak, a veteran legislator (the third candidate was the late State Assemblyman Antonio Olivieri). The experience was by no means discouraging, however, and the campaign served to introduce me to the entire state and to the sometimes byzantine world of campaign politics.

The winner of the gubernatorial primary and general election was Congressman Hugh Carey from Brooklyn, whom I had known since law school. Now he gave me my first chance at public service: he appointed me secretary of state. The position had been largely honorific, but Governor Carey allowed

*Now, twelve years later, one can look at the Forest Hills project, which has not only not disrupted the neighborhood but has stabilized it, and call the compromise a success —though, like most compromises, when it was put together it left some of the parties on both sides dissatisfied, even resentful.

me to redesign the Department of State and to involve myself in a series of projects that gave the office a new dignity and offered me an extraordinary education in state government.

I did well enough in the governor's opinion to convince him that I should run for mayor of New York City in 1977. The city was reeling in the early stages of its fiscal crisis, and he felt someone was needed who could see the situation from the state's viewpoint as well as the city's. I was reluctant, but with his strong commitment of support, I agreed.

There were six candidates in the primary, the best of whom proved to be Congressman Ed Koch of Manhattan. In a brilliant campaign, designed and managed by the resourceful and indefatigable David Garth and Phil Friedman, Koch was able to get 20 percent of the vote. Garth had been Carey's media consultant and the heart of his campaign in 1974, and the fact that I ran second to Koch with 19 percent of the vote, setting up a one-on-one nine-day runoff campaign, created a curious internecine confrontation. I knew and liked Koch and had earlier urged editorial boards to consider him as a candidate for mayor. Carey, who had asked me to run, knew him even better; they had served together in the army and in Congress. And Garth, who was an intimate of both Koch and Carey, was also friendly to me.

But all this familiarity did not prevent the runoff from becoming one of the most hard-fought—some people said bitter—battles in the history of New York City politics.

My side was badly beaten. In a quick series of coups, Koch and Garth were able to win the support of Herman Badillo, the city's most effective Hispanic leader, and practically the entire Black political leadership. That, plus a relentless pounding from the editorial pages of the New York *Daily News* and the *Post*, and an amateurish performance by me as candidate, resulted in a nine-point victory for Koch, who then went on to win the general election and become mayor.

Unlike my first defeat this one might have ended my political career. But the next year, at the last minute, Lieutenant Governor Mary Ann Krupsak broke with Carey and announced she would run against him for governor in the Democratic primary.

Down in the polls, already an underdog to Perry Duryea—the handsome, capable, long-time Republican leader of the state assembly—the governor sent his secretary, Bob Morgado, and Dave Garth to ask me to run in Krupsak's place.

From my point of view, the chance to serve in a position that was traditionally regarded as less than challenging was not appealing. No one on my staff liked the idea. After a few hours of discussion the sentiment was overwhelmingly against my saying yes and in favor of my running for attorney general or comptroller instead. It was also the staff's opinion, however, that a refusal on my part—only three days before the state's Democratic convention—might well be the final blow to Carey's chances.

Finally, about ten o'clock that night, I called Matilda and told her that I thought Carey would be better for the state than the Republicans, that I could help him win, and that I thought we should do it. She was not enthusiastic but went along with my judgment.

I think I was right about being able to help. Starting from a twenty-eight-point disadvantage, Carey and I ground out a tough come-from-behind campaign that had us catching Duryea and his running mate, former State Assemblyman and U.S. Congressman Bruce Caputo, in September, then passing them comfortably by election day. Garth and Friedman once again directed the Carey campaign, with a heavy assist from Bob Morgado, working from inside the government. My son Andrew and my old friend Jerry Weiss, whom I had known since our years together at St. John's Law School, worked well with them, and all together we proved to be a good team.

Life as lieutenant governor, however, was about what most of us had expected it to be. Governor Carey's management style was more like that of a chairman of the board than a chief executive officer. He left most of the day-to-day decision making and administration to Bob Morgado and to his director of policy management, Mike Del Giudice.

Though my relationship with Morgado was a good one, there was clearly no room for me at the governor's side on any regular basis: he was surrounded by his secretary. Instead, I presided over the senate (doing so is one of the lieutenant governor's few

constitutionally prescribed duties) and traveled the state promoting the administration's policies in the role of ombudsman.*
From time to time the governor's absence from the state required me to serve as acting governor, and on those occasions
I got a quick taste of what being number one might be like, but
for the most part I was kept in the bullpen on a "just in case"
basis.

Then, in 1980, the presidential election provided me with an
unexpected opportunity to play a leading role.

Although both sides had worked hard at it, the relationship
between the Carter White House and New York's Democratic
leadership was not strong; neither Governor Carey nor Mayor
Koch was satisfied with what Washington had done for New
York, state or city, and their disposition toward the president
reflected this. Eager to build a strong effort in what would be a
crucial state, the president's people, whom I had known for
several years (two of them, Gerry Rafshoon and Pat Caddell, had
participated in my unsuccessful 1977 run for mayor of New
York City), asked me to assume overall leadership of their campaign in New York, in the first instance against the challenge of
Senator Ted Kennedy.

After receiving the approval of most of the state's leading
Democratic officeholders who were not already in the Kennedy
camp, including the governor, the mayor, U.S. Senator Daniel
P. Moynihan and State Assembly Speaker Stanley Fink, I accepted and, working with Joel McCleary (who had been sent in
by the Carter team), Jerry Weiss and Andrew, set about constructing a campaign.

The primary, which Kennedy won after a debacle in the
United Nations that cost us much of the Jewish vote,† was tough

*The ombudsman's office was one of those I had designed for the Department of
State, as a liaison to local governments and contact point with "the people." Apparently
because the governor and Morgado preferred the lieutenant governor to be occupied
outside the governor's immediate sphere, they asked me to bring the function over with
me when I moved from the secretary of state's office to the magnificent antique beauty
that is the lieutenant governor's suite, adjacent to the senate chamber.

†On March 1, 1980, the United States supported a UN Security Council resolution
calling on Israel to dismantle its settlements on the West Bank and Gaza Strip. Two days
later, President Carter disavowed the vote, saying that he had really intended his delegation to abstain. Jewish leaders assailed Carter's flip-flop and helped swing the March 25
primary to Kennedy.

and divisive. It set the stage for another bruising battle at the Democratic National Convention in New York City in July.

By that time, the president had the nomination locked up, and Mayor Koch had joined the Carter forces. But Carey had managed to remain aloof. Then, just days before the convention was to begin, the governor endorsed the idea of an "open convention"—one at which the delegates would ignore previous commitments and votes for candidates, and start all over again. It was tantamount to rejecting the incumbent president, and as Carter's principal spokesperson in New York, I took a different view. The result was the spectacle of the Democratic governor and the Democratic lieutenant governor of New York State disagreeing over the question of who should be president. In the end, Carey's appeal was rejected, and Carter carried the convention, but the dispute put a strain on the relationship between the governor and me.

By the end of 1980, then, Governor Carey and I were halfway through our term—and I was looking ahead. It was uncertain whether Carey would choose to run again, even less certain whether I would be asked to—or want to—run with him, and little more than a guess as to what I would do if I didn't run with him. All during 1981—while our administration failed to get a budget past the state legislature; while my old adversary Ed Koch, piloted by David Garth, ran a triumphal campaign for reelection as mayor of New York, promising to be mayor for twelve years, and praising the ascendant Republicans to the extent of agreeing to run himself as a Republican; while what was left of my bank account fell to a new low—I worked at being lieutenant governor, and thought about what else to do with my life.

WEDNESDAY, NOVEMBER 5, 1980

I am beginning to get advice from all over about my political future. I don't need to make any decisions now, but I should decide on what my present posture should be. I haven't really analyzed it. Let me try:

I start by wanting to remain in public service if I can because I believe I can function better trying to help people than trying to make money with them.

The first rule and operating principle must therefore be that whatever preparation we make for the future, we use every day now to serve the people in every way that we can. Mostly that means concentrating on my ombudsman's office and on special projects, and articulating and advocating positions for change. It's difficult to know to what extent service requires working closely with the Governor. It's clear that he and Morgado find my failure to agree with Carey totally and my unpredictability inconvenient. I understand that, but they should have thought of that in 1978 when they asked me to run.

SATURDAY, NOVEMBER 8, 1980

Meeting with Garth at Des Artistes[1] at 12 noon.

Garth said that Morgado and he had met earlier this week. They have begun Carey's campaign for '82. Their objective is to pay off all debts and amass a war chest. They want MMC to be an integral part of the effort. The Governor is supposed to have said that to Garth specifically. He never told me. Garth says Carey could run for President in '84 and probably wind up a Veep. MMC would then be Governor. MMC should begin articulating the Carey record, then start on the national scene.

I didn't agree to anything, although I didn't disagree, either.

Garth thinks Kemp[2] will be the Republican candidate, will have $6 million to start. I disagreed. I said Kemp wanted to be President, not Governor. I guessed Caputo would be the candidate.

[1] A restaurant in Manhattan.
[2] Jack F. Kemp, Conservative-Republican congressman from Hamburg, New York, advocate of supply-side economics.

Garth says I wasn't hurt by the Carter defeat: that I actually won respect for staying with Carter when others didn't. He wants me to stay close and keep in touch.

SUNDAY, NOVEMBER 9, 1980

All day at home. What a pleasure!

MONDAY, NOVEMBER 10, 1980

President Carter called. He was tired. Who can blame him after all he's been through? I wanted to be able to tell him what a mistake I thought had been made; how I believed all the attractive prescriptions of his opponent would prove to be vain, but it didn't seem right. We lost. I told him, instead, that I was proud of what I had been able to do and wished I had been able to do more. He was gracious—strong, I thought. Just calling me required strength. Just going through it—I'm sure many times calling friends—required strength.

TUESDAY, NOVEMBER 11, 1980 (VETERAN'S DAY)

Coffee with Bob Keating[1] and Joe Hynes.[2]

A lot of casual talk. Apparently they want to bring me closer to Koch. They might even be concerned about my running against him for Mayor next year. I was noncommittal.

A new Carey story—in which he had the State seize property next to his Shelter Island home to give him more privacy—is damaging him. Breslin[3] did a piece comparing it to Corona. I'm trying to duck it. I tried to get Morgado yesterday and Garth today—they didn't call back.

---

[1]A lawyer friend from Brooklyn who went from the district attorney's office to serve as criminal justice coordinator for Mayor Koch. Now a criminal court judge.

[2]Former first assistant to the district attorney of Brooklyn. Appointed by Carey as special prosecutor of the nursing-home investigation in 1975 at my suggestion. Later appointed fire commissioner by Mayor Koch. Now a member of the State Investigation Commission.

[3]Jimmy Breslin, New York *Daily News* columnist.

During the day the Carey–Shelter Island story grew progressively more damaging. The dentist whose property was being condemned—one D'Arrigo—went on radio and TV protesting that Carey's argument that he needed the land for "security" was a "sham." Carey and the commissioners[4] were caught in inconsistent statements. Richard Rosenbaum[5] was on the attack for the Republicans. Jimmy Breslin wrote another particularly tough piece warning Carey the situation could bring him down. I talked to Garth and Phil Friedman and Sandy Frucher,[6] telling them they should get the Governor to rescind his action. Others did as well.

Frucher called at about 12:30 and said Carey had decided to rescind. I hope they've checked it out legally: as I recall, rescission of a vested eminent domain proceeding isn't simple.

SATURDAY, NOVEMBER 15, 1980

The Governor continues to get himself into difficulties. Yesterday he announced an effort to get raises for elected and non-elected executive state officials. Even if it were a necessary bill, he made a mistake by announcing it in the same week when he was attacked for having spent money at Shelter Island for "security" purposes that appeared, at least, to relate more to personal comfort. It was also the week when it was announced that he had been given a $500,000 cooperative apartment on Park Avenue by his brother, Ed. The result was that he permitted the press to get him involved in a discussion about damaging details, all over again.

Jerry Weiss moves ahead with getting up his own law firm. I've given him the names of firm attorneys, secretaries, even some legal printers. He's hoping to be able to open by Jan-

---

[4]The superintendent of the state police, the commissioner of the Office of General Services and the transportation commissioner.

[5]Former Republican state chairman, from Rochester.

[6]Meyer S. ("Sandy") Frucher, director of employee relations for Governor Carey; formerly with the administration of Mayor John V. Lindsay in New York City; confidant of Bob Morgado and Carey.

uary 1, if he can by then work out the details with Manus.[1]

All of this is great, because it helps me provide for the future. Right now I don't know if Carey will want me to run for Lieutenant Governor, or whether I would want to, or whether we could win if we did run. That might mean that, much as I'd like to remain in public service, I won't be able to, and I'd be out by the end of this term. If that were to happen, I'd have no law firm to go back to, because I gave that up to avoid conflicts. And Corner, Finn[2] is now gone. If Weiss and Manus are able to put something together, they might be able to take me in eventually.

Maria was back from school last night. She looks and sounds great. She's buoyed by the news that her cast will be coming off sooner than she thought originally. Carl picked her up and I shuddered internally when I remembered how close these two had come to getting killed.[3]

And Madeline has made the National Honor Society![4]

Now, if Margaret can find a good internship and someone who deserves her; Andrew can get law school behind him;[5] Maria can hit her stride at Iona; and Christopher can recover a fumble tomorrow! Well . . . then . . .

I spent a lot of time today thinking about how hard the last six years have been. I'm almost ashamed to admit that I feel I have deprived my family of so much. I don't blame Matilda for being a little resentful, especially since she knows others have done what I've done and still practiced law and probably gotten rich —legally. She has never agreed fully with my decision to give up the practice and the income.

I'm thinking that maybe I have to find some way to put my family—what's left of it—up higher.

---

[1]Justus Manus, Jerry Weiss's partner in the new firm.

[2]Corner, Finn, Cuomo and Charles, of New York City, my old law firm.

[3]My daughter Maria, a freshman at Iona College, and Carl Mattone, the son of our friends Joe and Irene Mattone, had been in an automobile accident.

[4]At St. Francis Preparatory School, where she was a junior.

[5]Margaret was in her last year at Downstate Medical School in New York, Andrew in his second year at Albany Law School.

MONDAY, NOVEMBER 17, 1980

Public service has never been as difficult for me since I entered
it in 1975 as it is now. And today pointed it up dramatically. I
traveled to Syracuse to deliver a speech at the outset of a convo-
cation of Human Services agencies. The subject was my conviction that one of government's basic obligations is to deal with the
"legitimate" needy. I don't know exactly how it went over, but
I think it was the right subject, the right side. That, it seems to
me, is why I came into this hard profession.

But the rest of the day was frustrating. Early in the afternoon
I received a call from a reporter who said somebody had somehow picked up from my car phone my conversation with Sandy
Frucher in Albany earlier today and recorded it. He explained
it was a fluke; that they were listening to fire calls at the
time.

The conversation concerned how Sandy should go about defending the Governor's call for salary increases in a press conference. I had been opposed to the idea of the press conference
because it would aggravate the problem created by an announcement of pay raises that had been poorly timed to begin with. In
fact, I was opposed to the philosophy behind the pay raises for
elected officials without passage of a conflicts-and-disclosure law
and a welfare bill. Sandy indicated he was getting a good editorial from one of the major New York dailies, and I said I would
be "shocked" if that were to happen, because of the strong
adverse reportage on the subject. Moreover, I felt that even if
there were to be a good editorial, it would only have the effect
of keeping alive the question.

In any event, the reporter said if it were up to him he would
run a transcript of the entire conversation.

I told him, and later his editor, that I believed that would
be illegal and certainly unethical and would encourage all
kinds of kooks to run around trying to do the same kind of
thing.

The editor said he wouldn't use the transcript but would do
some kind of story using the information as background.

I told Frucher about it later, and he was as shocked as I had
been that we had been listened to and taped.

This can be a hard way to live! With this and the State Senate Subcommittee still pursuing people over the so-called "street money" that Dwyer distributed[1] and all the aggravation of the Carter campaign just over and two more just ahead . . . I'm tired. People come into politics to serve, but so much time is spent trying to win office, defending yourself against attacks and game playing that it's difficult to spend enough time doing the kind of thing I did in Syracuse this morning.

So I find myself without a law practice, with our bank accounts depleted, with my kids borrowing money to go to college, with Matilda understandably unhappy with the fact that I haven't been able to provide her with the things her friends have and with only a limited opportunity to perform really good public service.

I wonder what Teilhard[2] would say about this kind of thinking. Is it a form of weakness? How do I deal with what he would call the diminishments of my own spirit and the diminishments imposed by the world? He would probably tell me that I must struggle with my own weakness constantly—and suffer all innocent diminishment in order to fulfill the experience of life and to earn eternity. And even in order to properly understand and enjoy what is not diminishment in this life.

TUESDAY, NOVEMBER 18, 1980

The news stories were not as bad for Carey as I thought they would be. And there were editorials supporting the raises. Frucher was right.

[1]After the 1977 mayoral election and after my law partner Peter Dwyer's death, his name was used in the course of a racketeering prosecution. A labor leader, whose union had supported our campaign, was accused of extorting money from various businessmen. His defense, in part, was that he was actually raising funds for the campaign. He claimed he had given Dwyer $50,000 in cash to be used on election day to provide the mechanics needed to get the voters to the polls—i.e., "street money." Of course, Dwyer was not around to dispute the charge. In any event, the jury didn't believe it, and the official was convicted and sentenced to prison.

[2]Pierre Teilhard de Chardin, the great Jesuit scientist and theologian, whose work, especially *The Divine Milieu,* first enunciated for me a central part of Christian truth: that God did not intend this world only as a test of our purity, but rather as an expression of his love; that we are meant to live actively, totally, in this world and in so doing to make it better for all whom we can touch.

THURSDAY, NOVEMBER 20, 1980

A Special Session[1] was called for Albany yesterday. Nothing much occurred other than a lot of fun with Senator Dick Schermerhorn and the other Republicans. Real work starts today, but I have to leave to make two speeches; I'll be back tomorrow.

Instead of going as usual to the Bella Napoli, I had dinner last night with Andrew at Cavaleri's. Ate too much but talked a lot, too. Afterward he went to the library and a birthday party and didn't get back until after 3 A.M.

Left Albany on 3 o'clock plane to go to New York City. Speech to Young Presidents' Association[2] at the Jolly Fisherman & Steak House in Roslyn. Al Roth of Bond's stores arranged it. Spoke for about an hour and 15 minutes with Q and A. All Republicans, fascinated by Kemp-Laffer supply-side economics. I created some doubts for them, but in an election everyone in the room but Al and me would be with Kemp—as of now.

From Roslyn to Terrace on the Park, where I spoke at a testimonial for Caesar Cirigliano.[3]

Matilda went out with the Breslins tonight to have dinner with the Winklers—Irwin and Margot Winkler. Winkler produced the *Rocky*s and De Niro's *Raging Bull* about Jake LaMotta. I was asleep when she got home, but I'm sure she'll have a lot to tell me. She had quite a week. Yesterday she was on the Barry Gray show for an hour and, I'm told, was great. I'm less and less concerned about how she'd manage if I were to die suddenly. All I need to do now is to find a way to earn a little money to keep my insurance and add to it to take care of Madeline's and Chris's education.

FRIDAY, NOVEMBER 21, 1980

Marian Neef[1] tells me—on good authority in her academic circle—that Bellamy[2] has begun to gear up for a race for Governor because Carey is definitely beatable. She's going

---

[1]Of the state legislature.

[2]An international organization of corporation presidents who are under forty years of age.

[3]An old friend in charge of lawyers at the Legal Aid Society.

---

[1]A member of my staff.

[2]Carol Bellamy, president of the New York City Council.

to run on my old "neighborhood preservation" platform.[3]

Tonio[4] reports someone from Buffalo says Fink says he's running. I've never talked to him about it but I don't see any reason why he shouldn't—he has all the qualifications.

It looks as though the Governor's political weakness as now perceived has excited a lot of ambitions. I suspect that as Carey regains strength those ambitions will waver. I would guess Carey can make himself very strong with heavy campaigning from here on in.

For myself, I'm tired. It's probably the natural result of the presidential election campaign—and the election results.

Today is supposed to be the last day of the Special Session. I'll have to fly back to Albany early for it. I'm leaving in two hours.

SATURDAY, NOVEMBER 22, 1980

5:30 A.M. here in Albany. The legislative session is "Special and Extraordinary" only juridically: in all other ways it is typical of our recent efforts. Confusion, inefficiency, what seems to be a lack of coordination have brought us to the fourth day without the pay raise bill or the banking bill[1] that were the principal reasons for the session. Actually, the banking bill was the principal reason: the raise bill has simply become the most talked-about issue. Last night I left before the Senate returned from a recess sometime around 9 P.M. because my presence was simply a waste of time. I came back to the apartment, watched a little TV and dozed off. I'm not going back tomorrow (today) because it simply means another day of delay, with activity in fits and starts. Probably by tonight sometime things—most of them, anyway—will be worked out as they always appear to get worked out despite the confusion. But I will not have had a significant role in it and so there is not much reason in my occupying space on the stage. The experience has been another confirmation of the wisdom of my

---

[3]In 1977 I created the Neighborhood Preservation party and ran for mayor on that line as well as on the Liberal party line (see pp. 147–48). Its platform was geared toward preserving middle-class communities in the city.

[4]Tonio Burgos, staff member since 1976.

---

[1]A law to deregulate the interest rates on most forms of consumer credit.

proposed constitutional amendment that would take me out of the
Senate (or at least take the next Lt. Governor out of the Senate:
the resolution would probably take that long), make the job
full-time and drop the other ceremonial chores now called for.

6:00 A.M.

Still dark out the window of the 10th floor of the Wellington,
muffled sounds of auto engines revving up in the background.
A car going by occasionally. Andrew's parrot—or whatever—
silent, standing perched on a lamp in the second bedroom. Andrew asleep. A good time to think.

Approaching 50. You will die as you must. Maybe today. If
you believe in nothing, you are not sure you would want not to.
So you try desperately to believe in "An eternity of peace that's
earned." But you don't understand eternity and you're afraid
you have not earned it in any event. "A full and happy life for
what's left of it." But what is there that I would want to "fill"
it with? Achievement? Has anything ever been so useless as the
momentary acclaim of a world that does not know you, no matter
how "public"? Glory? The fear of shame and rejection is much
more powerful a force than the desire for glory. Why? The
world's condemnation should be as irrelevant as the world's
acclaim. Then why? Why guilt over satisfaction?

Think:

How you reach a point of review and retrospection. I hope the
Lord grades me easily. How you are troubled to think that even
being troubled is cause for guilt. Because it's selfish.

"Selfish." That's the word. As long as you think about what
you need, *you* want, *you* feel—as long as you are selfish—you are
doomed to frustration. "Me" is a bottomless pit which cannot be
filled no matter how much in achievement, glory, acclaim, you
try shoveling into it. If only we were good enough to *do* perfectly
what we know would work perfectly. But we can't.

Why not? When I say "I can't" am I saying it too soon? Am
I saying it because I don't want to have to try? Because being
required to love denies me too many of the delights of being
loved or liked or applauded or smiled upon? And if that *is* the
case, then aren't you silly—as Matilda would say—because you
know those delights don't last. You've tried them. You've had

them. They don't work. A world filled with wisdom and stupidity came before you. And all that was wise told you that those "satisfactions" weren't really satisfactions—except in a terribly transitory way.

For God's sake, you know the truth! The truth is that the only way to make anything of your life is to be what you know you're supposed to be. You're kidding yourself if you prefer not to know. And you're kidding yourself if, in trying to be what you know you should be, you fail from time to time and use that failure as an excuse to abandon trying. You know—because it's the only logic—that the test is Timothy's: "to fight the good fight. To finish the race, to keep the faith."

I haven't. I've fought a thousand fights but not enough the good fight. I've been in the race but too often running in the wrong direction. I've not—truly enough—kept the faith. I've hurt people by bad example, even my own family. I have too often permitted people to know what I believed was right then witnessed my violation of my own truth. That is the truth and it is part of the pain in my chest.

Yes, I do know the truth. And way down deep I even feel the truth. But somewhere before the feeling reaches and marries with my knowing, another feeling intervenes: the imperfect feelings I know are wrong. The desire for the transitory.

So all that is left is to try again to *do* what I know I should do. And beginning this moment I will make the effort as I have not made it before because I have never been as old as I am now, and I have never known as much as I do now and I have never had as much to undo as I do now and I have never had as much to compensate for as I do now and I have never had less time than I do now.

7:00 P.M.
Another frustrating day in the Senate. Negotiations all day on various pieces of special session legislation. Bank bill passed us before 6 P.M.[2] Assembly is still arguing it at 7 P.M. It will almost certainly be over tonight.

[2]That is, passed the state senate, over which I presided as lieutenant governor. The bill didn't pass the other branch of the state legislature, the assembly, until later that night.

I've decided to leave to get a plane, even though they haven't done the pay raise bill or the Mitchell-Lama bill[3] yet. I have no real role in the negotiations, and that's probably good for the Governor, because there's a lot they're doing now that I don't agree with.

SUNDAY, NOVEMBER 23, 1980

Up again before the sun, reading and thinking . . . but not writing here: I didn't get to this until Monday A.M.

I took Matilda to Chris's last game with the Tomahawks.[1] He played right tackle on offense and by his coach's estimate he has come a long way in this, his first season. I had to leave at the half to be at the Catholic Guardian Society's luncheon honoring George Cincotta.[2] I enjoyed sitting next to Bishop-elect Joe Sullivan. My speech was rambling and disorganized. I didn't get a chance to prepare.

This afternoon with Madeline at a bazaar for the Immaculate Conception Church; all was quiet. Football game in the street and a walk with Chris. He's beautiful. Tall, sandy-haired, blue eyes. Sweet, loving, considerate—for a 10-year-old. I hope I can do more for him.

The coverage on the special session was straight. *Newsday* wrote another story about Carey's "excesses"—$10,000 to feed the kids and their guests at Shelter Island. But aside from that no negatives—yet. The politicians will get raises, but poor people will get no welfare increase.

Talked to Madeline A. on the phone again today. I can't say I have been able to detect much improvement, although her doctor says she is coming along. We'll continue to call her—and to pray.[3]

---

[3]A bill to provide funds to alleviate escalating costs at state-subsidized housing complexes established under the so-called Mitchell-Lama law.

---

[1]A sandlot football team in Queens.

[2]Former assemblyman from Brooklyn; at the time chairman of the Cable TV Commission (New York State).

[3]For several years Madeline Ansalone was my secretary at Corner, Finn, Cuomo and Charles and then at the Department of State and lieutenant governor's office. She was

MONDAY, NOVEMBER 24, 1980

The most impressive pageant I've ever seen. Matilda and I— together with a world of civic officials—witnessed the ordination of 3 Auxiliary Bishops for the Diocese of Brooklyn: Joe Sullivan, Anthony Bevilacqua and René Valero. They are a reflection of the new Church in the world's largest diocese. Sullivan, Irish Catholic, is from the ranks of the immigrants who built the church Matilda and I grew up in. So is Bevilacqua, except that he has concentrated on working with the new wave of immigrants. Valero is Hispanic.

The ceremony was over 2 hours long, but no one fidgeted. The music, the prayers, the ritual were beautiful and intelligent. I won't miss the next opportunity I'm given to share this kind of experience.

From there in the rain to Rochester, first to sit and talk with a group of sophisticated lay volunteers about criminal justice. They don't believe prisons work and want to talk about New York spending money instead on alternatives. I didn't do well. Slaughter said I was "so-so."[1] From her, that's condemnation. I'll try to recoup with a letter and some follow-up.[2]

Early evening

Tonio reported Andrew was trying to get me and that it was important. I called several times until finally I caught him from the Rochester Page airport at about 10:30 P.M. He had had his

a one-woman staff who did everything for me. One day she had a headache. A few days later it was found she had an aneurysm, and she was operated on. She has been recuperating slowly since then.

[1]Louise Slaughter was the Rochester representative of the ombudsman's office from 1975 to 1982. She's now an elected member of the state assembly from the 130th District in Monroe County. A close friend, she was, I always felt, too gentle with me in her appraisals of my performances.

[2]The letter was written and sent. It made clearer what I failed to make clear enough at the meeting. I have argued for a long time that we are wasting money on jailing people who would be better dealt with through one of a series of alternatives to incarceration, like work programs and supervised probation. Of course, violent criminals should be incarcerated, and New York State is spending a fortune to do that. But when we still need space for violent criminals who are not yet behind bars, it is foolish to use our expensive cells for nonviolent petty criminals who can be more appropriately—and more inexpensively—punished through alternative methods.

lip slit in a basketball game at the law school and he was trying
to arrange to go to New York to get it sewn. He talked to Uncle
Nick,[3] who told him it wouldn't be necessary. It didn't look
pretty, but I think he'll be all right. I don't expect to see it leave
a scar.

TUESDAY, NOVEMBER 25, 1980

I received a call late today from John Kiernan of Caemmerer's
office: Tom McLoughlin died today. First John Murphy, now
McLoughlin; no wonder Caemmerer's upset. The three were
close all through law school as students and later on with their
families. All three discovered they had cancer at about the same
time. Now two of them are gone.[1]

So many are gone. Dwyer's gone, too, and Hugh Carey's two
sons and my baby brother and my brother Frank's baby boy, and
millions by starvation and war, and now thousands in Italy in an
earthquake—buried alive.

WEDNESDAY, NOVEMBER 26, 1980

Up at 5:30 A.M. My first feeling of the day was regret at not
having done well yesterday. I was impatient with Matilda on
the phone and then when I came home last night. She resents
my talking on the phone when I'm home because I'm home so
little. She has more of a point than I have been willing to
admit.

The feeling was intensified when I heard a radio report that

[3]Dr. Nicholas D'Arienzo, a pediatrician, Christopher's godfather, Arlene's husband
and our close friend since we entered St. John's College together in 1949. He's not
related except through Adam and Eve and by affection.

[1]Thomas McLoughlin, John Murphy and John D. Caemmerer were classmates in law
school at St. John's and close friends. I had known all of them for all the years since then.
They had remained close through marriage and their careers, which saw Murphy become
dean of his alma mater, McLoughlin a deputy attorney general and Caemmerer one of
the strongest members of the New York State Senate. The grotesque coincidence that
saw both of his friends die of cancer within a year or so of each other was prophetic;
Caemmerer himself died of it in 1982.

Ella Grasso has learned that she is once again suffering from cancer. Valiant lady, faced again with what most believe is the most challenging reality—the end.[1] It reminds me that we are all faced with that reality, only we forget. "Death is here, only she hasn't announced herself yet" is what I said last night. I was right and I ought to live that way . . . starting again now.

THURSDAY, NOVEMBER 27, 1980 (THANKSGIVING)

A quiet day, surrounded by the things that should most inspire gratitude but don't . . . often enough. We were at Momma and Poppa's with Marie, Ted and their kids.[1] All the kids were there: I wonder for how many more years we'll be lucky enough to have that. Pop was better than he has been. He conversed well, had a reasonably good attention span, and got edgy only in the early evening. Charlie Raffa[2] stopped in at about 6: he was driving the AAA Emergency Service truck for extra money.

I argued too much as usual: even *I* found it unpleasant.

Chris's good day was spoiled by a toothache in the evening. He tried to stifle his crying while we watched *The Sound of Music* —again—in the den.

FRIDAY, NOVEMBER 28, 1980

Quiet day at the office: most people made it a long weekend. Spent most of my time dictating a draft of a speech on criminal justice for next Tuesday's Brooklyn Bar dinner. I want it to come out right this time, and it's a difficult subject to handle responsibly.

Spoke to Washington about the earthquake in southern Italy. Actually it struck the area where both Momma and Poppa come from. Mario Biaggi[1] went out front quickly with a series of good,

---

[1]Governor of Connecticut, Ella Grasso died February 5, 1981.

---

[1]My sister, Marie, my brother-in-law Ted Vecchio, and their three children, Mark, Lisa and Vanessa.

[2]My nephew, eldest son of Matilda's brother Sam and his wife, Pat.

---

[1]U.S. congressman from the Bronx.

intelligent responses: he's performing very well. I believe I can help by getting some of the voluntary agencies to coordinate their efforts. I have Rosemarie Gallina[2] trying to put together a meeting for next Tuesday.

This evening with Matilda at a reception for Bishop Sullivan at the St. Regis. Mostly people from Catholic Charities. A great party. Mrs. Sullivan is 80 and had 11 children; I think 10 of them were there. She sang—and did a little dance—and so did Bishop Joe. It was warmth and laughter and love. Matilda enjoyed the party so much she didn't want to leave at 11:30. I was tired, but I enjoyed it, too.

SUNDAY, NOVEMBER 30, 1980

Short visit to Grandma Raffa to see her newly refurbished kitchen and dinette area. Matilda worked hard to clean the place, and it looks good.

Mass at Incarnation—with Chris and Madeline. I was struck by how quickly we have begun to lose our children to the world: Andrew and Maria were back at school and Margaret away for the weekend on a skiing trip.

Aside from a few phone calls on the bar association speech for Tuesday night and the earthquake activity, I was able to stay away from work.

Last night's small anniversary party for the Molesphinis was our only stop for the evening.[1] So altogether it was a great weekend.

MONDAY, DECEMBER 1, 1980

The beginning of a new month. It's Advent, and I intend to take the season literally. I have made a firm resolve to get in shape . . . in every way I can.

[2]A member of my staff.

[1]Faye and Albert Molesphini are friends Matilda and I have known since his days at St. John's College and Faye's at St. John's Teachers College with Matilda.

Although the Governor chose not to include me on the Earthquake Committee he organized, I have gone forward on my own. Rosemarie Gallina has reached out to 12 or so groups. The response has been excellent: they'll be in my office tomorrow at 4 P.M. in New York City.

I finished my criminal justice speech and I think, for a change, I'll be ready tomorrow. I've even gotten out a release on it!

7:45 A.M. plane this morning, 8:00 P.M. plane tonight back to New York City.

TUESDAY, DECEMBER 2, 1980

Speech at the Brooklyn Bar Association dinner at the Plaza. I had worked hard on it over the weekend and thought it was a good effort. Not many people heard it in the room: during dessert, at the end of a long evening, and the acoustics poor in any event. Tonio was down about it.

Earlier in the day we had an extraordinary success when almost everyone invited showed up for the meeting in my office to try coordinating the many different agencies involved in the earthquake. It went so well we'll meet again tomorrow A.M. to formalize the effort. I even have a name for the group that we'll form: Italian Disaster Emergency Assistance (IDEA).

Home relatively early. Another day gone with no assurance of the number left. We have to use each one well.

Tonio down, too, because he chatted with Bill Stern,[1] who said that "heavy hitters" he was trying to liven up to support Cuomo were turned off because he was a "loser": he lost in '77 and with Carter—what kind of investment is that? Gee! What would they have said about Lincoln, who lost 6 times before he won the presidency?

---

[1] My supporter in 1977 and friend since then. He is now chairman of the Urban Development Corporation. He understood that if I were to have any opportunity to continue in elected office, we would have to work hard to gather the financial resources needed to campaign. He was always at it.

Thursday, December 4, 1980

The *Daily News* Brooklyn Edition was the only paper to cover my Brooklyn Bar speech on criminal justice, but it was a good story. The call for responsible change as distinguished from the overly simple—sometimes pandering—approach we've too often had is always well received when it's heard. The problem is getting it heard.

And nothing works like a good idea. Two things are hard to find: someone who can perform a task—even a simple task—predictably well and someone who is capable of producing good ideas regularly. I told Dave Garth yesterday on the phone I thought the Governor was making a mistake seeking to enhance his image by emphasizing people and episodes instead of ideas and programs. He's spending a lot of time trying to change the cast of characters in his administration—Meyerson, Holtzman, Burstein, Milonas are all rumored to be on their way in.[1] And planning events—ribbon cuttings, town hall meetings, etc. It's an old-fashioned campaign of endorsements and barnstorming. It tends to focus on personality and it's superficial. I believe what he needs is a campaign of ideas and programs. That's what accounts for most of Kemp's popularity. Two ideas that sound good, even if they're not—tax cuts and supply-side stimulation. And Carey has plenty at hand—local government expenditure review, expenditure cap, neighborhood preservation, a responsible response to crime.

I saw it work again today. There has been an explosion of activity on the part of well-intentioned people who want to assist the earthquake victims. Now IDEA has caught on, and our press conference this morning was a success, with an excellent turnout. One of the TV reporters who covered it told me on her way out, "This thing makes sense." That's the key—if it makes sense, if it's a good idea, the rest happens naturally.

[1]Bess Meyerson, former Miss America and consumer affairs advocate; Elizabeth Holtzman, U.S. congresswoman whose term was to expire on December 31, 1980; Karen Burstein, unsuccessful candidate for Congress in 1980; and Judge E. Leo Milonas of the New York State Supreme Court. Burstein was appointed chair and executive director of the State Consumer Protection Board.

What we need is more good ideas and a few people who can perform a task.

I also had a good chat with Fabian today.[1] We discussed the Ombudsman office, my job generally, criminal justice—and the old days. He has been a good friend, and as you grow older you realize how rare they are.

I'm writing now at 3:30 A.M. on Friday. My sleep cycle is completely off. I'll have to try to wrench myself back into a more decent schedule and one more compatible with Matilda's.

FRIDAY, DECEMBER 5, 1980

A typical week in my dealings with the Governor: he hasn't attempted to contact me in over six weeks, nor has Morgado recently. I don't know what they have in mind. They might even just be misreading my intentions.

Good meeting with Milt Mollen[1] this morning. A good man. Intelligent, wise, honest, tough and with me very generous. We talked mostly about how to improve the situation in the courts.

A WINS news conference was dull. I'm afraid being sensational and newsworthy on a regular basis—or even frequently—is not my forte. There are so many parts to the role I'm now playing as "executive type" in politico-governmental situations that don't appear to fit my style and likes. But that's always been true. I've not ever been able to match whatever makes up my composite of strengths and weaknesses with any situation that was anything like perfectly compatible. I've always felt just a little incongruous: baseball player, professor, campaigner, politician, father, husband—always a little too round for a square opening . . . or a little too square.

---

[1] Fabian Palomino, law clerk to Judge Adrian Burke of the Court of Appeals, assistant counsel to Governor W. Averell Harriman, legislative representative for Governor Carey, professor of law, practicing lawyer and my friend for some thirty years.

[1] A friend of over twenty years. Another St. John's Law School graduate, he became chairman of the New York City Housing and Redevelopment Board, State Supreme Court justice and eventually presiding judge of the Appellate Division for the Second Judicial Department. I had the privilege of reappointing him in January 1983.

Saturday, December 6, 1980

I canceled two drop-ins this afternoon because all the kids were around and I wanted to spend some time with them. Then I spoiled the afternoon by allowing an argument to develop with Matilda about my relatives in the earthquake zone. It was a silly dispute—like most family quarrels—and I should have been smart enough to handle it. Certainly, outside the house I would have had no difficulty in reconciling and pacifying. There is something about intimacy that tempts you to be less patient.

Margaret has been accepted by three of the hospitals that interviewed her. Andrew is looking for another car: he has a real fascination with automobiles that comes higher on his list of priorities than many other things, including studying for his classes. He'll pass anyway; he always has. But he has never tested himself intellectually. I think if he did he'd be surprised at his own ability.

Maria is trying to work it out to get in a course in the interterm recess to make up for the 6 credits she lost due to her accident. I'm not sure I wouldn't rather have her stay home.

Madeline is 16 and beautiful. But 16.

Chris did not get a good report card. He is bright but distracted in school, constantly in need of attention. I believe he is still reacting to the inattention he suffered in the mayoralty and gubernatorial campaigns. Matilda and I agreed we'll have to watch him more closely and pay as much attention to him as possible.

I was honored tonight by the Nassau Center for the Developmentally Disabled and Rabbi Mowshowitz[1] made the presentation. He was embarrassingly generous, and I felt like a hypocrite listening to him extol my "virtues."

At the same time Matilda was at her American Cancer Society, Queens Division, dinner at the Terrace on the Park, where I joined her later to make a presentation to Gloria McArdle.[2] The function was a success, as all of Matilda's efforts are: warm, well

[1] Rabbi Israel Mowshowitz, one of the nation's best-known rabbis and an old friend, now assistant to the governor for community affairs.
[2] Publisher of the Glendale *Register* and the Queens *Ledger*.

attended—some of our friends, the campaign group, Frankie and Marian[3] and Mom and Pop Raffa were also there—and had a good time.

WEDNESDAY, DECEMBER 10, 1980

Yesterday a headline on a *Daily News* story had me telling Mario Biaggi to stay home from Italy because his trip would be counter-productive. "Stay Home, Cuomo Tells Biaggi." It was unpleas-ant—and inaccurate. The truth is that following a meeting at the Italian Consul's office Monday morning, I reported to IDEA on the scheduled mission.[1] A young reporter for the *News* was there, as were many other electronic and print media. I said I had cautioned against handing out $100,000 on the trip to a list of beneficiaries prepared by local mayors. The reporter distorted that into an "attack." No one else in the room—Committee or reporters—heard it that way. I spent part of Tuesday trying to get a clarification printed and assuring Mario Biaggi and the Italo-American community of the truth.

The situation illustrated one of the difficulties of public life. Perception is often more significant than reality, and the two are often different.

Last night I flew to Albany to be honored at an "Appreciation Night" by the people of Buffalo for what I had done in connec-tion with our task force on economic development.[2] A few peo-ple—Jim Griffin,[3] Bill Donahue,[4] Bob Fierale[5]—commented on how unusual it was to have a nonpolitical, noncampaign "ap-preciation" night for an incumbent. There were over 500 peo-ple present. They gave me a beautiful watch and left me think-

---

[3]Matilda's brother Frank Raffa and his wife, Marian.

[1]Congressman Mario Biaggi had arranged to visit the earthquake zone to help distribute a fund raised in New York for the victims.
[2]My idea as lieutenant governor. It brought together all relevant state agencies with local officials in a common effort to enhance economic development.
[3]Mayor of Buffalo.
[4]Executive director of the Erie County Industrial Development Agency. I appointed him commerce commissioner in 1983.
[5]Buffalo business leader.

ing about how nice this business can be—even on a day when you've suffered a reversal in the press. I should be especially grateful to Andy Ciolek and his family, who worked so hard on the event.

Jack Watson[6] called from the White House yesterday. I'll probably be flying to Italy with a Presidential delegation for a fact-finding mission on the earthquake. I'm looking forward to it.

SATURDAY, DECEMBER 13, 1980

It's about 5:30 A.M. I've come to yearn for these early hours before my world wakes up. It's the only time in the day I have alone . . . to think, reflect, regret and reorder.

I've spent most of the last few days with a cold, then fever, both complicated by some inoculations I took in preparation for the trip to Italy tonight. It was particularly bothersome Thursday. That was a long and difficult day that started with a talk on anti-Semitism before 9 A.M. at a high school in Great Neck, followed by lunch with Jerry Weiss, a TV show with Bishop Broderick[1] on the earthquake, a ribbon cutting and finally a speech before the New Rochelle Bar Association. By the time I was through—at about 10 P.M.—I was shaking with the chills and I ached all over.

The day, however, was a worthwhile one, I think. It made me feel that what I've been telling my friends for two years is demonstrably true: the key for me and my supporters is to do as much good as possible in my role at Lt. Governor, on a day-to-day basis. The implicit assumption for many is that "everybody knows that a Lt. Governor can't do anything, so don't try—you'll look silly." In effect, that's what Will Stevens[2] wrote in his first UPI piece on me in 1979, and he repeated it to me on the phone. He said no one expects you to do anything in this office except be a standby and strong echo for the Governor. If you do anything else—or try to—you'll look overambitious, and people on the inside will resent you.

[6]Special assistant to President Carter.

[1]Bishop Edwin B. Broderick, from the New York Roman Catholic Archdiocese, assigned to the Catholic Charities effort.

[2]Veteran reporter and columnist with United Press International, a real professional.

I've felt differently from the beginning. I told our friends on inauguration night that we should work every day to do as much good as we could, even if it was a small good that was imperceptible to the public—so as to justify all our effort in achieving public office. That's why I gave up the practice of law nearly 6 years ago.

Thursday was a good example. What I had to say about racism and anti-Semitism had more impact on those high school kids because I spoke as Lt. Governor. IDEA is a good use of the office and will help provide relief to thousands of victims. The TV show will reach thousands of viewers and will also help the effort. My speech at New Rochelle allowed me to make good, strong points on the criminal justice system to over 300 lawyers and judges—and to the listeners on 2 or 3 radio stations. Mike Daly[3] called me Friday to say that a couple of minutes he heard on WINS was good. I had been asked about John Lennon and I made the point that a John Lennon dies every night somewhere in the city but goes unnoticed. I also talked about the "absurdity" of Nancy Reagan boasting she kept a revolver because she needed it—or at least needed it before she got Secret Service—to protect herself. I said that this was implicitly an invitation to the country to arm itself. If Nancy needs a gun, how about the people whose neighborhoods are burglarized every weekend? How about the ghetto-dwellers whose daughters walk the streets in constant danger of rape? How about the people who ride our subways?

These were messages worth getting across, and I did. It was, I believe, making good use of the office.

I also think that a lot of the time good use of the office will also be good politics—that Adlai Stevenson was right when he said "good government is the best political strategy." But this probably wasn't true on Thursday when I spoke against capital punishment, equated anti-Semitism and racism—which I'm afraid gets misunderstood—and criticized some of the disaster-relief efforts. Such things don't get you political points, but I don't really have a choice. There are times when one can afford to be discreet, but I can't spend my days editing out the things I believe because they are unpopular. Then, for sure, I would have to return to the private world.

[3]Reporter for *New York* magazine.

. . .

Tonight we leave for Italy in a delegation headed by Jeno Paulucci.[4] I have mixed feelings about it. Eight hours over, 9½ hours back without a movie, four and a half days away from home. That's a lot to give up unless a great deal of good is achieved. I'm not sure how much we'll learn about how better to support the effort, but we'll give it our best shot.

Matilda has done her usual good job of getting the house ready for Christmas. It's special this year because Joe and Josie, Mary Kay and Natalie[5] will be with us. In fact, Mary Kay came in yesterday morning, and I saw her when I got back from Albany at about 11:30.

The Albany Christmas party was "deadly dull," according to a couple of people there, but I thought it was kind of nice. Unfortunately, the jukebox conked out for a while, and I had to leave early because the pilots were afraid we would be snowed in. But I called from New York and the party was still going strong at that point, so it couldn't have been too dull.

Andrew Mark stopped by but was on his way to "their own" Christmas party somewhere in Albany. For a guy who complains a lot about Albany, he certainly finds a lot of fun things to do! God bless him!

7:00 A.M.
Time to get ready for the trip. Tomorrow . . . *Bella Italia*!

SUNDAY, DECEMBER 14, 1980

It's 2:30 P.M. Rome, 8:30 A.M. New York time, aboard an Air Force plane. I haven't slept yet. I chatted most of the night with Nancy Pelosi[1] and Don Dewey, editor of *Attenzione*. Nancy is

---

[4]A highly successful entrepreneur from Minnesota with businesses all over the world. Also a friend and supporter of Walter Mondale.

[5]Mary Kay and Natalie are my nieces from San Diego, daughters of Matilda's brother Joe and his wife, Josie.

---

[1]Chairperson, Northern California Democratic Party.

young, bright, a committed but practical politician. Mother of five children, she comes from a family with a long and proud political tradition, the D'Alesandros.

Earlier I talked with Paulucci. He's interested in IDEA and the possibility of expanding it into a national vehicle. He took my numbers.

Stopped at Torrejon Air Force Base near Madrid for refueling. Mass on the base for several of us. The priest was American and acknowledged our presence. He led the congregants in a round of applause for us. When politicians get cheered in church, it's time to review the ritual!

First briefing on the plane as we head for Rome. Jeno laid it out simply: the mission is to let the Italians know we care, investigate how best to spend the 50 million dollars of federal money and how the voluntary agencies can most efficiently assist. He mentioned "adopt-a-town," which Nancy is doing in California, as an idea worth considering.

We were met at the Ciampino Airport by Ambassador Dick Gardner, his lovely wife, Danielle, a red carpet—literally—*carabinieri* and various other officials. At my suggestion, Paulucci was interviewed alone by the media, and after picking up the baggage, we were off to the city.

What a ride! Narrow streets, mostly jammed, our bus led by two *polizia* on scooters moving in and out of the wrong lane—a hundred near misses! Tinny horns beeping wildly. For a few minutes it was like a Keystone Cops comedy.

We checked into the Excelsior. A quick walk alone down the Via Veneto to the Flora, then back to write this.

It's 2:50 P.M.; I should get a couple of hours' sleep before dinner at the Ambassador's residence.

Up at 5 P.M. Well, I said a couple of hours. This is what travelers would consider a luxury hotel. But many motel accommodations in New York are in ways superior to this good, elegant-looking European hotel. The bed is too soft for me, the lighting is poor. No TV, no radio. To one who is accustomed to the United States, the difference is noticeable.

It's extraordinary what we can find to complain about. That's true on a much grander scale than hotel accommodations. We complain about our simplest discomfort in Queens, and the Mezzogiorno swallows up 5,000 or so lives when the earth decides to take a big bite out of Italian humanity. We mourn for the loss of our John Lennon when every day a neighbor has suffered the loss of someone dear, without notice. Our joy increases our sadness; our comfort exaggerates our pain; our wealth of good things lowers the threshold of what we will consider deprivation. We have a distorted perspective . . . we are spoiled.

Called Matilda to say "all's well" at 6:20 Rome, 12:20 P.M. New York time.

It's hard for me to relate to the surroundings I was in this evening. The residence of the Ambassador in Rome is said to be one of the most beautiful in all of Italy. Huge stone arch entrance gates, tiled floors, tiled ceilings, rococo design throughout, patterned walls, chandeliers of tinted blue crystal, heavy velvet curtains, French provincial and Italian furniture. An Andy Warhol painting of Jimmy Carter—incongruous in its style—eccentrically obvious in the foyer. Circular stairs. Huge wall mirrors in gold-leaf frames. The confusion of baroque. Excess, near frenzy; anything to say it's real! Marble fireplaces. Elaborate gardens with—of all things—a bocci court.

Ambassador Gardner made a good, solid presentation: "Italy is an important ally. Italy is vulnerable because of the economy, the largest number of Communists outside of Russia and now the earthquake."

Increasingly, the political question comes to the fore: how the present government is perceived as handling the earthquake can determine its survival. The central government is making an all-out effort to do this thing right.

After the briefings, a bocci game, by flashlight, in the Ambassador's sumptuous gardens. Cuomo and Steve Aiello vs. Conte and Bob Georgine.[2] Both sides cheat. Contest declared a draw by Pelosi and Biaggi, referees.

Bed at midnight.

[2]Stephen R. Aiello, special assistant for ethnic affairs to President Carter; Silvio Conte, U.S. congressman from Massachusetts; and Robert Georgine, president of the Building and Construction Trades Department, AFL-CIO.

MONDAY, DECEMBER 15, 1980

It's 7:30 P.M., a free evening.

All day long we were surrounded by the antiquity and magnificent beauty of Rome. The Palazzo Chigi, where we met Prime Minister Forlani, the Palazzo Quirinale, where President Pertini greeted us, the Palazzo Madama, built in 1520, and the Palazzo Giustiniani, where we were feted, were each staggering in their grandeur. Marble, magnificent paintings, frescoes, wood carvings, architecture that has made the world gape in awe—all are a casual part of the life we were introduced to today, as we met the three Presidents.

First Forlani, President of the Council of Ministers and therefore Prime Minister. Sixtyish, slender, silver-streaked gray hair matching nicely a gray flannel suit. Very much the lawyer: discreet, careful. Very much the diplomat: charming, pleasant. He says the right and predictable things: "Thank you to President Carter. We look forward to working with President-elect Reagan. Thank you to the American people: you have always been our good friends. This is a terrible catastrophe but we will handle it . . . with your help."

President of the Republic Pertini is 83, a pipe-smoker and philosopher. Imprisoned by the Fascists, he is still fiery in his conviction. Sprightly. Quick to point out he has not lost his "sensitivity" to a beautiful woman, he flirts with Geraldine Ferraro,[1] to the delight of everyone. He emphasized that in reconstructing the devasted villages it would be essential to provide jobs for the residents through the encouraging of small industries. Sounds familiar if you're from New York City.

Fanfani, the President of the Senate, and his colleagues described the legislation he had passed, which among other things produced 1.7 billion dollars—in lire that would fill Madison Square Garden to the rafters—for emergency relief. That expenditure requires Italians to impose upon themselves a 10% increase in the price of gasoline—up to about $3.40 a gallon. For an economy already facing a terrible deficit, this is a big blow. And it's only the beginning. We heard today that the total cost

---

[1]U.S. congresswoman from Queens.

of reconstruction would be somewhere around 12 billion dollars. After all, 10% of the country's territory was struck. It's as though all of California had been victimized.

All day long we ask whether there has been corruption and exploitation of the earthquake situation. All day long the officials point out that whatever corruption and errors have occurred, considering the enormity of the confusion created by the disaster, they were not surprising. It seems to me that before Americans judge the Italian government or the Italian people, we ought to consider our own handling of the riots during the blackouts in New York City.

TUESDAY, DECEMBER 16, 1980

I did this morning what I haven't done in a long time—I overslept. I guess that's good. Nancy Pelosi had the same experience. We were both a few minutes late to the bus.

Forty minutes to Capodichino Airport in Naples by our air force plane from Rome. We drove past the old port areas from which my mother and father sailed a lifetime ago, past piles of containers ready to be reloaded for transportation back to the United States and other parts of the world. The containers, huge steel boxes in which goods are shipped, had been used as housing in the first few days after the quake. They have been replaced by tents and trailers and are being returned now to their more customary duty.

We arrived at the Palazzo Ammiragliato (Admiralty House) at about 10 A.M. for a meeting with Commissioner Zamberletti. The large, high-ceilinged, drafty old building showed us the first evidence of the quake—long cracks in some of the stone walls.

Commissioner Joseph Zamberletti. In his late 40's but looks older, probably because of his soft silver-gray hair. Fine features, pleasant smile, rimless glasses: smooth-skinned northerner, definitely not from the Mezzogiorno.

We sat at a long table and he described for us—through our flawless interpreter, the assistant to Ambassador Gardner, Anna Larson—what he has been doing and what he plans. We had heard much of it before: the early confusion and pilfering now largely under control; the vastness of the damage; 5,000 dead or presumed dead; 20,000 families needing housing in Naples alone; 240,000 people in tents; 20,000 trailers occupied by refugees.

Zamberletti won the delegation over entirely by his graciousness and apparent sincerity. He ended the meeting asking for our advice and counsel. Now there's a politician!

On the way out of the Admiralty House, Bob Georgine ran over to tell me some of my cousins were waiting for me at the bus. I met them—I hadn't before—and I was quickly caught up in embraces and two-cheek kisses. Benito Cuomo and some others whose names escaped me were simply glad to have seen me at all. They indicated they had some problems that they would talk to my mother about rather than "bother" me now. They asked if I could come back in the spring, and I told them I'd try.

A rushed lunch at the Italian officers' mess at Capodichino Airport, then into the helicopters.

Finally, we are in the earthquake zone. Flying low, some miles east of Naples, over stretches of farmland. Random houses, separated by flat fields, an occasional cluster of homes in developments, and then the mountains of Avellino.

Villages tucked in the crevices of the mountains—clinging to the sides of them, sitting at the tops. All the homes of stone or cement, many of them with heavy tile roofs, so heavy that if they fell, they would crush everything beneath them, floors and people, until they returned to the hard mountain earth.

This is the Mezzogiorno—the place where the sun always shines, where it's always the middle of the day. It is the southern half of Italy, relatively undernourished economically for generations. The poor, the uneducated, the undereducated, the unemployed, the underemployed. In the north is the industry, the education, the high culture, the refinement. My people and Matilda's come from the Mezzogiorno, and things have not changed here much since they left.

Here and there the signs of the quake. From the air, one can see an occasional pile of rubble dripping down the side of the mountain in a small river of stone and brick and clay.

The earthquake struck in a snakelike pattern, zigzagging through the mountains, missing some villages with its major force, touching them only enough to cause pain—but leveling others entirely.

The helicopter lands first at Sant'Angelo dei Lombardi in Avellino. A month ago it was 5,000 inhabitants in a mountain village that can be reached only by winding one's way up a narrow dirt road barely wide enough for two vehicles. Simple people, farmers, small merchants, shepherds, laborers, fiercely loyal to the only home they knew—as we were to learn repeatedly from the villagers we spoke to during the day.

Ninety-five percent of this town has been destroyed by the flexing of God's muscle. About 600 of Sant'Angelo's simple people are dead, crushed, battered or buried under the tile roofs and rubble.

Many were infants and children, left behind with the older people while their parents went north seeking work that the hard ground of Avellino would not yield. Six hundred more are still missing. Practically everyone is homeless. Some live in tents, others in trailers.

Nearly a month after the *terremoto* they walk the streets, those who for some reason remain, looking for signs that someone, somewhere, somehow will find a way to help them.

I walked down the muddy street toward the center of the town and met two young ladies. We talked for a few minutes. One of them was 17 or so. Big brown eyes, quick intelligence, sharp, cogent answers and observations. She's a student at the University in Salerno. "The north has never done anything for the Mezzogiorno, and the young people of the Mezzogiorno have never had much opportunity. That's why they went to the United States in the old days and go to Switzerland and Tuscany and Lombardy today. We don't expect the government to do much for us now. The things that have come to us—like the trailers and tents and clothing—came not from the government but from the good Italian people and others around the world." "Why do you not leave," I asked, "like the others?" "Because now there is trouble. Now I must stay because this is my place and my duty."

Lino Angelone—down the street farther. A technician. He was watching TV in his pajamas at 7:40 P.M. on November 23 when the current died. Immediately tremors started, the ground began to tremble, and in 1 minute and 10 seconds the "shocko" came. Wreaking havoc. With the first tremor he had bounded down the stairs to where his 4-year-old was on the first floor. He held him close and stood in an archway—that much the people of Sant'Angelo knew about earthquakes. He was injured, but he and his child lived. In the house next to his, they didn't. A family of four was crushed. He had seen them an hour before he had come into his house to lie on the bed and watch the soccer championship on Sant'Angelo's major luxury, TV. One minute and 10 seconds after the tremors began, his friends were buried in graves without crosses.

We walked past small hills of unused clothes from the United States, soaked from the rain and snow. If the clothes had been dry, they could at least have been burned for heat. Not even that. What a waste . . . why didn't someone tell us?

Politicians and TV crews mill around in the center of town. The people left behind are willing to talk. They spend little time describing how bad it was: we can all see that for ourselves. Instead they give advice: "Don't give the money to the government. Build schools; come over yourself with the money. Don't trust them."

Much the same story in Balvano, in the Province of Potenza. A smaller town—of about 2,500 people. Ninety-eight percent was destroyed. Eighty to 100 are dead, 100 not accounted for and many others injured. But there was an added grim irony in Balvano. Sixty people were killed, most of them elderly women with grandchildren, when the façade of the church collapsed, crushing them as they prayed.

About 100 feet from the remains of the church, I saw an evergreen decorated with colored paper ornaments—a Christmas tree, amidst the tents and mud, the rubble and sadness. I stopped a middle-aged-looking man who was walking past it and asked him what it was. He said it was for "*Natale*." I said, "Why aren't there religious symbols on it?" Perhaps I imagined it, perhaps I saw in his face what I expected to see, but for a brief second his eyebrows lifted, his face tightened. . . . I was sure he was about to condemn the very notion of religion. He didn't. He caught himself. With a shrewdness of instinct, perhaps an implicit reluctance to tempt the fates further—especially for no profit—he decided not to deal with the matter. "It's not our tree—someone broughtitinfromoutside."Andsohedismissed thehardquestion.

Jeno was in a different part of the village. He met a woman who grabbed hold of his coat and pleaded for a stove. She had spent her life "keeping the house," and the stove was her central, indispensable instrument. Without it she was lost. And here is the United States in all of its might: military, politicians, Secret Service, TV, radio, press, photographers. But when we departed that day, the woman was left looking for other lapels to seize— still without a stove.

Another woman was asked whether she would be willing to leave her homesite at the top of a mountain in the Sant'Angelo region. She said no. "But, Signora, the earthquake may come again!" "Makes no difference." "It makes no difference that you may die?" "There are two ways to die," said the old woman. "One is by earthquake, the other is by being forced to leave your home." Clearly, the problems of reconstruction will be more than technical.

I walked alone between the broken buildings. I talked to people. One cried—still another elderly woman. She will cry for a long time.

They are talking in New York about Mafia, corruption, ripoffs, foul-ups. That makes news. But this isn't a story of spectacular corruption or spectacular crime or spectacular bureaucratic bungling. The story here is one of spectacular disaster. Its dimensions are difficult to exaggerate. It's a situation the people of the Mezzogiorno do not understand. Nor do I. What I *do* know is that those of us who can respond must respond.

WEDNESDAY, DECEMBER 17, 1980

Breakfast with Ken Curtin and Jim Brown of the Red Cross. We discuss more ideas for IDEA. Adopt-a-Town, with the local representatives of AID putting up the towns for adoption and IDEA in the USA responding.

Ben Palumbo[1] joins us. "Ben, why not a commercial coordina-

---

[1]Governmental relations representative for Philip Morris, now with the public affairs firm of Palumbo and Cerrell, Inc., in Washington, D.C.

tor for IDEA? Why couldn't Philip Morris build senior citizens' centers in the disaster zone and call them 'Marlboro Houses'?" No commitment from Ben, but Ken and Jim love the thought. Multiply it by 100.

IDEA to go national. We all agree. Curtin will report when we all meet on the 23rd of December in New York City. As I write my first notes of the day—9:15 A.M.—the lights go out in my room at the Excelsior. It's not unusual for this energy-poor land. Another reminder of how relatively well off we are in the United States.

Lunch with Emilio Colombo. Twice Prime Minister; now Foreign Minister. Fiftyish, pleasant-looking, but with rounder features than the others. He looks more like someone from the Mezzogiorno, and he is, from Potenza.

We begin the trip home at about 2:30 P.M. A few hours later we stop at Shannon.

We arrive in Washington at about 8:30 and finally back to New York by about 10:15 P.M.

It's over. I think the trip will help us to help them. Lord knows they need the help, and we need to give it.

THURSDAY, DECEMBER 25, 1980 (CHRISTMAS MORNING)

Up at 5:30 A.M.

Christmas Eve at Grandma Raffa's. Sam and Pat showed up with their children, and that meant all the Raffas were together. They had their cousin Sal Raffa, his wife and children there as well.

A feast—as always. This time Sal—who is a chef—added some touches. Octopus in a dark sauce, shrimp cardinale, broiled striped bass, scallops, fried fillet, spaghettini with clams, broccoli, salad, wine . . . on and on.

Bitter cold. We drove back to our house, arriving at about 1 A.M. Chris a little moody. Margaret was dropped off by Andrew in Bay Ridge for a party. Andrew stopped on Flatlands Avenue on the way home to buy an enormous stuffed dog because Maria (with her cast still on) and Madeline had seen them being sold and said they wanted one. He's been great. He basically is very close to the whole family. I hope someday he has his own and the happiness he deserves.

Matilda's big effort comes today, so we'll let her sleep a bit. (It's 7:30 A.M.)

FRIDAY, DECEMBER 26, 1980

It's the morning after at 9 A.M. It went well, thank God. And for us, it's so simple. The kids were all here with Nancy and Bob,[1] Joe and Josie, Mom and Pop Raffa, Frank and Marian and their kids. Matilda's food was superb. Lasagna, filet mignon, a roast, spinach pie, vegetables of all kinds, salad, fruit, exotic desserts. Later in the day Bill Stern stopped by, as did Jerry Weiss and Joe Anastasi.[2] We played dollar-bill poker and chatted.

Chris had a really big day! Andrew got him an AMF bike. He also received the "Head to Head" computerized football game, which he played almost ceaselessly all night.

Otherwise nothing dramatic. No carol singing. No great traditional ceremonies. No real surprises. Just a basic, solid, simple, pleasant time, with—inevitably—a few spots of sadness.

SUNDAY, JANUARY 11, 1981

The holidays have passed: the political year begins anew in Albany!

Carey's State of the State message was described as "masterful" as a political effort by most of the media. It was a potpourri of benefits for various groups but didn't clearly reveal the costs of the benefits and who would pay for them. That will come in the budget. It's clear to me that the litany of nice promises, which was so well received when delivered, will become a severe burden before much longer.

I continue to have no contact with the Governor. At the last minute he attempted to insert my name in the State of the State

[1]Nancy and Bob Mazzola, Matilda's sister and brother-in-law.
[2]State trooper assigned to my security, who has been with me since I became lieutenant governor.

message as a "coordinator" of the Criminal Justice effort. But I
didn't think it was a serious effort: he hadn't even discussed it
with me and the message contained some recommendations I
was opposed to, so I told Del Giudice to take my name out of
the message. They were irritated, but to have left it in would
have permitted the Governor, again, to dispose casually of whatever my usefulness is. The Governor reached out at the last
minute to sit down with me, but we were cities apart and it didn't
work out.

Fink criticized the message.

Ned Regan[1] criticized Carey on the MTA.[2]

Bellamy criticized Carey and Regan on MTA.

The potential candidates arrange themselves in a flurry of early
anticipatory eagerness.

Vice-President Mondale liked IDEA at a meeting at the White
House on Friday (January 9), and at my suggestion Jeno Paulucci
was appointed to chair a committee to make IDEA national.[3] I
think if I'm aggressive about helping him, we can do something
worthwhile with Jeno.

WEDNESDAY, JANUARY 14, 1981

It's 6 A.M.

Maria's cast came off Monday. She was distressed by the ugliness of her shriveled leg and it upset her for a day or so. But
this morning at 2 A.M. she came home from a date (even a
shriveled leg won't keep her home) totally different in disposi-

---

[1]Edward V. Regan, Republican, New York State comptroller.

[2]Metropolitan Transportation Authority, public transportation system serving New
York City and surrounding suburban counties. Carey was accused of not paying enough
attention to its management problems.

[3]The first meeting of IDEA National was held on March 5, 1981, and attended by
representatives of the voluntary agencies and the Italian and U.S. governments. Eventually, USAID contributed $4 million (out of the original appropriation of $50 million)
to match funds raised by the voluntary agencies and to be used by them. In fiscal 1982,
$10 million was appropriated, to be shared by Catholic Relief Services, Salvation Army
World Services and Save the Children Federation. In 1983, $10 million was again
appropriated for Italian earthquake relief, with, however, only $2 million for the volun-
tary agencies (CRS, SA, SCF). Reconstruction in the Mezzogiorno is still far from
complete.

tion. She was nearly ecstatic about the fact that she had been able to stand on the leg only a day or so after she had the cast removed.

With some patience she'll be O.K.

Met with Morgado at length for discussions Monday and Tuesday in Albany. He "very much wants [me] working more closely with the Governor." The Governor walked in on our discussions a couple of times with desultory comments on a variety of subjects. I made some suggestions they both liked, on how to present the budget message. I dictated a 5- or 6-minute presentation for the Governor. Frucher and Morgado thought it was "great": we'll see if the Governor uses it.

Coldest winter I can remember. The heating bill pains me.

THURSDAY, JANUARY 22, 1981

The budget has been announced. It is the main work of the governmental year. This one is Carey's most interesting since his first. It lays out a plan for the decade. In parts it is—or would be if adopted—precedent-setting. It would impose a cap on expenditures at both the state and local levels and would mandate real-property tax reduction. It would call for clearer methods of accounting, a welfare increase, money for prisons and a lot of other politically—and substantively—attractive things. Perhaps its only political vulnerability is in the area of education, where it leaves a great deal of room for criticism by teachers and education lobbyists.[1]

The Governor has asked me to work aggressively to sell it. There are parts I will enjoy pushing, like the expenditure cap.

Matilda is ill again today with what appears to be a touch of the flu. Andrew is working at the gas station for the week he's home. He's going to need the money. He ran up $165 in tickets in Albany for leaving his car parked overtime while he was

[1]Because it would be perceived as not generous enough.

studying for exams. The car is in his mother's name, so they ran a story in the *Times-Union* referring to Matilda Cuomo, scofflaw!

THURSDAY, JANUARY 29, 1981

The Governor's budget has survived well the first days of discussion. I made the case for it in Rochester yesterday at the Gannett editorial board meeting, and it was well received.

I didn't do as well on a 10-minute appearance on Channel 21, the Public Service channel there. I looked fat, balding and baggy-eyed, and I was a bit testy. Probably tired.

WHAM went well: calls from Kentucky and New Jersey, among others.

A speech to the New York Public Welfare Association, consisting of professional county welfare administrators, was not well received. I made the point that our needy were threatened by calls for austerity that would inevitably prove to be austerity only for the underclasses. They seemed bored with the rhetoric. Barbara Blum,[1] who followed me (after I left), said that we should not "overreact" to the change in Administration. This morning I read that Secretary of Defense Weinberger said the Administration would probably have to reduce social programs! Overreaction?

Spoke to the Governor's new Counsel, Jack McGoldrick. Seems like an intelligent, capable, sensitive, nonpolitical chap. The Governor will be gone from January 31 to February 10, and Jack wants to be sure that we coordinate for bill signings and other details.

I recommended to the Governor that he keep a written record of his trip.[2] It will keep him in the papers, deliver the messages he wants delivered, instead of the ones the press would like delivered, and be fun. I suspect he may do it, since my advice on presenting his budget—and the material I wrote—was received quite well.

[1] Commissioner of the New York State Department of Social Services.
[2] The governor was going to Japan to try to persuade the Japanese to invest in New York State.

WEDNESDAY, FEBRUARY 4, 1981

I've been Governor for a few days and have concluded that it's better than being Lt. Governor. I enjoy the responsibility—however limited. Comptroller Regan issued a statement condemning the request for a welfare increase. I was required to respond—and did, in strong language. It was well covered in this morning's papers and on last night's TV. That would never have occurred if I had spoken as Lt. Governor. Yes, it's better being Governor: it gives impact to positions; it improves the capacity to help.

Dominic Baranello[1] called. He's distressed at Carey's apparent unpopularity statewide. I commiserated with him but said there was still a long way to go.

Andrew has begun to learn about the imperfections of our criminal justice system. He's been waiting three days for the trial to be reached in the case of the bus driver who struck and killed James Spirio. Andrew is a principal witness.[2]

WEDNESDAY, FEBRUARY 11, 1981

The term of Mario Cuomo as Acting Governor ended tonight at 5 P.M. when the plane carrying Hugh Carey crossed the air space into New York. It was fun—and, I think, successful. I told the Public Employees' Conference this morning, in the presence of the legislative leaders, that during my term there were no tax increases, no loss of jobs, no strikes, no vetoes overruled and 90% good weather!

More serious is the publicity that each day increases the speculation that Carey is seeking to "get rid" of Cuomo. There are leaks and rumors about Carey talking to Schuler[1] and other

---

[1]County leader of Suffolk County and state chairman of the Democratic party of New York State.

[2]The bus driver was convicted of a misdemeanor and received only a ninety-day suspended sentence—another example of the imperfections in our system.

[1]Ray Schuler, former transportation commissioner under Nelson Rockefeller, Malcolm Wilson and Hugh Carey. Now—and in 1981—president of the Business Council of New York State.

possibilities for a running mate in 1982. No one knows where they come from, and there does not appear to be an intelligent political design to the activity, but they are damaging to everyone involved. The Governor hasn't spoken to me about them, nor—I'm sure—will he. The Governor has made it clear that he will talk to me only when he needs something.

THURSDAY, FEBRUARY 12, 1981

I was wrong about hearing from the Governor.

Yesterday, after I had made my notes, he called me from New York while I was still in Albany. He had apparently decided that the best defense was a good offense, and he started by suggesting that I was somehow responsible for the rumors that he had spoken to Schuler about being Lt. Governor. I was outraged and made that clear to him. I had been reliably informed that he did talk to Schuler in '78 and gave him the impression he might want him, and that he also spoke to him in November of 1980 and expressed his dissatisfaction with me and, incidentally, Bill Hassett.[1] We know, and the *Daily News* knows, of this because it was one of their reporters who discussed it with me. My discussion with the Governor was crisp and firm from my end. I told him I was not interested in his discussions with Schuler or anyone else; that it would be unseemly for me to ask him about them—or to complain. I told him he would make his decision about Lt. Governor and I would make mine, independently. I told him even if he asked me, I might not run for Lt. Governor: I did not say what I *would* do. He asked me to be at the press conference today at which he would announce his major achievement from his trip. What he really wanted—I thought—was to put an end to anything that suggested I might run against him. I told him I wouldn't be there—and I wasn't.

I had the impression from my conversation with him that the Governor had been stung by a Breslin column which attacked him mercilessly on his trip and that he was about to overreact by overstating what he had been able to achieve on the trip. Despite

[1]Governor Carey's commerce commissioner at the time.

our personal differences, I was concerned that he might promise something like a Japanese plant somewhere in New York, which he might not then be able to produce. I was also concerned that he might take our relationship for granted and indicate a commitment I had not made yet and might never make. I warned Morgado and Del Giudice about both.

They instructed Carey, and he took the instruction. At his press conference, he handled the question about me by saying simply that he had not yet decided what he was going to do about running. He said, "When I decide, I will talk to my family, then I will talk to Cuomo."

Home tonight, having driven myself in the Checker[2] leaving Albany at 6 P.M. It was a good drive. What a difference from Sunday night, when I had to drive through a snowstorm.

Tuesday night in Albany with Joe Bellacosa[3] and Sol Wachtler[4] celebrating Woodie's birthday.[5] This is an annual event. We had 6 pleasant hours of jokes and discussions. I think Sol is really eager to run for Governor against Carey. He'd make a good candidate, too.

Sunday, February 15, 1981

It's 5:30 A.M. Andrew has just come in, and it's clear he's spent a lot of time tonight talking about my future with some of his friends. He thinks that Carey will find it very hard to win again because the personal dislike which he overcame in '78 has now become "disgust." Andrew agrees with me that Carey doesn't deserve this low appraisal by the public at large, but he is convinced it's a strong and unchangeable opinion. Given the public's desire for "a change," which makes even a good record academic, there is no doubt there's something to what he's saying. The trip to Japan has proven to be a small fiasco. Carey is

[2]A Checker Marathon, my personal "limousine."
[3]Clerk in the New York State Court of Appeals (and an old friend).
[4]Associate justice of the New York City Court of Appeals, and former county executive of Nassau County.
[5]I met Woodie Fitchette, former crack newspaper reporter for the Gannett chain, while he was covering the 1974 campaign upstate. He joined my staff, and we became close friends.

trying to explain away "gratuities" and an expensive retinue when he should be getting credit for an exciting and potentially lucrative move. His unpopularity with Democrats active in the party and potential rivals like Abrams[1] and Fink and Koch (who is potentially a rival vicariously; I doubt he would ever run) also hurts him. Nevertheless he is gearing up to run and at this point it appears unlikely anyone could dissuade him.

My position has been to remain uncommitted even as to whether I will run at all, for Governor or Lt. Governor.

SATURDAY, FEBRUARY 21, 1981

I've spent most of the last week at home working by telephone because I tried to get too much raking done with Christopher last weekend. I was able to get in at the tail end of the week to meet with Bill Stern and Arnie Biegen[1] about a fund-raiser and have a staff meeting. Yesterday I did a dull ½-hour show with Bob Keating about crime and the Guardian Angels[2] at WCBS and then did the Sabbath sermon for Temple Sholom in Glen Oaks. The Temple is unique: they have a young woman rabbi, Rabbi Susan Abramson, and a young woman cantor, Ellen Sussman, with an extraordinary mezzo-soprano voice. I enjoyed the ceremony a great deal, especially the communal nature of it: perhaps a dozen of the congregation participated in readings. I spoke about anti-Semitism: I read the Shabbos Goy speech.[3] That was well received. The question-and-answer period was a different matter. A decade ago you would have expected a group like this one to be sensitive to the concerns of the minorities, open-minded, compassionate—in a very general sense, "liberal." No such thing today. There is a fear, an insecurity and an impatience with government that makes these embattled middle-class people leery of any suggestion that they be called upon to make sac-

---

[1]Robert Abrams, attorney general of the state of New York.

[1]A lawyer from New York; a friend and supporter for seven years.

[2]A group of young, mostly Black and Hispanic volunteers organized by Curtis and Lisa Sliwa. Now found in various cities across the country, they started as citizen anticrime patrols in the subways of New York City.

[3]This particular "Shabbos Goy speech" appears on pp. 399–405.

rifices for the people economically beneath them. For the most part, this group would not even understand that the recent closing of a "white" school in Rosedale was required by the Constitution. They oppose busing, period! They don't wish the "Blacks" any evil; they just don't want to risk their convenience or life styles to help them. They might be less unwilling if they believed the government's policies might work; but that—especially—they find difficult to believe.

Governor Carey's popularity continues to wane. No matter how good his substantive performance, small embarrassments have created an aura of "arrogance of power" that's tough to overcome, whether true or not.

This evening I took Matilda, Chris and Nellie[4] to the Northstage Theatre in Glen Cove to have dinner and see *Man of La Mancha*. I enjoyed it more than I did the first time we saw it on Broadway, although the singing and production were not quite as good. The management wanted to pick up the tab, but I wouldn't let them. Too bad—it cost me over $100! I didn't let Matilda know.

Chris is still at the fidgety stage and it wasn't easy for him to sit through the performance, although dinner, as usual, he handled quite well. He didn't fully understand the plot, which was a good deal more didactic and subtle than I had recalled it to be. I remembered the original as nicely moralistic and simple. The main theme came through to him, however, and it was a good one: believing is better than not believing; believing in goodness, virtue, improvement will give you a better opportunity for peace than not believing.

SATURDAY, MARCH 14, 1981

Steps decided upon today at a meeting with Jerry Weiss, Bill Stern, Joel McCleary, Andrew and myself at J.W.'s office.

The operating principle is that Gov. Carey may decide not to

[4]Nellie Vitale, an old friend from down the block in Queens.

run because he doesn't want to or because he believes he can't win. Joel reports that political leaders in Washington who were associated with Reagan before and after his campaign say Carey will be eminently beatable and that the only person they would be concerned about would be MMC. I'm not sure I like to hear that: why should I become a target?

In any event I suggested the following and all agreed: (1) Stern to find a nucleus of 6–10 strong contributors who would be willing to pledge their involvement. They could be approached on a contingent basis, but we would prefer to get a war chest immediately. MMC to get list of names and work with Stern to put this group together as soon as possible and meet with them. (2) Nail Mondale down to a date after August for a fund-raiser. Build around him, announcing it as soon as possible. If we get Mondale, I would then ask Koch, Moynihan and perhaps even Kennedy on a flier: I've agreed to put my name down on a number of fund-raiser efforts for the Kennedy debt. (3) Stern will go over all cards with Tonio as soon as possible. (4) We will rent a pre-campaign office where we can poll as soon as possible. (5) I will continue to work as hard as possible, concentrating on the city of New York and on Westchester, Rockland, Nassau and Suffolk counties. (6) We will meet regularly.

There is no question that Jerry and Joel are eager to see me run for Governor even against Carey. I have told them repeatedly it would be difficult for me to do. Even apart from my personal feelings on the subject, unless there was a clearer rationale than now exists I don't believe my decision to run against the Governor I had served would be well received. On the other hand, if he were perceived as a loser, then the dynamics would change. The difficulty with mentioning this, even to a small, tight group, is that it begins to tempt those who want me to run into projecting the image of Carey as a loser, and that I don't feel comfortable doing. I still believe my best course—although it does not have a high degree of likelihood—is to get as ready as I can and stay reasonably close to the Governor and the apparatus of our government—at least as close as they'll let me.

I think Andrew is inclined to agree with me. He doesn't like the idea of running against Carey, because he doesn't think there is an acceptable rationale.

So, the planning begins in earnest. It seems the campaigns never really end. It is necessary in the hurly-burly and excitement of this kind of thinking to remind yourself that the basic objective is not to win an election, or power, or fun, but to help improve the conditions of people's lives. It's not easy.

There are other distractions. The wind destroyed part of our rotting fence in the backyard yesterday. Margaret is graduating, and we will want to have a nice party. Matilda is all set for a trip to San Diego with Maria, Madeline and Chris, to visit Joe and Josie for Easter. Altogether we will need a good deal of money before the Fall. I'm getting closer to the bottom of the barrel: all I have left that amounts to anything are the 2 certificates that don't come due until June.

I can't blame Matilda for being angry at my refusal to make money as a lawyer even while serving. She doesn't see it as a commendable effort to create no false image of conflict: she sees it as selfishness on my part. This is one of the things that really make my position difficult, but I have no one to charge the discomfort to but myself. It would be so much easier if I could blame someone.

WEDNESDAY, MARCH 18, 1981

The country still thinks President Reagan is on the right track, and most are not willing to believe that there is a better way to get there than the one that's been taken. Today, the editorial boards of the *Times-Union* and *Knickerbocker News* showed their strong, dogged, almost obstinate conviction that any attempt to criticize the federal budget is an attempt to abandon the direction toward austerity. Again, there appears to be very little subtlety in the public at large, and that situation seems contagious. Many leading Democrats either don't disagree with Reagan or are afraid to say they do. I think the budget is bad because it will be ineffective in achieving the results it promises and most people hope for;[1] it is unfair especially to New York and the Northeast,

[1] Among other things, an end of inflation without recession and a balanced budget after three years.

and it dramatically reverses the proposition that all parts of the country should work together. We saved the South after the Civil War—built the TVA, highways and the infrastructure that made it viable. When I say "we" I mean it was done with money that came largely from the Northeast. Now they propose to direct efforts away from the Northeast when it is disadvantaged and weakened.

I told the Governor today (by memo) that I believed he should be leading the attack against the Federal budget for the Northeast. He appears reluctant. His political judgment is usually better than mine, but my sense of it is that *he* should be leading now. He appears to be deeply involved with Mrs. Evangeline Gouletas, a widow from Chicago, and that may be distracting him. I'll try again in a few days and in the meantime I'll continue to do what I can.

Andrew is thinking of working with Jerry and Fabian this summer and perhaps even next year, by transferring down to N.Y. I like the idea but I don't want to push him.

Madeline is still working hard on a diet and a full social life, and Christopher grows taller and sweeter.

Matilda has lost a good deal of weight and looks great. The activities she's found to occupy her energies, like the American Cancer Society and St. John's Auxiliary, have been very good for her. They all began with the campaigns and that's one good thing I can say for them.

WEDNESDAY, MARCH 25, 1981

The Governor appears to have dyed his hair again and that is being perceived as a sure sign he's running again. I'm sure he is . . . but I don't know if it's for Governor, for President, for Evangeline Gouletas or for all three!

In the meantime—and in the dark—I'm going forward with fund-raising and a poll and a temporary meeting place, to be ready for whatever.

. . .

Still no state budget, with less than a week to go.[1] I like to think I would do it differently and better, if I were Governor. I wonder if I'll ever know.

THURSDAY, MARCH 26, 1981

I'm told Koch is angry about my comments concerning capital punishment. I was quoted as saying that in '77 he should have told people we'd have to spend money on police, prosecutors, courts, etc., and he didn't. I also said I thought it would be good to have a debate on city services. Weiss and Burgos and others are unhappy that I have "unnecessarily" incurred his wrath—which can be considerable. The question is, did it serve any good purpose? I think what I said was clearly true and accurately reported by the *Post* (although they left out the flattering things I said about Ed). But I doubt that it will—or did—affect people's judgments on the question of crime, capital punishment or services. Under those circumstances it was, indeed, probably "unnecessary."

MONDAY, APRIL 6, 1981

Five days past the budget deadline without a budget. Sinning gets easier with repetition: this is four years in a row. Some say the pressure of the deadline is necessary in order to generate incentives to trade. I don't believe it: it wasn't true before 1978.

We had a "special session" called by the Governor at Fink's request. It forced everybody to Albany on Saturday but—the way it worked out—didn't achieve anything else. Carey and Fink agree on a budget $1.4 million higher than last year. Anderson[1] suggests a $1.8 million increase. Carey wants to start by getting Anderson to identify the $400 million in additional revenues he would spend. Anderson says, "It's there!" He wants to get right

[1]By law, the state's budget must be adopted by April 1, the beginning of the fiscal year.

[1]Warren M. Anderson, majority leader of the state senate, Republican from Broome County.

into negotiation with Fink and Carey on all items. Alphonse and Gaston. No progress in sight. Meanwhile, the Governor has announced he'll be getting married on Saturday.

One difference between this year and the last two is that I have been more usable in the negotiations this year, and that has attracted some reporters' attention, with mixed results.

I've tried distilling lessons from my participation of the last few days.

The first thing that occurs to me is that what is required here is not just experience but basic abilities and qualities as well. The pressure, the confrontational style are made to order for a lawyer's skills. All three of the principals have those skills. It's best to be quick, glib and knowledgeable. It's also extremely useful to have a strategy, long-range and immediate, that sets overall objectives, and short-term day-to-day goals in the matter of tactics. Here I believe we've been a bit weak. At first Carey wanted one or more of his conceptual predicates—Medicaid pickup,[2] state expenditure cap, local expenditure cap and GAAP.[3] Now, with the real danger that hospitals and nursing homes will be in trouble because of a failure to approve payments,[4] the objectives have been reduced to just getting a budget. My guess is Carey will not get Medicaid pickup or the expenditure caps, unless something changes tomorrow. (GAAP is now perceived as more attributable to the Comptroller than to anyone else, so achieving it will not benefit Carey much politically.) That leaves them as issues for next year.

Still, and increasingly, speculation goes on as to whether the Governor will run again. We'll know when we know.

WEDNESDAY, APRIL 8, 1981

Impasse on the budget continues:

Warren will not consider the Medicaid pickup by the State; Carey will not allow consideration of the rest of the budget

---

[2]Carey wanted the state to assume ("pick up") all or a portion of local governments' share of Medicaid costs.

[3]Generally accepted accounting principles, a standard method of accounting, not then in use in the state government.

[4]The delay in adopting the budget jeopardized the timely payment of the state's share of Medicaid costs, as well as other funds.

without it. Nursing homes and hospitals will soon be out of cash.
The Governor had the Assembly pass a special bill appropriating
$75 million to take care of the situation. Warren will not call
back the Senate to consider it, saying: "I won't do the budget
piecemeal."

We will work on Del Bello[1] and Crawford[2] tomorrow to see
if we can get some help on Medicaid. Meanwhile, we will hope
to build the pressure. I'm afraid it will not work, since the Governor's wedding on Saturday will eclipse everything.

THURSDAY, APRIL 9, 1981

Irving Green[1] at the Algonquin for breakfast. He wanted to
convey two messages: I should talk John Dearie[2] out of running
for comptroller against Jay Goldin;[3] I should allow Abrams to
run for Governor and I should run for Attorney General. Buttenwieser[4] will have $750,000 to start an Abrams campaign. I
told Irving I would have $1,000,000. Why not!

SUNDAY, APRIL 12, 1981

The uncertainty of the budget and the Governor's imminent
departure because of his honeymoon have required me to cancel
my plans to go with Matilda and the kids to San Diego. I'll do
what I can to try to compensate with Chris by scheduling a whole
series of things for when he gets back.

The wedding went flawlessly yesterday, ending with a dinner at the Mansion, finishing at about 1 A.M. Matilda enjoyed
it.

[1] Alfred B. Del Bello, then Westchester County executive.
[2] Edwin L. Crawford, of Albany, executive director of the New York State Association
of Counties.

---

[1] A pseudonym for an old friend and supporter.
[2] John C. Dearie, assemblyman from the Bronx.
[3] Harrison J. ("Jay") Goldin, comptroller of the city of New York.
[4] Lawrence B. Buttenwieser, a New York lawyer and leading fund-raiser for Bob
Abrams.

This evening there was another leadership meeting at the Chamber.

The discussions have become increasingly personal and acrimonious between Warren and the Governor. At the meeting tonight Warren suggested the Governor go on his honeymoon and turn the Government over to "Mario." It seemed a calculated effort to annoy the Governor and to lay the groundwork for exploiting his imminent departure from Albany. I did what I could to handle it with the press thereafter.

This morning I spoke at Temple Israel on 75th Street in New York City. (Reform singles group. I would guess 60% of them were conservative Republican types.) It's clear to me the trend is strongly toward the right, and we, the Democrats, have lost much of our formerly presumed constituencies. We certainly can't take the Black or Jewish voters for granted anymore.

We must find ways to make the things we believe appealing to middle- and right-leaning "reasonable types." It's not easy to do without abdicating. My guess is that we have to make clearer, here in New York, our feelings about tax cutting, jobs, waste fighting and common sense. We must use fewer labels; the labels we like—such as "progressive" and "liberal"—can be misleading.

We should talk more about family, too.

MONDAY, APRIL 13, 1981

The budget impasse continues. No relief in sight.

TUESDAY, APRIL 14, 1981

Joe Wasser, member of State Commission of Corrections, Sheriff (formerly) of Sullivan County, and well-known political person in Hudson Valley, came in today to say he was disillusioned with Carey and wants me to run—against him if necessary. He promised me support geographically in his area and in the law-enforcement community. I told him I was getting ready to run if Carey didn't but that I did not intend to run against him "in disloyalty."

Mike Armstrong[1] called and said he was going to go on a list
for Koch. He wants me to endorse Koch, too, so that I win points
in case I want to run for Governor. I told him I'd get back to him.
He said I should talk to him and Cy Vance about it.[2]

Eli Guggenheimer, former Commissioner of Consumer
Affairs of the City of New York, told Burgos today I should run.

This kind of thing can be expected to occur more frequently
now that there has been a series of embarrassing stories about
Mrs. Gouletas-Carey.

Bob Keating says the Koch people think now the Governor
is "mortally wounded."

"I honestly don't believe it" was my response. "This may even
get the Governor some sympathy."

In any event, now that the Governor is under attack, I'm
inclined to defend him.

WEDNESDAY, APRIL 15, 1981

There has been a change in the public image created by the
Governor's wedding. It was all plus Saturday night: tonight the
Governor is seen as the object of pity and sympathy. I don't know
what it means politically, but I feel for the Governor and I'm
struck, again, by the unpredictability of this political life. So
much of the planning is for nought because of the unexpected
events which occur with such frequency. Watergate made for a
Democratic sweep, which made for Carey. Duryea's tax returns.[1]
The UN vote. The Cleveland Debate.[2] Iran. A helicopter that
wouldn't work. None of these things could be analyzed. Nor
could a love affair and then the revelations of the last few days.
A husband who was supposed to be dead is resurrected at Easter-

---

[1]An old friend and chief counsel to the Knapp Commission, which investigated
corruption in the New York City Police Department in 1970.

[2]Cyrus Vance, former secretary of state under Jimmy Carter and long-time prominent
member of the Bar of the State of New York, was at the time a strong supporter of Mayor
Koch.

---

[1]In the campaign of 1978 Perry Duryea refused to disclose his tax returns for a while
and some analysts believe that it turned the campaign against him.

[2]The presidential debate between President Carter and Governor Ronald Reagan. A
turning point in Carter's campaign in many people's opinions, including mine.

time, there is another husband who wasn't counted at all . . . who would have figured on it!

It's had some interesting effects. I think Koch is convinced Carey is either not going to run or will lose and is staying loose so that he can pick the next Governor. His people have cooled on any efforts at rapprochement with me, probably because they don't want to be perceived as getting closer to me as the vacuum occurs.

Whatever happens to Carey, Phil Friedman has made clear that he believes I am "not strong" in New York City. He says my numbers are only "fair" in the City. He says he doesn't know what to attribute it to except that I am perceived as still negative to Koch, and that's hurting me. That might make sense. My major image formation here in New York City was the '77 campaign. That's probably still the dominant force. Phil thinks I need a specific issue and association with Koch. He also properly points out that the office of Lt. Governor is such a fuzzy one it's hard to project a favorable image.

Bob Sullivan[3]—whose judgment is the best I've seen so far—tends to discount Friedman's analysis. He says that even if Friedman's poll figures show me only to be "fair," that's not bad. He's sure that, outside the City, no one's numbers are better and that I could improve the rating by campaigning. He reminds me of Bess Meyerson and so many others who started high in the polls as "favorable" and lost.[4]

The polls are useful, and I'll be taking one, but it would be a mistake to overemphasize their importance.

On the other hand, I do have to work at my image in New York City. More visits here should be helpful.

EASTER SUNDAY, APRIL 19, 1981

Matilda, Chris and Madeline, still in San Diego with Joey and Josie, were sorely missed, but the rest of us—the "older" kids and I—enjoyed dinner at the Douglaston Manor. I can't re-

---

[3] A member of my staff, and one of the brightest people I've ever met.

[4] Bess Meyerson, initially far ahead of her nearest rival in the polls, ended up losing the 1980 Democratic primary for U.S. Senate to Elizabeth Holtzman.

member when Margaret was so relaxed. Maybe as medical
school ends, the pressure will be relieved. I hope so.

Maria came in from San Diego last night and looked great. As
we waited at the airport for Margaret, she was telling Andrew
that she might want to live there after college. I wouldn't be
surprised: why should my children be immune to the lure of the
Sun Belt!

I am grateful for a really good day.

WEDNESDAY, APRIL 22, 1981

I think in the long run the Governor's present embarrassments
will prove not to have hurt him badly—if at all. In a way they
show him to be vulnerable, and vulnerability can be an antidote
to the perception of "arrogance" with which he was previously
charged. And his performance in the budget struggle is clearly
winning him new respect from editorial boards and upper-
echelon politicians, even if the message hasn't been fully trans-
mitted to the people.

Rumors of polls are beginning to emerge. Abrams is "best-
known" state figure. Bellamy, most popular. Cuomo—so-so. I
can believe it.

FRIDAY, APRIL 24, 1981

Doug Ireland and the *SoHo News* ran a piece headlining a quote
from me: "The people around the Governor are cowards and
phonies and you can tell them I said so." I regret it; it makes me
uncomfortable even to think about it. Actually, it's taken out of
context. I was really referring to those "unnamed people around
the Governor" who, Ireland said, were saying disparaging things
about me that I knew were lies. I reacted in irritation and made
an intemperate statement. Sometimes I think we learn very
slowly, if at all. I'll have to try harder on this as on so many other
things. Accurate or not, the story widens the chasm between the
Governor and me.

WEDNESDAY, APRIL 29, 1981

Carey and Anderson agreed to break the impasse.

SUNDAY, MAY 3, 1981

I write on the plane—the State 604—to Oneida County to do the United Food and Commercial Workers' dinner for Sam and Joe Talarico.[1] They've been good friends.

I have the feeling that the vise is beginning to tighten. I did a "Newsmakers" show this morning, and trying to answer questions about my political future dramatized for me how hard answers are going to be to find.

I said that I wasn't going to run for Mayor and would probably support Koch, who has been a good Mayor. I also expressed reservations about his performance, but overall I was commendatory. As to Carey, I simply said it was too early to know. When Vincent Cosgrove of the *Daily News* said, "What if Carey dumps you?" I was stung. I don't think that it makes any sense, but I was annoyed to think anyone is considering it a reasonable possibility.

Carolyn Walsh[2] didn't like my supportive remarks concerning Koch. Marian Neef didn't like my supportive remarks concerning Carey. Neef wants me to commit now to a race against Carey if he runs. Walsh is not so sure. And in these two people are the most popular points of view centered.

Garth and Friedman say Carey definitely wants to run: they both hint that he may not be able to, but they don't hint strongly.

The hardest question for me is, What does MMC do if Carey asks point-blank whether MMC will run?—which he probably will soon.

Say yes, despite the difficulty of the position and the unlikelihood of winning, without strings?

Say yes—on conditions? A more useful role?

Say no and run for Comptroller?

[1]Joe is president of the Amalgamated Meatcutters. His brother Sam is director of internal operations for the union's District Local 1.
[2]A member of my staff.

Say no and run a primary?

Say no and quit politics and government?

I don't have an answer now; I don't have to.

What I'm sure of is that I don't want to be forced into worrying about it.

SATURDAY, MAY 9, 1981

The Governor and leaders announced another budget settlement. After last week's blew up, people received the news of this one more cautiously. I said in the beginning of the week we all look bad. Everyone is saying it now.

MONDAY, JUNE 1, 1981

Met with Phil Friedman for breakfast. In effect he said the following: There's a poll being taken now that may show Carey weak enough so that Garth might not handle him, although this is not likely. If Carey doesn't run, Cuomo will have a chance, but it will be tough in a big field. Bellamy is eager to run. Public doesn't know how "intelligent, sensitive, caring" Cuomo is; would cost big money and big campaign to show them. Did not say who Garth would handle; interested in working with Sullivan (at my suggestion); would like to meet Neef (at my suggestion); doesn't think I have rationale to run against Carey. "MMC would make a great Senator." D'Amato[1] may run for Governor.

WEDNESDAY, JUNE 3, 1981

Last night Margaret had her commencement. My daughter the Doctor! I don't have the words to describe our pride and gratitude. She will be a great Doctor: I only hope it brings her joy.

[1]Alfonse M. D'Amato, U.S. senator (R) from New York.

. . .

The Governor has alienated Fink and Ohrenstein[1] entirely. They are now putting together their own programs with the Republicans.

Howard Rubinstein[2] called to say that Rupert Murdoch[3] said he is going away for 3 months and won't be back till after Labor Day. He (Murdoch) assumed I wanted his endorsement. He said he would do nothing until he got back—for me or anyone else. Howard said he sounded friendly.

Haven't heard from the Governor since he got back from Japan in February except for leadership meetings.

THURSDAY, JUNE 4, 1981

Meislin[1] of the *Times* told me last night that Carey had "knocked" me for "not being around." Meislin said it was a "stunning" and "inexplicable" attack and it would be big news in tomorrow's *Times*. He said Carey said he didn't know what I was doing with my time and suggested I wasn't helping him. I told Meislin I was surprised to hear the Governor say he didn't know where I was when I had been all around the state for his programs at Morgado's request, presumably on his behalf. I have no explanation for the Governor's conduct, but it's clear he's letting me know how little he thinks of me—at the moment. I would have preferred it if he had told me face to face.

FRIDAY, JUNE 5, 1981

Yesterday afternoon at the AFL-CIO convention I mentioned at the beginning of my remarks that I was surprised Carey could say he didn't know what I was doing. I also made it clear that I was

---

[1]Manfred Ohrenstein, state senator (D) from Manhattan and minority leader.

[2]A public relations expert and old friend. We began our careers at about the same time in Brooklyn.

[3]Publisher of the New York *Post* and *New York* magazine.

---

[1]Richard Meislin, New York *Times* bureau chief in Albany.

annoyed; I shouldn't have. The *Daily News* ran a headline
"Cuomo: Carey Doesn't Appreciate Me," which had a whiny
quality I didn't like. One cheap shot in reply to another cheap
shot makes 2 cheap shots . . . nothing good!

Our 27th Anniversary. Matilda and I went to see *Four Seasons*
in New York and then to Lenox Hill Hospital to see Rosemary
Breslin. It appears to be only a matter of time for her. Jimmy and
the kids seem to be bearing up well. Of course, the worst trauma
lies ahead.

SATURDAY, JUNE 13, 1981

Poppa is dying. Everyone does, billions have, there are crosses
and reminders everywhere. Rosemary Breslin did last week . . .
but this is Poppa. He had a stroke. Momma was at the hospital
yesterday with me and looked down at him, tubes and pipes and
needle marks everywhere. He was trembling and twitching as the
dull signs of massive seizures continued. I could barely take it.
Momma cried and patted his head gently. *"Studa y luccha,* Andrea," she teased, pathetically—"Turn off the lights." Poppa's
endless cry for austerity in the house. She was trying to tell herself
how right she was for all those years when she warned him he was
trying too hard to save, to scrimp for old age, for the kids.

Momma is magnificent. So are Matilda and the kids. It pains
me so, remembering my moments of impatience with him,
remembering all I might have done to help him, remembering
how much he gave us.

Nicky D'Arienzo, as usual, has been solicitous and constant.
Jimmy Breslin came to the hospital and met Momma on the way
out. He was able to do all you can do—he kissed Momma and
said he was sorry. He's still trying to feel exactly what his own
loss will mean. I think he'll probably learn a little more about it
every day for a long time to come. But he's already made something beautiful out of Rosemary's passing. The eulogy he delivered at the Mass was published in the *Daily News.* It is a message
of love and hope and humility that is one of the best homilies
ever read here.

Late tonight, on my valet, Madeline left me a personal note—probably for my birthday and Father's Day—that was more beautiful than I deserved. It thanked me for setting a good example. How guilty it makes me feel!

Also, a big New York *Times* story saying I may run against Carey because our division has finally become public. All my people are pleased; right now—I don't care much.

TUESDAY, JUNE 16, 1981

Poppa has been in a coma since Friday. We see him every day, lying still now, his seizures having stopped. He's breathing by use of a respirator machine but gives no other signs of life. Momma, a few times a day, stands by his bed, her hand on his temple, gently calling his name.

Matilda is depressed. With this coming on top of Rosemary's death and her own father needing an operation, she thinks a great deal now about death and life. I never worried more about hurting her . . . and others.

WEDNESDAY, JUNE 17, 1981

Garth is back from Israel and asked me what was going on with Carey. Of course, I didn't know and couldn't tell him. He had no advice for me, but I get the feeling he is mildly concerned about the fact that Carey has hired a "media" type from Chicago—Michael Colopy—to do what Garth is supposed to do.

I met with Koch at 7:15 A.M.: Bob Tierney[1] was present. Good meeting, on the issues mostly. We talked about undocumented aliens, criminal justice, real-property tax. The Mayor was cordial. Later in the afternoon George Artz[2] reported Koch said, "Cuomo would make a great Governor." That statement could be worth a lot if printed.

[1] An attorney, member of Koch's staff.
[2] Reporter for the New York *Post.*

WEDNESDAY, JULY 1, 1981

Poppa died tonight. I was just back from a radio show at WGY
in Schenectady when Andrew called to say, "Pop, I have bad
news—Grandpa passed away."

   We all knew it would happen at any time, but it's still not easy.
I can't relate to it: I'm afraid to try, to feel the guilt of all that
I did and all that I failed to do. I know the only right response
is to love more deeply—more intelligently. I'm flying back now
at 11:30. I wonder how long it will take me to forget how good
he was. I hope I don't live that long.

THURSDAY, JULY 2, 1981

Arrangements have been made after a day of tears and bickering:
it will be done Momma's way. She decided against the crypt after
seeing it, in favor of a plot we bought for her and Poppa at
St. Mary's. There will be a wake: we didn't want one; Momma
did.

TUESDAY, JULY 7, 1981

We buried Poppa yesterday. As it worked out, Momma was
right about the wake. We didn't publish a death notice, but the
word got out anyway: the wake was well attended. Momma
was superb: strong, intelligent, dignified. As Poppa weakened
over the last few years, Momma appeared to get stronger. In
fact, all that was happening was that the strength and capacity
Momma always had—that had been sublimated in her life with
Poppa—came to light. In a way, it's the story of women of this
generation: we're only now allowing their strength to be seen
and used.

   Poppa and Momma are beautiful. They taught us so much. It's
difficult to be reluctant to go forward with any worthwhile effort
after thinking about how courageous they were. We have to
remember.

SUNDAY, JULY 12, 1981

I was at the *Festa* of Our Lady of Mount Carmel to see the dancing of the Giglio.[1] Al D'Amato was there as well. Last year they didn't know him; this year he was the center of attention. I also had what the pros would call a "high recognition rate."

It's getting closer to the time to decide. Carey will probably be announcing soon, and when he does, my time for decision will be forced. I've been meeting with leaders and telling them I believe I can run and win the governorship if Carey doesn't go.

FRIDAY, JULY 17, 1981

Matilda is finally showing signs of recovery from the skin lesions that have been tormenting her for the last couple of weeks: I think by next week she'll be O.K.

Margaret is studying hard for her board exam in early September or late August. I don't see much of her.

Andrew appears to be progressing nicely with Jerry's firm. Madeline and Maria are working hard, and Chris grows taller and taller.

I continue to make the rounds politically. This afternoon I met with Steve Berger.[1] He's close to Bellamy but feels he owes Carey an obligation. If Carey runs (and I think Steve hopes he doesn't), he will help him. If not, he'd be inclined to go with Carol. I explained why I thought I would be the strongest candidate against Kemp, who seems the likely Republican candidate. We agreed to stay in touch.

[1] In Greenpoint, Brooklyn. The Giglio is a pole representing a lily, topped by a statue of St. Paulinus of Nola, that is carried by dancers in the annual parade on the saint's feast day.

[1] Long-time political consultant who had served as commissioner of the Department of Social Services; now a member of the board of the Metropolitan Transportation Authority.

MONDAY, JULY 20, 1981

Jerry Weiss, Jack Bigel[1] and I had breakfast. Jack is dry, slightly
sarcastic, bright. We all agreed that MMC was a poor candidate
in '77. I did not say that I was prepared to run against Carey: I
did say I was getting ready, just in case.

He was not overly negative.

He indicated I wasn't sufficiently well known by the labor and
big business constituencies. He says Fink is and is doing very
well. He suggested that I get around to people like Sandy Weill,[2]
Walter Wriston[3] and Dick Ravitch.[4]

George Douris[5] came in with the Court officers for pictures.
He thinks I can win and is eager to help any way he can. I've
always liked him: we go way back to the Long Island *Press*–Long
Island *Star-Journal* days, when they covered my appearances at
the Board of Estimate.[6]

JULY
SUNDAY, ~~JUNE~~ 26, 1981

I'm not surprised I got the month wrong; I've been up all night.
Matilda, Chris and Andrew went to the lake,[1] and waiting up for
Maria and Madeline consumed so much of the night that I didn't
bother going to bed.

---

[1]Economist, union consultant, expert on pension plans.
[2]Sanford I. Weill, chairman of the board of Shearson/American Express.
[3]Chairman of the board, Citicorp.
[4]Chairman of the Metropolitan Transportation Authority.
[5]Formerly a reporter, a public relations consultant in 1981.
[6]A quasi-legislative body, consisting of the mayor, comptroller, president of the city
council and five borough presidents of New York City, that passes on various land-use
plans. Before I entered politics I often appeared before it representing neighborhood
groups.

---

[1]Lake Hopatcong, New Jersey, summer home of my father-in-law.

WEDNESDAY, AUGUST 5, 1981

Felix Rohatyn[1] for lunch. He believes Carey cannot win. I told him I would run if Carey didn't but didn't know what I would do if Carey ran. Felix is impressed with Stanley Fink, as appear to be many of the "heavy hitters." He has had the opportunity to function and has—impressively.

TUESDAY, AUGUST 11, 1981

How quickly the summer passes and the years. I already have the feeling that I've wasted so much time.

Christopher has had his birthday at the Lake. He's there with his cousin Vinny Romano, with whom he enjoys almost everything. Matilda and Madeline are there as well, and I hope to get a few days this week.

I met with Del Giudice for lunch at the Palm Court. I think he's a big loss to the Government[1] and would try to have him if I were Governor. He assumes Carey is running. Although he didn't take any firm position vis-à-vis my running against him, his questions indicated a negative view of it. He seemed to feel I would have as little rationale as Kennedy did against Carter. I told him that if I chose to run against the Governor I could sharpen my rationale to the point of saying the following:

"The polls, my feedback from editorial writers and everything else tell me Carey cannot win against the Republicans and I can. I think the Democrats must win." If you assume we are both true to the Democrats' principles, the Democrats who vote in a primary—who know these things best—should be given a chance to decide who they believe can most effectively represent them. We will have a fair, not a war: he can display his wares; I mine

---

[1]Nationally renowned investment banker. He helped structure the devices that rescued New York City from bankruptcy in 1976. In 1981 he was an adviser to Governor Carey. He now heads the Municipal Assistance Corporation.

---

[1]Mike Del Giudice had resigned as Carey's director of operations, effective October 21, 1981.

—without negatives or slander or pouring paint over each other's works of art. To make sure we don't damage our chances against the Republicans, we'll agree not to spend a lot of money, since the Democrats know both of us well anyway.

If Michael's failure to dispute the rationale could be fairly read as meaning he thought it was a good one, then he did.

He also put the question to me of Carey's accepting the Liberal Party endorsement and saying that he would do with it what Cuomo did in '77: he would stay on the line in November even if he lost the Democratic primary. I said if I did that again it would be consistency; if Carey did it, it would be hypocrisy, because of the position he took in '77.[2] I think that gave Michael food for thought as well.

I don't know what's going to happen, of course—no one does. But I believe the strategy of generally staying ready to run is a good one for now.

Our success in softball is clearer! Tonight we defeated Carol Bellamy's team 15–12![3] I only played four innings and went 1 for 3. I'm 4 for 9 for the season—2 singles, a double and a home run. Maybe I should have stayed in baseball: it was easier for me.

MONDAY, AUGUST 17, 1981

Stanley Fink called because Bill Cabin had been talking to Dave Langdon, of Fink's staff, about a position on one of Fink's commissions. Fink didn't think it sounded right for my Chief of Staff to be seeking other employment. I explained that Bill probably felt a little vulnerable and now that he is putting down some roots in Albany, he wants something more secure than I can give him. Fink still doesn't like it and I don't expect it to go anywhere. I called Cabin and told him.

Stanley and I talked a bit about other things. He was eager for me to know how much he has done in 2 areas that interest me especially, planning and high technology. We'll exchange materials.

[2]See p. 148 for an explanation.
[3]"We" were the softball team of the lieutenant governor's staff.

He seems as confused as most of us about the political situation. He thinks whatever support the Governor has is very "soft" but is not prepared to suggest that anyone run against him. It's still early as far as Stanley is concerned.

We met on the fund-raiser for October. Conovitz[1] will take a leave to help and to make sure everything is okay.

THURSDAY, AUGUST 20, 1981

Met with Howard Samuels[1] for breakfast. As usual he was gentle, sincere, friendly. He says he will do in-depth polling on Carey in September and October and then will decide what to do about running himself; I don't believe he will run. He doesn't think Carey can win and believes he will have difficulty getting money. Howard said he would help me with the fund-raiser on the 21st and would like to be invited.

Koch was quoted today as saying he thought either Bellamy or Fink could beat Carey in a primary. He didn't mention Cuomo. I don't know what it means: it's clearly not a judgment supported by the polls, except for Bellamy.

Elaine Stouber[2] called to say she was reluctant to have me visit senior citizens' centers in Brooklyn because Shirley Weiner[3] says Fink is going to run for Governor and "we should help the Brooklyn boy." Stouber was not totally consistent on the subject, but I told her I would straighten it out with Esposito.[4]

Garth called. He hasn't heard from Carey and doesn't know what he's doing. Thinks I should "de-escalate" my efforts because if I get out too soon a "fresh face" can do it in March of next year and I'll be stale. He wants me to endorse Koch now. I sent over a letter I'm sending to people who ask me, telling them why I'm voting for Koch.

---

[1]Ellen Conovitz, a member of my staff.

[1]Successful businessman, candidate for governor a number of times, including in 1974 against Hugh Carey, and first president of New York City's Off-Track Betting Corporation.

[2]A friend; director of the Abe Stark Senior Citizens' Center.

[3]Coleader of Brooklyn's Democratic party.

[4]Meade Esposito, long-time head of the Democratic party in Brooklyn.

I wrote a piece on Monday describing a new approach to negotiating with the legislature for the Governor. I released it today after the Governor received a copy but before he responded. Fink took a shot at it, saying I was being too political. I don't think I handled the release as well as I might have, although the substance was good. The dilemma—and it's a constant one—is created by the fact that people don't expect a Lt. Governor to work. If he does, they regard it as purely self-promoting.

SUNDAY, AUGUST 23, 1981

Madeline's 17th Birthday. Wow! Dinner together; all of us but Margaret.

Last night Matilda, Chris and I made it to the movies, *Raiders of the Lost Ark.* It was a fun fantasy-type picture. A lot more fun than the political realities we're living with.

Phil Friedman called. He believes Bellamy will run against Carey. He has poll numbers showing Bellamy—40, Cuomo—23, Carey—22 in a primary. He doesn't know what I should do: every time he talks to me he expresses regret that I didn't run for the Senate last year. He doesn't really see a role for me next year. He thinks I should keep going forward with my preparations—money, visibility that's heavily issue-oriented.

THURSDAY, AUGUST 27, 1981

The Governor has been away on a belated honeymoon and I have served as acting Governor again. It does make life a good deal more interesting. I've had discussions with Jim Larocca,[1] Morgado and Jim Introne (who will be replacing Del Giudice) about the new energy plan,[2] the deaths at South Beach and

[1]Commissioner of the New York State Energy Office at the time. Now transportation commissioner.
[2]Statewide plan projecting future energy needs and how they would be met.

Rockland psychiatric facilities[3] and the State of the State message for '82. On Monday, the troopers brought down rendition papers,[4] which I signed. I try to low-key the "Acting" role, but it's more fun than what I do usually.

It now seems clear that Fink and Bellamy want to run and are doing everything they can to get ready, as I am. Last night we had a cocktail party for our October 21 fund-raiser. There were pledges of 51 tables, over $250,000. That's a pretty good start if all the money comes in. It's going to be exciting . . . if we can finally get involved in a race.

WEDNESDAY, SEPTEMBER 2, 1981

New York State Fair in Syracuse yesterday.[1] Inevitably now, the press and media generally will attempt to escalate the political "struggle." I believe it's too early to be as prominent a potential candidate as I now am, but I have little choice.

FRIDAY, SEPTEMBER 4, 1981

Last night the Feast of Santa Rosalia in Bensonhurst, Brooklyn, and Democratic cocktail fund raiser for New York County at the Tavern on the Green in Central Park.

Carolyn Walsh felt I was well received. It's probably just a result of my having developed a greater identity in the community by moving around politically. I don't know the relationship between strength in the political community and strength at the polls but I know that gaining strength in the political world is a matter of working at it.

---

[3]Patients had recently died in circumstances requiring investigation and explanation.

[4]Official instruments, requiring the governor's signature, that return to another state a person accused of a crime by that state and captured in New York.

---

[1]It was in my speech at the fair that I first referred to the "family" of New York. See pp. 406–12.

Koch was "warm," as he was again today at the PBA[1] Convention at the Pines. He said I'd be a great Governor. That's nice, but I must remember his opponent is named "Barbaro" and I serve his present purposes well.[2]

Matilda and Chris are back from a short stay at the Lake. I missed them.

This weekend I must apply myself to the matter of raising money: it's becoming more and more evident that financing may be the key to the next election. If I want to run, my instinct tells me I should now accelerate all preparations while keeping a low profile (in terms of candidacy) with the media. No mean feat!

WEDNESDAY, SEPTEMBER 9, 1981

Bill Hennessy[1] at 55th Street office for meeting. Loyal to Carey. If Carey doesn't run, he wants to support MMC—he would quit the Department of Transportation in January to do it.

Tom Regan.[2] Of all people. He and the Governor had a personal disagreement. Carey wants him to have a job but not his own role. He thinks Carey may not run. Now, that's interesting.

Both Regan and Hennessy think I should be careful about being perceived as bringing Carey down. I agree, and I'm trying to avoid that.

As usual, when one considers running for office, hypersensitivity is a threat. Every time a rival's name is mentioned favorably, there is a tinge of resentment or even fear. How stupid we are. When will we learn? If one wants to run, one should simply run; put your head down and go if it's worthwhile. Aristotle's rule for success: decide what you want to do and do it.[3] I think I'll try that this time around.

---

[1] Police Benevolent Association.
[2] Assemblyman Frank J. Barbaro (D) of Brooklyn, Italian American, was running against Koch in the Democratic mayoral primary.

---

[1] Governor Carey's transportation commissioner.
[2] A close friend of Governor Carey and a member of his staff.
[3] Actually, it was my mother's rule for success. But, as I once told New York *Times* reporter Mickey Carroll, "No one would listen unless I said it was Aristotle."

FRIDAY, SEPTEMBER 11, 1981

Spoke to Ray Corbett.[1] His poll shows "Mario Cuomo doing better than anyone." Taken in 6 cities. He says in New York City, Carey slightly ahead of Cuomo but that's not head to head. Bellamy does well in New York City but not upstate. Kemp not known in New York City.

Ray says, "Mario, you can do it." He wants to have lunch with me.

Reporter Fred Dicker called. They (Albany *Times-Union*) have polled 50 upstate Chairmen of the Democratic Party! 20 want Cuomo if Carey doesn't run. 8 Fink, 2 Abrams, rest undecided.

16 want Carey to run again.

40 want Cuomo as running mate if Carey runs.

MMC's comment: "Too early to poll. If this means they are satisfied with my work over last 7 years, I'm pleased." "Would you tell Governor to run again?" MMC's response: "Whatever I would tell the Governor—if he wanted to know—would be told to him even before I told it to Matilda."

Tim Sheridan[2] called. I think he will be quitting next week.

This evening I spoke in Albany at a 40th Anniversary Dinner for Erastus Corning. He has been Mayor of Albany since 1941. Before that an Assemblyman and Senator. What a man! And always a gentleman. His position is that Carey is odd but a good Governor. If Carey doesn't run, he'll be for me.

I spoke about politics as a beautiful profession.

We'll have to come back to Albany for a special session on Wednesday to reschedule the primaries that were delayed because of the delay in meeting the Voting Rights Act requirements.

WEDNESDAY, SEPTEMBER 16, 1981

Last Sunday in the Albany *Times-Union* a story appeared describing the poll taken by its staff. The results indicated dissatisfaction with Governor Carey and a considerable body of opinion

---

[1]President, New York State AFL-CIO.
[2]Staffer to Governor Carey.

among upstate county chairmen that Cuomo should run. I am not sure what its implications are, but I know the Governor and all the other players will note it and react, even if not publicly.

I saw Bronfman[1] yesterday. Dick Clurman, his assistant, was with him. We talked a good deal about Israel.

I told him it was increasingly unlikely I would be able to run with Carey, but if Carey could prove he was the best bet against the Republicans, I would be obliged to support him one way or another. I said I wasn't asking for a commitment but would be back when I decided what I wanted to do.

Andrew hurt his back. He needed x-rays. He went to his sister Margaret. How lovely!

MONDAY, SEPTEMBER 21, 1981

A roller-coaster day, like so many in this world of politics if one measures by acceptance. The truth is that the power to function politically—and therefore to help improve the conditions of people's lives—depends upon being sufficiently acceptable to get elected. It follows that one who is interested in helping people through politics must be interested in his or her acceptability at any given moment. That's theoretically sound. The reality, I suspect, is that most politicians react to evidences of acceptance or rejection more out of some personal need for the consolation of approval than a desire to serve.

In any event, today was a day like many in a campaign: some success mixed with some rejection. This morning at the Food Merchants' Convention in the Catskills, my speech was greeted by unrestrained and what seemed to be unanimous enthusiasm. The reception following the Brooklyn Red Mass[1] was also a warm exchange of greetings with old friends. There was encouragement all around.

Tonio was especially pleased because I was being accompanied

[1] Edgar Bronfman, of Seagram's.

[1] An annual mass for lawyers celebrating the commencement of the court year.

by Frank Lombardi, who is doing a piece for the *Daily News Magazine.*

But the Holliswood Civic Association meeting at night was an embarrassment. All went well until I got into the subject of capital punishment. Many of them want it—desperately. Some think it will make them safe. Some need it to satisfy their desire for vengeance. Some want it just out of fear. I found myself swept into a tough argument—mostly hostile from them—with no real chance of convincing them. On the way out a couple of people shouted insults that nearly enraged me. It's difficult to be reminded how many of the people you seek to serve simply disagree with what you believe. It raises difficult questions. And it hurts.

So you step back and you try to remember why you do it. It is in order to serve because it's good to serve. And, if despite my best efforts, I am not given the opportunity to serve as Governor, I should find another opportunity. Sometimes—as now—I need to remind myself that what we feel as personal hurt could be evidence of our own hypocrisy.

TUESDAY, SEPTEMBER 22, 1981

John Zuccotti[1] for breakfast at the Regency.

I told him that I thought I could do a better job than Carey, but if he is perceivable as a winner against Republicans, I will support him. If Carey doesn't run, I will definitely run.

I didn't ask him for dollars.

I didn't ask him for support. I told him I hoped he'd be willing to help if I ever became Governor.

(We agreed to stay in touch.)

Some time ago, Morty Baron[2] called to say that I would be receiving a call from Martin Brown,[3] a very heavy Republican who wanted to tell me something confidentially. I eventually

---

[1]Former deputy mayor of the city of New York with Mayor Beame. In 1981, an influential New York City lawyer.

[2]Supervisor of the town of Ramapo, in Rockland County.

[3]A pseudonym.

heard from Mr. Brown. He described himself as a friend of
President Ford, wealthy, a widower. He said he was calling me
to warn me that Carey was trying to drop me and that I should
regard it as a blessing because I should be Governor. He said he
wanted to meet with me. We missed connections a couple of
times after that and he, apparently, became irritated and told
Baron that. Baron in turn told me at the Nyack Hospital Dedication (8/25/81). I called Brown and set the date for today's
luncheon, which he hosted.

He spoke flatly and bluntly to me and said, in effect, the
following: I could be Governor. I was intelligent, a good
speaker, honest, and I am for the people. Carey has had it. "If
you continue to do what you're doing, get a little more publicity,
you can be Governor. Now is your opportunity, don't miss it. I
am a friend of Howard Baker, Jerry Ford and a lot of important
people. I know what I am talking about. With me or without me,
you can be the Governor."

I asked him why he wanted me to be Governor, and he appeared to be irritated. He said he was very rich and didn't need
anything. Later in the conversation, after more encouraging analysis by him and prodding by me, he said his son someday would
like a good Committee assignment for no money. He never got
specific, never asked for it, never suggested it as a quid pro quo.
Just mentioned it, when I asked whether his son had any interest
in politics. He appeared to know most of the outstanding Republican candidates and said I could beat any of them. He said the
people in Washington know I am their biggest threat. I told him
I was flattered and I would like to stay in touch. He said he is
going to speak to some important Republicans this weekend and
then he will get back to me.

WEDNESDAY, SEPTEMBER 30, 1981

I had an important meeting with David Garth at lunch today. It
lasted well over two hours. David will not handle Carey but
won't announce that until after the end of the year. He would
like to help me, although he's not sure I can win. He won't do
a Republican and doesn't like Bellamy's or Fink's chances. He

thinks Koch may go with Fink but could possibly go with me if I played it right.

He wants me to stay close to him for the next few months: I should call him regularly.

He's at war with Newfield[1] and Breslin and doesn't like the fact that I'm friendly with them both.

He believes I should not "give everything up" so quickly. . . . I should hold things back to create a little mystery.

He wants me to meet with Koch, do a TV commercial for him: ask him for his advice.

He doesn't think I should work as hard as I'm working now: it's still early . . . also . . .

I need staff.

I shouldn't hire pollsters yet.

I shouldn't wear a vest.

I should collect money!

Meet Steve Ross.[2]

Not tell anybody we're meeting.

THURSDAY, OCTOBER 1, 1981

It was reported to me today that a Washington columnist mentioned to Pat Caddell he had heard I was "anti-Semitic." Penny Kaniclides[1] reported something similar last week. I don't believe it was coincidental. As the likelihood of my candidacy escalates, opponents will stoop to conquer. It is part of the ugliness of this business and must be dealt with if one expects to succeed . . . or even survive. I've asked Joel McCleary to set up a date with the columnist: I'll do what I can to disabuse him.

Met with Dale Horowitz of Salomon Brothers for lunch. He'll send a check. He said he likes me and will be helpful if ever I get to become Governor.

Ray Corbett and Howard Molisani[2] tell me I'm doing well in

[1]Jack Newfield, senior editor, *Village Voice.*
[2]Chairman of the board of Warner Communications, Inc.

---

[1]A friend and supporter.
[2]Secretary-treasurer, New York State AFL-CIO.

their AFL-CIO poll. They will buy tickets. They would like me
to declare against Carey.

Met Carl Rosen of Puritan Fashions (Calvin Klein jeans) at
breakfast (7:30, before 9 A.M. breakfast with Corbett) with Jerry
Weiss.

Most people believe Bellamy will run. Phil Friedman thinks
she's almost "unbeatable."

But it's still early.

SATURDAY, OCTOBER 3, 1981

A brief step back:

Carey is generally perceived as weak, but analysis reveals it's
mostly attributable to a perception of him personally as unlikable
and distracted from the business of government. Not a great deal
is said about his performance: to the extent his performance is
judged by the conditions of things in the state, he can make a
good case.

But the role of the Governor is not understood well, especially
in New York City. There, the Mayor delivers the services and
the people's relationship to the Governor is remote, so he tends
to be measured by his personality and the few substantive matters
that the people do understand. At the moment, capital punishment is one such issue.[1]

There is a considerable amount of strength clinging to the
Governor, mostly because he is the incumbent and partly because people believe he has the ability to rise again like the
Phoenix. Victor Gotbaum[2] and District Council 37 and the seafarers' union[3] are in that category. Other unions, such as Morty
Bahr's CWA,[4] like him despite it all and will remain with him
to the end. The Civil Service Employees Association is negotiating with him and must not abandon him.

Baranello will be with Carey if he goes—period. So will Fink

[1]Carey is opposed to capital punishment.
[2]Head of District Council 37, American Federation of State, County and Municipal
Employees (AFSCME).
[3]Seafarers International Union of North America (SIUNA).
[4]Communications Workers of America.

and Ohrenstein and Bellamy and Abrams and all the other Democrats, if it comes to a primary between him and me (which is unlikely).

Wall Street and the bond houses will be with him. He will have money and unions and troops. But the question remains: who would get the votes?

I would guess that Carey believes he can win a primary and a general, and that he will. He probably figures I won't run and if I do he can make me out to be a "crybaby" or another Krupsak. I would guess he's not taking me as seriously as some other people are.

The Carter team believes I'm running.

Jerry Weiss is hoping I will.

There are great reservations about my potential candidacy in many quarters. I have a blurred image. I have a reputation for not having run well in the past. I am perceived as in a position (Lt. Governor) from which one cannot run gracefully against the incumbent. I don't have money like the Governor's.

On the other hand, there are Congressmen like Tom Downey[5] and other legislators like Gorski and Bianchi[6] who would be eager to see me run despite it all.

The October 21 fund-raiser will be significant if it raises more money than expected. Frank Lynn[7] and one or two others have written that I expect to clear $50,000–75,000. If I can surprise people by raising $200,000 instead, it might supply some impetus.

The State of the State, which Carey asked me to submit by November, is also significant.[8] That can provide the rationale, or part of it, that I need. It will require a good deal of thought.

[5]Democrat from Nassau.

[6]Dennis T. Gorski and Icilio W. ("Bill") Bianchi, state assemblymen from Erie County in western New York and Suffolk County, respectively.

[7]Political reporter, New York *Times*.

[8]Each year I was lieutenant governor, I submitted a suggested State of the State message for the governor's use.

TUESDAY, OCTOBER 6, 1981

Kal Finkel[1] came in to see me.
He says MMC's negatives are:

—not a political pro, not a "winner's image."
—Jewish problem because of affiliation with Carter and Carey.
—didn't keep in touch with Jewish community.

He says the negatives are curable.
What we need to do:
"No more Stevensonian musings. In answering questions—
answers first, then reasons."
If Finkel is involved, he wants to be part of the group on the
inside.
Wants an analysis of where the vote is and scheduling to be
related to that. (Burgos will give it to him.)
He's a real help. I told him that if we declared, he would be
part of the inner circle.

Vice-President Mondale had a fund-raiser at Abe's Steakhouse. I went and met Abe Margolies[2] and Nate Landau[3] from
Washington. Margolies says he will help me whatever I do. He's
an old ballplayer, and we got along well.

WEDNESDAY, OCTOBER 7, 1981

Spoke to John Heiman[1] at breakfast. Will help me, although I
suspect that, despite disappointment with him, he would support
Carey in a pinch.
Spoke to Chaikin[2] at lunch. He'll introduce Mondale at the

---

[1]A friend—bright, Orthodox—who helped me in the 1977 mayoralty campaign.
[2]Owner of Abe's Steakhouse, supporter of Walter Mondale and a former basketball
player.
[3]A large contributor and fund-raiser for Walter Mondale.

---

[1]Former U.S. comptroller of currency; at that time chairman of the executive committee of Warburg Paribas Becker, an investment banking firm.
[2]Sol ("Chick") Chaikin, president of the International Ladies' Garment Workers'
Union (ILGWU).

dinner and give us $5,000. Jerry Weiss was there and called it a score and a half.

Matilda is very busy on her own ventures, but I believe, with the children leaving one at a time, she's thinking about loneliness, too. I must do something.

MONDAY, OCTOBER 12, 1981

A good mass at St. Patrick's for Columbus Day. Then the march, with Tony Bennett as Grand Marshal. The crowds seemed thinner and less enthusiastic than in the past. Relatively few appear to have come for the parade. Most seemed to be passers-by. I don't enjoy waving at strangers—I feel as though I'm presuming on them. John Nikas[1] says that's why I lose.

Dinner with Arnie and Ann Biegen at Nanni Al Valletto. Fun but outrageously expensive. The bill came to $200. It's so large I'm not going to let the campaign pay for it. But I won't go back —at least not when I'm paying.

WEDNESDAY, OCTOBER 14, 1981

Howard Samuels told Ellen Conovitz on the phone today that he's upset because I didn't endorse Dinkins.[1] He also says I have no one around me: no "family," no one to talk to. He is apparently telling people I don't have staff and therefore can't win. Howard is a good man and means well. I ought to deal with his objection, even if it is somewhat overstated.

---

[1] A staffer who has been with me since 1977.

---

[1] David Dinkins, New York city clerk and clerk of the council, ran for Manhattan borough president in 1977.

THURSDAY, OCTOBER 22, 1981

How unpredictable the world! Last night we had a fund-raiser that stunned insiders in New York City and New York State, politically. Mondale spoke. Koch said I'd make a good governor. Over $250,000 at $500 a seat was raised by a person who has not announced, who has no leverage, without a professional fund-raiser and with an incumbent Governor who is at the very least discouraging participation. A great success.

And tonight I learned that Bill Cabin has been ripping off the State with several fictional names on the payroll. Woodie Fitchette found out about it somehow and flew down from Albany to tell me. If it is what I think it is, it is a staggering blow—not because I'm personally culpable but because I'm responsible. And I should be. For years, I have been painfully aware of how vulnerable we are to the fates, to forces beyond our control, to the vicissitudes of life. Now, as I sit at my kitchen table writing these notes, feeling the impact of this development, it's difficult even for me to think clearly and to analyze the situation. What is apparent about it already—that Cabin simply added names to the payroll (forging my signature on the records sent to the comptroller), took the checks for them, and kept the money— is enough for me to know that once the public is informed, as inevitably it will be, he will be destroyed and I will be hurt, quite apart from the fact that I am totally innocent. I will have been the victim of my trust for this individual, my chief of staff. "If you cannot choose a chief of staff who is honest, how could you hope to run the state?" I can hear it now.

FRIDAY, OCTOBER 30, 1981

It's been a difficult week. From the first word of Bill Cabin's crimes there has been deep concern, anger, sadness and trepidation about the future throughout the staff. The general feeling is that it is, or will be when publicized, a heavy to devastating blow. For myself, there is the beginning of resignation to these events. I am not at all convinced that they will cripple us, but if they do I believe I will be prepared.

I have done what needed to be done. I went immediately to D.A. Sol Greenberg of Albany County and told him to pursue the matter to whatever ends. Only 4 days later, on Wednesday, October 28, the State Police confronted Cabin. They showed him evidence that they had indicating he had placed false names on the payroll and received checks for them for his own account, to the tune of about $170,000. About $128,000 of that was received by Cabin; the rest was taxes withheld.

Cabin asked to see me. He came in with the police. He said he was "sorry." He had earlier told the police he was sorry he had done this to Cuomo, because "Cuomo was good to me."

I told him I was sorry, too. And I am. His life is badly damaged, if not ruined. It is the classic case of the cop who has confused his roles. He has been pursuing wrongdoers for years.[1] He learned how to do it and decided to try it for himself.

He seemed not to be fully aware of what is going on. He apparently believes he can make it all go away, perhaps by making restitution.

Well, we certainly want restitution made, but I can't believe he can escape without a felony conviction—nor should he.

As for us, I expect we will pay a heavy political price. We'll know soon how heavy—and how well we handled it. I see it as a challenge to our strength and maturity. I'll approach it in that way—aggressively. I suspect, in the end, a great deal will depend on how I communicate it. I'll focus on 4 elements: (1) Cabin's résumé, showing he was a good choice; (2) the effective disclosure from *within* my staff; (3) my decisive and strong action; and (4) the likelihood of restitution. After that, all I can do is keep my fingers crossed.

---

[1] When I first met Cabin he was an investigator with the New York State Welfare Inspector General's office. He was a principal figure in the state's investigation of nursing homes and testified at the trial of a nursing home operator eventually convicted of a felony. As executive director of the New York State Board of Public Disclosure and in his other capacities, he placed a strong emphasis on investigation and detection of all forms of political and governmental corruption.

TUESDAY, NOVEMBER 3, 1981

I had an hour-and-a-half meeting with the Governor yesterday morning and then later in the day had a press conference to announce the Cabin affair.

The meeting with the Governor was unpleasant, puerile, intensely personal. All of our frustration and hostility showed, perhaps for the first time. He is even more sensitive and defensive than I and much more so than I had expected. There's no question that whether he wants to run or not he is frustrated and angered by his belief that I intend to challenge him. What he really wanted was for me to say I was with him. I didn't. He also tried to tie me into an agreement to travel around the State saying his government was "superior." I told him I would say the government was "good but could be better." He's displeased, to put it mildly.

The Cabin affair was more important to me. I wrote the statement and Sol Greenberg agreed to stand alongside me. Woodie Fitchette and Len Schwartz[1]—who have performed superbly all through this affair—were on hand and said the conference went well. The newspaper accounts were not bad, considering Cabin has himself been telling "all" to reporters. It's bizarre! He said to Paul Browne of the Watertown *Times* that at another stage in his life he might have committed these crimes just to experience prison. Can you believe it?

SUNDAY, NOVEMBER 15, 1981

Fourteen days after I went to the District Attorney, Bill Cabin had been "caught, convicted (on a plea of guilty) and canned." He is even now sitting in the Albany County jail awaiting sentencing on November 30. The taxpayers should get all their money back: he'll make restitution from the buildings and real estate he invested in.

In the end, the taxpayers will not be hurt: Cabin's family will suffer badly, Cabin will be driven into a different kind of life, but

[1]A member of my staff.

I suspect—judging especially by his remarkable unflappability—
that he will accommodate himself relatively easily. Almost certainly I will be hurt politically, if only because the affair makes
it more difficult for me to talk about "management" and my
"hands-on" style. The truth is that it would be difficult to fault
me on a management basis if one were being purely analytical
about the situation. The Comptroller has virtually conceded that
it could happen with any legislative agency. Jerry Kremer[1] told
me last Sunday morning he was sympathetic because his "ways
and means" payroll is larger than my staff's and he is vulnerable
exactly as I was. But a large number of the voters will not be
analytical and logical about their conclusions. They will operate
from superficial impressions and I'm sure they are mostly bad.

We proceed with our preparations in any event. Every Saturday morning Bill Stern, Joel McCleary, Jerry Weiss, Len
Schwartz, Tonio Burgos, Bob Sullivan, Ellen Conovitz, Andrew,
Carolyn Walsh and I meet. Bill has organized the effort into a
series of "projects." The most important one is fund-raising.

The general strategy is to get ready to run without commit-
ting entirely to running for Governor. There is still a great deal
that can happen unexpectedly. There always is, as the Cabin
affair reminds us. At the moment, despite indications that the
Governor plans to run again, something gives me the feeling
that he's decided to hang it up. But I go back and forth with
my guesses.

Joe Crangle[2] criticized me this past week for being "disloyal,"
and I talked with him. He thinks Carey will run. He likes the
Governor a good deal less than he likes me, but he's cautious and
is not so sure of my ability to win.

Don Manes[3] is trying to find an office to run for himself.
Probably the only major party leader statewide who might con-
sider coming to me if there were a primary involving me and
Carey is Stanley Friedman of the Bronx, and I'm not sure of him.

The story is similar with the unions. Gotbaum appears not to

---

[1]State assemblyman, head of the powerful Ways and Means Committee.

[2]Chief administrative officer of the New York State Assembly; long-time chairman,
Erie County Democratic party, from Buffalo; state chairman at the time of Carey's
election in 1974.

[3]Chairman, Queens County Democratic party.

like me at all, although he doesn't care for Carey either. Most of the municipals will go with the incumbent—they have to do business with him. I may find some strength with the AFL-CIO private sector.

Local government officials will also be with the Governor because they have to do business with him.

The Governor, in sum, is in a good position to gather up most of the establishment strength for various reasons, including some continuing respect for him and his performance, the need to "do business" with him and a fear that his opponents are not strong enough—or serious enough—to beat him.

There was a developing sense that my candidacy might be formidable, especially after the successful fund-raiser. The Cabin affair has slowed that down, and unless we can find a new momentum, I will not even be under consideration in a few months.

One possibility is the emergence of polls and other indications that Carey can't win but I can. Kemp, who last week announced he would not run for Governor, referred to a Republican poll by Robert Teeter that shows that he and Ned Regan both beat Carey at the moment. Jack Ferro[4] says he has been told that the poll also shows I run better than any other Democrat. That's the kind of thing I'll have to get out if I'm to recapture any momentum.

All of this can be absorbing. It's not difficult to be consumed by the effort to serve and to win. Little wonder that there is such a high incidence of divorce and disorientation among the children of politicians. One could easily spend all one's time thinking only about the problems of the state and the next campaign. And too many days, I do.

It's important from time to time to adjust the perspective. I'm not a single, unattached public servant. I can't devote myself totally to public service without abandoning other major obligations. I have a wife and children—two still at home, both badly needing and fully deserving of my time, attention, advice and manifest concern. I've tried to do the right thing by them, but too often I haven't succeeded. I'll have to try harder.

[4]A member of my staff, from Buffalo.

FRIDAY, NOVEMBER 27, 1981

We had all the kids with us for Thanksgiving yesterday. How quickly we grow older and things change. It's hard to understand that Margaret is now virtually on her own, Andrew gone from the house, Maria as well, Madeline on her way to college. We miss them already.

It's difficult to avoid thinking about how lucky we've been with the kids. They have had no really serious problems. Their health is good, disposition sound. Of course, they've had the accidents and the traumas and the difficult moments. But when I think of all the people around us whose lives have been spent dealing with drug addiction or crime or abortions or nervous breakdowns, I feel almost guilty about our good fortune. That's the case generally where I'm concerned. I've always had the feeling that I've been given much more than I deserve and much more than most others and that most of my life should be spent trying to give something back. It's important to be even. Although I've never been able to figure out exactly why.

It's a bit of a lag time politically. The power of the incumbency is at work. The day belongs to the Governor, who is campaigning everywhere, apparently without untoward incident. He is getting stronger with the insiders and the politicians as a result. This is predictable: all he has to do to be strong with the party leaders and unions is look as if he's going to run and take care of the constituencies—which, of course, he's doing. Yesterday it was announced that the Governor had abandoned the idea of a nuclear waste repository in central New York. Why? Because it's unpopular, and that's the name of the game this week. Meade Esposito told me last week that he would be with the Governor because he's doing very well with him: he says the Governor has shown him a lot of "respect" recently. I wonder how "respect" translates into appointments.

It's not clear yet to what extent this activity is changing the minds of the voters. And it has never been very clear to what extent the party and union leaders *can* change the minds of the voters. On the other hand, there is no question in my mind that the unions can make some difference and the Governor will have them all.

SUNDAY, DECEMBER 6, 1981

Tempus fugit. Every day, a thousand lost opportunities: every day closer to the end. If only everything we did, we did in light of that, how differently we'd act. We would have so few regrets. But now I look back on nearly fifty years and I'm pained by the memory of so many hurts, so many mistakes, so many missed opportunities. So much weakness. It's a hard game, but "the game is lost only when we stop trying." So, on with the effort!

A busy weekend with Tita and Joe Monti's annual fund-raiser for the Don Monti Foundation[1] and Julie Mattone's[2] wedding. They were both lavish affairs, and Matilda enjoyed them. I took the opportunity to begin telling people that I was considering running for Governor, although I wouldn't be able to announce it for a while even if I decided definitely to do it. Clearly, once the word goes out that I am definitely running, all sorts of things occur. Some money will become available that isn't now, and volunteers will be heard from. But it also buys negatives, the big one being the opportunity Carey and his people have to move on the budget and everything else. I used this weekend as a feeler to give us some reaction so that I could better gauge the situation. The next couple of weeks will give me additional input and information. Today, at lunch, I hope to get some clearer answers from Dave Garth about what he thinks I ought to be doing. Last week on the phone, he was quite encouraging. He and I are both skeptical about growing rumors that Carey might choose not to run, but it does appear to be a real possibility . . . again. Bellamy is getting more active and has announced she will run either for Governor or Comptroller. I doubt she will run against Regan, so it is important to know whether he will seek reelection or to move up.[3] Lehrman has emerged as a "strong candidate" virtually overnight. While he is attractive, conservative and eager, his strongest asset is obviously his wealth. In this

---

[1]Set up by Tita and Joe, friends of ours, to help in cancer research; inspired by the death of their young son, Donald.

[2]Daughter of Joe and Irene Mattone.

[3]Ned Regan was considered a strong candidate for reelection as comptroller, which he had been since 1979 (and still is). There was speculation he might try for the Republican nomination for governor.

absurd system we have where wealth is so important, his affluence has provided him with instant credibility.

Meanwhile my Saturday morning group continues to inch along in its organization effort, led by Bill Stern. Following this week's meeting I met with Tony Schwartz.[4] I like him and his work but doubt he'll be able to help us, because I'm pretty sure he'll be working for Moynihan. I'll continue to meet with media people until Christmas. Sullivan has begun his focus groups,[5] and I'll begin pushing the field organization now to get ready for petitioning.

But most of all, *tempus fugit.*

WEDNESDAY, DECEMBER 9, 1981

All day in Buffalo. Their first snow of the year. In and out of cars all day, without rubbers on; I'm sure to have a cold tomorrow.

There were what appeared to be negatives everywhere. Some Buffalo Chamber of Commerce members walked out of their meeting with me this morning because I was too hard on "Reaganomics." A story in the Queens *Daily News* saying I had been "booed" by people who thought an answer I gave on welfare was "too liberal." Dyson[1] attacking me, saying I was "dishonorable" and "disloyal" for attacking Carey. He said I should resign.

But then I heard from a writer today that the Teeter poll showed the Republicans beating Carey by 30 points and being even with me, statewide. I'm still weak in Buffalo, however, despite all my time here. That's what my poll shows, too, and I don't really understand it.

Sandy Frucher—today—is convinced Carey is not running. He talked with Bellamy yesterday, and she thinks Fink is the real threat. Without Carey in the race, Fink would get the Wall Street

---

[4] A media consultant.
[5] A relatively new opinion-gathering technique involving concentrated in-depth discussions by a carefully selected cross section of people, led by a professional who elicits opinions and reactions in designated subjects.

---

[1] John S. Dyson, chairman of the Power Authority of the State of New York, appointed by Carey.

money and other financial money Carey would get if he were running. And if Carey runs, Fink will not run against him. The word is out in Brooklyn as well that Fink is running if Carey doesn't, and Esposito is supporting him—all the way.

Fink would be tough. He's smart, experienced, with a good record. He would have many of the unions with him.

The only thing that's clear is that there is still a long way to go. The best thing I can do now is raise money.

WEDNESDAY, DECEMBER 16, 1981

It's the middle of the day. Political activity is picking up. Teeter poll was leaked to *Post*—it showed Carey losing by 30 points to Regan. I called the *Post* and argued that they should, in fairness, publish the part of it that showed Cuomo and Regan virtually neck and neck. No other Democrat does that well.

Today the *Post* has a story saying Moynihan is afraid of running with Carey.

THURSDAY, DECEMBER 17, 1981

Christmas is upon us: I had hardly noticed. So quickly the seasons come and go. Each year repeats itself: always I feel there was something I was supposed to feel that escaped—or passed—me.

Politics knows only one season—the political season.

This morning I met with Mike Del Giudice. He was helpful with suggestions without making any commitments. He is a person I would want close to me in any campaign. He is beginning to suspect Carey may not run. But today a poll was announced in Rochester indicating that county leaders statewide now support Carey almost unanimously. What's the difference from three months ago? A visit to the Mansion. It's called the power of the incumbency.

SATURDAY, DECEMBER 19, 1981

Last night we had a meeting of our early and strong financial supporters. I told them that, from all I know and feel, Carey will not run.

This morning our Saturday morning group spent a few hours talking about structure for the campaign.

Almost without noticing, we have moved from tentativeness to commitment. There could be a turning back, but it would have to be a reversal; we have set our course. While we will not have to announce it for a while, we should rapidly accelerate all practical preparations now. The big sticking point is still Garth. If we knew we would have him, everything would be much easier, but we can't wait much beyond the first of the year to know.

MONDAY, DECEMBER 21, 1981

Met with Mayor Koch this morning at 8:15 A.M. Pete Piscatelli[1] and John LoCicero[2] were present. I talked about my willingness to help with Medicaid takeover as I did last year. I suggested it would be wrong to try precisely the same formula we used last year because Warren Anderson would have to reject that again. I suggested enhancing it with education dollars for upstaters on the theory we would have to do that anyway if *Levittown*[3] is affirmed.

I talked a little about ways the Ombudsman's office could be used to help generate volunteer support for government and about working on something for small-home tax-assessment procedures and community services for the deinstitutionalized. The Mayor said he would call James Brigham,[4] who's working on a Medicaid pickup task force, and tell him to get me involved.

I also suggested to the Mayor that he travel upstate himself because his popularity extends from New York to Canada.

[1]Lobbyist in Albany for the city of New York.
[2]Director of Special Projects for New York City.
[3]A case that affected the legality of the present system of financing elementary education in New York.
[4]Former New York City budget director.

On the political front, I told him I was getting ready to run for Governor. I didn't know whether Carey would or wouldn't. The Mayor didn't indicate any position, favorable or unfavorable. He asked, "Why not run for Comptroller?" I said that would make Regan governor, and I didn't think that would be good for New York.

On the way out, Pete Piscatelli told me Fink was getting more serious and Rupert Murdoch was very impressed with him. Peter, who has always been a friend, made it clear he thought it would be a very tough go for me if I tried running for Governor. The meeting left me with the impression that Koch wouldn't be comfortable dealing with me and would prefer a number of people—even a Republican—to me.

SATURDAY, JANUARY 2, 1982

Matilda and I went to the reinstallations of Koch, Bellamy and Goldin as Mayor, Council President and Comptroller of New York City. Bad weather drove us indoors. That reduced the crowd, confused seating arrangements, and somehow "depressed" the occasion. There did not appear to be much in the speeches that was "inspirational" or even different. That isn't because our people lack eloquence. I think it's because they—we—are faced with problems that are much easier to describe than they are to resolve. There's nothing inspirational about a grim litany and constant protestations of noble intent, without at least the outline of an idea that might work.

The Mayor made clear he is going to test Governor Carey—if Carey chooses to run again—by making him "produce" on Medicaid takeover "before the primary." Well, of course, the only one in a position to make the test real is Stanley Fink, who has a Democratic Assembly and can pass the pickup anytime he wants. It looks very much as though the Mayor has begun a "cat and mouse," "carrot and stick" ritual. It's worked before: the question is whether it will wear thin before it works again.

Another pleasant holiday, after the installations. At home with

Momma, Umberto and Anna Maria,[1] Frank and Marian and the kids, Mom and Pop Raffa. This time Andrew was missing. I guess he needed a day to himself. It gets harder and harder to keep the kids next to us. That's natural, of course, but it doesn't make it easier. "We grow too soon old, and too late smart" goes the old German American beer hall sign. It was written by a wise person, probably a very old wise person.

A good time to reflect again on where we are, where we should be trying to go. You can hardly do too much of that. What are the alternatives, as I move into the second half of the 50th year of my life? How should I try to spend the rest of my time so that I hurt as few people as possible and help as many people as possible? It gets clearer and clearer—easier and easier to see the logical thing and the "right" thing, if right and logic are the same. All that I believe tells me the only worthwhile way to live is to spend the time loving, by doing.

But wanting to do is not the same as being able to do, because imperfection intrudes. So many instincts, so many impulses that from moment to moment confuse, distract, mislead.

How shall I try? Shall I leave public office voluntarily and commit myself to practicing law and teaching and perhaps finding a position from which I might continue to articulate?

But this is an option I will be left with even if I am forced out of public service by a defeat in a campaign, so I don't have to sacrifice any other opportunities to achieve it.

Well, then, how about staying in public service? In what position?

Being Lieutenant Governor again makes no sense. I don't believe that if he chose to run I could make Governor Carey a winner. Even if I could, it would leave me in a relationship that obviously doesn't work.

I could run for Comptroller. A lot of people like the idea, and if Regan runs for Governor, as he has announced he'd like to, I could probably beat anybody who runs in the primary . . . probably. But I don't want to be Comptroller.

Abrams will run for Attorney General and win. That's a position I would have been happy with in 1978.

---

[1] Umberto Serio, my father's sister's youngest son, and his wife—cousins from Italy.

I'm left with the possibility of running for Governor or stepping aside. That's the case as of this moment, and things are sure to change, maybe even dramatically, but I mustn't do nothing while I'm waiting for all the facts. What I will do now is go forward even faster and harder with all preparations for the race. Things may change—let them. If I run, I will be a long shot, but so were Momma and Poppa.

SUNDAY, JANUARY 3, 1982

The new year begins. A year closer to the end. A chance to begin again the time that's left. A looking back—almost always in regret because of what I have failed to do or did poorly. A new resolve: to remember the purpose; to be what I am supposed to be; to show the love—to live it.

Matilda is exhausted after having spent herself entertaining, shopping, putting up with me and the kids. I must do more to make it easier for her.

Maria will be going back to Iona and we won't see much of her for a while. I'll miss her.

Madeline gets closer to her decision on college.

Chris—still a bit supercharged—is a delight. I must try harder to do more for him. He is bright and sensitive. His sensitivity permits him to enjoy . . . and to suffer. I must be more gentle with it.

Andrew is ensconced in his apartment in Albany pursuing his own life, trying to help here at the same time. I must do everything I can to make sure he gets past this last six months in school and then the Bar.

I did my weekly Sunday night call-in show on WMCA. Matilda is right: it takes a great deal out of our weekend. And though the reviews have been good for all the time I've done it, I've never been satisfied. I'm constantly uneasy about not having all the detailed information I need to answer each question on hand, immediately. I'm also struck by the difficulty of offering solutions to most of the issues that are raised. Sometimes it is—or seems to be—nothing more than an exercise in futility. So many of the problems—crime, unemployment, the homeless, the disabled, a chaotic tax structure—seem totally beyond our capacity to solve at the state level, or at any level of government. The temptation is to turn away, to give up the effort.

It's clear that this lack of confidence, even disdain for what government can do, is helping push the population of the city and state dramatically to the right. It's not just capital punishment and toughness on the poor. It's a general rejection of anything traditionally perceived as "liberal," unless the one offering the opinion is the immediate recipient of the benefit of the program. A welfare mother will be liberal on welfare. A prisoner will be liberal on penal reform. But even a welfare mother and a prisoner will be less than liberal on the programs that don't affect them. The senior citizens who are not rich are conservative on everything except Social Security and programs for the elderly.

Of course these are not universal truths, but they are dominant trends, more clearly pronounced than any opinions I've yet observed since I have been measuring public opinion.

Almost always the tendency is to see things from a narrow self-interest without the embarrassment that used to accompany the admission that one was self-seeking. It's now recognized, understood, accepted that the name of the game is taking care of one's self.

That leaves the politician with choices. Go along with the dominant trend and try to give the people all that they want to assure yourself popularity, enough to win the chance to serve. Then continue to behave that way in order to continue to earn the right to continue to serve. That's "good politics": it wins.

Another choice is to try to lead—at least in opinion—by pointing to what you think is a better way. This requires disagreeing with the people's dominant opinions from time to time and trying to convince them they are wrong. This is risky politics, and today it does not appear to succeed often, but it's the only kind of politics I'm comfortable with.

What is clear is that it is not just risky but suicidal, politically, to disagree with prevailing opinion and not to offer alternatives. Too often I am perceived as doing that.

I will have to take greater pains to be sure that when I disagree I show the alternatives.

TUESDAY, JANUARY 5, 1982

Umberto and Anna Maria left for home today. They had a wonderful five days. Matilda says that, at the airport, they told her
they felt as though they had known us for a lifetime. I'm pleased
for Momma.

Card from Margaret indicates she's having a good time in San
Diego. More good news.

The political world is becoming energized. Tomorrow is the
Governor's State of the State, and the media will look for political signals. They will describe the message mostly in terms of its
political import and that, then, is the way it will be interpreted
by the world at large, since the substance will remain largely
obscure. Some few people are holding out for the possibility that
the Governor will announce within the next two weeks that he
is not running again, on the theory that the appropriate time for
such an announcement would be with the submission of the
budget. I don't see it that way. I believe he will hold on until
April at least without making an announcement. He has nothing
to lose.

Phil Friedman agrees with me. He believes the Governor will
reserve his options until the last possible moment. He thinks he
will not be able to win but that Garth may still decide to help
him. That Bellamy will run for Comptroller. That I have only a
slim chance to win. Phil and Garth now operate together only
occasionally.[1] I told Phil I would love to have one of them. He
said it was too early for him to know what he would do but he
didn't think it likely he would be doing anyone in New York this
year, except possibly Bellamy for Comptroller. He suggested I
talk to Michael Kaye from Los Angeles and Tubby Harrison, the
pollster. I will.

The thinking on Bellamy progressed from the fact that Regan
is assumed to be running for Governor and not Comptroller. I
think that assumes too much: I'm not at all sure he has the
Republican nomination locked up. This means he may have to
go back to Comptroller, which, in turn, may drive Bellamy into
the Governor's race.

[1]Friedman had opened his own consulting firm.

The great danger for anyone who would be Governor is that so much time will be spent on the speculation that the effort won't move forward. I will not make that mistake.

I spoke with Basil Patterson[2] this morning at his office. He was generally hospitable, advises patience and indicates a general interest in running for Lt. Governor if he were reasonably sure he would be everybody's choice. That won't happen unless he makes it happen.

I attended Don Manes's installation[3] at noon. Koch and I were the only speakers other than Manes himself and Surrogate Judge of Queens County Lou Laurino, who served as Master of Ceremonies.

Phil Friedman suggested Andrew would make a good campaign manager. They worked closely together in the 1978 campaign. I'm leery about his being too distracted from his law studies, though, and will have to think hard about it.

WEDNESDAY, JANUARY 13, 1982

I was hit by the flu and spent two days recovering at the Wellington.[1] The nausea and fever and achiness reminded me how fortunate I've been in my good health. Andrew, Maria and Madeline joined Chris, who came down with it last week. Nick D'Arienzo says it's an epidemic. Matilda, so far, has been able to avoid the full impact of the bug and has spent her time tending the kids.

I might have had plenty of time to think, over this period, but constant calls and the delivery of the daily mail kept me busy. I could have taken the phone off the hook, but rumors are circulating so ferociously that I wanted to be sure to hear and analyze as many of them as I could.

They come down to this. Morgado has taken a terrible pounding in the *Daily News* for a week about personal business dealings with a man who does substantial business with the state and,

---

[2]Former state senator, secretary of state, Democratic candidate for lieutenant governor in 1970 and deputy mayor of the city of New York.

[3]As borough president of Queens County, a post to which he has been reelected every four years for as long as anyone can remember.

---

[1]The hotel in Albany where I had an apartment.

although there has been nothing illegal, the stories have eclipsed
the good press the Governor might have received for the State
of the State message.

At the same time—and perhaps partly as a result of this latest
bad luck—Morgado, Frucher and Garth have all indicated to me
in the last few days that they believe there is a good possibility
the Governor will not run. All encourage me to be nice to the
Governor publicly, on the theory that if I'm not he might be
forced to run, if only to avoid the public impression that he has
been driven out by me. Apparently, the Governor believes I've
turned on him and been unkind to him. I'm not surprised: I think
he thinks that about a lot of people.

THURSDAY, JANUARY 14, 1982

This afternoon it was announced that the Governor would
make a surprise announcement tomorrow at a press conference
in Albany. Morgado and Frucher won't let me know what it's
about, except that both indicate it will affect me. There are so
many possibilities. He could be calling for a political moratorium until the budget is adopted. I had suggested that to Baranello. He could attack me somehow, perhaps by saying he
would not be running with MMC. He could be announcing
he's not going to run, perhaps joining that with a call for a
moratorium.

I spoke with Morgado and Frucher again in the late afternoon,
but still no hint.

By the end of the day the rumor was that Carey was not
running. By midnight the rumor was confirmed and was being
dictated to editors by reporters from Albany. The mad scramble
is about to start.

FRIDAY, JANUARY 15, 1982

Carey announced he's not running. He didn't invite me to the
announcement. He told me about it formally, in a phone call
afterward.

Dave Garth at home. He said he will definitely do my campaign. I have a date with him 12 noon Saturday at Des Artistes.

Ray Harding [vice-chairman of the Liberal party] shifted our date to Saturday at 9 A.M., Plaza Hotel.

Vince Albanese [an old friend and former state committeeman]. He will try to reach Arthur Emil,[1] after I missed him twice.

Woodie Fitchette. He will go over message for today, which will be generous to Governor and low-key on MMC.[2]

Mike Del Giudice. He said he "would be helpful, down the road." Right now "he didn't know how the pieces would fit." I said I'd like to be able to use his name as soon as possible.

Garth called again. "Play it cool. Confident. Not overly self-deprecating but not defensive. Not moralistic."

Mayor Erastus Corning said he's for MMC. MMC said, "Great."

John Kelly [president of Office and Professional Employees International Union] called to wish me luck. I called back. He'll be with me.

Evelyn Aquila [state committeewoman in Brooklyn]—just advice.

Harold Fisher [an attorney and former chairman of the Metropolitan Transportation Authority] will help me—doesn't know yet what role. I need to go to dinner with Betty [Fisher] and Matilda.

MMC called *Mario Biaggi*—said he would like to talk to him. Biaggi said "anytime"—over a bottle of wine.

John Sullivan [counsel to the State Democratic Committee] gives MMC his support.

Stopped by at Donald Manes's home—he is with me—all out. He's hoping I will be able to help him run for Mayor three years from now. This is a real big break. There are so many ways Don helps my effort.

TV and radio spots. I tried to avoid discussing my plans, but it was impossible. I said that my intention to run is clear and I would be announcing plans specifically by mid-March.

[1]Partner in the law firm of Surrey & Morse, New York City. Fund-raiser for Hugh Carey and a supporter of mine in 1977.

[2]I applauded the Governor's work for eight years and said nothing about my plans.

I'm told that Fink is calling upstate chairmen and doing well. Abrams, Bellamy and Dyson will all be moving tomorrow, I'm sure.

SATURDAY, JANUARY 16, 1982

Met with Ray Harding and David Garth separately. Harding is well disposed to me at this point but by no means ready to commit. Garth, on his way to Spain with Ed Koch for 10 days, gave me a great deal of advice and reassured me that he would be doing my campaign—allowing only for the slim possibility that Ed Koch would run for Governor. Garth thinks he's unpredictable enough to consider it.

My Saturday morning team met and worked on the fund-raiser —nothing is more important than money now.

Governor Carey had a long press conference in which he gave indications that my suspicion that he would try to freeze me out was justified. He attacked my qualifications, saying I hadn't come forward with programs that he hadn't advocated and he thought I had changed my position on the death penalty. He's wrong, but if he continues on this tack, he can hurt a great deal.

Fink is clearly the most formidable opponent. He would have Carey (at this moment), Koch, newspapers, unions and money. In this up-and-down world where we live through a thousand crises, reversals and turns in a campaign, today's assessment would have to be a negative one for me.

Tonight, Chris asked why I stay in this political life. A good question.

I've never been totally satisfied with having to deal publicly. I tell myself I do it because public service is "good," but then I doubt I would be so selfless about it. So I continue to inquire.

I've always preferred privacy. Loneliness has never been the threat to me that the world has been. The more deeply I have become involved in opening myself, revealing myself, discussing myself, the more vulnerable I have felt. Nor do I see this life as proving any kind of personal success. My mind tells me the "success" is little more than good luck attached to efforts you make that aren't much different from the efforts of many others who don't get touched by the good luck. Why, then, am I in politics at all? I take power too seriously to be totally comfortable with it. It's not the notoriety: I'm reasonable enough not to attach significance to that. Indeed, on those occasions when acclaim does come, when the applause is loudest, I am the most uncomfortable, because at those times I judge myself so much more harshly than others do. When the rejection comes—the defeat, the disdain, the inattention—I feel it. But I am not allowed even the luxury of feeling sorry for myself, because quickly the intellect reminds me that however "natural" the hurt is, it is inconsistent with the truth as I know it, which is that the ultimate virtuous condition is selflessness.

Always, the feeling is one of being out of place. Not enjoying fully the things most enjoy, not even being allowed the consolation of self-pity. Always, the nagging truth is that I should be something else—a person who gives only to give, who works only to provide, who speaks only to soothe or persuade for the good, who strives only for others. And always there is the depressing reality that I fail utterly at that truth, that my emotions are at war with it—or at least are too strong to surrender to it.

In the end, I am a man who knows what to do but knows even more sharply that he has failed by his own standards to do it as well as it can be done.

I am now in the midst of a campaign I cannot win. If I am successful at the polls, I will challenge the motivation that drove me to it, and wonder about the life it then requires. If I am not successful, I will feel again the sharp pain of rejection and "humiliation" and will dislike myself for feeling it. But I am in the midst of it. For however long it lasts, it is here. The anticipation, the frenetic work, the perpetual motion, the frustration of a thousand tasks to perform without the time to perform them; the concern about the public appearance, the debates, acceptance by the editorial boards, trying to win the favor of a union or a contributor or an important leader without losing your soul; the exhilaration of the contest, the waiting for a hundred verdicts, the victories, the coups, the soaring prospects, the defeats, the losses, the betrayals, the depths, the fear of slander, the bitter-

ness, the embarrassment, the tears, the satisfaction, the pride, the
happiness. The campaign is on, and I will be part of every part
of it—and I will always be out of place.

SUNDAY, JANUARY 24, 1982

In a week the Governor's race has already changed rapidly. In
the beginning was Bellamy, then Fink; now the most formidable
opponent is said to be Abrams. He has a huge war chest and his
supporters say he has great strength with the Black and Jewish
communities. They feel if Abrams is in, all other Jewish candidates—including Fink—will drop out and it will be Abrams vs.
Cuomo alone. There is no question he would be formidable, but
I think with a good campaign I can beat him.

MONDAY, JANUARY 25, 1982

Herman Badillo [former U.S. congressman, former deputy mayor, and
long-time political power in New York City]—breakfast at Regency.
He is "sympathetic." Suggests I build a coalition with him, Biaggi,
Carey and Blacks. Believes a Koch candidacy could be a source of
strength to me since it would be easier to organize such a coalition
against it. I told him I would pursue the agenda of action he recommended and get back to him in a couple of days.

Meade Esposito said he would call me next week for lunch. I said his
name is being used "against" me. He said we will talk.

Jim Introne. He'll stay close to me for the next year and I'm glad—I'd
like to have him around.

Stanley Friedman thinks Abrams would be "big trouble" for us. He
would like to use Koch to keep Abrams out and will talk to him
tomorrow if possible.

Bob Morgado wanted my view of the "Draft Ed" movement.[1] I told him
I was going forward. Asked him to help me with Liberal party. He said
yes.

---

[1]An editorial entitled "Let's Draft Ed Koch" had appeared in the New York *Post*,
published by Rupert Murdoch.

Mayor Pawlinga [of Utica] will see MMC in Albany—10:40.

Steve Berger: "Talk about yourself, what you will do. Answer question: 'Why should I vote for Cuomo?'"

Harry Holman [a pseudonym]. It was the Mayor himself who encouraged Murdoch to run the stories and start the "Draft Ed" movement.

Barry Feinstein [president, City Employees Union, Teamsters Local 237]. Fink is not running. Wants to know where Garth is. Will talk next week.

Lillian Roberts [commissioner of labor]. She was glad I called. I told her I would send her the job report.

David Burke [former secretary to Governor Carey] pleased to have me stay in touch.

Al Vann [assemblyman from Brooklyn]. I said, "I want your support if you can see your way clear and Stanley doesn't run." He'll get back.

Major Owens [state senator from Brooklyn]—no return call.

David Garth—a little more tentative than he has been about supporting me. I think he's beginning to believe Koch may run after all. Back from his trip to Spain, Ed refuses to discourage the *Post* "boom" movement. He says that he will not close any options and that while he once said, "Life in Albany would be worse than death," he now says, "Everyone has to die sometime." Garth tired from jet lag. He said he needed a "couple of weeks." I said I would talk to him tomorrow. Looks like Koch may be serious. If he is, that may change a lot of things.

We suffered a disappointment in the evening when Alan King said no to a fund-raiser he had agreed to because he has known Howard Samuels and Bob Abrams so long; he said Howard called him and asked him not to help me.

It's like a ball game . . . or a war. The fortunes vary from day to day . . . and a coward dies a thousand deaths.

I'll try to be more aggressive tomorrow so as to avoid any serious demoralization in the ranks.

In addition to the Badillo meeting I had a good meeting with Rohatyn. Felix said, in effect, that I was his personal favorite and that he would say so if asked, although he didn't expect to endorse anyone formally. I will stay in touch with him on substantive matters.

TUESDAY, JANUARY 26, 1982

Jack Bigel [consultant to unions] gave me names: said keep working.

Bill Scott [officer of the United Federation of Teachers]—tips on dealing with Shanker![1]

Mayor Robert Wagner [former mayor of New York City] is going away for a few weeks. Will call. We'll have dinner with him and Phyllis.[2]

David Garth: "Play it 'cool.' It's going to work out. I don't believe Koch is going to run. If he does, we have to look at it again. Wait a couple of weeks."

David Rubenstein [former staffer to President Carter] gave me names of people to call: Dobelle, Kling, Peter Kelly, Shorenstein, Wasserman, Nate Landau.

Nate Landau: "Do whatever I can for you. Have your man talk to me."[3]

Mike Del Giudice: "Stay cool. At one point you'll have to talk to Fink. I'm talking to Harding all the time." He'll stay in touch.

Nick Mancuso [president of the Firefighters' Union of New York City]. He wants to hear the issues. He'll put my name down.

Armand Magnarelli [president of the Common Council of Syracuse]: "I'm with you. Some of the people who are with you are losers. We'll talk."

Charlie Rangel [U.S. congressman from New York City]: "We'll talk over the recess."

Tom Carty [Democratic county chairman, Westchester County]. I told him, "I'd like your support, Tom." No commitment from him. He's writing for Al Del Bello to give him a signal.

Ed Costikyan [a lawyer and friend]: "I'd love to talk to you about it."

WEDNESDAY, JANUARY 27, 1982

Peter Solomon [now a New York City investment banker, formerly deputy mayor for economic development with Koch]. Doing nothing for a while. We'll see later.

[1] Albert Shanker, head of the United Federation of Teachers (UFT).
[2] Phyllis Cerf Wagner.
[3] Landau never gave anything. Neither did any of the others.

David Garth (again). He said he is 99% sure to do me if Koch doesn't run. I don't know why it's not 100% sure. He said to ignore *Daily News* story that says Koch is holding out for Fink because he doesn't like Cuomo.

THURSDAY, JANUARY 28, 1982

Andrew operated our hospitality suite at the State Committee meeting, and it went well. It was regarded by the media as well organized, and that's a real plus.

Mike Kramer [columnist for *New York* magazine]. Garth told him that Koch might run for Governor, Cuomo might conceivably wind up running for Mayor.

Dominic Baranello wanted to be assured—without a commitment—that I did not "disfavor" him as Chairman. I told him I didn't. He wanted to be consulted on coordinator for Suffolk. He's apparently concerned about Joel Girsky,[1] who's a friend of mine and a political enemy of his.

Herman Badillo: "Koch thing is serious. Get after Carey."

Phil Caruso [president, New York City Police Benevolent Association] told Richie Hartman[2] to convey message that I'd like to talk to him.

Woodie Fitchette died last night while reading a book at home. I got a call from the hospital at about midnight to tell me. He died too soon: he so much wanted this campaign. He was a man who won the respect of everyone who knew his work as a journalist and a public official, a man who won the affection of everyone who ever had a glimpse at his gentle soul, a man who was better than most of us and made most of us better. He's a very great loss to me and a lot of other people. Tomorrow will be tougher.

[1] Vice-chairman of the Suffolk County Democratic Committee.
[2] A labor lawyer noted for his work with the Police Benevolent Association.

FRIDAY, JANUARY 29, 1982

Chick Chaikin. Meeting with him and ILGWU leaders. No formal endorsement but fully aboard. He suggested people like Weissman[1] and Carl Rosen he could help with. Wants me to go to AFL-CIO leaders in Miami. I told him that Drozak[2] would like to see him lead the labor movement for me.

Ray Harding. I told him I was beginning to look at running mates for Attorney General.

Jack English [former Democratic county chairman, Nassau County]. Carol Bellamy is running for Comptroller. He'd like me to meet Ted Kennedy.

SATURDAY, JANUARY 30, 1982

Charles Rangel (accompanied by one Al Bermet)—breakfast at the Regency. It was pleasant. We disposed of a previous misunderstanding. He promised me an opportunity to present myself to the Black leaders. He'll wait to hear from me.

Gene Goldman [former client, long-time friend] says he's working hard on the fund-raiser but it's difficult to get people to bet on a long shot.

MONDAY, FEBRUARY 1, 1982

Walter Diamond [adviser to Barry Feinstein] wants me to reconsider announcement date, to speed it up in order to discourage Koch.

Barry Feinstein doesn't think Koch will run, says: "Keep going, Mario."

Jackie Llewellyn [a friend]. She will do whatever she can to help me.

John Russell [a supporter on Staten Island in 1977]. He's with me.

Bob Garcia [U.S. congressman from the Bronx] thinks it's a little premature. "Let's see what develops."

Gloria D'Amico [clerk of the Board of Elections]: "We're with you!"

[1]George Weissman, chairman of the board of Philip Morris, Inc.
[2]Frank Drozak, head of the Seafarers International Union of North America.

Stanley Stachowski [zone chairman, Erie County Democratic Committee]: "You're doing well, Mario."

TUESDAY, FEBRUARY 2, 1982

Joe Bellacosa: "You should talk to Breitel."[1]

Tom Wilmot [one of the owners of Page Airways in Rochester]: "Mario, I'd like to speak to you down the road."

Bobbi Wilson [a supporter from Rochester]: "Mario, I'd love to speak to you, down the road."

I wish I could get more of them to talk to me now, at the beginning of the road.

How rapidly the political landscape changes shape. Every day now the speculation mounts that Koch may run. Dave Garth is telling people he has advised him against it but thinks that Koch is seriously considering it nevertheless. There's no way of knowing exactly what it will mean to me. Most people have simply stated that they will not run against Ed. I have not said anything other than that I don't expect to address the matter of Koch's candidacy until it is a reality. Meanwhile, I will continue to move forward: issue papers, headquarters, staff—the works. If Koch announces, we will be in place. If he chooses not to run, we will have picked up ground on others who are now lagging.

WEDNESDAY, FEBRUARY 3, 1982

Meade Esposito. Koch shouldn't run. Too early to talk to me. "Is Adam Walinsky with you?" I told him, "No. I think he's with Lehrman." Meade said, "Good. I don't like Walinsky."[1]

David Garth. He still did not seem ready to believe that Koch was running. He found Koch's recent statement that Carey should recon-

---

[1]Charles D. Breitel, former chief judge of the New York State Court of Appeals.

[1]Former assistant to Robert Kennedy and one of the first people to encourage me to run for public office. He had since made the trip from the left of the political spectrum all the way to the far right and was piloting Lew Lehrman's campaign.

sider to be inexplicable except on the assumption that Koch couldn't
live with any of those who might replace Carey. He suggested I treat
it as lightly as possible. He still thinks it may "work out" to my advantage. He said—kind of plaintively, I thought—"I've given him [Koch]
my advice [not to run]. I don't know what else to do."

After an interval for thinking, I called Garth again and told him I
would be announcing my March 18 "Announcement Fund-Raiser" and
that when the question came up, I would have to say I was going to stay
in the race, no matter what. I also said I would talk about: (1) Koch's
position on Reagan in '80;[2] (2) his abandoning of New York City.[3]

I said I would invite Koch to a fund-raiser—like the last one.[4] I'm
consistent. If Koch runs, I'll run on the slogan: "Cuomo for Governor
—Koch for Mayor."

Stanley Friedman. Murdoch says Koch has *not* made up his mind. He
agrees that Koch would not want Bellamy as Mayor using him as a
scapegoat, and that's a strong disincentive.

Lou Resnick [Ulster County Democratic chairman]. MMC called to say,
"I will be in your county next week." Lou said, "Theoretically, I am
with you. I'm the kind of guy who moves slowly, then goes all the way."

There was a leadership meeting at the mansion this morning
for presentation of the Governor's criminal justice message. In
the course of Tom Coughlin's[5] presentation, I made an observation to the effect that we were making arrests and getting convictions in only a small percentage of the crimes committed and
whatever else we did would not serve as much of a deterrent,
given that fact. The Governor's response was brusque and harsh.
His bad blood continues to boil.

Jerry Weiss reports Chaikin is with me but wants to hold until he sees
what Koch will do—"out of respect." This is not an uncommon situation.

---

[2]Although he had announced his support for President Carter in 1980, the mayor's
actions with respect to Reagan, including inviting him to Gracie Mansion, the mayor's
home, were interpreted by everyone as good for Reagan and damaging to Carter.
Subsequent statements by the mayor throughout the campaign enlarged that perception.

[3]After having just been reelected mayor on the promise that he would be mayor for
twelve years.

[4]In October, when Koch, for the third time, said I would make a good governor.

[5]State commissioner of correctional services.

Frank Weil [an attorney in Washington]. He's interested in being helpful in governing. "More with less" is the way. Must structure a parallel organization of private-sector people.

Phil Friedman: "Keep going. Don't get angry. It's only a couple of weeks—if he decides to run, they'll ask you to run for comptroller."

Ed Koch: "None of the Democrats can win except me in November." That's what Ed Koch said to Hugh Carey today, according to Bob Morgado. He asked Carey to reconsider and said if Carey doesn't reconsider, then "I [Koch] must go because I am the only one who can save the State and the City."

SATURDAY, FEBRUARY 6, 1982

The early campaign continues to dominate our lives—except there are all the moments when you pause to reflect how Margaret has suggested that much of this is an ego exercise that has produced an abdication of real responsibility. The hardest part of it is wondering whether she's right, whether it's even right to try.

But we are trying. Koch has now replaced all other forces as the principal element. It is generally assumed that if he chooses to run—and the speculation is intense that he will—he will be unbeatable in a Democratic primary. Surely, no Democrat of any standing is expected to oppose him, except me. His formidability is such that it dissuades many of those who might have considered investing in other candidates' campaigns, including mine.

Of course, no one but Koch knows his motivation. He has expressed no persuasive rationale. His argument that no other Democrat can beat the Republicans is disingenuous, because the polls clearly show otherwise. I think the truth is, he's simply reluctant to have to deal with anyone who might win, like MMC, especially since the city continues to have financial difficulty. He is also concerned about losing his position as the most prominent Democrat. His suggestion that the "power has moved to Albany" is also transparent. It's not true to begin with, and if it were, to many it doesn't justify his abandoning the commitment he has made to the City unless he intends to pervert the Governor's office into a power base for helping the 40% of the people of the State who live in the five boroughs.

In any event, I believe having MMC as Governor and Ed Koch as Mayor would be better for the City and State than having Koch as Governor, an unknown quantity as Mayor, and Cuomo eliminated from public service. So I am prepared to run against Koch, probably one on one.

If Koch decides to run, he will become an immediate favorite. I believe, however, the weakness of his rationale will eventually erode his position. I have a strong case—"A vote for me is a vote for both of us: keep Koch as Mayor and get me as Governor" —unless Koch decides to step aside as Mayor to make the race, and I don't believe he is that gutsy.

My people were nervous and intimidated for most of last week. I think they feel better now. There is something exciting about being David—as long as you believe it's possible the stone will find its mark on Goliath.

Monday, February 8, 1982

Mayor Tom Sharpe [of the city of Mount Vernon] called. He said he was still committed to me but he was clearly uneasy about the prospect of a race with Koch.

Al Lamb [a pseudonym] of Elmont, Long Island: "Elmont thinks Koch is crazy: you should run anyway."

Mayor Corning: "Straight ahead, Mario!"

Herman Badillo. I told him I was going forward. He said, "Good. Tell Basil."

Basil Patterson: "Good! Go forward."

Jim Featherstonhaugh [attorney for the Civil Service Employees Association]: "We won't do anything until June or so, but we can help, short of an endorsement." He said he thought MMC had a chance against Koch, although it would be difficult. He talked to Ned Regan (they are working together on the Pension Fund Committee, where Jim represents the CSEA). Regan would rather run against Koch than against Cuomo.

Harold Fisher. He was interested in the fact that I will run even if Koch does—but very guarded.

Stanley Friedman was worried about the situation.

Yesterday David Garth appeared on the Gabe Pressman show. He said a number of things that may become significant in the course of this campaign.

At one point he was asked whether Koch was the only Democrat who could win in November. He said there were one or two others. He didn't name MMC. On other occasions he has said specifically to MMC that MMC was a good bet in November if he could get past the primary. Overall, he appeared somewhat sheepish and embarrassed to have to admit that he had intended to go with MMC, but now would have to go with Koch if Koch decided to run. He said that if Koch did not go (and he wasn't prepared to treat it as definite) he would do Cuomo, "if Mario wants me." He repeated that today on the phone to Sandy Frucher.

Phil Friedman, who is apparently increasingly remote from Garth, called a couple of times yesterday and suggested I remain "cool." He doesn't know what is happening but believes that Koch will run. He asked me what my intentions were, and I told him the following:

I intend to run. I know that with the Mayor in the race I would be the underdog, but I am convinced that it would not be a worthless effort to oppose Koch. I believe his rationale for running for Governor is so weak that he will lose strength in a campaign. I think the common sense of it is that we are far better off with Cuomo for Governor and Koch for Mayor than we would be if we lost Koch as a "good" Mayor—replacing him with a less-experienced person facing a $1.3 billion deficit and making him a Governor who might be out of place—and lost MMC to the public service.

Money would be a problem, but I would seek to generate as much free publicity as possible by debating Koch as often as possible.

On Wednesday, after seeing Mayor Koch, I will announce that I'm sticking with my original schedule of a formal announcement in March, and that I see no reason for changing that schedule because of any of the many threatened candidates. I will not emphasize my visit to Koch and I will not ask Koch not to run. I will be respectful, concerned, but not intimidated. I will say I always knew it was going to be difficult. I will use the occasion to announce a headquarters, a finance committee and other specifics. I will try to mention the $1.3 billion deficit New York City is facing.

If Koch decides to run and my effort proves to be an "impossible dream," he will have time to force me out before the Convention. If he chooses not to run, I will have gained a large advantage by being the only candidate that has stood up.

Phil Friedman thought I was right and was encouraging.

In the course of Garth's presentation on the Pressman show, he sought to explain away Koch's ignoring of a commitment to George Clark[1] not to run for Governor when he asked Clark for the Republican line in the '81 Mayoral race. Garth's answer was a transparently weak one. He said there was a commitment, but circumstances had changed. I called Ray Harding, who had seen the program, and pointed out to him that the same logic would allow Koch egress from a promise to the Liberal Party to stay with them in November. If they went with Koch, and he lost the Democratic Party and then withdrew his support, they would get under 50,000 votes because they'd have no real candidate, and would lose their standing as a Party.[2] Harding is troubled.

I can feel my people—or at least many of them—weakening. A tentativeness comes into the voice, sometimes almost a sadness—a little bit of embarrassment at the bold assurances of support that they had already given; a hope that they might be let off the hook, a ducking. I've seen it before, and I recognize it. As quickly as it comes, it can go. Let Koch announce he is not running and all will be euphoria in the Cuomo camp. Let him even slip a bit on TV and there will be a surge of confidence. It is as though the soul were being puffed up by a bellows operated by the hand of Fate. To do this thing right, or to do it at all, you have to be able to look beyond the moment. I'm trying very hard to do that.

[1]Chairman of the Republican party in New York State.
[2]See p. 147.

WEDNESDAY, FEBRUARY 10, 1982

Billy Kessler, our restaurateur friend from Brooklyn, says that he has taken an informal poll and that I will beat Koch. He knows a lot of people, and I wouldn't discount what he says entirely, although every professional in the place disagrees with him.

But Kessler's view is plausible in light of an unconfirmed rumor about a Moynihan poll done by Dressner[1] that is supposed to show the following:

Most popular Democrat for Governor—Moynihan
Koch v. Regan—Regan wins
Cuomo v. Regan—Cuomo wins
Koch v. Cuomo—Koch by 10 points

Today I announced that I would be running for Governor regardless. I did it after a meeting with the Mayor.

At the meeting, the following occurred:
He had John LoCicero, Bob Tierney, Tom Goldstein[2] with him.

I asked about Warren Anderson's Medicaid proposal.[3] He said he liked it as a bottom-line alternative. I asked him about the Rubin Commission, and he said they were delighted with the report, and they would try to get as much as they could.[4]

I told him I would be formally announcing on March 16th. I said I'm ready; I've been prepared for a long time; I believe I can win—I know I can win—especially with his help. If I won, I would be mindful of the City's problems. I said that I was from the City; that I had a deep commitment to help the people; that the people in greatest need are the people who live in the City. "I can help balance with the upstaters."

[1]Richard Dressner, a pollster.
[2]A member of Koch's staff.
[3]A proposal to have the state assume a portion of the Medicaid expense of the city of New York and the fifty-seven counties of the state outside the city. Carey had proposed a total pickup. The partial pickup was eventually adopted.
[4]The commission, named for its chairman, Max Rubin, had been assigned to study the system of state aid to public school education in New York City. Among other things, it recommended a lot more money for schools in poor districts, including New York City.

I said I believed the Mayor should be the voice of the cities of the Northeast and Midwest. I think the Mayor was impressed by my observation. I said that if he became Governor, Carol Bellamy would be the voice of the City—that her picture would appear on the cover of *Time* magazine immediately. I think that concerned him. I emphasized that the Governor is not the strong voice of the cities because the Governor has other concerns. I pointed out that Governor Rockefeller was not the voice of the cities, that Lindsay was; that Carey was not the voice of the cities, that Koch was; that whoever is Governor will not be the voice of the cities, the Mayor will be.

Koch responded by saying that he has told four candidates (he didn't name them) that he has not yet made up his mind. He said he believes he can win, and would probably be the favorite, but there are other considerations, including personal ones. He said he would announce by February 24th. He mentioned twice that life-style judgments were important to him.

He said that if he chose not to run, his selection of a candidate to support would be limited to the Democratic candidates. He said that on that score he might sit out the primary but he would definitely not endorse the Republican.

He surprised me by saying that Breslin and Newfield would be a serious problem for him in considering me. I spent several minutes explaining to him that neither controls my judgments, although I would certainly not disavow them as friends. He said my critics point out that nobody affects MMC's judgments—he said it sarcastically. He added that he was concerned about the personal relationship between him and me, and how Breslin and Newfield might affect that. I tried to reassure him, but I don't think it worked.

He said he didn't expect me to get out of the race once I announced, any more than he would. He said he wouldn't ask me to. That was the end of the meeting.

And when the energy and preoccupation with the campaign are at their most intense, threatening to obscure the other things in our lives, events occur to remind us how one-dimensional we are becoming. Iris Malone[5] has had a mastectomy. The early

[5]A pseudonym.

indications are troublesome. Matilda and I saw her last night at Mt. Sinai. She was "carrying on" admirably. Her daughter was there and said "Pop" wasn't doing as well. What would he trade to get back Iris's freedom from this ugly menace? What would I give if, God forbid, it were to happen in this family? What are we trading every day—and for what?

Harold Holzer[6] called. Normally he's full of gossip and questions and wisecracks. He called today just to say that he was sad . . . at the sudden death of his good friend Bob Rickles, who had been a commissioner with John Lindsay and a constant political partner of Harold's since then. And what is Harold trading?

The coverage of my press conference was extensive. The story that I will run, regardless of what the Mayor does, has been played on every radio and TV outlet. The *Post* did an afternoon story that wasn't bad, especially considering I'll be running against their candidate. Ed's reaction was gentle because my approach was so flattering to him. A lot of the people on my staff and others, like Jim Introne, didn't like my argument, which was, in effect, that Koch is too good a Mayor to make Governor: it gives him too much and doesn't give me enough, in their judgment. If this were July or August and I knew Ed and I were in the race, then of course I might use a different emphasis. But as long as there is a chance he can be kept out, my approach, I think, is better. Here, as in so many cases, people tend to take extreme views. Almost always in this complicated business there are such powerful and evenly matched considerations at work that solutions and approaches need to be subtle, filigreed, works of art. There are times for the one-sided, uncompromising, head-down "full steam ahead" approach. More often, however, one has to cover more than one base at a time. That can be a strain, and is often misunderstood, but that's what government—and politics —is like much of the time.

We haven't heard from our friends like Don Manes or Stanley Friedman or other leaders for a while. They're all biding their time, waiting for Koch. But Corning has been there. God bless

[6]A friend; a talented writer and public relations expert, now in the private sector. He worked for a while in my 1977 campaign for mayor.

him! I must ask him to be an Honorary Chairman of this campaign. The whole campaign should be upstate and downstate; women and men, black, brown and white; multi-religion; reform and regular.

Generally, an up day. Down deep, people on my side feel today Koch won't run. Yesterday, they were sure he would, but the press conference today saturates with confidence everyone who is a partisan of the Cuomo effort. Tomorrow will be down. Then up, then down, then who knows? *Sempre Avanti!*

FRIDAY, FEBRUARY 12, 1982

Spoke to pollster analyst Tubby Harrison on the phone. He said: "You would have a serious problem in any election: you have no image, negative or positive. You need to be seen as a person associated with one or two issues and a vision of the state."

"Vision is the key."

He also said he doesn't believe that Garth knows anything about primaries. Organization and turnout are everything.

Ulster, Dutchess and Putnam trips went very well, according to Martha Borgeson.[1]

Howard Rubinstein says we're doing well, and it's not hopeless. Murdoch does not seem to be upset. *Post* got only 14,000 coupons, not a lot. Newfield says they buried some of the negatives, although they admitted to 1,000 or so.[2]

Jim Introne: "Your press conference didn't get the coverage you should—you need better staff." MMC: "Agreed, Jim—find me some!"

---

[1] A member of my staff.

[2] The *Post* had asked readers to send in coupons indicating whether they thought Koch should run. The *Post* said the result was about 14,000 to 1,000 in favor of Koch's running. Some people, including Newfield, were suspicious. Newfield said the coupon was like a Soviet election because you couldn't vote no; the coupon only had a "yes" box.

SATURDAY, FEBRUARY 13, 1982

It's clear that "management" will be discussed a great deal in the upcoming campaign. My old friend Howard Samuels has apparently told the Mayor—and others—that I can't manage. Cabin will come back to haunt me. I have to find ways to combat it. Using Stern as a "Manager" of the details and business side of the campaign and Jerry Weiss as a "Spokesperson" and David Sawyer[1] or someone like that as "Political Consultant" should help. Also announcing the kind of people I'd like to have in government would help.

Met with Sawyer. I like him. He'll wait to see what happens with Koch, but if Koch does run, he'll consider doing me.

My back is gone! I don't know why, but the pain is intense. Here we go again.

SUNDAY, FEBRUARY 14, 1982

We'll know this week if Koch will enter. If he does, his people will probably try to get me out of the way. How? A suggestion I run for Comptroller? Or manage the campaign, then be in the administration and run for Senator in 1986? Or Mayor next year?

If Koch were to run, all the polls would show me an underdog, and the polls would be right. He would have the political establishment and the money. Those in the City would be afraid to say no to him: his reputation for "getting even" is self-proclaimed, and he will not step down from the Mayor's office to run. He will also have going for him issues like capital punishment; his successful management of the City; his enormous public acceptance; Garth. It would be Goliath vs. David—without a slingshot.

I might get the Liberal line. If that's the case, I might be able to trouble him in November.

Altogether, it doesn't seem to most that I could be a serious

---

[1]A professional political consultant.

threat. That suggests I should quit as soon as he announces. But the fact is I see it differently. I believe I would be a better Governor than he, and under those circumstances I should at least try to take him on. And, I think the rationale is all with me. If I'm wrong and it's a foolish effort, I'll know before the convention, and there will be plenty of time to do the "prudent" thing.

If he doesn't run, I'll be a favorite for three days, until others come back into the race, and even then I'll be a good bet.

Why? is the big question. Why do we do what we do? Too often we forget to ask. Having asked—having cross-examined myself again—I feel better about going forward. I'm even getting eager for the game to start: we've spent so much time warming up.

TUESDAY, FEBRUARY 16, 1982

Dominick Scaglione [a banker and leader in the Italian American community]. He wants to help.

Bob Morgado likes my suggestion about asking Koch to resign as Mayor if he runs. Morgado is talking to Garth.

Bill Hennessy. He's with us: Koch can't win in November.

Jeff Sachs [a Carey staffer]: "We'll do everything we can for you. Los Angeles *Times* ran a story that Koch would announce next week that he was running. You can see our people begin to fold—or at least some of them."

Harvey Kelly [reporter from *Time* magazine] wants an hour for an interview.

One thing for sure—nothing's for sure in this business.

Charlie Pace [a pseudonym for a well-known investment banker]: "I'll give you some money no matter what. We like to encourage good candidates." They give it to everybody. I'll call him back in March.

Linda Fallon [a pseudonym]: "I have news. Koch is definitely running: a friend of mine was in the room when Josh Friedman got a call asking him to become Koch's campaign press person."[1]

[1]Friedman has since become a reporter for *Newsday*.

There are rumors everywhere. It's typical. Everyone wants to be part of the action. The vast preponderance of the rumors is negative—perhaps, indeed, bad news does travel fastest, even if it's imagined bad news. My people would take Koch's decision to run as very bad news. Many people would. So the rumors that he's running are intense.

I'm guessing that the Mayor hasn't made up his mind and that personally he is leaning against running. If I'm guessing right and he says he's not running, he'll probably talk in terms of his personal commitment, his life style and a love relationship with "the greatest city in the world" too strong to allow him to leave even if he knows he will win. I think he has great instinct and senses a weakness in his rationale for moving to Albany . . . or trying to. I called Garth. He stressed to me—as he apparently has to the Mayor—that it will be difficult for any Democrat to win in November, and a tough primary will only make it tougher for us. David expects Lehrman to win the Republican nomination and to have 8 to 12 million dollars for his campaign. Strange, he should be this precise as to amount: he must be talking to Walinsky.

Wherever I can (or almost wherever, because I didn't with David) I stress the point that Koch's refusal to resign as Mayor would create a series of campaign years in the Mayoralty that would not be helpful. Clyde Haberman made the point independently in the *Times* today, so maybe we'll hear more of it.

WEDNESDAY, FEBRUARY 17, 1982

The *Post* published a poll showing Koch ahead of Cuomo 42–18, with Bellamy at 8 and the others—Fink, Abrams, Samuels—out of the running. I saw some encouragement in the 24% margin. Carey-Cuomo were behind Duryea-Caputo 28% in '78 at a similar stage. Last week I predicted a 35% margin for Koch. 58% of the people voted for someone other than Koch, and in a two-man race that will be significant. When one considers that the Mayor has had unique and unprecedented exposure . . . yes, I see the result as encouraging, though most do not.

I sense from the media a tightening of their coverage of Koch.

They gave him an "ordination" last year. They don't intend to do it again.

THURSDAY, FEBRUARY 18, 1982

It seems definite that Koch is running for Governor. Phil Friedman called today to say perhaps I should think of running for Mayor next year. He feels I'll get hurt critically if I take Koch on. It was bound to come. I expect before it's over, there'll be more of this.

I don't know if it's simple perversity or the freedom that comes from being an underdog, but I feel better and better about the race.

Tomorrow the AFL-CIO meeting in Bal Harbour, Fla., will consider the possibility of endorsing me. I expect to get some of them; if I receive a lot of support, it could be a big story.

If I work hard, I can get good Black support, good Hispanic support and the unions. Their common antagonism for Koch makes them natural allies of mine. Add the disabled: Koch said in Baltimore last year that the Democrats were doing too much for them. With a strong effort in the Italian community, that could be good. I could argue in the Jewish community, "Vote for Cuomo. Then you'll have Governor Cuomo and Mayor Koch both fighting for Israel. If you vote for Koch you lose one voice."

Andrew is doing an excellent job organizing the campaign. He, more than any of us, has appeared to profit from the political involvement of the last 8 years. He is competent, respectful, dedicated—and liked.

Matilda has been a star. She is always well received. Her charm and good looks, her obvious sincerity make her a much more effective spokesperson for my cause than I am. I'm troubled, however, about what the involvement is doing to her personally.

Chris is sensitive and aware. As long as we can spend time with him—at least Sundays—he'll be all right.

All of life, in a year. That's what it seems to come down to in a campaign. The best and the worst of people. A new challenge almost every day. The timid quit, the bold proceed, the stupid make fools of themselves. In the end, almost everyone is seen to have been pursuing his or her own narrow objective. Few are altruistic—but there are a few. Few are doing it for the "best" motives—but there are a few. Few will play it by the old-fashioned rules—truth in a handshake, the importance of commitment, fairness. Machiavelli is a more popular source than the New Testament. But then Jesus never won a race for Mayor of Jerusalem.

Margaret called. She was crisp and cool—being a doctor isn't the most relaxing profession. I asked her what she thought about the race. She said she thought Koch would win. She may be right, but I felt like crying.

FRIDAY, FEBRUARY 19, 1982

Garth called me back. He says he's not sure what Koch is going to do; he might not run. He gave me a good deal of advice that would apply whether Koch won or not. It was an extraordinary conversation, considering all that's occurred . . . and is occurring.

Herman Badillo is going away for a week. He said "stand firm"—don't let them talk to you about comptroller.

Many of the AFL-CIO unions have let Koch know they'll go with me. Bill McGowan[1] called specifically to let me know.

SUNDAY, FEBRUARY 21, 1982

I had perused Teilhard's *Divine Milieu* again in preparation for a speech I am writing for the Labor/Religion Conference on Monday night at St. Joseph's in Valatie, Columbia County. I was up at 4:30 A.M. to do it.

By midafternoon, despite all the speculation and rumors, I was excited about "functioning." Back to grabbing rebounds and spearing line drives.

[1]President of the Civil Service Employees Association (CSEA).

Sometime in the afternoon I got a telephone call from Joe Slakas[1] saying that Mayor Koch was going to announce he was running for Governor. I was sitting in the den. I hung up the phone, thought about it for the few seconds it took me to walk to the kitchen, then called Andrew and a few others to let them know. There was no mistaking their disappointment. Whatever brave language is used by our closest friends, the impression clearly is that the Mayor is unbeatable.

About an hour after I received the word, the Mayor called to tell me personally he was running. He said he didn't know what I was going to do. I told him I was surprised to hear that and, "Of course, I'm running." I said I was prepared to conduct a long, tough, intelligent, decent campaign. He said whatever happened we would be friends. I said, "I'm sure of that from my end."

I spent the afternoon and evening doing television,[2] trying to buoy up the spirits of our people, and then driving to Albany.

---

[1] At the time, a member of my press staff.

[2] With Koch in the race, I was getting increased attention in the media.

PART II
The Primary

So, despite polls that showed Koch the winner, I proceeded with the campaign, surrounded by a group of tough, intelligent, loyal long-time friends and a few newcomers who proved indispensable.

What my staff lacked, at least at the beginning, in the way of high-powered professionalism—Dave Garth naturally went with Koch—they more than made up for in intelligence and commitment. Bob Sullivan served as economic adviser, pollster, analyst and writer. Bill Stern handled the finances. Ellen Conovitz did a little bit—indeed a lot—of everything. Carolyn Walsh, Elaine Ryan, Ethan Riegelhaupt and Mark Gordon were all bright, issue-oriented troopers, who, like Ellen, were useful with everything from issues papers to organizing a community. Mike Nussbaum, an old hand at clubhouse and convention politics, and Tonio Burgos, who had been involved in it from the time he learned his alphabet—in Spanish and English—knew the arcane rules of New York's electoral system, the players and even the referees who had to be watched. Jerry Weiss was the legal expert, and Andrew the central organizing force.

In March we were joined by Harvey Cohen, a talented advertising man whose previous political experience was limited to three or four campaigns, two of them against Garth and both of them successful. Then Bill Haddad—a man of a thousand talents perpetually in search of a cause he feels worthy, who had been in a dozen campaigns, including several of the Kennedys'—came along as campaign director at just the right time to give us credibility with the media, many of whose members he knew. Finally, Gene Spagnoli, a veteran newspaperman respected and liked by everyone who ever knew him, agreed to join us, another convincing proof of our seriousness and professionalism.

Perhaps the most important task of the staff of any candidate in a major race is to maneuver him or her safely through the maze of the election laws while taking maximum advantage of such favorable developments as endorsements from prominent people and editorial boards, street fairs, TV debates and (especially for the Democrats) the Labor Day parade. In New York State, the requirements for election, compounded of the legal and the traditional, are enormously complex.

The general election in November presents candidates from each of the currently established parties—that is, those parties that are entitled to a place on the ballot because they received at least 50,000 votes in the last gubernatorial race. Today the established parties are Democratic, Republican, Conservative, Right-to-Life and Liberal; each one has a "line" on the ballot for each of the positions being contested: governor, lieutenant governor, comptroller, attorney general, et cetera.*

The established parties choose their candidates for each position at a convention of the members of the "state committees" —individuals selected by the party in each county and legally independent, although they will usually vote at the convention for the candidate favored by their county chairperson.

The state convention "designates" a candidate for each position by majority vote, and if there is no legally qualified challenger to that selection, the designated candidate's name appears on that party's line on the general election ballot without more ado. For one to be a legally qualified challenger, one must receive at least 25 percent of the vote at the convention, or get a prescribed number of signatures from party members in a statewide petition. If there is such a challenger, then there will be a

---

*Other candidates able to amass a prescribed number of the signatures of registered voters on petitions may also have their names added to the general election ballot, and several always do. Called "independent" candidates, they run under such labels as "Libertarian," "Socialist Workers," "Civil Service Workers," and so on, but seldom amass enough votes—even cumulatively—to be significant; though if any one obtains 50,000, his or her party is thereby established for the next election.

primary election preceding the general election, and the winner of the primary becomes the official candidate of the party in the general election.*

Thus, one of my tasks in the first part of the campaign—the Democratic convention was scheduled for June—was to try and assure myself of at least 25 percent of the convention vote for governor. Failure to do so would mean either a petition drive, which would have been extremely expensive and highly uncertain, or dropping out.

There was another task as well, one at least as important and involving quite delicate matters of politics.

In the general election, a candidate can be the choice of more than one party, that is, run on more than one line on the ballot. In 1982, Lew Lehrman, for example, was the nominee for governor of the Republican, Conservative and Right-to-Life parties, and his name, therefore, appeared in three different places on the ballot. As for me, getting the endorsement of the Liberal party —the "Liberal party line"—appeared to be indispensable to victory: in New York's modern history, no Democratic candidate has won statewide office without both the Democratic and Liberal lines. Nor has any Liberal candidate succeeded without the Democratic line.

On the other hand, if I once "got on" the Liberal party line, I could not get off except by moving out of the state, accepting a judicial nomination or dying. Hence, if I got the Liberal line, then lost in the Democratic primary, my name would still appear on the general election ballot as the Liberal candidate and technically I would still be in the race—in opposition to the Democratic candidate (presumably Koch). Further complicating the situation was the legal requirement that a party must receive at least 50,000 votes in the race for governor or forfeit its life as an established party. That meant, in effect, that if a candidate on the Liberal line were to stay on it but, for whatever reason (such as having promised to "support the Democrat" in the general election), were to make no serious effort to get votes, the very existence of the Liberal party would be jeopardized.

---

*One of the peculiarities of this system is that the candidates for governor and lieutenant governor run independently in the primaries. As a result, one's running mate in the primary might not be one's running mate in the general election.

These intricacies were even more complicated in my case by some personal history. In the 1977 race for mayor of New York City, Governor Carey had been able to persuade the powers of the Liberal party that I should be their candidate, and they had designated me before the Democratic primary. I, in turn, had promised them that I would remain in the race on their line even if I lost the Democratic primary—that is, that I would campaign actively as a Liberal in the general election. They believed that Governor Carey had also assured them of his continuing support. But faced with the reality of the hard choice after my defeat in the primary, the governor decided to switch from my candidacy to Koch's—to "support the Democrat." Political professionals understood the governor's dilemma and accepted his decision without much criticism or surprise. Less-sophisticated observers, especially many who had supported me, criticized it as a flip-flop. Then, when, campaigning as a Liberal (against Koch as well as the Republican, as I had promised I would), I came surprisingly close to Koch in the general election, some of my backers believed that the governor's support would have made the difference, and they didn't hide their anger and disappointment.*

It was inevitable, then, that the interested parties would recall what had happened in 1977 when the whole matter of accepting the Liberal line and agreeing to remain on it came up again in 1982. Koch, the heavy early favorite for the Democratic party designation, argued that I was a "spoiler"—that is, I was willing to ruin the Democrats' chances in November (remember, no Democrat had ever won a general election without the Liberal line) because I refused to say I would "support the Democrat" if unsuccessful in my own party's lists. To do this, I would have had to violate any pledge I might make to the Liberal party to campaign in the general election on their line alone if I lost the Democratic primary, as I had done in 1977. I responded to Koch's attack by saying I would render the issue moot by winning the Democratic primary—it would be a lot simpler than

---

*I was never seriously bothered by the governor's decision to switch to Koch in 1977. Down deep, I felt that since my own poor performance as a campaigner and my refusal to drop out after the primary had created his dilemma, I was more to blame than he was for his change of position. But most of my supporters never understood that.

dealing with the conundrums that would otherwise be created. But that, of course, did not make the issue go away.

So Koch and I squared off, in a campaign that was seen as "a rematch of the tough race for mayor in 1977." Conceptually, it was a little different. Koch had moved much further to the right in the interval, capping his transition with his 1980 speech at the Democratic National Committee meeting in Baltimore, in which he attacked "traditional Democratic philosophy." He had also been perceived as sympathetic to Reagan in 1980, had run as a Republican as well as a Democrat in the 1981 mayoral campaign, and throughout his mayoralty had escalated his calls for reinstatement of the death penalty in New York as a deterrent to rising crime (a position that was and is politically popular but to which I was and am opposed).

Koch's move to the right was perhaps suitable for a general election in New York, when Republicans and Conservatives vote, but the mayor decided not to press it in the Democratic primary, where respect for "traditional principles" was still high. He chose instead to ignore philosophy—at one point even to deride it—in favor of his "record of executive experience," suggesting thereby that there is a difference between having a philosophy and running governments. I responded that I thought eight years of the Carey administration had proved one could do both.

So there we were. A hundred obstacles to be overcome. Most people saying it couldn't be done. Even our closest supporters doubting our chances. But then, all our lives we had seen our people make it against the odds. Why not again? The race was on.

TUESDAY, FEBRUARY 23, 1982

I made a mistake yesterday by giving the press the impression
that I took it for granted I was losing the party organization's
support. I spent much of today trying to contact the leaders to
correct the impression.

David Garth called. He said he felt terrible: he had a cold. He said he
was worried about what would happen to Koch and Cuomo in November if I persisted in running. I said I saw the problem but I wasn't
responsible for it unless Koch is to be presumed to win. I told David
that I am the "logical" candidate, not Koch. I told him he would get
an intensive six-month debate on the issues. I said "good-bye," and he
wished me luck. I don't think I'll be talking to him for some time.

Meade Esposito didn't get back to me. Louise Slaughter talked to Nick
LaPorte,[1] who tells me he is with Koch.

Joe Crangle said he is holding himself open—he likes talking to me.

Marty Mellman [chairman, Nassau County Democratic Committee]
said he would hold himself open as well.

Mayor Jim Griffin was a big disappointment. He was inexplicably harsh,
saying things like, I had never helped him and that he didn't owe me
a thing. On the other hand, he didn't say he was going with Koch,
although it seems clear he will. He is one of the unhappiest surprises
so far.

Barry Feinstein is also still open, as is Al Vann, with whom I met today.

Maurice Hinchey [assemblyman from Ulster County] says he will endorse me. He also told Joe Martorana.[2] I spoke to him on the phone
this afternoon and he told me, "Anything you want." He's a man you
can believe.

Former Assemblyman Armando Montano [from the Bronx] is with me. I
asked Tonio to get up a meeting with him.

Assemblyman Bill Bianchi is with me. He came to my office to say so,
and I was delighted. *Assemblyman Lew Yevoli* [from Nassau County],
however, will be with Koch. He thinks Koch is strong in his district.
They both came to my office at the same time, but Lew left early.

[1]County chairman, Democratic Committee, Richmond County.
[2]Member of my staff.

Increasingly I find the idea of Orin Lehman[3] as Lieutenant Governor appealing.

Denny Farrell [assemblyman and Manhattan county leader, and a key to my political support in the Black community] made some good points: "Be positive on MMC, don't attack Koch; make more of the Lieutenant Governor's status; call Dave Dinkins; get Bella Abzug's[4] endorsement; follow the UN debates and make comments where appropriate on Israel." He also said he thought it would be a mistake to make the Black support too prominent too early.

Dick Ottinger [U.S. congressman from Westchester County] called me to endorse me—what a nice bit of news and a surprise. He will be very useful in Westchester, and elsewhere, too.

Bill Finneran [state assemblyman from Westchester County] was in the office today to tell me I would win, and he's with me.

A reporter called to say Koch had done an interview with *Playboy* some time ago that will appear in the April issue. Koch apparently said some embarrassing things.[5] I learned later that the *Times* would have a piece on it tomorrow.

WEDNESDAY, FEBRUARY 24, 1982

Spoke to Don Manes at the Forge Diner.[1] I told him that I had spoken to Stanley Friedman last night. I explained that I had no intention of getting out of the race and that I would do everything I could to beat them both. I told Meade Esposito the same thing as strongly as I could on the telephone.

All three of them said they would stay on "hold" for the time being. I doubt they will for long, given the realities of politics in New York City.

[3]State parks commissioner.
[4]Former U.S. congresswoman; irrepressible, perpetual activist.
[5]Among others: "Have you ever lived in the suburbs? I haven't but I've talked to people who have, and it's sterile. It's nothing, it's wasting your life. . . . [A]nyone who suggests I run for governor is no friend of mine. It's a terrible position, and besides, it requires living in Albany, which is smalltown life at its worst. I wouldn't even consider it."

[1]A diner conveniently located on Queens Boulevard near the Queens Borough Hall.

Larry Kurlander [attorney from Rochester and a friend since my first political effort; also former district attorney of Monroe County] called from Rochester. I can win. He wants to be part of my inner circle.

Ken Butterfield [supervisor of the town of Huntington] called to say he endorses me. He will also call Bob Herbert at the *Daily News* to react to the Koch announcement. He feels I can win.

Spoke with *Stanley Friedman* again and told him that I could not afford to have him go with Koch without a struggle. He said that it was silly for me to stay in the race.

Bill Stern says the money people have tightened up.

Ed Koch was on the radio all night talking about how he is warming up to the Liberal Party. "What matters is winning."

Sandy Frucher called to say that I have to get out, the Liberals are going with Koch. Garth is going to "kill" me.

At the moment, therefore, it looks like we won't get the money, we won't get the Liberal Party, we won't get the leaders. It's been a tough day—and night.

Gail Shaffer [state assemblywoman from Schoharie County] was extremely effective with comments from Albany. She has a great future.

Joel McCleary was in to see me. He pushed Caddell and Squier.[2] He can't be campaign manager because he's tied up with David Sawyer.

David Sawyer can't be campaign manager because he's tied up with helping Senator Pat Moynihan.

I did "Live at Five"[3] and made the point that Koch's *Playboy* remarks could cost the city money because they begged for hostility from Albany. This will be a story for a week.

Liberal Party meeting was frustrating. They are in danger of being wiped out as a party. Koch will be Mayor no matter what, and that's a reality they must deal with. They badly need jobs: if they go with me and lose, they have none, no matter how well I do, although they'll keep the party, because I will get them more than 50,000 votes.

[2]Robert Squier, political analyst. Pat Caddell eventually joined the campaign.
[3]A WNBC-TV presentation of news and interviews weekdays at 5:00 P.M.

We're caught in a circular problem. The Liberal Party, many of the unions and many of the money people are reluctant to commit to me. They are waiting for signs of organization and potential success before they "invest," but they are almost indispensable ingredients in forming up the effort in the first place.

I must get a "name" campaign manager and a headquarters as soon as possible.

THURSDAY, FEBRUARY 25, 1982

Supervisor Larry Bennett called from the Town of Newburgh to endorse me. I took a picture with him last year, and he remembered. He is the only Democratic official in the town.

Stephen Berger was encouraging today. He would not be available to be a campaign manager, but I think he will help. He said he thought I could beat Koch, although it would not be easy. He said he has no relationship with Koch.

Bella Abzug is waiting for the lines to be drawn to decide whether to run for Congress. It was a friendly conversation, and I think she will agree to endorse me down the road.

There's no question that the Koch candidacy has been damaged by the *Playboy* interview. It's so early in the campaign, however, that the chances of the damage being permanent are slim.

FRIDAY, FEBRUARY 26, 1982

Jay Goldin. I told him to consider the possibility of our doing something together. He said, "You never know." That's "no."

Terrence Benbow [lawyer, former president of the Staten Island Citizens' Union] apologized for having rejected me on behalf of the Citizens' Union in '77. He said it was a mistake. Would like to help me in any way he can.

The value of a Garth is clear from the way our campaign is shaping up—or, rather, isn't. It has no form. It is not being driven by anyone along any particular path. Although the Koch candidacy is now—and only for now—reactive to the *Playboy* blunder, they have the capacity for overall strategy with design, form, evolution. Garth and Friedman provide it themselves by application, on a saturation basis, of their attention and their talent. Eventually, it will involve the media heavily, but even before that, they set about to achieve specific objectives by specific moves and feints. We must supply that capacity. I think we can. It requires polling and an ability to analyze the results. Sullivan, with Green,[1] can do that, I expect, as well as anyone. They will tell us what message we need to deliver. The next step is to find a way to deliver it. That requires creativity. By issue paper, endorsement, event, commercial? Linda Fisher,[2] perhaps, with Ethan Riegelhaupt and Len Schwartz should be able to do that, with Burgos and Sullivan and Nussbaum sitting in. This on a regular basis—perhaps daily.

SUNDAY, FEBRUARY 28, 1982

The movement of the political establishment to Koch continues, almost inexorably. They are concerned about Koch as Mayor whether he wins or not as Governor, and few of them have the courage to take him on, although many of them will say privately he is doing the "wrong thing." It is a demonstration of the political system at its weakest. Survival—not the good of the government or the people it serves—but survival for the politician becomes the test.

Traveling to Kings County reform groups and Queens regulars, I detect a sense of Koch's formidability. At this stage, the political people are not prepared to believe Koch can be beaten and therefore will not risk taking him on. To change things we need another mistake by Koch, a show of strong support for me, a show of money or a dramatic change in a poll—all of those things . . . or some of them.

[1]Roger Green, a young, relatively unknown pollster who was willing to work for us. Not many were, at this stage of our effort.
[2]A member of my staff and former press aide to Paul O'Dwyer, one of the great figures in New York State politics.

Sandy Frucher, who just concluded his negotiation with CSEA and was distracted by that more important subject, delivered to me what is essentially the Koch line: can you get the money? I must get it. I'll spend the next three days calling people.

My first few calls today indicated that some unions are hanging back—Morty Bahr especially—waiting for Shanker and others to come forward. Again, the vicious circle. I must break it.

MONDAY, MARCH 1, 1982

I stayed in my room at the Wellington this morning to make calls.

There are some who are enthusiastic largely because of their dislike for Koch. Others will help because of a similar dislike, but feel there is no real chance for success. That feeling communicates itself.

The unions appear to be disconnected at the moment. Morty Bahr, who was so vigorously out front for me in Florida, appears to have gone back. He told me yesterday he is waiting for others to go forward. Gotbaum said he is getting bad vibes from some Italian local leaders who prefer Koch. Even Charlie Hughes, a Black leader who supported me in '77 and Carter in '80, is going to Koch. That's because Koch is the Mayor, with a reputation for getting even, and he will be Mayor even if he loses.

Chaikin, today, was noncommittal.

I have been concerned about how to get Sandy Frucher's help. He could hurt me with CSEA, which until today has been accommodating, if he were to come out against me. Today Jim Featherstonhaugh called and indicated they may have to delay their endorsement. It sounds to me like Frucher may have been talking to them. I'm pushing for an early endorsement, on March 10th.

Bill Hennessy remains a stalwart. I wish he had as much influence in New York City as he does upstate. He's been talking to everybody, although Morgado is watching him like a hawk. The Carey policy, ostensibly, is total neutrality in the Democratic primary. As for me: it is clear that Carey and Morgado are seeing to it that no one on their payroll goes out of their way to help me.

Armando Montano came in the office today. He's with Herman Badillo. He points out that Bob Garcia and my good friend Robert Rodrigues[1] will be with Koch. To them, as with most, it's a matter of going with the people who can help you politically.

I met with Arthur Eve[2] late last night. It was a rambling discussion but a good one. He talked about creating an independent party of his own. Although he didn't say it explicitly, he clearly doesn't think I can win. He indicated it by dropping remarks like "Patterson doesn't want to run for Lieutenant Governor because he doesn't want to serve with Koch." We left it that we'd be talking again within the next few weeks.

TUESDAY, MARCH 2, 1982

5:30 A.M.

It's frustrating. The Koch people have spread the word that I would not be able to "put it together" in the month of March. Stanley Friedman revealed that as a criterion when he indicated that he thought March would be a critical month for me. Jack Newfield has called to say the "Kennedy" unions—i.e., those that were with Kennedy in 1980—are upset at a takeover of my campaign by the "Carter" unions.

A central problem is not having the strong individual to put it all together for me. Andrew is terrific, but I am still left without a campaign manager who can do the job and command the respect of the political press and political forces. Stern is excellent as an organizer of economic ventures but has no political identity. Nussbaum is a good man but more useful as a consultant than a manager! Weiss is well known by the press but only as an articulator. The few who might be able to do the job are not willing. Frucher is trying to talk me out of running. Others like Walter Diamond of Teamsters, Norman Adler of D.C. 37[1] and

---

[1]City councilman. We were allies in 1977 and thereafter.
[2]Deputy speaker of the assembly, from Buffalo. One of the state's leading Black elected officials.

---

[1]District Council 37 of the American Federation of State, County and Municipal Employees.

Jan Pierce of CWA are part of the "Kennedy" unions now on hold, at least for the month of March. I'll try calling them directly again today.

Last night in Albany was difficult. Koch was treated like a "triumphant King" at the Association of Counties' reception, and I was insulted by an elderly, conservative businessman at the 50 Club—fortunately, with no press.

Before that, I was with Stanley Friedman at the Bronx Legislators' party. They were uncomfortable with me there. Olga Mendez,[2] who had previously indicated strong support for me, took me aside to tell me how she had to be "discreet" for now.

And at night Andrew explained how the new headquarters possibility at 51st and 8th Avenue was not as good as it appeared at first blush.

Later in the day
No campaign manager, no headquarters, no press person, no contact with media, and this after months of preparation. And Stern says the fund-raiser's not going well.

This afternoon in Albany I spoke before the telephone executives. The talk went well, but none of it was repeated in the press. Instead, the media quoted a reference I made to Koch in answering a question by Greenspan.[3] I pointed out he had called the Liberal party "slime." Koch now, however, is seeking their votes. I said that was tantamount to "swimming in the slime." Koch attacked me in return for personal invective. It wasn't, but I shouldn't have given him the opening. This campaign "stinks" already, and now it's partly my fault. It's such a hard business. It's a business that allows you—indeed, forces you—to see yourself at your dumbest and your worst.

It's a business that can make you forget—at least in the frenzy and heat of the campaign—who you are, what you are, and what you're supposed to be. Because the goal is so dramatic, the pursuit of it so complete—taking so much of one's energies and concentration—unless one is very careful, everything else is eclipsed. That happens in life all the time: a temporary delight

[2]State senator representing the 30th District, in New York City.
[3]Arthur Greenspan, then a reporter with the New York *Post.*

can be so tempting that it makes us forget a greater good. It happens in a concentrated way in a campaign.

The attraction of the victory offered in the campaign—what it offers the ego, if not the soul—can be a powerful distraction from the greater good. The greater good for me has to be to remember that anything which is not an expression of love—or silence —is probably wrong. The greater good for me is to remember that it's not whether I am accepted or liked or admired that counts but that I have not done wrong that matters. The question is whether one can conduct a campaign that is politically successful and still remember all of this. So far, I haven't succeeded at either—the right conduct constantly or real political success.

WEDNESDAY, MARCH 3, 1982

I have been calling Senators and Assemblymen.

Marty Connor's[1] response today said a lot about my present situation. He said that he did not believe Koch ought to be Governor, and was hardly convinced he was a good Mayor. He thought his club in Brooklyn (and Staten Island) would prefer me. But he wasn't ready to endorse, because people weren't sure of my candidacy. Some were saying that Koch would make a deal with me; others, that I couldn't raise the money; others, that "Cuomo has no one around him"; others, that I was simply too inflexible for politics.

It is almost amusing how these images hang on. I say "almost" amusing, because they are really quite serious. They all arise out of the runoff of '77 and ignore completely my history before that nine-day period and my history after it. But the images have to be contended with. It is so important that we look and sound organized, for the next month especially.

This was the second day of the "slime" story. The *Post*— believe it or not—ran a headline saying that I was attacking Koch. Today Koch went to a *Playboy* luncheon. He was apparently enormously entertaining and sought to make himself the victim of slander by George Clark and Mario Cuomo. To anyone

[1]State senator from Richmond County.

who knows the facts, it is a preposterous position. But in this business, where whole worlds of truth often separate perception and reality, he may be convincing large numbers of people.

FRIDAY, MARCH 5, 1982

6:15 A.M.

I've not yet formally announced and already the campaign seems 6 months old. I've suffered my first major faux pas—at least in my opinion. My reference to Koch's "swimming in slime" was a quick, spontaneous attempt to pin him with the use of the ugly word "slime," but it allowed Koch to paint himself as the victim. Koch is *always* painting himself as a victim. In every campaign he's in, at some point his opponent is accused of dirty tricks. He never misses the opportunity even if he has to create the opportunity. Now he's dragging out his old charges about the attacks on him in 1977.[1] Clearly, Garth is up to his old tricks. The campaign is not a discussion of issues or records; it's a series of posturings to create psychological moods. Garth wants the primary voters to think of me as a thug and Ed as an underdog. Neither is true, but that, of course, is almost irrelevant in this business. It remains to be seen how well Garth will succeed. I must remember to do nothing to contribute to the ugly atmosphere and, instead, to look "gubernatorial." It's not easy when you have mud all over you.

Meanwhile there is still the tentativeness among potential supporters. Barry Feinstein has been put on hold by Garth. Morty Bahr and the "liberal," "Kennedy" unions are on hold as well. If I can look reasonably good at announcement time—with an organization and some money and some support, and some recognizable and worthwhile themes—I'll be ready for a breakthrough. Another important factor is the "numbers." Many—like Mort Kornreich[2]—have been told that the "numbers" aren't there in a Democratic primary. That means that, judging from the past and treating certain parts of the voting population as

[1] Much was said in 1977 about rumors, allegedly started by the "Cuomo" camp, that Koch was a homosexual. I believed the Koch camp encouraged the rumor.

[2] A supporter of mine in 1977.

predictable, Cuomo can't win. There are two possible flaws in this argument: (1) history isn't being properly read and (2) the predictable is exaggerated.

Rabbi Mowshowitz confirmed all the negatives for me at breakfast yesterday. Support he thought he could get me is disappearing because people are afraid Koch will hurt them, win or lose. His reputation for getting even is being used like a club—perhaps without his knowledge, but very effectively. The Rabbi, God bless him, is doing everything he can despite the problem. He'll set up meetings with influential friends and make calls around the State to other Rabbis.

Bill Bernbach[3] will also help. The greatest ad man of the last 50 years, he wants to advise our young Harvey Cohen on how to do his work for me! It is help we couldn't afford to buy, and that wouldn't be available anyway, were it not for his friendship. I had a delightful hour and a half at lunch listening to his wisdom and gentle wit. He is a lovely, soft, brilliant . . . legend. It is a privilege to know him. I was troubled to see how pale and drawn he looked. I shudder to think of what illness he may have.

Ed Costikyan called tonight with some suggestions. He'd like to talk some more after he's convinced I can win. He thinks I have the potential on the merits; he wants to see if I'll get the money.

Ray Harding and Dick Wade[4] before lunch. Dick will help with themes. He is convinced I can win with "independent" Democratic votes. He suggested a couple of people to help write speeches.

Some good news about important things: this evening Matilda and I met Bob Perpignano, who has been dating Margaret, at Grandma Cuomo's house. We both liked him—he's quiet, intelligent, respectful. He's a Syracuse-trained architect in the real estate development business. His family and ours—it develops—have a lot of friends in common. Momma liked him, too. She said he's "serious." That sums it up for her—"hard-working, mature, sober, reliable . . . a good husband!"

[3]The legendary William Bernbach, of Doyle, Dane & Bernbach.
[4]Professor Richard Wade of the Graduate Center of the City University of New York; historian, lecturer, political expert and a good friend to me, especially in 1977.

Madeline is doing very well on her moot trial. She's a natural for the law. Chris is well. So is Maria. *Deo Gratias!*

SATURDAY, MARCH 6, 1982

5:30 A.M.
I called David Garth yesterday morning. My purpose was to let him know that I didn't intend to see the campaign degenerate into a mud-slinging contest and to let him know that I would call on Ed as soon as possible for a discussion on the issues. He was not testy, but he was tight and contained. He probably wasn't sure why I had called.

John Gerity[1] called to say I shouldn't attack Koch. Everybody says that. It shows how good Garth is. That's why I called David: I didn't feel right about what I have contributed to the campaign dialogue so far.

I talked to Linda Fisher. I badly need to have a group to make strategy and plan for me on a daily basis. I think I ought to be saying something about the Reagan cuts, reminding people that I was the first voice against Reagan while Koch was being ambivalent. I told Linda she ought to try to get Chaikin's ILGWU endorsement on Monday and CSEA endorsement on Wednesday to reflect that theme. Generally, I suggested following this outline: we need a Governor who knows the State, knows the problems, knows the solutions, can negotiate, and can be a strong unequivocal credible voice against Reaganomics; MMC is all of that.

Buffalo trip yesterday. Things appear to be fairly good in Buffalo, but then Koch hasn't made his move there yet. Joe Crangle is on the fence.

The Liberals (sans Ray Harding, who is out of form because of an accident suffered by his Dad) met with Black leadership. Theoretically, they're talking about the possibility of an independent candidacy for the disaffected Blacks and Hispanics. Actually, the best likelihood is a coming together behind my

---

[1]One of my oldest friends—since St. John's College; a lawyer, activist and constant supporter. He and his wife, Sally, have been with me in all my efforts.

candidacy. That helps. It also hurts, with people who don't like the notion of "liberal." Overall, however, especially in the primary, it is a help.

There are already so many competing and contradictory forces apparent. People who like Koch as Mayor and want him to stay and ∴ might vote for me for Governor. People who don't like him as Mayor but would want to get rid of him so will vote for him for Governor. People who like Bellamy and will vote for Koch w/o liking him to get Bellamy as Mayor. People who don't like Bellamy for Mayor and will vote for me to keep Koch as Mayor.

Joan Kaufman[2] reports again the obvious: disaffection among some like Geraldine Ferraro, whom I was hoping I could count on. It's a hard time. There will be plenty like it before this is over.

Saturday night

The day was to a large extent typical. It had good, not so good and discouraging results.

The Queens Women luncheon was a smash. Koch spoke, before I arrived, to 1,000 Democratic women of Queens County. I'm told he was acceptably received, but not enthusiastically received. As soon as I walked in the back entrance of the main ballroom of Antun's, people recognized me and started applauding. When Manes introduced me and after I spoke, I received a standing ovation from some. Ed had already left.

Ed talked about voting for the Democrat in November. He may be getting ready to face the loss of the Liberal line. I said I had no concern because I would be the Democratic candidate. I think a better answer would have been to say, "Fine, so vote for the Democrat—the real Democrat!"

The line I used that worked well—because it left no one out —was: "When you vote for me, you get Koch and Bellamy, too." Cuomo for Governor, Koch for Mayor, Bellamy for President of the City Council.

That was well received again tonight at the Harry S. Truman Democratic Club affair at the Palms in Sheepshead Bay. The "Keep the Mayor mayor" concept has an attractive logic. We

_____
[2]A friend from Queens and a volunteer.

ought to consider running a "third-party" effort[3] that makes just that point.

I also spoke to the Chiropractors' Association. No promises to them except a sympathetic ear: I'll listen to their complaints and requests.

Late tonight Bill Stern indicated he wanted to leave the role of General Chairman. He said I haven't relinquished enough authority to him. I don't believe that's the real reason. I believe his particular, semimilitary style just doesn't work with the kind of people who are involved in political and governmental life. And there is a struggle between him and others—for authority. It's a serious problem at this stage of our organizational effort, especially for Andrew, who is carrying the heaviest part of the burden.

MONDAY, MARCH 8, 1982

Events are happening so rapidly. I've decided to make these quick notes at 6:30 A.M.

Yesterday I met with Sam Brach, an Orthodox Jewish gentleman, his son-in-law and daughter in Kew Gardens Hills. Ellen Conovitz had set it up and was there. He was strong in his language of support, although he cautioned that he would not be able to come out for me right away because he had been backing Koch until now. He says he has decided Koch is not going to win and he wants me to. He will help by talking to Rabbis, especially the Satmar Hasidim[1] and others. At one point he took me aside and asked how much he would have to give me to be on the inner circle. I told him there was no figure and that it didn't make any difference, because if his ideas were good, they were good and would be recognized on the merits. I told him I was sure he would be hearing from our campaign. He gave me a lot of good advice. For example, he suggested I only call the Mayor "the Mayor," because the no-

---

[3]Creating a separate legal entity by petitioning for it, in order to gain an additional line on the ballot and another opportunity to make a case.

[1]See p. 223.

tion of that commitment to the office of Mayor being violated was a good one for me. He's right.

I marched in the Purim parade in Mr. Brach's neighborhood in the rain, then to Saul Weprin's[2] fund-raiser in the afternoon.

I was asked by the *Times-Union* (Dicker) whether I would support the winner of the Democratic primary and refused to say I would. That has created a story that I don't like because it has me on the defensive. I have to take that argument away from the other side. Of course I can't commit to the winner of the Democratic Party, not without giving up the chance to get the Liberal Party line. Neither can Koch. He started the day saying he would go only with the Democrat and then hedged to say only if the other side commits will he. It is clear Ed first figured he had lost the Libs and wanted to box me in. I spoke to Notaro[3] about it —then Koch changed his public statement from "I will support the winner" to "I will support the winner if he promises to support me." I suspect the Libs got back to Koch to make sure he didn't shut them out.

I should be positive. I should simply say I intend to win and will not be pushed into thinking about losing.

WEDNESDAY, MARCH 10, 1982

Over the weekend the flap concerning whether I would support the Democratic nominee attracted Chick Chaikin's attention. For a brief while Monday morning, I thought it would cost us the ILGWU endorsement, which we announced today—my first big one. Already a little apprehensive about not backing Koch, whom he had supported in both Mayoral elections, Chaikin didn't want to go too far out on a limb. I tried to explain Koch was simply trying to deny me the Liberal Party line because he's convinced he's lost it. We managed to get through the press conference with a minimum of embarrassment, although there was a perceptible difference between us on the question of fealty to the eventual Democratic candidate.

[2]Assemblyman from Queens; a supporter of mine and a friend for years.
[3]James F. Notaro, then secretary of the Liberal party.

Earlier Monday morning, Frank Drozak headed up a meeting of a dozen or so unions, all of whom will be coming aboard. I'll need to orchestrate the endorsements so my candidacy doesn't become one-dimensional.

Both Morgado and Introne indicated to me yesterday they would be helpful after the budget was resolved in early April. I think they detect a glimmer of hope for my candidacy.

Saul Weprin was surprised that over 40 Assembly men and women responded to an invitation he extended to meet me Monday evening to discuss the issues. Some of them seemed clearly to be Koch people bent on embarrassing me with their questions. I don't believe they were successful. Denny Farrell and I chatted for a while after the meeting. He's astute and appears to have tied his future to mine in the race. He's trying to accomplish the difficult objective of getting Black and Hispanic support without painting me as excessively liberal.

Every campaign for major office is a complex effort. This one, however, has more facets than usual. Every day new cross-currents appear. I'm more and more convinced that the difference here will be the result of whose intuition and judgments are best—provided, of course, they are accompanied by a healthy portion of good luck.

In my Albany apartment Tuesday (3/9) morning, Assemblyman Bill Bianchi and Cary Kessler[1] continued to be supportive.

Yesterday afternoon I appeared briefly with Governor Carey at the Maritime Port Council in Albany. After he left I was only mildly well received. I expect I wasn't more enthusiastically applauded because I discussed the death penalty again. It is clear that my position will cost me votes. On the other hand, if leaders do not lead, who will?

I did it again with the death penalty at the Plainview Jewish Center on Tuesday night. I wound up making it the most powerful part of my presentation, when I wanted not to. The Jewish community in the suburbs seems fiercely pro-Koch. On the other hand, Cary Kessler reported to me that my appearance was described by the President of the Men's Club as having been "fantastic." He said I changed a lot of people's minds. What is now

---

[1] An aide to Assemblyman Bianchi.

perfectly clear is that most of the voters have no clear picture of
Lieutenant Governor Mario Cuomo. It is also clear that those
with whom I've been able to spend some time are less apt to be
negative.

The question now becomes whether we can reach enough
people, and that gets to the matter of money for television and
radio. It is at that point that one begins to become discouraged.

I drove to Albany this morning for a Leaders' Meeting in the
Governor's office regarding the budget, and will drive back to
New York City this evening to tape WABC-TV's "Eyewitness
News" show at one o'clock.

Thursday morning I return to Albany for the CSEA endorsement—then back to NYC again for the New York *Times* Editorial Board at one o'clock.

Because it is so complicated, the election is already fascinating.
The Republican side has already taken a turn. It is my guess that
Lehrman will have Ned Regan out of the race by the time of the
Republican Convention, if only because of his ability to spend
money. That would mean that even if the Mayor wins the Primary, I would have a chance to win in November if I decided to
stay in the race on the Liberal line (assuming I get it). I would be
the only moderate-to-liberal in a field of moderate-to-conserva-
tives. I would have the Blacks and Hispanics. I would also be the
only Catholic, except for the Right-to-Lifers. I would be the only
one against the death penalty and the only one with 7½ years'
experience in State government. And certainly the poorest!

Bill Scott of the UFT called me. He's Al Shanker's right-hand
person. He said Al wants to talk. That can only mean he's considering endorsing me. The Teachers are perhaps the most effective
of all the State's unions. If they go all out, it will mean telephones
and vigorous statewide support. It will also mean some money.
I would have had them in 1977 if it had not been for a clumsy
meeting I had with Shanker. I must see that I don't make the
same mistake again.

Biaggi called me back. He was friendly but admitted he was
under enormous pressure from Koch. I told him I had heard the
Koch people were offering everyone the Mayoralty and to be
careful not be made a fool of. Biaggi said he is anguishing over
the decision.

Doctor Harrington[2] called. He is asserting himself as Chairman, and I'm sure that's troubling to Harding. Ever since we discussed Teilhard de Chardin in 1977 he's been a friend. He said he was heartened at the meeting with the Blacks that the Liberals held last Friday.

Our organization still lacks the strong central force that will organize the components. Stern is very aggressive as to business and structural questions, but has no political experience. Harvey Cohen is only now getting involved and doesn't even know me. The result is I have had to do most of the thinking politically so far and will have to do so for a while, at least unless and until we find someone else.

The campaign is only beginning, but already I'm afraid I won't stop often enough to smell the roses.

FRIDAY, MARCH 12, 1982

Even for me, the pace has been killing, and it's beginning to show—only days before the announcement. The lack of a single strong, well-known chief-of-staff type and a speech writer I can rely upon has made it especially tough. My family, however, makes it easier for me. Andrew has been superb. He impresses everyone. He is bright, patient and relentless. Matilda makes no demands on me and has been working hard herself. The girls are all off doing their own thing, and beautiful Christopher is simply out of it. I regret that and I have to see to it that Sundays are his.

Perhaps most wearing of all are the constant reminders that Koch is considered "unbeatable." Of course, no one is. But the perception often produces the reality, and it is disconcerting that even the *Playboy* interview did not cost him a great deal of strength in the polls. Barry Feinstein has been telling people that he saw the Teeter poll for Ned Regan and it shows Koch's strength to be totally overwhelming. He bumped into Weiss and Burgos at a Senate fund-raiser and, for a while at least, shook them with the news. That kind of thing can be handled—and is —but it's harder when you're tired.

[2]Dr. Donald S. Harrington, chairman of the Liberal party.

The most debilitating thing of all is to feel a loss of self-esteem. There can be a nobility in facing an uphill struggle, even one that seems nearly impossible, but only if you feel good about yourself and what you're doing. Don Quixote never despaired because he believed deeply—indeed, irrationally—in his own rightness. When, as will happen from time to time, you do something or say something or even feel something that makes you think yourself unworthy—or guilty—then it is difficult to avoid despair. I must feel good about my intentions and my conduct or I feel only emptiness. In that condition, even victory would be sour—it would taste of hypocrisy.

Over the last few days some events occurred the significance of which it is too early to determine. Ned Regan's stepping aside divides the field conceptually into two camps—with me as the only "progressive." I believe Koch will try to move to the left against me in the primary. My basic strategy will be not to give him the room. Being the legitimate voice against Reaganomics and a traditional Democrat is the way to do that. Getting Kennedy somehow to look favorably on me would also help.

The biggest problem for me will be the suburban middle-class vote. It appears dominantly and almost unshakably for Koch. I don't know, of course, but I think it's that he appears to express their frustrations perfectly. He provides them with a catharsis. He especially pleases them when he is perceived as tough on the Blacks and the unions. Everyone seeks scapegoats, and those who feel they were driven out of the city—and that is the middle class generally—have many among them who believe Blacks represent crime and neighborhood deterioration, and unions the waste of public and private money. The truth is, of course, that it's not the Blacks *qua* Blacks, but poverty and oppression that cause the social disorientation. But it's easier to believe it is the Blacks. As it is easier to believe that the private unions are the principal cause of inflation and the public unions the principal cause of unbalanced budgets. People are susceptible to simplistic —and erroneous—answers. The whole criminal justice system needs rehabilitation, unemployment must be relieved, a loss of spiritual values has created a vacuum—but many people believe the answer is the electric chair. It's easier to believe that. I have to find a way to tell what I believe is the truth—and get it understood. What Koch is telling them is what they believed to start with—and I don't think it's the truth. The ultimate question is, can you beat the man who starts by telling the people what they want to hear? Incidentally, I don't think Koch is conning them either. He believes what he says on these major points. But then—because he's one of them—in a sense people would be leading themselves, if they select Koch. It happens often. Will it happen again?

The notion of an independent Liberal-line candidacy in November also becomes more relevant now. It's not likely, but it's possible that if I were reasonably close to Koch in the Democratic primary and lost, my November candidacy on the Liberal line alone would be plausible. If I could keep the Blacks and Hispanics and Italians statewide—and some of the unions—it could be interesting. The polls will tell the story when the time comes, because few will invest in the effort unless something tells them it's a winner.

The CSEA endorsement was—and continues to be—a big boost. Tonight in Suffolk County there was a whole table of them, and they were very enthusiastic. I wish they were all Democrats!

SUNDAY, MARCH 14, 1982

I had written a long announcement address which was inadequate. I left it to the team to work on and they produced something worse, after trying to rewrite it with a committee. It leaves me at the 11th hour without a speech.

After 3 speeches today, I wound up the evening with Ray Harding at Ray's apartment in Riverdale. Among other things, I got the following suggestions:

1. The *Times* is important.
2. Campaign credibility is the key—money.
3. Orchestrate your endorsements.
4. Don't try to detract from Koch's popularity; turn it against him. "Keep the Mayor mayor."
5. MMC's 4-year pledge shouldn't be used till later.

6. Use focus groups to determine why Koch as Governor is a bad idea.
7. Garth is waiting for me to kill myself: they think they have me on the run.
8. Add up the money he[1] has asked for New York City. How does it relate to commuter tax?[2]
9. Libs can get money for general election. Then you can allocate it to the campaign, thereby legally increasing amount you can spend on the campaign.
10. Challenge Koch to debate later.
11. Must show people their self-interest is served by MMC's election.

TUESDAY, MARCH 16, 1982 (ANNOUNCEMENT DAY)

It's like getting married. Everyone knows it's going to happen. As a practical matter it's done already; we have long since passed the point of no return. But still, it's the exchange of vows that makes it real—and irretrievable. So today we officially announced in New York City and Albany. My Mom and Pop Raffa and all the kids were there. They were great. Andrew's organization of both the Halloran House and LaSerre (in Albany) announcement press conferences was superb. The speech, which I finished writing early this morning, was fair. I think it was a good official start.

That assumes, of course, that the reality of the announcement is consistent with the perception of the reality after it has filtered through the media. There, I think, we have a mixed bag. Some suggested the campaign would be a referendum on the death penalty. Of course it shouldn't be, but enough stories like that and it will be. Some focused on my reference to a possible $1.3 billion budget deficit in New York City next year as an "attack on Koch." That's particularly unfortunate, because I'm afraid that kind of thing will be repeated. The media want a "fight" between Koch and Cuomo; it makes better press. They're in a mood now to take any excuse they are given to talk about "at-

---

[1]The mayor.
[2]A tax on people who work in New York City but commute back and forth from homes outside the city.

tacks," and "slaps," and "charges." For example: if I talk about
unity—which I have talked about for seven years and long before
the *Playboy* story—the press may suggest I am attacking Koch as
being divisive. If I point out that he has a fiscal problem, which
won't get better when he comes to Albany, they say I am attacking him for mismanagement. When my family appears on TV,
Frank Lynn reports that I may be trying to attract attention to
Koch's bachelor status. This puts me in a position where whatever virtues I have can't be referred to, if Koch doesn't share
them, without my being accused of accusing.

Another complication is that we started this campaign with
preset, predisposed media people working from fixed images, set
in 1977. It's surprising how the images linger, but it's a real
problem, and I have to deal with it. Much of dealing with it will
involve a fundamental question: how far should a candidate stray
from what he or she truly believes in order to create the impression that is necessary to win the power that is necessary to do the
good he or she wants to do? Should a candidate who believes
things that appear obviously unpopular, and appear to threaten
him with a loss of votes, state them? Should the campaign be used
to try to educate and enlighten? Is that arrogant? Is that stupid?
And if you choose to suppress the truth or to move away from
it, what do you do when you win? Do you return to the truth
as you see it, in which case you have deceived the population?
Or, do you pursue what they think is the truth, in which case you
are not a shepherd but simply a part of the flock?

THURSDAY, MARCH 18, 1982

What happens in campaigns is that you go up and down as
though you were speeding over a long series of hills. It makes
it difficult to know whether overall your progress is up, down or
just chronologically forward. Over the last day we've been on a
down motion—or at least that's what I felt. "A cool reception at
the St. Patrick's day parade for Cuomo" was reported by Pressman. It rained, I was in the middle of the line of the Emerald
Society of the Transit Authority Police, where I wasn't expected,
and I didn't wave, so no one saw me. But Pressman's report

creates a belief that will surely—for the moment—cost us something. Then an interview with the *Daily News* that's mostly death
penalty didn't go well. And all day I hear about Andrew and Bill
Stern and our people killing themselves to put tonight's fund-
raiser together. The fact that we have to put so many people out
hurts. The fact that so many say "no" hurts. The fact that Koch's
presence appears to intimidate so many, like Nick Lark,[1] a friend
who should be a supporter—not because Nick wants Koch as
Governor but because he is afraid of him as Mayor: all these
things hurt.

Upstate chairmen that I was always close to now appear to be
charmed by Koch. Actually, there is an aura of invincibility that's
affecting them. I must use this upcoming trip to break through
that.

Jan Pierce of the CWA has been difficult. He was apparently
the only negative voice the AFL-CIO heard at the convention on
Tuesday in Albany. I've tried reaching him, but he won't return
my calls. Gotbaum says he's playing a game. Gotbaum has a
meeting with him and the Teachers on the 25th. Feinstein has
been frozen in place by Garth, who has him convinced Koch
can't lose. I'll talk to him again, but I'm told he's gone.

Stern is fiercely at odds with people in the office. Andrew is
exhausted and uptight. Matilda is completely absorbed. It's as
though she sees, hears, feels only the effort. It's the secret of much
of the "success" in the world: concentration. It's particularly
effective for her because she's so attractive while she does it.

Overall, the announcement has gone very well. I hope the
fund-raiser will, too. Now is the time for serious campaigning.
I'll have plenty of sideline advisers—pretty good ones, at that.
Like Featherstonhaugh and Bill Finneran.

SUNDAY, MARCH 21, 1982

The newspapers carried not a word of our successful fund-raiser
last Thursday. Perhaps we should be grateful. Arthur Greenspan
had indicated that he was going to write that there were no

[1] A pseudonym.

"heavy hitters." Bill Stern pointed out to him that there were: that we had people in the room who were among the wealthiest in New York City and that unless a "heavy hitter" was defined as one who gives to more than one campaign, we had plenty of them in the room.

In any event, the word will go out to the insiders that we did well. We netted about $240 thousand.

I was well received in Buffalo on Friday, although I wish the whole family had been with me. In Buffalo "family" is an unmixed blessing: in New York City some people will try to use it as a negative, as we learned in 1977.[1] Jack Ferro did his usual competent job. The local Buffalo police, Dan Tauriello and Pete Tulty, together with the usual State Police contingency of Norm Birner and Dick Genora, were, as they always are, accommodating, friendly and a pleasure to be with.

The surprise of the day came immediately after the press conference, when Jack Ferro reported that Jimmy Carter had called New York from the White House. At first I thought someone was pulling my leg—I received the message from Jack on the way out of the room, and the last question at the press conference had concerned Carter's possible participation in the campaign. I said I'd be pleased to have a former President support me. After confirming with New York, I called the White House and, sure enough, they put me through to the former President. I didn't ask, but I believe he was either in Plains or Atlanta and that the White House merely places and conveys his calls. The President said he was pleased to see that we had announced and that he wanted to help. He said that I would make a good Governor and that he thought it was important to the nation that I win. He also said that I was a "truth teller." I don't know what the politicians and analysts will say about the efficacy of his assistance, but I was flattered and felt good about his calling me.

Friday night in Harlem was rough. I met with a group called "The Community of the '80s." They have many real problems like housing and crime and unemployment. All of them want Koch to lose and most of them want me to win. Some of them

[1]In 1977 I was accused of using an emphasis on "family" as an indirect way of condemning homosexuality and forcing the issue into the campaign.

understand that a blatant attack on Koch by Blacks may only make him politically stronger. A few suggested that the Mayor baits them into attacking him for that reason. A lot of them, despite this, wanted me to call Koch a "racist." I told them I wouldn't, and they were unhappy. They were also displeased that I am against quotas and would not guarantee to put a Black on the ticket.

Saturday morning I met with Jan Pierce and then with Victor Gotbaum. I am getting closer to getting both the CWA and D.C. 37 aboard. The visits were necessary as a matter of protocol and to clarify some misconceptions.

Gotbaum suggested, without stating, that he might need to be assured that I would not oppose Koch on the Liberal line if I lost the Democratic primary. Gotbaum says he fears Lehrman even more than he dislikes Koch. I did not agree to anything. In fact, what I told Gotbaum was that he was assuming two things: that I would lose and that my staying in would hurt Koch and make Lehrman a winner. I said that even if I lost it was possible that I might be able to win on a third line in November and that, in any event, I would probably hurt Lehrman more than Koch. I left the conversation without any resolution.

Harvey Cohen is apparently doing some work for Al Shanker and the Teachers. Shanker is supposed to have said to him that he might sit this one out because, although he couldn't stand Koch, he's unsure he wants to go with Cuomo. Asked why by Harvey, Al was supposed to have said, "Mario is a bright and nice guy, I just don't think he can knock heads the way he has to."

Actually, the only way to convince people that you can do the job is to do the job. My difficulty is I haven't yet been given the opportunity.

I knew my interview with Sam Roberts[2] hadn't gone well. There's a piece on me today in the "View" section killing me— out of my own mouth. It had me as evasive, ambivalent, pedantic and a loser. If I hadn't been through all of this in 1977, it would hurt more than it does. But even as a seasoned participant in this tough game, I found the piece disconcerting. When something

[2]Then of the *Daily News,* now with the New York *Times.*

like this happens, the temptation is to run for cover. Instead, I ran more vigorously—into the Stephen Wise Synagogue—and made one of the best presentations I've ever made to any group. I was well received, and I could see people around me, like Ellen Conovitz, Joe Slakas, Len Schwartz and Joe Anastasi, were picked up a bit by the reaction of the people and the media.

The long view, the long view . . . we need to keep the long view.

WEDNESDAY, MARCH 24, 1982

This is an extraordinarily hectic pace for so early in the campaign. There is activity everywhere. To some extent, it's organizational in nature—with all the chaos that accompanies the attempt to build a complicated mechanism for an enormous statewide effort, with limited funds and limited expertise. We've had some problems, but thanks mainly to Bill Stern and Andrew, our effort is moving ahead nicely now. The headquarters at 39th Street and 5th Avenue opened this week and that will help make things easier to manage.

I appeared as a guest speaker for another ADL function this week—this one for the publishing industry. Smith of *Playboy*, Guccione of *Penthouse*, Oliva of *Oui* were all there and—facetiously, I'm sure—suggested *Playboy*-type interviews for me. I said no.

I appeared at a meeting of a day-care group in the Mall[1] and was greeted enthusiastically by Blacks and Hispanics. Autographs, pictures, kisses. The works. I don't see these things out of perspective, but there's no denying events like this one are good for the spirit.

President Reagan came to town and said he thought Koch would make a great Governor. Why not? Koch left the impression he thought Reagan would make a great President. I took the opportunity to suggest that Koch's politics would understand-

[1]The Albany Mall, where the Capitol and other state government buildings are located.

ably please a conservative Republican president. The point was a good one, but overall, the publicity simply increased Koch's aura of near-invincibility.

Despite the polls and the predictions, however, I feel very comfortable. It's not so much because I believe I will win but because I am so sure that I am better equipped to be Governor than the others who are running. It helps to feel "right" about what you're doing—and that's the way I feel.

It showed at the Police Conference meeting early this morning (9:30). Despite my death penalty position, I was warmly received.[2]

Jerry Weiss appears to be having some personal difficulties— he looks down, and it doesn't have to do with the campaign. That troubles me.

Matilda and the kids are O.K.

Upward and Onward, Excelsior!

FRIDAY, MARCH 26, 1982

Koch's strength at the moment is the perception of his strength. Everywhere—even upstate—political leaders, whose political lives depend upon being with the winner, are putting aside ideology and even personal likes in search of the probable winner. And at the moment, most of the time that appears to them to be Koch. Of course, there are the exceptions—those relatively few who are strong enough to sustain their principles and convictions and live with them—like Mayor Corning. But if I am to make a major breakthrough with the political establishment, I will have to appear stronger. Canceling my around-the-state trips over the last week in order to stay closer to Albany and the budget process hasn't helped. I'll have to work harder now to compensate for that.

This evening's stop at the Women's Division of the New York State Democratic Committee did help. I was very warmly received even as I entered the room. Stanley Friedman was present, escorting Mayor Koch's sister Pat Thaler, and he must have noticed the enthusiastic reception. A party after the dinner—in

[2]The text of the speech appears on pp. 413–19.

Rosalie Abate and Marianne Oldi's suite—jammed with women from Albany, Buffalo and Queens and elsewhere. For the most part, these women are the nonreform, old-line women of the party. I talked to them about the need to preserve traditional Democratic principles and philosophy, and it went well. I believe I'm beginning to turn Mayor Koch's "loyalty oath" approach[1] against him by pointing out how he has endorsed Republicans over the years. If I'm able to turn the issue against him, it will be a real strategic—or, at least, tactical—victory for us.

Jack Newfield called. He said Bob Caro[2]—who wrote the Moses book—says I'm coming across "whiny and political." I've been told that before, and I'll have to try harder to talk about the issues exclusively.

Newfield and Breslin, too, have an extraordinarily good sense of how things are perceived by the public. That shouldn't be a surprise, considering what they do for a living and how well they do it. They've also managed not to let our personal relationship affect them professionally. Neither of them has ever been reluctant about disagreeing with me and saying so. It hasn't always made me happy but it certainly has won my respect.

I continue to receive reports that Harding is trying desperately to avoid endorsing me. I'm told he simply believes I will not win and is trying to find a way to save his skin. I don't believe that, but his refusal to have the party endorse me until "later" is straining my confidence. How I'd love to surprise him! Harrington called this afternoon and asked me to write him a formal request for an endorsement now; Harding wants to postpone it until the Democrats produce a primary winner.

After midnight I woke up Tonio with a call. Apparently, the people from the office didn't respond well to Andrew's invitation to a headquarters-warming party. Andrew was—according to Tonio—hurt and a little discouraged. I hate to hear that kind of thing. He must be very tired. It made me feel guilty again for getting everyone involved. I'll call him.

And thinking about the people who have a tough job: how

[1]The mayor's attempt to make the Liberal party endorsement an albatross for me by suggesting that we both pledge to support the Democrat if we lost the Democratic primary.

[2]Robert A. Caro, author of *The Power Broker* (New York: Alfred A. Knopf, 1974), a biography of Robert Moses.

about Bill Stern, Mr. Independent? He's done everything on his own for his whole professional life. Now, every day he gets rejected over and over in his requests for contributions. Sometimes the cracks are cruel. He's been told more than once that we're wasting people's time by running. That our effort is a "joke." That Cuomo's just dragging down his friends. It's not easy for him, but he won't quit.

SUNDAY, MARCH 28, 1982

Andrew has decided not to take the Bar exam until February of 1983. That bothers me. It makes me feel I'm making the people around me pay too much for this campaign.

In retrospect, yesterday's breakfast with commodities exchange members Arthur Levitt, Jr., and Frank Santangelo was encouraging. Levitt says he very much wants me to win and I expect he will be helpful before this is over. He reminded me that his father had asked me to run for Comptroller. I wonder what people would say if they knew that Louis Lefkowitz[1] suggested I run for Attorney General in '78, Levitt, Sr.,[2] suggested Comptroller in '78, Garth said Senate in '80, and I wound up as Lieutenant Governor. No wonder some people think politics is not my game.

Saturday afternoon at the NYSUT[3] convention at the Hilton Hotel I received a standing ovation—perhaps the single best reception I've ever had. It may have happened because I threw away the prepared speech. I talked about basics—the importance of emphasizing fundamental skills, discipline, respect, especially for teachers; the primacy of the public schools.

In any event the affair has improved my chances for getting an endorsement, though at the moment all I am sure of is their neutrality: they don't like Koch.

I have now had three standing ovations in a row—Police Conference, Women of the Democratic Party and Teachers—

---

[1]Former attorney general of New York State.
[2]Arthur Levitt, Sr., was comptroller of the state of New York from 1955 to 1979.
[3]New York State United Teachers.

and nothing in the newspapers. Koch heard some boos at the Teachers, I'm told, but the *Post* did a piece saying he "warmed" them.

Met with Senator Cranston of California for an hour today. He's exploring the race for the presidency. I like him: he's bright, progressive, pleasant, determined.

Saturday night at Peter Vallone's Astoria Civic Association party and this afternoon at the Greek parade, it was clear how popular Mayor Koch is. He's a kind of male "Evita." It can be disconcerting to march alongside him and hear the electricity he creates in a crowd. Can you beat electricity with light?

Herman Badillo is dedicated to my cause, I suspect mostly because of his dislike for Koch, but he will be a big help whatever his motivation.

Jack Perry[4] has been beating me up in Rochester. Apparently he wants to be Lt. Governor with Koch.

Mayor Koch has appealed to politicians' ambitions very cleverly all through the upstate areas. Everywhere north of New York City he has suggested possible candidates for Lt. Governor: Lee Alexander of Syracuse, Jim Griffin of Buffalo, Jim Tallon[5] of the Southern Tier, Al Del Bello of Westchester. It's helping him for the moment, but I'd like to be sitting in the front pew when all these brides get to the altar at the same time.

Koch made a blunder. He tried showing that I had supported a Republican the way he has in the past. He accused me of endorsing Tony Gaeta's opponent in a race for Staten Island Borough President. He was wrong, and now he's had to apologize for it. Score one for us: they're not as well organized as they ought to be.

Esposito told Badillo he'd give us the 25% at the State Convention if I promise to support the Mayor after the primary. The Koch strategy is clear: it's to do everything possible to keep me off the primary ballot, or, failing that, at least to assure that I will not stay on the ballot after the primary. They apparently believe that their best chance is without a primary, so

---

[4] State senator from Monroe County.
[5] State assemblyman from Broome County.

their choice is to deny me the 25%. The notion that a primary you're sure to win can be good for you as an energizer is not appropriate here—because they're not as sure as they say: Garth knows that Koch could blow a primary by saying something outrageous; that constant discussion of the issues will make him weaker; that even if he wins it will cost a great deal of money and alienate some of the voters. If they cannot avoid a primary, then they must at least try to assure that I will not be around in November on the Liberal line. Their judgment at this time is that I could divert enough votes away from Koch to make myself or Lehrman the winner. Garth knows—even if the Mayor doesn't—how fragile the Mayor's popularity is statewide and how considerable is Lehrman's ability to use TV, thanks to his great wealth.

Garth is trying to achieve his objectives in a number of ways. The first stage was the phone calls from Phil Friedman and others suggesting the possibility of running for something else. Friedman said I should consider Mayor. The second was the effort to convince people I couldn't put together a team by mid-April and that I would demonstrate by then my inability to organize. The third was to discredit me as a Democrat by suggesting I was disloyal for not pledging to support the winner of the Democratic primary while at the same time trying to keep me from getting the Liberal line. Hence Esposito's offer.

The initial efforts to talk me out of the race have failed. The prediction that I would not organize has been dealt with. The attempt to discredit me continues, except that it has not worked out for Koch the way he wanted it to. It has focused attention on his own qualifications as a Democrat. I have tried to keep that issue alive by reminding people how he has accommodated Republicans, and on Tuesday at the State Committee I'll serve him with a formal request that he disendorse the three Republicans he has endorsed. He won't. He'll try to toss it off as "ridiculous" or ignore it. We'll then have to find new ways to keep the issue alive.

Of course, if I can keep a substantial amount of support intact on an "all the way to November" basis, it changes the outlook radically for their side. If Herman, Al Vann, Jan Pierce and the CWA and some others all are clearly committed to going all the way with me even if I lose the primary, and Lehrman is the likely Republican candidate, it's going to be difficult to see how Koch can win.

The Liberals are in the midst of a serious internecine struggle. Notaro and Harrington on the one hand are opposed to Harding on the other. Here's my guess: there are at least two parts to it. Harding wants to stay on the best possible terms with Koch; if he could find a way to support Koch, he would. At the same time, if he can't find a way and must go with me, Harding wants to know he has my loyalty and gratitude, in case I win, which Harding doesn't expect. He also wants—I'm sure, although it hasn't come up—to know that if he goes with me and I lose the primary, I will be flexible enough for him to work something out with Koch that saves his skin. Notaro wants to go with me, although he's nervous about it. Harrington is straightforward and unadulterated: he thinks Koch is bad for the State and he likes me. Harding has been walking a very tight rope. I have let him know—in various ways, subtle enough not to spoil our relationship—that I suspect him of accommodating Koch by delaying his endorsement of me; it fits into Koch's strategy for undermining my effort. I've also told Harding directly that while I will make no illicit arrangements in order to get the Liberal line, the gratitude he naturally might have expected because of his support will be diminished by the extent to which he delays and plays games.

My strategy must be to get as credible as possible; look as well established as possible; line up a coalition of Blacks, Hispanics, unions and ethnics, and add random pieces as we go along. I must hope for 25% at the Convention while talking of getting the 51% designation and remaining ready to petition or run independently if I must.

MONDAY, MARCH 29, 1982

Harding spoke to me and Weiss. He was explicit about saying he will "do" Cuomo; he can't do Koch. Jerry is not sure whether to believe him: in this business that's not unusual. I believe him and think that this simply means our strategy is working better than theirs—for the moment. We'll see.

The basics are still simple and obvious: "Decide what you want to achieve; do everything to achieve it."

Stern thinks all of the analysis I've gone through over the past few weeks is unimportant. He believes the only important thing now is to figure out my politics and whether my positions are salable. Way down deep he thinks the people simply don't want what I believe and I can't convince them.

TUESDAY, MARCH 30, 1982

A thought: If the Liberals reject Koch on principle, then say they will not support me except if I agree to stay on the line after the Democratic primary if I lose it, my argument is simple. No Democrat can win without both lines, and I'm the only one who can get them both.

Again today I was reminded that perhaps the greatest danger of all in a campaign like this one is forgetting why you are doing it—or at least why you should be doing it. The temptation is to measure everything as though victory is more than the most important thing—it is the only thing. A bad day in the press, an important rejection, a slumping poll—and the spirits sag, frustration, depression, sometimes even anger set in . . . because we forget that what is really important is the effort: doing it well, trying it well, living it well.

I don't like hearing from people: "You're a fighter; very competitive; everything is a challenge to you; you must win for the sake of winning. I think Andrew is like you." I hope he's not! And I hope I'm not. The political power one wins is good for the good it can do. The acceptance is good for the political power it gives. The joy of winning is the joy of having an opportunity to do the good. Losing, not having the acceptance that gives the political power, is being denied the chance to do good. But trying for it—for the right reason—is a good by itself. I'm so sure this is true that it's hard to live with the reality of my departure from it.

THURSDAY, APRIL 1, 1982

I called Jim Notaro. The machinations in the Liberal party are so complex I am beginning to lose my way. He thinks the following: Harding is now ready to do my candidacy because he has no choice; Harding will encourage Koch to do a write-in, which might be a problem for me. That way Harding can cover both bases. Notaro says Koch's strategy is to deny me the 25% at the Convention, then get me to walk away from it without petitioning and pull the rug on me on the Liberal line with a write-in vote.[1]

Koch gains political strength. Lee Alexander[2] and a couple of other important names will endorse him soon. I think it has little to do with their liking him or his abilities. They will tell you privately they wish he weren't running. But they expect him to win. The impression is created simply by the enormous publicity he receives. There is a tendency to convert notoriety and celebrity status into popularity and success. The intellectual process in campaigns—at least until you get into the booth on election day —is terribly superficial and at times cynical. It can be depressing to hear people tell you over and over that while they prefer you "on the merits" they want to be with the winner. And the more that's felt, the stronger it becomes: it feeds on itself.

My being compelled to stay in Albany on the budget for the last week or so has been damaging, because I've been unable to do anything to reverse the impression of Koch's strength. I had hoped we could bring Bill Haddad aboard and that his appearance would give us a jolt forward, but now that move has been bogged down in a disagreement between Bill Stern and Haddad over how much money he should get.

One of our difficulties is the inability to get publicity that naturally goes to a Mayor of the City of New York, especially one as charismatic as Koch. This week, for example, the Senate and Assembly, in the still of the night, asked a repealer of a

---

[1] It is possible in some races to "write in" the name of a candidate who doesn't appear on the ballot. The idea was that Koch, having avoided a primary by eliminating me at the Democratic convention, would proceed to garner most of the Liberal vote by asking them to write him in, instead of voting for me, on the Liberal line.

[2] Mayor of Syracuse.

special capital gains tax on real-property transactions above a million dollars in the City of New York. There seemed to me to be no good reason for the repealer other than the fact that the real estate industry wants it. They are, obviously, strongly in Koch's corner. I'm told American Express will save $18 million as a result of the repeal.

I got out a release with a cute line from Ben Liebman[3] calling it "Carte Blanche for American Express." All I could get was two lines in the *Times*. Maybe it will be better when I get out on the road.

We suffered a setback Wednesday night. President Sandro Pertini[4] was being feted at the Waldorf. I was supposed to address the group but was stuck in Albany, and Mayor Koch replaced me. He made points with 2,000 Italian leaders. The next morning when I got home, bedraggled and annoyed at how the circumstances had conspired against us, I ran headlong into Matilda's frustration. She was there last night and, being totally committed to victory, was unhappy that I was not able to make it. She started the morning by making that clear. That can be a difficult way to start the morning.

So this has not been a particularly good period. There will be many periods like it and many better periods before this is over. It's a little bit like being in a championship prize fight. There's no point in trying to figure out who's winning on points in the middle of the fight. What you have to do is land as many blows as you can each round, trying to duck as many as you can at the same time, then hope for the best when the judges file their ballots.

Then again, anything is liable to happen in a fight, in a ball game, in life generally and certainly in a campaign. For example, it's clear that Koch will refuse to make public what he said in the 13 hours of tapes made by *Playboy* that never appeared in print.[5] That's bound to be an issue and could be an important one. Many

---

[3] A member of my staff.
[4] Of Italy.
[5] The *Daily News* demanded the *Playboy* tapes under the Freedom of Information law. Koch claimed that the tapes were personal and that they did not fall under that law. The *Daily News* chose not to bring the lawsuit, apparently because it would not have been resolved before the end of the campaign in any event.

other presumably unanticipated events will happen before this is over. Together, those things we're not now anticipating will eventually make the difference.

MONDAY, APRIL 5, 1982

The vacuum in my campaign that was created by canceling the around-the-state trips so that I could stay in Albany has been even more damaging than I thought. Missing President Pertini and allowing Mayor Koch to take the whole limelight helped create a general impression that I was either not serious about the campaign or incapable of sustaining it.

One inexperienced with political campaigns might not realize how significant this kind of impression can be. The rapidity with which rumors and impressions travel—and their extraordinary reach in a campaign—are difficult to appreciate until you have been in the fray. All the players on the inside are extremely sensitive even to nuances. They read conclusions on the basis of them, and their conduct is definitely affected by them. The most expert political manipulators know how to create and exploit these nuances. I am sure the Mayor's people are doing that to me now by suggesting that I will never be able to go the distance. The last two weeks helped them make that point.

Saturday we tried to make a positive move by going to the Great Neck station and talking about the commuter-tax increase which is proposed by Mayor Koch and which I oppose. We were able to get no press at all. If I had not called *Newsday* myself and argued very hard, there would not have been a mention. Even with that effort, all I could get was a small box on a back page. Actually, I got more than a box. I came away with a cold, because it was raining and I didn't have a hat.

Saturday afternoon I spent reading, writing and making telephone calls.

Christopher was the Altar boy at the 8 o'clock Mass on Sunday. It was the best hour and 20 minutes I've had in a long time. The new ritual calls for a kind of theatrical presentation of St. Mark's Passion. I didn't think I was going to like it but I did, a great deal.

Sunday night I was involved in an entirely different kind of religious experience, the Lubavitcher Rebbe's birthday.[1] Hundreds of the Lubavitchers were jammed into their auditorium at 770 Eastern Parkway. They were literally hanging on each other's shoulders. Bodies had to be pushed aside in order to make room for passage. It was like walking through a cornfield, except the stalks were harder to push. There was an intensity of emotion in the room that I haven't seen for a long time. There was chanting in Yiddish, singing, people shouting. They used the occasion to reassert their allegiance to the group. They were expressing their confidence born of their communion. There was something about the congestion that created a power. Some of them cheered the Mayor when he came in. I had the feeling that they would have cheered the Mayor even if nothing he ever said pleased them. The bond between them is much stronger than issues or superficialities.

I saw Barry Feinstein at breakfast this morning. He's leaning toward Koch. I like Barry, but there's no question in my mind that if he goes for Koch, it will have very little to do with ideology. Why should it?

I spoke to Don Manes. All the indications are that Manes is going to go with Koch. I expected it but made a last effort anyway. Today I told him two things: The polls are showing a softening of support for Koch (he agreed). I told him that if he went for Koch, he would probably never get to be Mayor even if Koch won, because Koch would have to go with Bellamy or Biaggi, whom he's trying to reach, or Goldin, who is helping him, or Fink, who is a friend, or remain neutral. On the other hand, if he went with me and I won, his chances would be excellent. For the moment, I may have made him think. But only for the moment.

Saturday morning I met with Jerry Bloom.[2] I like him. He's old-fashioned about things like loyalty. He's bright, experienced and could be a big help to me in Brooklyn. At the moment, he's considering the possibility of running for Lieutenant Governor or Comptroller. I think, in the end, he will decide not to do it,

---

[1]Rabbi Menachem Schneierson, religious leader of the Lubavitcher Hasidim, was celebrating his eightieth birthday.
[2]Former state senator and state committeeman. He died October 2, 1983.

but I didn't discourage him. Actually, I think he could be useful as a running mate. He's leaving for Florida and will get back to me next week.

TUESDAY, APRIL 6, 1982

A bad day!

A story appeared on the front page of the *Times* telling the world that Koch has the Convention locked up. It was an extraordinary decision by the *Times,* placing a political speculation on the front page. Given its power, this paper can kill you with a story like this one. Another story appeared in the Gannett papers saying Cuomo was in trouble because he's not getting publicity. How ironic.

Koch has indicated that he'll do a write-in in the Liberal party. With money alone he could win that. If he did ten mailings at $15,000 apiece, and I couldn't answer, he'd win.

Even a really good meeting with Jan Pierce, Al Vann and the Black trade unionists wasn't enough to make up for today's negatives. And on top of everything else, there was a blizzard —yes, a blizzard in April. We drove over four hours back to the Capitol so that I could be sure I'd get to Utica tomorrow.

The press came in to see me in my Capitol office shortly after I arrived in Albany, and I was testy—especially with Fred Dicker. That's not helpful, because the press reads testiness as weakness, and they're right.

FRIDAY, APRIL 9, 1982

Actual campaigning—the full day of speeches, cocktail parties, handshakes and editorial boards—has strong effects. The impressions formed by the reception the candidate receives from crowds or groups or the media—even if in relatively unimportant voting areas (i.e., where the vote is relatively small)—can have value as an energizer. It can also produce dejection. The trip to Utica, Syracuse and Rochester had good results. I was well received—even enthusiastically received. Bersani[1] and Slaughter saw to it that I was respectfully and respectably treated by local politicians, and the comparisons to Mayor Koch, who had preceded me, were favorable. The upstaters particularly like a scrappy, rousing style, and that's what I was for 2 days. If I were like that in Metropolitan New York City, my "people" here would probably tell me I was being too tough.

Thursday, which was Holy Thursday, produced one depressing incident. We were in Rochester and I thought it might be nice to stop at three churches, as has been the custom for years in the old neighborhoods. We couldn't find one open—in the middle of the day. They were all locked—and in some cases wired—against burglars. More than any cold statistics, it reminded me how far we've fallen and how deep a sickness crime is in our community.

The *Playboy* tapes emerged as an issue again. The Mayor has turned them over to *Playboy* hoping to shield himself from the *Daily News'* demand for them. It seems clear to me that he's not legally entitled to immunize himself that way. Moreover, he has a transcript, or at least so it is reported. But as a practical matter, it gets him off the hook because bringing suit would take so long —nothing could happen soon enough to be useful. The real question is why the Mayor, who boasts of his candor and asks people to judge his insults "in context," is unwilling to give up the context. It won't go away.

Nor will his proposal to repeal the capital gains tax on real estate transactions in New York City. He is so wrong there that it is bound to become evident if I keep describing the situation.

Bill Haddad is aboard. He has a high energy level. He produces ideas as if they were coming off an assembly line. Some of them are too exotic or harsh for my taste, but all of them are interesting and some of them are excellent. He gives us credibility with the inside political people and the press, and that will help. I think Bill Stern is adjusting to him, and that's a relief. Stern's not happy about the money we have to pay him.

Haddad wasted no time in having his presence felt with the

[1] Hank Bersani, a member of my staff since 1975 and a political pro.

media. He and Dick Wade together got an excellent opinion piece in the *News* that helped offset the *Times* piece by Lynn that said I wouldn't get past the convention.

We still need to beef up the press operation and continue to be weak at political organization. We need help there. It's amazing how much work there is to do.

This is Good Friday. A day for recollection and renewal. A good day to remind ourselves why we're doing all of this.

Matilda took Chris to Aunt Nancy's because Mary Kay is in from California. I haven't seen them since Monday. I'm afraid there will be many more weeks like this one ahead of us.

The invisible but felt "wave" is at work again. Subtle impulses move through the political community. They are unwritten, unverifiable but almost unanimously felt senses of momentum or decline. No one knows exactly what produces them or whether they are accurate. Maybe they are imagined, but repeated enough to become real factors. In any event, the insiders talk about it constantly. Well, today—despite our problems—it's reported by the likes of McCleary, Walter Diamond, Jim Notaro, second stringers on the second floor in Albany and others that the Cuomo thing is "coming together"! Koch believes we're more formidable than he at first expected. Already his people seem to be moving away from the "denial of 25%" strategy—instead of making us look weak, it made us look strong. I'm not sure this is reflected in the polls or is even a report of the polls. But it's happening.

SATURDAY, APRIL 10, 1982

This is worth recording, just after it happened, because it's happened a lot.

I called Congressman Joe Clarke.[1] I gave him my pitch. He said, when I was through: "I'm not going to endorse anyone in this primary. I don't like Ed's positions. I think they would be

[1] A pseudonym.

bad for New York and the country. I'm a lot closer to you philosophically, but I don't think you have a good chance to win; so I see no value in endorsing anyone [value for Clarke]. So unless you have someone else talk to me, I won't endorse anyone." Now that's what I call principle.

SUNDAY, APRIL 11, 1982 (EASTER)

After a while, important races like this one apparently become more and more controlled by the media. The media become more than reporters and recorders: they are players. The reality becomes what they say the reality is. If they say you can't win the state committee vote, then state committee people are inclined to read it, believe it, decide not to go with a loser and *Voilà!* The report becomes the reality. So much of the contest—especially in this State—becomes a matter of persuading the media. Their comments are much more potent than their reports, although their reports are also significant.

So far it's not clear how the media people want to see this race. Left untended by my side, which is what has happened at least until Haddad, most of them will take the easiest path. That is the path which says Koch is going to win, and that's what most of them have been writing. How do they know? The few polls, their sense of it and Garth's relentless press agentry. In any event, Haddad will have to turn it around if we're to have any chance.

We're beginning. Actually this was the first real week of campaigning, and we didn't do badly. In fact, my "Inside Albany" appearance—the bad interview with Dicker, etc.—and a less damaging but still not good interview on "Newsmakers" were the weakest part of our effort. But I was finally able to get some attention on an issue—Koch's repeal of the capital gains tax for real estate and his proposed increase in commuter tax. I have to keep dragging the media into discussion of the issues because I don't win the political arguments.

Madeline was going to give up a trip to Florida to work on the campaign. She's been convinced by Maria to go. I'm relieved.

With all the sacrifice the campaign has already caused, I didn't want to add to my guilt.

I'm convinced the campaign is going to be decided by something as yet unexpected—a big surprise or two. I can't wait to see how it comes out.

For the moment—and probably until I get on television (and if I don't get on TV, there's no campaign)—the polls will continue to show Koch way ahead.

THURSDAY, APRIL 15, 1982

The thing you miss most is privacy, solitude.

I sat back from the kitchen table in the midst of my early morning reading of materials and, all of a sudden, felt the way I have from time to time since I was a child. I remember being behind the store, alone, with the boxes of pasta piled high and the sacks of rice and coffee. I remember pushing over the sacks and tying a cord to the two gatherings at the top of the sack that stuck up like ears and riding the sack like a horse. I remember a thousand days being alone in my own quiet world while all the neighborhood's activity was going on steps away on the other side of the door with the glass window and the curtain over it. Alone, but not really lonely.

I've felt it late at night in the library surrounded by failed efforts to find a precedent, stopping to smoke my 50th cigarette of the day—in the days before I gave them up—struggling for another and better idea—walking through the empty halls and rooms of the law office I loved so much.

I've felt it when I should have been feeling other things. Word of victory comes from the Court, and I go for a walk to think about it, instead of having a party to celebrate it. Poppa dies, the unhappy returns are in, Chris is born, the moment to leave arrives, the middle of another wedding, Margaret's commencement—and I want to close my eyes and think and feel . . . alone.

I felt it this morning. For a moment my only relationship to the others in my world was to be sure that I did not hurt them,

that I help them if I can. But there is no sense of wanting anything back from them. Acceptance, approval, maybe even applause as its evidence, but only so that I have the opportunity to
lead and to help. But no sense of wanting to share joy and
certainly no sense of wanting to share my pain. A comfort in
silence, in introversion, in the quiet hours before it's time to start
another day wearing a tie for 18 hours. Back to the back room,
and the boxes and the sacks and the door separating me from the
rest of the world—their world. I get the feeling that I'm ready
for the passage out and always have been. Yet, in just a few
minutes I will be as deeply immersed in the swirl of life as anyone
can be—totally involving my mind, my emotions—to communicate, to cajole, to react, to persuade, to laugh . . . to cringe. If
I could, I would reverse the order. I would prefer to spend the
18 hours as I did the few minutes this morning and the briefer
intervals of the day being involved. But that comes after the
passage out.

It's clear that we were right about the repeal of the capital
gains tax on lucrative real estate profits in New York City. To
many knowledgeable observers, it is indefensible. There have
been a few pieces on it here and there, but basically it's only an
insider's story. Mayor Koch, I think, has been stung by it because
he has been bitterly personal in his attacks this week. Lew Rudin[1]
called me to explain the tax and its repeal. He was pleasant but
not persuasive.

This evening I changed plans at the last minute to allow a stop
in Goshen, Orange County, to receive the Orange County
Dems' unanimous endorsement. I had to speak at the Town of
Bethlehem dinner in Albany County before the meal, then drive
down. It was tiring but worth it. At Goshen the spirits were high.
I was in the midst of an old-fashioned political event—straw hats,
ribboned "Cuomo" supporters, music—the works. It was fun.
And encouraging. Of course, Orange County has only about
40,000 Democratic voters—about two districts in Brooklyn.
Nevertheless, it's difficult to think that the feelings they expressed tonight are unique to this county. What it means to me
is that if I could get everywhere I would do much better.

[1]One of New York's largest real estate owners.

FRIDAY, APRIL 16, 1982

Quiet at home. Chris stayed with Aunt Nancy and Uncle Bob for the week and Madeline went to Florida with her girl friend. I barely saw or talked to Matilda this week: I called a few times during the day and she wasn't home, and when she was in I was out campaigning. I think about it a lot . . . and about kids not being around.

I did well with the IBEW[1] and assorted other unions on the Island, notwithstanding that someone from the machinists beat me up on the death penalty.

Spoke to Ray Schuler. I should get along well with him if and when I become Governor.

This morning Haddad and I met with Harding. Harding appears to be taking it for granted that the Liberals will endorse me. He says I ought not to be concerned about the write-in possibility. I think he and Haddad have talked about what to do in September in the event we don't win the primary—they haven't said anything to me, and I'm glad of that.

That meeting was immediately followed by an off-the-record meeting with *Times* editorial people. I thought it went well. Haddad said it was "good"; he sat in without commenting.

Yesterday I had lunch with Meade Esposito. I never challenged his going with Koch. I showed as much "respect" as I could, telling him he would be the first person I call after I win the primary. He liked that and promised he would deliver $250,000 in campaign contributions if I won. He also gave me "permission" to go after his leaders.

I met with Fabian and Jerry Bloom at night at the "Philanthropies" building[2] in Manhattan and brought them up to date.

Another good issue is developing. MTA is planning to buy 800 or so subway cars from Japan. I am not convinced that a sufficient effort has been made to build them here. It seems to me wrong to send all this work overseas when we need it so badly. I've called for a task force to look into it. I'll push the issue everywhere.

[1]International Brotherhood of Electrical Workers.
[2]Headquarters of the Young Men's Philanthropic Association.

WEDNESDAY, APRIL 21, 1982

I have just completed preparing a speech for tonight's dinner (Town of Colonie Democratic Committee) that sounds stale even as I read it to myself. I've been putting too many words on paper, but unless we find a speech writer, I don't have much of an alternative.

Saturday night in Stevensville, at the Middle Atlantic Corrections Association, I delivered a paper on the criminal justice system that was well received.[1] I couldn't help thinking, as we drove to Albany late that night, how characteristic of my situation that evening was. I believe the ideas are good and, in terms of the realities of governing, more practical than those uttered by most candidates. But they are subtle and complicated and difficult to communicate in 22 seconds on a TV commercial. Where the truth is clear to me—as in my position against the death penalty—it hurts me politically. Where the truth might help, it's difficult for me to make it clear.

Monday night, while I was at the Holocaust Memorial ceremony at the Hillcrest Jewish Center, Matilda and Chris were accosted by two muggers. Neither was hurt except for a fright that they won't be able to shed for some time.

The media took the report from the police blotter and quickly blew it up into a major story: it captured the entire front page of the *Post*. The tragedy is that it is actually not a front-page story—it is only a statistic. This kind of thing, and much worse, happens every day to people who don't get their names in the paper. It has become so commonplace, so pervasively frightening and disgusting that it is difficult to understand. Sometimes it makes you feel that there are no answers. After Maria's incident, and Margaret's some years ago—and two burglaries—an enormous revulsion sets in.[2] It is sad and confusing. It is also easy to understand the indignation and anger that has led so many of our people to ask for death as a solution.

[1]This speech appears on pp. 420–26.
[2]Margaret was accosted by a young thug when she was about fourteen years old, Maria when she was eighteen, and everybody, it seems, who has a house has been burglarized twice.

A number of friends called to see how Matilda and Chris were. Chris became an overnight hero because he chased one of the muggers down the street. Not bad for an eleven-year-old. I hope he doesn't grow into disenchantment.

Koch "announced" earlier today. I guess they liked it so much the first time they decided to do it again! He didn't make a more persuasive case than he did the first time. From the beginning, he's had difficulty finding a rationale. He started by arguing that the New Federalism requires that he go to Albany. Now there is no New Federalism. He said at one point he would have to go to Albany to save New York City. That, of course, doesn't work politically statewide. Now he's saying he is a great and experienced leader who has done wonderful things in New York City. He took credit for additional jobs and higher reading scores. But the fact is, the State saved New York City and controls its destiny even now, and services in the City are not as good as they might be.

All of this, however, seems, as a practical matter, to be beside the point: the Mayor's progress seems to have little to do with these realities. His image and personality eclipse them. For that reason he is a difficult candidate to beat, and I see that more every day. Whatever the truth is, he is reaching a lot of the people who vote.

THURSDAY, APRIL 22, 1982

Last night at the Town of Colonie Democrats where about 900 loyalists assembled—I was better received than I had been for a long time.

A lot of it had to do with the traditional nature of the affair. There is a deep, old-fashioned "party" attitude in Albany. It is probably the last of its kind in the State.

I spoke very late and threw away the speech: that often seems to help. The spontaneity that you gain when you don't read the text scored last night. I talked about involvement, the differences between Democrats and Republicans, and the future of the State. I finished by reminding the audience that we are the sons and

daughters of the people who achieved even more than we aspire
to, without the resources we have. This group liked feeling hope
—and so do I.

I was mobbed by people asking for autographs and with volunteer offers. It was exciting. As usual, however, the instant I
began enjoying it, my mind began analyzing it, and I remembered how little of this kind of reaction I get in New York
City.

One of the reasons became clear again early this morning. I
spoke to Jane Harris.[1] She wants to be with me, but has a job that
Manes could kill. I hear this over and over. I heard it from
Assemblywoman Rhoda Jacobs[2] yesterday.

One of the biggest things Koch has going for him is the
intimidation factor. That will get him names, and posters, and big
gatherings. But I wonder how many of those people will support
him when they get into the privacy of the polling place. I'm more
than ever grateful for secret ballots.

FRIDAY, APRIL 23, 1982

My recent appearances have been extraordinarily successful.
Colonie went well and so did the Nassau Democratic Committee. Despite that, however, the Koch strength is very clear.
George Blue,[1] a presumed "liberal-thinking" Democratic State
Committee member in Nassau County, told me on the phone,
"Mario, he's so popular! My friends all like him because he told
off the minorities and the unions!" I argued with him that Democrats shouldn't win by telling off unions and minorities. He
thought I was "simplistic."

The race could decide whether the Democratic party believes
in anything that makes us different from the Republicans—or
whether the only difference is that they wear an elephant on their
lapels and we wear a donkey.

[1] A pseudonym.
[2] Of Brooklyn.

---

[1] A pseudonym.

SUNDAY NIGHT, APRIL 25, 1982

We're finally beginning to get into more substantive discussions, although they remain pretty much at the surface of the issues. This weekend we began arguing about the respective roles of the Mayor and the Lt. Governor, a comparison which I like. In Syracuse today, Mayor Koch took some—what I thought were ridiculous—shots by asking what I had done to put together the State budget. When told about this by Steve Geiman of the Binghamton press, I reacted sharply by saying it was naïve to suggest that the Lt. Governor is responsible for the failure to make the budget. Eventually, however, I concluded that this was an excellent ground for me and expanded the discussion by comparing roles. I was also able to show that if Koch wishes to get credit for the good things that have happened to the City, he will also have to take blame for things like homicides and families who leave.

It was a tough weekend. It started Saturday afternoon at the Liberal party, where both the Mayor and I appeared. The charade of the Mayor seeking to make an albatross of the Liberal party, while at the same time he seeks their endorsement, continues. The media appear not interested in it. I thought I was well received, although one never knows. We will see where the final decision is made.

Some people are worried that I have alienated my "base"— which they think is Catholics and homeowners. Their analysis is that the Liberal wing is mostly Jewish and it will vote for Koch no matter what and that therefore I ought to stay close to the center. That's suggesting I place myself according to the polls. It's easier for me just to place myself where I'm comfortable, issue by issue.

I will continue to talk about traditional Democratic principles and put the emphasis on how those principles helped the immigrants to become Americans.

Bad scheduling produced a situation that required Hank Bersani to drive me back to Albany from Syracuse. I was unhappy about that: it's much too long a trip for him to make back and forth in the same night.

WEDNESDAY, APRIL 28, 1982

Incumbency is a mixed blessing when you are campaigning. There are, of course, advantages because so much that is properly governmental is also useful politically. But there are disadvantages as well. Politically, the very existence of a record creates a vulnerability as well as a strength. Those practiced in the art of verbal manipulation and fact distortion can find material both pro and con in any record. That's especially true if the positions you had were Secretary of State and Lt. Governor. The Mayor in recent days has tried to make the most of this by pointing to himself as a "superb manager of the second-hardest position in the United States," while Cuomo has "never run anything."

Those are effective arguments, because few people will get beneath the surface. The truth is, if it weren't for the Emergency Financial Control Board and the State's strong influence, the City would never have escaped bankruptcy. Moreover, it faces a $1.3 billion gap in next year's budget, which is difficult to reconcile with the boast of superb management.

It seems to me—although I can't say it this way in the campaign —that the real question is whether the truth will win out. The Mayor has no real case for running except that he wants to get out of New York and move in what he perceives to be a generally upward direction. I think he contradicts himself conceptually. But he does it with spectacular political deftness. While I wish he weren't so effective, I admire his ability to play this game.

There's a tendency to try to keep score on a day-to-day basis that can frustrate you. Channel 5 last night indicated that they had traveled around the State and concluded that Mario Cuomo was unknown because they asked four or five people at random, in different cities, and they didn't know who Cuomo was. Matilda was all upset and called me in Albany early this morning to say, "You have to do something about it."

Obviously that kind of publicity doesn't help. But there's such a long way to go that it's wasteful to react strongly to any individual bit of news—good or bad.

I said something like that today to Bob Morgado, who is suffering because of the unkind newspaper comment about his business dealings. He's pained mostly, I think, because it hurts Marylou and his children. I'm sure his perspective is off because he's the subject of the piece. He's forgetting that in a little while the whole matter will disappear from people's recollections. I tried to get him to take the long view.

And if you want to concentrate on small events, why not pick happy ones—for example, our fund-raiser Monday night? It was at the Italian American Community Center in Albany. Two nice people, a Doctor DelGiacco and Mrs. DelTorto, who had never done this kind of thing, decided to try to raise some money for me. They are both friends of Al Levine,[1] and I'm sure that had a good deal to do with it. Over 200 people came at $50 apiece. That's a really good result, although they, as amateurs, expected more. It was a good party. It started slowly because a lot of people there had never been to this kind of event and weren't sure of themselves at first. But the wine and the accordion and the fact that a lot of old friends were there warmed up the atmosphere by midmeal.

Mayor Corning, as usual, was a picture of elegance, class and charm. I spoke. I didn't give a speech. I talked about Momma and Poppa and what they represented. It was loose at points, disconnected, rambling and overly long. But it came close enough to the lives of a lot of people in the room so that it held them, as it did me. What a shame that my kids' children won't remember Momma and Poppa, Ellis Island, broken English, near-despair and old values.

FRIDAY, APRIL 30, 1982

A.M.

I had the PRID[1] club debate last night at the Grace and St. Paul's Lutheran Church in Manhattan. It seemed to me I clearly had the advantage, especially on the repealer of the capital gains tax. On the way out, people were feeling sorry for my opponent, Carol Bellamy. Her friends regretted she had to be present to defend Koch. My people thought it was one-sided in my favor. I opened the newspaper at 6 A.M. this morning to read the good news. It described—in the middle of another story—a brief exchange,

[1] A member of my staff since I served as secretary of state in 1975.

[1] Park River Independent Democrats.

which appeared to favor Bellamy, and one person quoted as complimenting her. I could hardly believe it, but then that kind of thing has been happening repeatedly in the press—or at least that's the way it looks to me.

Meanwhile the *Post* carried a piece about Poppa Raffa owing the City $140,000 in back taxes. It made him sound like a criminal. A tough old immigrant refused to abandon his commercial properties despite deterioration and tried to pay off his taxes legally. He winds up in a story sounding as though he's ripping off the City. A tough business, this is.

SUNDAY, MAY 2, 1982

Before flying up to Rochester for a meeting in Genesee County I had breakfast with Rabbi Mowshowitz and David Mack.[1] The Rabbi is pushing very hard for me in the Jewish Community. He tells me he has run into a great deal of opposition but none of it because of personal animosity to me. Many of his wealthy friends are invested, one way or the other, in the City and they are afraid of the Mayor's memory. I don't believe the Mayor is as vindictive as some think he is, but the appearance works well for him. I expect Mack will be of some help anyway. He is an attractive, genial sort of fellow who has wealth and tries to use it well. He likes to keep his hand in politically—with more regard to candidates than to political philosophies. He supported D'Amato last year.

The meeting of Western New York County Chairs on Friday in Batavia and a meeting of 14 Chairs in Saratoga on Saturday were similar. The Mayor and I appeared separately. I think it went well for me both times. The Buffalo *Courier-Express* ran a headline after Batavia that read: "Koch wins laughs; Cuomo wins cheers." If that becomes a general reaction, I can't lose.

The Koch rationale, for the moment, is: "I ran the City of New York well. Proof? Balanced budget, reading scores up, jobs coming back. I can win: I've beaten Cuomo twice. Cuomo has never run anything."

[1] A businessman, philanthropist and community activist from Nassau County.

He used lines like: "Cuomo's been practicing; I've been doing." (I said, "If you look at the results in New York City, you'll see he should have practiced first.") "Don't vote against me so as to keep me Mayor." (I said, "If they vote against you, Ed, it will be to make you finish the job you admitted wasn't finished when you pledged 12 years of service to the City.")

I have cast the Mayor as saying, "I will do for the State what I have done for the City."

I am responding by saying, "I will do for the State what we have been doing for the State, and more."

If I can keep these 2 lines going, it will force a comparison of the City record and the State record, where we are much stronger, since the State saved the City. It will also reinforce the appropriateness of him remaining in a City context and me in a State context. That's exactly what Sam Brach was getting at when he said, "The Lieutenant Governor should be Governor and the Mayor should be Mayor." That implicit logic—implicit in the very situation—is the heart of the matter. I believe if that can be conveyed, it may be enough to make me a winner.

The Mayor also continues to call me a "spoiler" upstate. Here again he is playing games, but in some places they have been effective. They give frightened Democrats who think he's going to win but can't find any other reason to support him an excuse for doing so. I've been hitting back hard over the last few days, but this hasn't made it to the public at large, especially in the New York City area. I point out the following:

1. Koch has endorsed Republicans, admitted it was a "sin," but refused to disendorse them.
2. He supported Reagan and says he was right to do it.
3. He has attacked the Democratic party.
4. He is seeking the Liberal line, and if he got it he couldn't legally get off any more than I could, so what he is suggesting now about my position on the line[2] is a ploy.

I point out that when I ran as a Liberal in 1977 I was true to Democratic principles, emphasizing that it is philosophies and

[2]That if selected to run on the Liberal line, I would campaign on it in the general election no matter what the outcome of the Democratic primary.

programs and beliefs that matter most. This scores in small groups and is having a political effect in the places where I've done it. But it's too early to say what effect it will have on the public at large.

I also remind people that the Mayor doesn't keep pledges: "Asking me to trade pledges[3] with Ed Koch is like asking Henry VIII's third wife to trade fidelity pledges with Henry the VIII." The press seems to enjoy lines like that. Here are two others I used this week that they enjoyed: When asked whether Mayor Koch had saved the City, I said: "He saved the City the way a passenger on the *Half Moon* discovered the Hudson." And, in the PRID debate, Carol Bellamy, standing in for the Mayor, started by saying, "Now I know how the Christians felt when they had to face the lions." I said, referring to Koch's refusal to face me, "Carol, the difference is the Christians had to show up!" What a business—these one-liners get more attention than the speeches or the position papers.

I have a general sense—an apprehension of things, more than a perception of them—that there is a movement away from Koch. I think the inappropriateness of his position manifests itself now that there is an actual contest and people begin to focus on the question before them. It is still very early and not many people are yet, in fact, focusing, but there is definitely the beginning of change. If I'm right—and nothing happens to change the direction—the media will begin to detect the movement and write about it. Once that happens, the movement will accelerate. I've felt from the beginning that it simply makes more sense to have us both, him as mayor, me as governor, and I think that is beginning to show.

THURSDAY, MAY 6, 1982

6:45 A.M.
I just left the Wellington. It's the kind of morning that makes you wonder. It's beautiful, clear, bright, promising to be a day that drives the state workers onto the lawns of the Capital, stretching

[3]To "support the Democrat" in the general election.

their lunch periods to enjoy God's good effort. The kind of day that reminds you there is a beauty at work—and what "intelligent" humans might call an "intelligence" at work—that we barely understand and that some of us abuse, out of ignorance and confusion.

Which gets me back to the campaign.

This morning Mayor Koch will be endorsed by four of the five leaders of the Democratic organization in New York City—all except Denny Farrell of Manhattan. It has nothing to do with what they believe "traditional Democratic principles" require, and probably very little to do with whom they would rather see as Governor. It has to do more with a practical judgment as to who will win and what would happen if they went the wrong way. There are other practical considerations. Manes wants badly to move up and thinks his best chance is if Koch moves out. If I were a favorite in the polls at this moment, I would be his best chance and he'd be with me! Instead, he'll go with Koch and try to hedge a little by agreeing to help me get on the ballot. That, incidentally, is exactly what Esposito did for Carey in 1974 when he backed Howard Samuels in the primary. The Death Penalty, Reaganomics, A Vision for the State—none of this means anything except insofar as it may affect the possibility of success in the race. All they want to know is whether the horse will win.

Of course, I knew it was coming, but it hurts a little anyway. It threatens to arrest what seemed to be a little momentum we developed from doing consistently better than Koch upstate and in the northern suburbs, and from some good press this week. Koch's press conference was timed to blunt our own announcement today of support from the Amalgamated Clothing Workers and Harry Van Arsdale's coalition.[1]

On the plus side for us is that our unions will produce money and troops all summer long. I don't believe the Democratic "organization" has as much strength. Its leaders' principal contribution is to get you on the ballot at the convention by giving you —or helping you to get—the 25% vote that's needed. In the end, the primary will be decided by what gross perceptions are created in the minds of the 1 out of 5 or 6 Democrats who will

[1]The New York City Central Labor Council, Harry Van Arsdale, president.

go to the polls on September 14.[2] Unfortunately for the nonrich, that is done mostly on television.

In a couple of weeks the Liberal party will be announcing its decision in my favor. We have to use their support to maximum advantage, and I believe that means someone other than me getting out the notion that MMC could be formidable even if he had only the Liberal line in November. That will irritate some Democrats, but it also makes me a better bet. The irony here is that Democrats are concerned I will stay in if I lose—and so are some Liberals! I'm sure they (the Liberals) want to be in a position to deliver something to Koch, should he win the primary, so they won't press me for a pledge.[3] I, on the other hand, don't want to be in a deliverable condition, because that would reduce the Liberals' desire to see me win the primary. I want to be the Libs' only horse to make sure their support helps get me to the finish line first.

I have been surprised at some of the reaction I've received upstate. The women appear to be more active than I've seen them recently. In Rensselaer on Monday night all the questions were from women. They cheered my answers on privacy and the death penalty. In fact, there is often a strong favorable reaction to my stand against the death penalty even when it seems clear most people in the room are for it. I think the opponents of the death penalty have more passion on the subject.

I am continually being advised by people around me to avoid discussion of the issue because it is a negative for me. It probably is, although one never really knows. But it's not easy for me to avoid discussing—maybe even at length—the fundamental issue we deal with—life and death.

There is current at the moment an analysis of the election that has Koch beating me because he does so well in Nassau and Suffolk, where they like what they think he has done to "keep the minorities in their place" and to tell off the unions. The theory is they see him as the expression of their indignation. I don't believe that sentiment will be strong enough with enough people to make the difference. I'm afraid that if it is, I won't be

²This was the original date for the primary election. It was moved to September 23 because of complications created by a court decision on redistricting.
³To campaign on the Liberal line alone if I lost the Democratic primary.

able to change it with a series of speeches. We'll see. Again, I'm reminded of how much of this business is perception.

SUNDAY, MAY 9, 1982

Actually, I don't think the endorsement of the Mayor by the four New York leaders produced the impact they expected. At the same time, we were endorsed by some 20 labor unions with a pledge of massive support, and the contrast as it appeared in the Friday papers was at least a draw—perhaps better for me.

When asked about the "power" of the leaders to produce a winner, I said that the last time 4 leaders in this area agreed on a candidate in a tough contest and won, the four leaders were Chiefs of the Iroquois Confederacy. No matter it's historically incorrect to suggest the Iroquois Confederacy ever convened in New York City—the political history is accurate. Ask Meyerson, Samuels and Carter.[1]

Our fund-raiser at Antun's on Thursday produced a reasonably good crowd and about $90,000 at $100 a ticket. Many from the old group were there, and it was very much like a wedding or bar mitzvah. Warm, friendly—unlike most of these events. Our strength is in the loyalty of our hard-core supporters, many of whom have never been involved in a political campaign before.

People liked my talk,[2] except Harvey Cohen, who made what I thought was a trenchant observation. He said I couldn't win with the kind of talk I gave because I had a tendency to talk to people about other people's problems and Koch talks to people about their problems. He also said I often sound morally righteous.

Organizationally, there have been difficulties. Stern, Haddad and Cohen are all strong personalities with intense biases and competitive instincts. They are constantly at one another. Andrew is bearing the brunt of the load, and it's a real strain. I'll try to help by having a meeting with all of them and then have them meet regularly. We won't be able to get the thing running

---

[1]Bess Meyerson, who lost in the 1980 Democratic primary for the U.S. senate; Howard Samuels, who was defeated by Hugh Carey in the 1974 race for governor; and Jimmy Carter in 1980 were all endorsed by the four leaders.

[2]About politics, family and Americanism.

perfectly—one never does in a campaign—but we can improve
it.

Another "debate" Thursday. Koch again didn't show up himself. He is ducking me while at the same time telling everybody
he's going to "cream" me. I'm thinking of challenging him to a
debate at the Convention.

Governor Carey is still neutral. I suspect he will stay that way
unless there is strong evidence that one or the other of us will
be a winner. Rumors circulated again this week that he might try
himself for the nomination: I doubt it! He'd rather stay out of
it and dislike us both.

Mother's Day. Thanks to the forces that are that we have all
three of them.

Some thoughts for tomorrow in Utica.
"They that govern the most make the least noise." (John
Selden's *Table Talk*—17th Century.)
"Cuomo is not an entertainer—he's a performer."

MONDAY, MAY 10, 1982

There are the insiders and the outsiders, politically. The insiders
number about 4,872. They consist of candidates, leaders, press
and other media that cover politics, wives—and parts of the
families of the aforedescribed. Then there are the outsiders—all
the rest of the people. Only some of them will vote, about 1 in
5 of those who could if they wanted to. The insiders are always
talking to and among themselves. They get a distorted view, or
at least a view different from that of the outsiders. The poll and
the analyst are supposed to teach the insiders what the outsiders
are feeling. Or you can use a dozen smart outsiders, like your
mother—if you're lucky enough to have one who is not involved. My mother tells me (and so would a poll, probably) that
people think Koch is going to win: that Cuomo is a nice guy but
Koch is too strong for him. My mother is not sure, however,
whether the people who feel that way will vote for Koch because
they want to be "with" the winner, or at least want to feel they
haven't wasted their vote. Now, of course, my mother can't be

sure of her feelings or the people's, but Momma is mostly right.

I know I get the same emanations from the outside, a general feeling that Koch is strong and getting stronger the more he is seen and heard. He impresses people with his style and with his record—Mayor of a Great City, popular enough to be reelected by a 70% vote, generally regarded as competent and charismatic. It makes a strong case—on the surface. It is vulnerable to analysis, but it's not easy to get voters to follow analyses that take them beyond the surface. The key to communication here—as in many places where large numbers of people are involved—is to keep it simple.

I spoke at Cooperstown to the Society of Newspaper Editors, and it went fairly well, except that I got a little testy with the editor-in-charge, who I thought had given me a fast shuffle on the schedule. I let him know it and I probably should not have. Koch is going to be there tomorrow.

TUESDAY, MAY 11, 1982

Koch showed up at Cooperstown and when asked what county he was in said "Oneonta." When he was told that Oneonta and Cooperstown were both in Otsego, he indicated amusement. I wonder for how long he can turn lemons into lemonade by being flip.

WEDNESDAY, MAY 12, 1982

I told the New York State Professional Firefighters about Koch in Cooperstown, and said that it was all right for a Governor or a Mayor to be ignorant of what county he was in, but if he asks for a job as Firehouse Dispatcher—don't hire him!

At 10:30, I met with Ed Murphy, who was representing a Vietnam Vets' group. He described these vets as a group that ought not to be thought of as a version of the VFW. He sees them as eager to get back into government and politics. I had the general feeling that he was confirming my belief that there is a large number of people—of all ages—who want badly to believe in something worthwhile. That's what the nuclear freeze is all about. It responds to the desire to have a cause.

After the legislative session, to Buffalo. We had three excellent stops. A strong endorsement from a Polish American group, following one from an Italian group over the weekend and a good meeting with Arthur Eve and some Black leaders at a Baptist Church on Sunday. Koch has Crangle and Mayor Griffin; I have the "people." An interesting line-up.

While I was in Buffalo, so was Koch. He allegedly said I should drop out of the race for the sake of party unity! Was it a clever device to make me look like a sure loser? Probably. An act of desperation? I doubt it. Chutzpah? Partly.

I think I should answer by saying he should resign as Mayor and watch his support go down the drain. Many of his endorsements are tied to his Mayoralty the way an unborn child is attached to its mother.

THURSDAY, MAY 13, 1982

Mayor Koch announced a work camp proposal that was—I thought—a politically effective and substantively unwise response to a complicated, severe social problem. Three-card monte players and other petty criminals are to be sent to a work camp on Hart's Island as a "deterrent." The DA's—or most of them in the City—applauded the notion. I believe it is popular, but simplistic and wasteful. With arsonists and rapists going undetected, and the City with nearly 10,000 fewer police than in 1972, with not enough room in the prisons for violent criminals, the Mayor is proposing a major expenditure (more than $3,000,000 a year after capital costs) for petty criminals. But it sounds tough and works politically.

Met with Joe Napolitan, one of the "original" political consultants, before whom the business of packaging and selling candidates was left basically to politicians and volunteers. He didn't say anything new, but he said it all so clearly and comprehensively and succinctly that it brought the campaign into perspective for me. The most obvious feature of the campaign as far as I can tell is that there is no campaign as far as the general public is concerned. I am simply *not* being portrayed to the public with any kind of detail. There is no concerted, cohesive attempt, through the media, to picture me as believing in anything particular. The image is being formed only in the minds of the relative handful of people we can reach in the course of the personal appearances I am able to make. That's too few to make a substantial difference, and even among them I have no sharp identification. Generally, I am perceived as fairly competent and knowledgeable. But because I tend to be eclectic and extended in my presentations, even the personal appearances don't create the kind of quick, unmistakable profile that a "tax-cutting," "defense-minded" Reagan has. Or a "no-nonsense," "tell it as it is," "tough on crime/capital punishment" Koch has. And I am getting virtually no media attention, not through any fault of the media but because we simply haven't gone about it intelligently.

For the moment, therefore, this race is dominantly Koch against Koch, and Koch is winning. His popularity is still high, although I would guess it is not as high as it was 2 months ago. The decline, however, is only because there is beginning to be a contest, not because I have brought people to my side by what I have been perceived as saying.

All of this is troublesome, because Gannett will publish its first poll this weekend, and it can be a self-fulfilling kind of thing. I'm afraid that if it does not show me having closed the gap a bit, it will set us back considerably. And I'm afraid I have not closed the gap a great deal. My guess is that it will show me somewhere between 15 and 20 points behind and that people generally will not think this close enough to make me real. We'll see.

Lately, too, I have allowed myself to work too hard and to get very tired. I can feel myself beginning to get irritable and taking my eye off the ball.

FRIDAY, MAY 14, 1982

Tomorrow afternoon we will be told the results of the Gannett poll, and I still feel some apprehension about it. If I had my way, there would be no polling at all—certainly none until everyone has had the chance to campaign. I haven't been on TV or the radio, and we have had little press "on the merits" of my case. Koch therefore is bound to do well. If he does so well that the press writes me off now, this race may be over before it really starts, at the convention. I am convinced that we have the ingredients for success. I am also convinced that this has not yet been perceived by the public. The poll comes too soon.

Generally, the last few days have been difficult. I've tried to keep Stern, Haddad and Cohen in some kind of balance, but it is very difficult. All three are constantly concerned about being diminished by the others.

And tonight in beautiful Columbia County produced a few moments of discomfort. I was struck especially by a 61-year-old former basketball player for Hudson High. Cheery, good-looking brash Irishman. He was immediately friendly at the K. of C. Hall where the locals were throwing a cocktail party for me. He cautioned me against "talking too much about the poor. What about my problems? I have to send kids to school." He's absolutely on target with what I hear everywhere: people want to be told what government will do for them, not what we will do for someone worse off than they are. I have not been doing that effectively. I have been talking to people about other people's problems, as Cohen points out. If I am to succeed, I must convince people we can give them safety with *effective* criminal justice (that doesn't just *sound* tough but *is* tough); tax reduction (while N.Y. City's taxes were going up, N.Y. State's were going down); secure employment (we won't lose jobs, we'll gain them); security in their old age; a good education system. And I must convince them without selling out the poor. The key is to keep the alliance between the middle class and the poor together or the alliance of the middle class and the rich will crush the poor, and that will be bad for the entire society. If there is to be peace and security, there must be justice. Social disorientation cannot be confined to the blocks of the neighborhoods where the poor are forced to live. The answer is the "traditional" Democratic coalition.

MONDAY, MAY 17, 1982

I was wrong about the poll: it was much better than I expected. Overall, it showed Koch with a 10-point advantage—beating me in the City, thrashing me in the suburbs, but losing upstate. Since

I haven't begun campaigning down here yet, that's encouraging. I frankly don't believe the situation at the moment is as rosy for us as it appears in the poll, but in this business, where the perception often produces the reality, the poll can get us money and political support and a more attentive press.

Whether it was related or not, the poll was followed by a full day of successes. Indeed, Saturday night, when the poll was announced, I was warmly received at Westchester's County Dinner. Koch followed me, called me a "three-time loser" and got hissed in return. I was asked about the Mayor's reference to my having lost to him three times. I said, "That's what the people who owned slaves said about Abraham Lincoln before he was elected President."

Koch is obviously either following Garth's instructions to try to bait me into intemperate remarks or he is occasionally out of control.

Sunday I received an award from B'nai B'rith Women, won the NDC[1] endorsement on the first ballot with over 70% of the vote, was complimented, publicly, by Ted Kennedy at Agudath Israel,[2] and was well received as Guest Speaker for Rodeph Sholom's[3] 140th Anniversary at the Plaza.

Everything was "up." Our own people are all infused with new energy. The press has a new interest. Bill Stern is sure it will mean money. Koch has been defensive. It has indeed been a good weekend. But the weekend is over.

TUESDAY, MAY 18, 1982

Driving to Albany from the Police Conference at the Pines in Fallsburg, I was struck by the loveliness of the land here. In fact, when I think about the possibility of not serving the State next year, it brings to mind all the extraordinary beauty I would be missing: the rolling hills of Columbia County, the Kinderhook Inn and the Public Square outside it, together a postcard from

[1]New Democratic Coalition.

[2]An organization responsible for an international educational movement of Orthodox Jewry.

[3]A Reform Jewish temple in Manhattan.

the last Century; the craggy magnificence of the Adirondacks; the Finger Lakes, sparkling like diamonds when seen from the air; the Hudson Valley, especially in the Autumn, when it's painted with a dozen colors and a hundred shades of colors; the almost flat land of the Southern Tier, with nature's lawns mocking the cultivated lawns of the cities; the breathtaking spectacle of Manhattan in lights from 2,000 feet at midnight; the incomparable beaches of Suffolk County. I have been taking them almost for granted for seven and a half years. Maybe it's been because I was so busy noticing the people, who were just as varied and almost as beautiful. I wonder if I'll see it better now for the next six months. I wonder if I will have to memorize it all or whether I'll be blessed with 16 more seasons.

Koch is, for the moment, trying to isolate me on the left side of the party upstate. But downstate he doesn't talk about me being liberal. Indeed, on "Newsmakers" in New York City, Koch referred to me as more conservative than he. I wonder how many people notice the difference. It's a great argument for doing everything on statewide TV.

Paul Curran has come into the race.[1] He's a good man, but it's kind of late to take on megabucks. He's for the death penalty. That makes me the only one in the race who's not. Plus or minus? A political minus. How much? We'll never know for sure, win or lose.

WEDNESDAY, MAY 19, 1982

A full day in Buffalo and Rochester. As usual here, I was well received. An endorsement this morning from former Chief Judge Charles Desmond was exciting for me.

Then a strong speech to the UAW, who yesterday voted for "neutrality," which I regard as a victory for Koch, although 80%

---

[1]Paul J. Curran—former state assemblyman, chairman of the State Investigation Commission, a United States Attorney for the Southern District of New York—is a moderate Republican. Lew Lehrman's radical conservatism had put him at odds with the party's moderate wing, and his lack of political experience had upset party regulars. Hence Curran's challenge.

of the locals—according to Tom Fricano[1]—will be willing to help me.

Two fund-raisers in Rochester for a total of about $15,000. A mad drive to the airport to catch a 9 o'clock flight to Kennedy.

Home, beat.

THURSDAY, MAY 20, 1982

No one will ever know how much a specific episode contributes to the final result on election day—whether negatively or positively. The campaign consists of making every point you can without pausing to calculate how heavily they weigh overall.

The Commission on Social Justice[1] had a conference yesterday. It was the Italian American Community at its best. A careful, professional research project was published. It showed that Italians are depicted in unfairly negative ways on prime-time television. The dominant image is the buffoon, the bigot or the bum. We said so yesterday to a full room of media without hyperbole, without stridency, without asking for boycotts or censorship. It was done reasonably and maybe even elegantly. At least two of the networks ran it in their 6 o'clock news segments. It remains to be seen if this way works.

At night the Rockland County forum with Vince Monte, the Rockland County Chairman. He confesses he wants to be with me but suggests that they are bringing "terrible pressure" to bear against him. Koch was on before me and was, I am told, mildly well received. He set a new record for political agility by abandoning his old position and making himself a champion of nuclear freeze.

[1]Regional director of United Auto Workers in Buffalo. Since transferred to New Jersey.

[1]A group I helped organize in 1980, putting together the Sons of Italy and the Anti-Defamation League of B'nai B'rith.

Tuesday, May 25, 1982

7:00 P.M., on the plane from Albany to New York
Trying to rest is impossible in the midst of this effort. There are
so many things to think about—issues, events, ideas for releases,
problems—that I find it impossible to empty my mind of the
campaign.

Seeing things objectively also gets more difficult as we become
steeped in it—more and more, deeper and deeper. Generally, I
think, things have moved toward us. The polls created a reality
that may not have existed previously. Today no one would write
an article that said Cuomo can't win, although most are still
saying I won't win. And Senators and Assemblymen increasingly
are finding the occasion to drop by and say something encouraging. It's a sure sign the polls are being read.

Small things happen that should be remembered. Red Miller,
the greatest Budget Director the state ever had,[1] came to my
headquarters opening in Albany today. Tall, gaunt, unsteady:
he's been very ill. He walked slowly, struggling to put one foot
before the other. But he insisted on walking alone. His voice was
shaky, but as he walked into the headquarters, into the mikes,
lights and open notebooks of the Albany media, he was sure of
what he wanted to do. Without warning, he grasped my hand,
raised it in a victory salute, and said—as loudly as he could—
"The next Governor of the State of New York!" We exchanged
compliments before the group, and Linda Fisher drove him
home. He cried a little in the car. Ill, retired after years of
relentless activity, he cried in disappointment: being remembered by some of us made him remember how many had appeared to forget him.

Sunday's Salute to Israel parade[2] was another sadness. The
people in charge, apparently eager not to have the Mayor's dominance challenged, saw to it that I wasn't allowed to speak at the
same time as the Mayor or even to march at the front of the
parade. Eli Zborowski, a Holocaust survivor and a colleague of
mine from the Holocaust Commission, was humiliated. He

---

[1]Howard F. Miller was state budget director from 1978 to 1981.
[2]In New York City.

called me today to apologize. I told him to forget it and that it was just part of the pettiness that all political campaigns seem to generate.

For some reason, a number of my speeches have been extraordinarily well received. Saratoga's County dinner,[3] the IUE[4] endorsements in Schenectady, the sanitationmen[5] this morning—all gave me standing ovations. It's hard to believe, but my presentation on the death penalty often gets a strong favorable response. Generally, as I told Ed Murphy of the Vietnam Vets again today, I get the sense that people are eager to find something to believe in. They badly want a cause. That's why nuclear freeze is so popular. My whole case is an affirmative one that is aggressively confident of our ability to help ourselves. Most people like that more than they like surrender.

In 1802 the Duane Mansion was built in Schenectady. Jim and Barbara Featherstonhaugh now live in it. They gave a $10,000 dinner party there last night. It was fun—except for 45 minutes on the death penalty and a suggestion from one of the guests that we sterilize welfare mothers after their second child.

FRIDAY, MAY 28, 1982

8:00 A.M.

In the course of the campaign, three or four times we will spend a day or two with a reporter doing a profile piece. It almost always means being driven into yourself with probing questions about why you are running, what's the lure, etc. Most of the time, candidates are prepared with quick, glib, attractive answers like, "Ever since I read my first Carl Sandburg, I knew I wanted to be like Abraham Lincoln." It's a good way to do it—if you don't, you're apt to confuse reporters. That happened to me in 1977, and I wound up being described as "Hamlet" because of my articulated introspections to Doug Ireland.

I've just had a couple of days with a fellow by the name of Jim

[3]See pp. 427–31.
[4]International Union of Electrical, Radio and Machine Workers.
[5]Uniformed Sanitationmen's Association.

Sleeper, who is writing a piece for the *Village Voice*. He was so
pleasant that I lapsed into enjoying myself instead of giving "I
love Abe Lincoln" type replies. We'll see how it comes out.
However the article pictures me, at the very least we had some
fun. He told me a couple of great stories, and I was reminded
about my "turtle" story. I should tell it again sometime. Actually,
I remember it vividly. Earl Andrews, patrician, white-thatched,
elegant rich Virginian and a client of our law firm, patronizing
me—a young lawyer—at lunch as the son of "immigrants":
"Isn't that nice. Even someone like you can make it to this great
City, and eat with the most successful people." Then asking for
a clam in his clam juice and giving me a lecture on how that
ensures "freshness." And the burst of laughter from everybody
at the table but Andrews when I ordered "turtle soup—with a
turtle in it!" Sometimes I think the best thing about the past is
20 stories like the turtle story.

I have a guess but only that. At the moment, the polls have
closed to a gap of somewhere between 6 to 10 points. They will
probably not change much from that unless and until I start
making a positive impact beyond the impact I've had so far. This
race has been Koch v. Koch and now Koch is slipping. But not
enough for Koch not to be still the winner. In the time remaining, I have to tell people about Mario Cuomo. And there is not
all that much time remaining.

And something more than a guess, unfortunately. In 1977,
during the Koch campaign, I was accused of being anti-Semitic
in a letter circulated through the American Jewish Congress just
before the holidays and the runoff. Considering my record of
support for the Jewish community in so many ways and for so
many years, I was stunned by how easily hostility toward me was
generated.

In 1974, the Garth campaign for Carey implied Samuels was
anti-Jewish.

In 1981, Koch painted Barbaro as making racist and anti-
Semitic comments. In *Playboy*, he called the *Amsterdam News*
anti-Semitic. And now someone is beginning to do it in this
campaign. A woman came to our office to say she had been
polled by telephone. When she responded that she was voting

for Cuomo, the pollster asked her religion (her name was Ross). When she answered "Jewish," the pollster asked, "Would it affect your opinion if you heard rumors that Mr. Cuomo was anti-Semitic?" The news disgusted me. Haddad is now trying to figure out how to handle it. In a few days we should know exactly who the "pollster" is but, there is a danger in even raising the issue—a danger for our candidacy. If you are picking up mud, even to clean it from your place, it makes you dirty. It underscores the viciousness of the tactic.

MONDAY, MAY 31, 1982

Memorial Day weekend has so far been relatively free of the campaign except for a few phone calls. I've spent the time reading, making outlines for a couple of speeches, talking to Chris, meeting Margaret's Bob for a second time—we like him more and more—and going to my mom's 80th birthday. There may not be another weekend like this one from this point on.

TUESDAY, JUNE 1, 1982

Uncertainty is the characteristic that makes the campaign exciting, fascinating, frustrating. In the end, everything—or at least, victory or defeat—will depend on decisions made privately by an unknown number of people behind a curtain. There is no poll that can tell us with any real certainty what people are thinking before they go in or what they thought when they voted. Surely the result never reveals the reasons. So, too, there is no sure way of affecting them. We don't really know whether they weigh integrity more than agreement with their views on one or more issues. How "looks" are counted. Whether ethnicity really is a factor. We guess. And because we don't know, we tend to think everything that can possibly be an influence is important. Every handshake at the subway, every mention in the paper. Everything goes, because we don't know what will really count.

I'm gripped by a strong revulsion—I'm sure it's only tempo-

rary, but it is for the moment very strong. Al Finn[1] of Rochester
has come to the conclusion that he will be for Koch. Barney
Erhart of Wyoming and Mary Louise Walter of Seneca have
changed their minds and are coming out for Koch. Basically it's
because they want to win.

Two things are possible. Either, despite the polls, Koch's
strength as a campaigner and Garth's mastery of the press have
reasserted themselves. Even before he goes on television, he is
coming across as strong, effective, successful. Or political people
simply want a winner—sometimes even before principle or platform.

More and more, I come to understand Governor Carey's disdain for the behavior of many people in this process: what's
practically good for *numero uno* is what he will do. The difference
is that we have the right to expect something more from people
in the public service.

SUNDAY MORNING, JUNE 6, 1982

I have to catch up in the office tomorrow. It means canceling the
Conference of Mayors. It's really too bad, because I'm well
prepared with a speech. We'll issue a release, which won't get
nearly the coverage the speech would have gotten.[1]

Events have been moving faster than my ability to record
them. June has always been a month of exciting family events for
us, but yesterday set a new record. It was our 28th Anniversary.
I can hardly believe it was that long ago that Frankie and I went
to the store, all dressed up in our morning tails, and took pictures
weighing out 5 pounds of potatoes for Artie Foster's mother
before the wedding.

It was also Andrew's commencement day from Law School.
What a joy!

Madeline also graduated. Matilda and I were there with Maria,

[1]A pseudonym.

[1]Because I don't want to die with nobody having read the speech, I include it here
on pp. 436–40.

and it was beautiful receiving the congratulations of teachers who went out of their way to describe Madeline as "beautiful," "warm," "sweet," "the best."

Then, Margaret chose to make it her official engagement announcement day!

And just to make it 5 events, because that's always been our lucky number, the Fates arranged for me to be awarded an honorary degree by the Albany College of Pharmacy. (To show how hectic schedules get at this point in a campaign, I wound up having to drive down to the Concord from Albany to speak at the Sons of Italy convention as well.)

The New York *Post* pointed out what was happening on the 5th and referred to it as the American Dream come true. It was a lovely story. Poppa came in 1926 without a penny. Half a century later the family he and Momma started here are enjoying the milk and honey of the greatest and most abundantly blessed nation in the world. Just the idea that I am considered a possible choice for Governor is a dramatic illustration of what this country means. It is the definition of the word "opportunity." I finished the day yesterday wondering if I will ever be able to repay the enormous kindness I have received.

And always, the funny things happen, too. Earlier this week, sitting behind the desk dictating my commencement speech for Saturday, I heard sounds in the crawl space above the high ceiling of the Lt. Governor's chamber in Albany. Pam Broughton[2] heard them, too. The second time we heard the noise, I looked up to see a bat suddenly darting down toward us. I flailed at it, first with my fist, then with my suit coat. That had the same effect a toreador's cape does. I'm told bats are blind: this one appeared to be charging the flailing jacket. When I wasn't able to get it with the cape and couldn't find any better weapon, we got out. I left for the Wellington hoping that overnight the cleaning people would figure out a way to handle it. One of the Capitol guards suggested shooting at it—in this chamber of irreplaceable oak and mahogany paneling over a hundred years old!

---

[2]My secretary in Albany. She first came with me in 1975, when I became secretary of state. Since then she has become a tower of strength in every circumstance.

I told them I thought there might be a better way. There's almost always a better way.

Jimmy Carter had his killer rabbit: now I have my deranged bat.

Peter Johnson has joined us.[3] He'll be traveling with me. Twenty-two, good-looking, bright, he appears to have a great future, in television, or whatever he chooses to do in this life.

I traveled through Manhattan for a couple of hours on Tuesday after receiving Herman Badillo's endorsement. I visited a garment factory called Lord West on 18th Street. It was exciting. You could see there the American mosaic replenishing itself with Nicaraguans, Hondurans, Italians, Greeks and some few Southern Blacks. I was well received, except on one issue that seemed to be very important to them. It was like the Sons of Italy convention last night, where I was also very well received except on one issue.[4] On Friday in Syracuse I had another good day, except on one issue. Wherever I go it comes up. Often, when it does, some people will plead with me to change my mind. They want the electric chair. At least they think they want it: they really want to do something about crime and "electric chair" is the way they say it. I can soften their stand—even change it sometimes if I'm given 5 or 10 minutes with them. But I'm afraid I won't be able to do that in this campaign. If I can get past their hostility on the issue—and win despite it—then I will have a better chance to discuss it and address it as Governor. I will have their attention and can create opportunities—for example, a 5-minute presentation on television. Indeed, that "fireside chat" approach to government is something I will do more of as Governor.

I have the feeling that our campaign is lagging. I am not yet creating a clear, affirmative image of myself through day-to-day exposure in the media. Koch, by virtue of his position as Mayor, dominates the Metropolitan television and radio. He's anchor man on most 6 and 11 o'clock news shows. That would remain

[3]As a member of my staff in the press office.
[4]The speech to the Sons of Italy appears on pp. 432–35.

true even if we were doing everything we could to get radio and television coverage—and we're not. Bill Haddad, who certainly has the capacity, has spent most of his time in political discussions and organizational work. I've been impatient with that and said so. Now I have to do something about it by becoming more actively involved myself. I have always felt—despite the shibboleths—that I should be aggressively involved in my own campaigns.

One event yesterday will get us a good deal of space. The Liberal Party Policy Committee announced it was supporting Pat Moynihan for Senate and me for Governor. There are obvious pluses. It is an affirmative development, and "success" seems to breed "success," especially in this business. If people think you're doing well, they will suspect maybe they should be with you. It also means that we are almost definitely assured the line for November. I will try to use that for leverage at the Democratic convention with this reasoning: Koch and I both wanted the Liberal Party line because we both knew that in modern times no statewide Democratic candidate has ever won without it. (Holtzman lost when it went to Javits, O'Connor lost when it went to Roosevelt, Ottinger lost when it went to Goodell.)[5] If now I have it, then I am the only Democrat who can win!

Koch will try to counter by suggesting that, if it is true that a Democrat can't win without it, all Democrats should agree to give it to whomever the Democrats choose. That sounds good until you ask, "How do you do that?" There's no legal way to get off the line except by moving out of the state, becoming a judge or dying. Koch will say we should therefore agree not to campaign on the Liberal line, but announce that we would support the Democrat. At best, however, that would be hypocritical —to have your name on the line but to ask that people vote for a different candidate. It would also probably be illegal to try to impose such an agreement on the candidates at the Democratic convention. Fabian and I have discussed it and agree that the

[5]Elizabeth Holtzman lost the 1980 U.S. Senate race to Republican Al D'Amato when Jacob Javits received the Liberals' endorsement; Frank O'Connor lost the 1966 governor's race to Nelson Rockefeller, with Franklin Roosevelt, Jr., on the Liberal line; Republican James Buckley defeated Charles Goodell (Liberal) and Dick Ottinger (Democrat) in the 1970 race for the U.S. Senate.

State Committee cannot impose limitations on the credentials of candidates that are not imposed by the statutes.

Koch may simply say, "Cuomo intends to be a spoiler." Or, "Cuomo should decide whether or not he is really a Democrat." Or, "I will beat him anyway." Or, "I will not have the tail wagging the dog!"

But whatever he says, he has to respond to the question: "Why did you endorse Republicans?" Etc.

It all needs a lot of thought.

SUNDAY, JUNE 13, 1982

A busy week. Yesterday the Nuclear Freeze rally in New York City was an enormous success. I carried the Torch that has been carried from Greece: it was the Olympic Torch used at the last Olympics. The day confirmed what I have felt from the beginning of the campaign: there is a great yearning for something worthwhile to believe in. The nuclear freeze is the simplest possible morality: life is better than death; peace better than war; love better than stupidity. It is hardly more than an affirmation, and yet it brought nearly a million people together. I could tell, just from their faces, that everyone felt good about the day. There was none of the hostility and tension that attended the rallies of the '60s. The only groups not in evidence were minorities. Perhaps their concerns are so fundamental and serious that they saw this massive philosophizing as unrealistic.

We won a big victory at the VID[1] by taking their endorsement away from Koch. On Thursday, he won the New York County Committee by one vote (4 of my votes, including Bill Nuchow, a union leader, were "encouraged" to stay home). That same night I got the ADA's[2] endorsement with 81.6% of the vote. That failed to make the paper. There is no question that Koch's being mayor is getting him a disproportionate amount of publicity, but there's little I can do about it, other than to get Haddad to concentrate on it more.

[1]Village Independent Democrats, a group from Greenwich Village.
[2]Americans for Democratic Action.

I had a good night at Co-op City, although Engel[3] has them committed to go to Koch.

Brooklyn opening on Friday. Jerry Bloom endorsed me. Nikas will work with Fabian Palomino. We need more strength here.

More than two centuries ago in Poland, a band of Jews were drawn by the marvelous tales of a great Rebbe to a place called "Satmar," to form their own religious community. They created a strictly regulated regimen which controlled every moment in their waking hours. Diet, marriage, role in life—all were regulated by the Torah. A strict hierarchy of rabbinical courts, headed by a chief Rebbe, was put in place.

Today they live in Williamsburg, Brooklyn, and are known there as Satmar Hasidim. Williamsburg was, when they arrived, already a deteriorated community. They have kept their portion of it breathing, although by no means elegant.

They still wear the black hats, beards of their ancestors—much like the Amish. After an arranged marriage, they have as many children as their inclination will allow: there is no birth control. They educate children in their own schools but, again like the Amish, discourage them from going beyond secondary school unless it is to Rabbinical Seminary. Extremely loyal to the group, they nevertheless pursue individual economic goals. Many of them become wealthy without ever leaving the cluster. They own shops, work in the diamond exchange, and come home every night to a house without television, without card games, or movies, or dates, or sports, or anything commonly thought of by our society as recreation.

Despite the regimen, they are quick to smile, at least with me. They have been kind to me for the eight years of my public life, and I have never understood exactly why.

Earlier today, on this rainy Sunday afternoon, I sat in the home of the Chief Rebbe, Rebbe Teitelbaum. His residence is totally out of character with the rest of the Satmar community: it is spacious and sumptuously appointed. The Rebbe himself seems uncomfortable in these surroundings—or perhaps just distracted.

[3] Assemblyman Eliot L. Engel.

I was attended by 15 Rabbis before meeting Rebbe Teitelbaum. There was nothing to drink or eat—that would have been
wasteful. The conversation was ritualistic, much like the ones I
had with the Iroquois.[4]

They seem pleased by my ability to make them smile: over the
last eight years it has gotten to be almost a game with us. Today
we even got Rebbe Teitelbaum to smile.

More than that, he gave me his blessing as Chief Rebbe. He
doesn't deal in political endorsements: the 15 who attended me
will do that as "individuals," if they choose. I suspect they will
have a meeting in a couple of weeks with the community leaders
and discuss the possibility.

Unlike other groups of Hasidim—the Bobover and Lubavitcher, for example—the Satmar are probably more emotional
about their endorsements than they are pragmatic. Winning or
losing doesn't mean as much to them as it probably should.
That's why I stand a better chance with them than I do with most
political leaders.

THURSDAY, JUNE 17, 1982

Last night Andrew showed the first real signs of concern about
getting 25% at the Convention. The Queens, Brooklyn and
Bronx leaders are taking proxies so that they will be able to
control the vote. Their dominance at the Convention will allow
them to dictate whether we get the 25% or not—at least that's
Andrew's fear. Manes has told Weprin that he (Manes) will try
to help me get the 25%, but it will be tough because Koch is
insisting I be "killed."

A hard session with Mellman in Nassau. Jan Pierce and I spoke
to him for about an hour, and I think I've softened him a bit.
We'll see at the Convention. One thing I've learned about con-

---

[4]In 1974, some traditionalist Mohawk Indians from the Iroquois Confederacy seized
property near Moss Lake in Herkimer County, claiming that the state's title to it was
illegal. For nearly three years neither lawsuit nor negotiation was able to resolve the
matter. In 1976, Governor Carey asked me to negotiate with them, and after several
months of discussion we arrived at a compromise as part of which they voluntarily moved
off the land to another location in Clinton County in the north country.

ventions is that they can produce a dynamic of their own that generates developments never anticipated. At the Republican convention, Ronnie Lauder's name popped up for Lt. Governor at the last minute.[1] He hadn't ever campaigned but was rich. Just as quickly, a deal developed that made Jim Emery first a candidate for Governor, then the consensus candidate for Lieutenant Governor within hours, although he had denied his interest in the position for weeks.[2] That kind of thing may occur next week at our convention.

Tuesday, the 15th, was my 50th birthday. We had five birthday parties, in Manhattan, Albany, Brooklyn, Westchester and Queens. The logistics were tough, but we made it—and about $150,000, too. The last party of the night was at the Waterfront Crab House in Queens. It was another of our old-fashioned "wedding"-type affairs. Even Joe Austin and some of the Celtics were there, as was Don "Cess" Poole—who came all the way from California.[3]

Brooklyn was another "love-in" with the people I spent 20 years working, learning, practicing law among. It's tough to have to ask them all for money and sacrifice over and over. Knowing that a victory could make it all worthwhile for them is a great incentive.

We received the endorsement of the Reform Caucus,[4] but I didn't have the feeling that they are enthusiastic about me. I haven't spent the time cultivating them and, in the end, with these political structures, a great deal depends on personal attention. Issues are not the only considerations.

[1] Ronald S. Lauder was finance chairman of the Republican State Committee.

[2] The Republican convention was held June 15–17, 1982. Lew Lehrman, of the highly successful Rite Aid drugstore chain, received 69 percent of the convention vote for governor. His challenger, Paul Curran, received 31 percent of the convention vote. Thus Lehrman and Curran faced each other in the Republican primary. James Emery, Republican minority leader of the assembly, did not face a primary opponent for lieutenant governor, and was thus the designated candidate for the general election. The designation for comptroller went to Ned Regan, who had been comptroller since 1978, and for attorney general the delegates chose Fran Sclafani, a former student of mine.

[3] Joe Austin coached the Celtics—the sandlot baseball-and-basketball team I played with as a kid. Donald Poole and I first met at St. John's Prep in 1945. We have been friends ever since.

[4] The Democratic party is proud of its diversity and expresses it in various ways. The Reform Caucus is made up of members of the Democratic party who like to think of themselves as more liberal and progressive than the rest.

Increasingly, I have a sense of the difference between campaigning and governing. The political structure that is so important, especially in this phase of the campaign, will have little to do with governing, if recent history is any indication. I'd like to find a way to elevate the structure to make it more useful as an instrument for reaching every part of the State.

Our organization efforts in Metropolitan New York progress strongly. We have to build our own because the "clubs" and the "regulars" are mostly with Koch. Weprin in Queens and Bloom in Brooklyn are our building blocks: two good people who have been loyal to me and who can make an important contribution to government.

We have begun the local campaigning in earnest. Today we opened our Queens Headquarters in Saul Weprin's club, opened an office in the Greek community in Astoria, met with Black Ministers in South Jamaica, did the Senior Citizens at Italian Charities and the Orthodox Rabbis in Kew Gardens, and were endorsed by the Federation of Italian American Societies in Queens.

The reception is good everywhere, except when the subject of the death penalty comes up downstate. I am almost universally condemned on that subject in New York City, especially by the senior citizens. I must find a way to convince people that I know about crime and what to do to improve our criminal justice system, despite my view on the death penalty. There appears to be no chance to convince them on the capital punishment question itself, at least not in the 1 or 2 minutes we are allowed.

Responses to our calls from headquarters now indicate that we will have the 25% we need to get on the ballot but that won't be clear until it happens.

Mayor Corning is in the hospital. Bill Keefe[5] tells me it's emphysema. I hope it's not worse.

Late tonight it was announced the *Post* would publish a poll showing me 16 points behind.

---

[5]Executive assistant to Mayor Corning.

SATURDAY, JUNE 19, 1982

The Liberal Party endorsed me today. They also endorsed Pat Moynihan, Bob Abrams, Bill Finneran and Harold Baer, Jr.[1] The value of the endorsement has not yet been fully analyzed by the media and probably by only a few political people. It's a unique circumstance: this is the first time the Liberals have endorsed before the Democratic convention.

Last night was the "People's Convention" conducted by Angelo Del Toro and his Hispanic colleagues. Herman Badillo accompanied me. It was exciting. Disco strobe lights, noisemakers, cheering, people jumping up. It had the kind of passion not seen in most of our politics. I was compared to Vito Marcantonio.[2] Some of them understood: most, I suspect, didn't.

I couldn't help thinking how much like rallies in the '20s this must have been. The people at the bottom, the uneducated and the undereducated and the deprived, appear always to have the greater passion. Here passion is an expression of need.

In order to govern, I need to understand both these people and people like Colby Chandler, who runs Kodak. Chandler will provide the jobs that eventually will provide opportunity to the people who attended the People's Convention.

I have found using Herbert Lehman as a symbol of the things I'm trying to project to be very effective.[3] He was a Lt. Governor who was against the death penalty, about whom it was said he was "not tough," "too pensive," "not political enough." I like it.

SUNDAY, JUNE 20, 1982

Left to their own devices, the Mayor and his political directors have recently made a series of errors and miscalculations. First they allowed him to say too much. He said things like: Cuomo

---

[1]Baer, a bright, practicing lawyer who was not well known politically, got the nod for lieutenant governor. Moynihan was nominated for senator, Abrams for attorney general, Finneran for comptroller.

[2]A legendary, progressive politician who fought hard for immigrant groups—Italians and others—in lower Manhattan in the 1930s and early 1940s.

[3]Lieutenant governor from 1928 to 1932, Lehman was governor from 1932 to 1944, and U.S. senator from 1949 to 1956.

is supported by "leftists," Cuomo is talking "racism"; and generally fed the issue of his outrageousness. They then misplayed a series of political situations, like the VID and the Liberal Party. They had Harding on the ropes early in the game but let him escape by allowing the Mayor to repeat his "slime" epithet about Dr. Harrington. They've continued to feed the notion that Koch can't win in November since I now have the Liberal Party line and won't be able to get off it. And to top it off, by handling New York County clumsily, they gave us a 2-day story when we reversed the vote.[1] I'm sure what Garth will now do is try and win back the momentum by announcing some polls and Koch's convention nomination, then low-key Koch personally with a modified rose-garden strategy and go deep, wide and continuously on TV. I will not be able to match his TV. The question is how much we can compensate for that with a pullout operation.[2]

From time to time the tough physical pace creates a fatigue which invariably produces doubts. The tendency is—for whatever brief intervals—to yearn for privacy, quiet, the time to think and be left alone. It continues to be the greatest tension I feel —wanting to be remote and having to be immersed.

MONDAY, JUNE 21, 1982

On to Syracuse for the Convention!

We arrived at the airport simultaneously with the Mayor. For some reason he went past the press directly on to the hotel. Burgos, Bersani and Company had arranged a receiving line for me. It was well done, and the press interviews seemed to go well. On the way to the hotel I was surprised to see the entire route

[1]The New York County (Manhattan) Committee at first failed to endorse my candidacy notwithstanding the fact that its chairman, Herman D. (Denny) Farrell, Jr., fought hard to get it for me. The Koch forces were able to prevent the endorsement by inducing a few fence-sitters not to show up for the vote. They then trumpeted their "victory," underscoring the importance of the New York County Committee's position. Having elevated its significance, the Koch people were embarrassed when Farrell applied his own pressure to the absentees, got them to show up, and won an endorsement for me the second time around.

[2]That is, identifying likely support on election day and facilitating their getting to the polls.

marked by Cuomo posters. I can imagine what that did to the Mayor when he took the trip.

There was a small rally outside the hotel of 100 or so people. It was basically to produce publicity and some more interviews.

We had a boat ride for our delegates—two boat rides, as a matter of fact. They took us down the lake and were great fun. Chris and I steered the ship for a while wearing Captain hats, behaving silly and loving it. The trips were more than a diversion; they were designed to shelter our delegates from further arm twisting. Apparently, there has been a good deal of that, and we won't know how effective it has been until the vote is taken.

There were a few receptions at night in the increasingly exciting hotel environment. Delegates streamed in from all over the state until midnight. The Mayor didn't wish to appear with me on Channels 2 and 4, so we made separate appearances. On the way back from the Civic Center, we stopped in at the local restaurant and stayed too late.

TUESDAY, JUNE 22, 1982

One of the things the convention was to test was our ability to organize. Hundreds of details had to be dealt with. Just the hotel arrangements for staff and guests could have kept two people busy for a week. The complicated floor arrangements, transportation requirements, PR capacity, interrelationship with a convention committee dominated by the opponent—all created a massive challenge. By the end of the convention, it was absolutely clear to all knowledgeable people that Andrew and Tonio and all the others on our staff, mostly young people, outshone every other group involved. Our rallies were longer, louder, more intense and apparently more sincere. In fact, it seemed to me, on the flight home tonight, there wasn't a single area in which my team did not outperform Koch's.

Yesterday, Andrew had all the bosses on the other side believing we were in danger of not getting our 25%. The Koch people were afraid of giving us that issue, so they relaxed efforts to twist arms. Actually, Andrew was sure of much more than the 25%. The relaxation and the euphoria created by our demonstrations and, I think, a resentment by the upstaters over the behavior of the power brokers combined to produce a 39% vote for Cuomo. That was higher than Carey got in '74 and gave us momentum that we never dared hope for a week ago.

I got up at 5:30 this morning to write my convention speech. In the crowded quarters, telephones ringing, another radio interview every 15 minutes, no one to dictate to and tired from the celebration of the night before—it was the worst set of circumstances in which I ever had to write a speech. And I never wrote a better speech.[1]

It was typed by a volunteer from the CSEA and handed to me as we rushed out the door to the convention center. I had to mark up the copy because of typos, and by the time I got to the convention center, I was afraid I mightn't be able to read it.

Sitting in the dressing room, I listened to Koch's speech attacking Reaganomics, and it provided me with three quick response possibilities that I scribbled into the speech. They proved to be the most effective part of the delivery. One was a reference to the "selfish spirit" that gives capital gains taxes back to rich real estate developers. Another one was a reference to Watergate that gave me an opportunity to write in a line about openness of government and a veiled reference to *Playboy*, and the third was his attempt to become the champion against Reaganomics, which allowed me to remind the convention of 1980. I did it by scrawling into the margin the following sentence:

"We should have been the party that attacked Reaganomics in 1980, when it was so popular, instead of waiting until now, when the error of our acquiescence is clear."

I am told, too, that my speech was much better received than the Mayor's even by the Mayor's people. Here again, my team outnegotiated the Koch forces. The rules originally called for the Mayor and me to speak at approximately the same time but not back to back. After our 39% vote, the shocked and angry Koch forces tried to change the speaking order to put the Mayor on first and then me five speakers later—after the hall would be emptied out. Haddad was at his histrionic best, threatening to have press conferences and raise the "bossism"

[1]See pp. 441–45.

issue. The Koch people surrendered. Indeed, they overreacted and moved me up the list of speakers so I appeared right after Koch.

Their original strategy was to have a big demonstration, then pull large delegations that they controlled off the floor before I spoke, to make it look bad for me. But in a backstage meeting, Andrew and Fabian put it to Piscatelli[2] and Baranello. They told the Koch lieutenants that if they tried to get away with "this blatant, obvious power play," the Cuomo people would just walk out of the convention and make as dramatic a point of it as possible. Andrew and Fabian won the chicken game. They won them all.

The Mayor spoke with applause leaders sitting in the aisles directing the delegates when to cheer. Lee Alexander had brought in locals from Syracuse to assist in the demonstration. But for all their efforts, they got drowned out by Cuomo partisans in the gallery, who threw cold water on their demonstrations with their "We want Cuomo" chanting.

SATURDAY, JUNE 26, 1982

The difference between reality and perception in the political game was manifest again by the convention aftermath. Those who were at the convention know that our side won the day, if not the vote. We were greeted with more enthusiasm, our speech was better received, our performance in the vote was better than expected and our organization by far better. The upstate press conveyed much of that, and the TV as well, although the TV coverage was very limited.

But that's not the perception in the New York City area. The *Times* downplayed the entire convention. The most prominent thing it used was a picture of Koch's team—with Del Bello, Gallagher and Abrams[1]—on the front page. A *Times* reporter

---

[2]Pete Piscatelli had become Koch's campaign manager for the 1982 campaign.

---

[1]Al Del Bello, Koch's choice, had won the convention's designation (the majority of the votes) for lieutenant governor on the second ballot. In the primary, he was challenged by Carl McCall, former state senator from Harlem and deputy ambassador to the UN,

had told other reporters at the convention he thought my speech was one of the best he ever heard—that wasn't mentioned in the article. The *Daily News* did a piece that was a real "downer"; the reporter explained that three paragraphs of his piece as written were dropped. The *Post*—which made Koch a candidate—continues to be the best thing we have going for the time being.

It's no conspiracy. The perceptions are a combination of things: Garth's mastery of media technique; Koch's ability to be colorfully succinct; his position as Mayor, which provides him with endless opportunities; my reputation for being "philosophical" and my refusal or inability to package things for the media —and, to some extent, Koch's being perceived as the winner. The *Rocky* theme is nice—but only if it's *Rocky II*, where he won. This is by no means universal, but I suspect it is the dominant feeling.

I noticed at the Irish Fair in Brooklyn[2] this morning a warmth in the reception people were giving me that didn't quite fit the analysis I've just suggested, unless they are getting the feeling— somehow—that I'm going to win. Madeline and Maria also report that our literature (we still have only the one basic piece) is better received in the streets than it was in '77. How I remember '77! One morning particularly. I was in a phone booth in midtown Manhattan. As I was making my call I watched some of our young volunteers handing out literature. Person after person would glance at it, then throw it down, sometimes with a look of disgust. Each one was like a slap. It probably wouldn't sting as much today, since my skin has grown thicker in the last 5 years, but nevertheless—and fortunately—it appears not to be happening as much. The general assessment is that there is no strong dislike for my candidacy. It is the kind of thing I began to feel near the end of the 1977 race when—as it developed— I almost caught up with Ed.

The most effective thing I am able to do on a stage is make people laugh. It happened twice yesterday at the Irish Fair. After a long series of politicians—incumbents—had lauded Ireland, I

who had received 30 percent of the convention vote on the first ballot. Raymond Gallagher was the party's nominee for comptroller, and Bob Abrams had received the nomination for attorney general.
[2]A two-day fair benefiting Catholic Charities of the Diocese of Brooklyn.

said they had thereby proven their ability to remain in office: "Moynihan should be Senator for 6 more years [cheers]; Golden, Boro President for 4 more years [cheers]; Consul General O Huiginn should remain [cheers]; and Koch should be Mayor for 12 years [loud cheers]!" Also, after Moynihan, referring to his "Beyond the Melting Pot,"[3] pointed out that 24% of people claim to be Irish, 20% English, etc., I said, "and 1%, the Politicians, claim to be everything!"

TUESDAY, JUNE 29, 1982

The New York *Post* debate is scheduled for July 7th, and the focus shifts gradually to the real confrontation stage. Most of the insiders expect the debates to make a big difference. I don't. I don't really think they did in 1977 or 1978. But they provide the candidates with a stimulus. It's not unlike getting ready for the Bar examination. I kind of enjoy the challenge. I'll spend as much of the next week or so as I can reading and relaxing.

Tomorrow the Financial Control Board will vote to approve Mayor Koch's one-year plan instead of a four-year plan. The Mayor will claim a victory, but actually it's a rejection of his four-year plan because of uncertainty.[1] More and more the fiscal future for the state and the city looks menacing. Bob Morgado suggested today that the Governor's job is not worth winning. We'll see!

There are indeed moments when you wonder whether it's worth all the abuse. I stood in the rain at the AFL-CIO Jobs Rally on the Capitol steps this afternoon, waiting for a chance to speak. My friend Ray Corbett decided it would be too political! I don't know why he did it, but it certainly seemed less than fair for a Lt. Governor who has been fighting labor's cause for years. *C'est la vie—la vie politique.*

The CSEA meeting this morning at the lovely Granite Hotel

---

[3] *Beyond the Melting Pot,* by Nathan Glazer and Daniel P. Moynihan, published in 1970.

[1] The Financial Control Board, an ad hoc state agency set up in 1976 to monitor the finances of the city of New York, whose profligacy had lost it the confidence of the investment community, was empowered to approve the city's financial plan.

in Kerhonkson was more fun. Only an hour and a quarter from
Albany; it was a beautiful ride. I'm always well received by them.
If I can keep their enthusiasm high, it may help offset the advan-
tage the Koch money gives him. We'll have to do it in the streets.
But to do that well we will need a better organization than we
now have in place. I'll have to get after Andrew.

Dyson called today to say he was dropping out of the race for
Lt. Governor.[2] No one is sure what that means. The most popular guess is that he's made a deal with Koch to get out to give
Del Bello a better chance. I don't believe it. He called me to tell
me about his decision, and I don't think he would have done that:
he's not duplicitous. We need time to analyze the significance of
the event.

WEDNESDAY, JUNE 30, 1982

It seems that the poll which appeared in the *Post* is probably
confirmed by Caddell's polls. Koch has moved back from an
8–10-point lead to a 12–16-point lead. There's no real explanation for it, except that the race continues to be Koch v. Koch,
with Cuomo not really being a factor, and as Koch has withdrawn
from the field, kept quiet, not made errant statements, he has
improved his position in the polls. Garth's modified Rose Garden strategy is working.

Probably there will be no deviation by Koch from this strategy, and his strength will be increased by his going on television
—extensively and effectively. Poll analysts would say that the
only chance I have is to go on television myself—first and effectively. I won't be able to catch him with posters, trips to the
Catskills and occasional free spots on radio and TV. Poll analysts
would say, therefore, that the questions now are: how much do
I have to spend and how good is my TV?

If the polls are accurate and the poll analysts correct, the

[2]John Dyson had won 29 percent of the vote for lieutenant governor on the first
ballot, Al Del Bello 41 percent and Carl McCall 30 percent. Since none of the candidates
received more than 50 percent of the vote, another ballot was necessary. On the second
ballot, Del Bello received his majority—66 percent of the total—and the designation.
Dyson's 29 percent on the first ballot gave him the right, however, to run in the primary,
as did McCall's 30 percent. Unlike McCall, Dyson decided against doing so.

picture is discouraging. So much of this contest for power comes down to manipulating the perceptions and relatively little of it to what would "naïvely" be called the merits. Or is that an early indication of sour grapes?

Then again—maybe the polls don't tell the story. Maybe there is an intensity of feeling and a network effect among my supporters that hasn't yet manifested itself. And maybe—as is more likely—unpredictable things are still to occur which will make a difference before this is over. The best advice for the moment has to be Winston Churchill's "never give up."

The hardest practical problem is trying to sustain the confidence of the money people and the volunteers. If the Gannett poll shows that Koch has resumed a wide lead, that will hurt with the "investors." I don't think we can get on TV fast enough to change that, so we'll have to find a way to explain it or do something other than TV to change it. The debates and a really aggressive campaign may do it. In fact, we haven't had either yet.

Yesterday I told Haddad I wanted him to get completely out of organization and into strategy and press. Today I will see that it happens.

THURSDAY, JULY 1, 1982

I spoke with Dominic Baranello yesterday on the phone and spent part of today thinking about him and regretting what I thought.

Dominic became State Chairman of the Democratic State Committee after I said no to the opportunity and recommended him to Governor Carey through his secretary Dave Burke in 1976. In 1978 he asked me to give up running for A.G. to help him and the party by running for Lt. Governor, because Mary Ann Krupsak had left them in a hole. When I said yes, Dominic said I was "owed" the next shot at Governor. I was clear-headed enough not to take him seriously. In 1980, when Dominic was afraid Carter's people would embarrass him by going around him as State Chairman, he spoke to me and I saw that it didn't occur. Early in 1981, Garth and Morgado suggested we get rid of him, and I objected.

After all of this—and a dozen platforms shared and a hundred embraces exchanged—Dominic, having told me he was neutral, ordered his delegation to vote with him for Koch at the Convention.

I called Dominic yesterday to talk about things. He sounded a bit tentative. He said that he was going in for a bypass operation and didn't want to "take on any more pressure."

I made a joke, tried to make him feel comfortable, and kind of felt sorry for him. The bypass was only part of it.

Then I wondered about the whole thing, the whole idea of putting up with all of this—again. This act of running for office is an intention that collapses without regular reinforcement.

I traveled to the Catskills yesterday after a press conference in New York. Mickey Carroll of the *Times* accompanied us. We talked most of the way up—with me answering all questions, being as open as I could be on even the tough questions like the implications of religion and ethnicity. I've gotten into trouble doing that. Anyone can pull 2 or 3 lines from a long discussion and twist its meaning. But if I have to develop a guarded style to deal with the press—especially reliable pros like Carroll—I think I will lose some of the credibility I've earned by being open for the last eight years. On balance, I think it's better to be open. We'll see how the Carroll piece comes out. It should appear in a couple of days.

SUNDAY, JULY 4, 1982

It's the Fourth of July. Outside I can hear dozens of muted—and occasionally not so muted—explosions. Once in a while a brightly colored rocket sprays a hundred sparks. But only for an instant. Enjoy it—quickly—because it will be gone before you can capture it: nothing but a quick puff of smoke gone almost as fast.

Sic transit gloria mundi.

Yesterday was the mass at the cemetery to commemorate the First Anniversary of Pop's passing. It's hard to believe it has been a year.

Tempus fugit, memento mori.
And that's about all the Latin I remember.

Everyone's out of the house. They left me behind to do some reading for the debate on Wednesday. I think the campaign moves into a new phase then. Koch has lost all he will in the polls on his own. Now it's my turn to make a move. To this point the people don't really know me well enough for me to close the gap. The debates will be the beginning of a new focus by the media and then the public. I should start my television, too, at the same time. The question that confuses our analysts is how exactly to "posture" me. I'm not getting involved with the question. I'm going to do the things that are to me most obvious.

THURSDAY, JULY 8, 1982

I don't know if it will mean anything a year from now, but I think yesterday was a turning point in the campaign. The "Great Debate" took place. At the *Post*'s invitation, over 600 business and professional leaders filled a ballroom at the Sheraton Centre. The panelists and podiums for the contestants were on the stage. All the media were there. Cameras jammed onto a platform at the back of the room, tables of press people around the platform.

It was a Koch crowd at the outset, although, thanks to Haddad's negotiating and Andrew's extraordinary crew, some of our people—150 or so—were able to get in. I tried to make the most of the fact that it was Koch's paper and his crowd by nailing that fact down psychologically. I told Haddad the night before that I wouldn't come for the breakfast preceding the debate because I didn't want them depriving me of my alien status with a plate of scrambled eggs. It wasn't a bad idea, but it produced a much larger advantage than I expected. Actually, I was late getting out of the house and was in danger of not making the 9 A.M. starting time. I got to the Sheraton and dashed up the stairs—with Matilda and Maria—to hear an anxious Howard Rubinstein say, "You have 2 minutes!" I walked in the back door of the crowded ballroom and an extraordinary thing happened. Some people began applauding. As I moved toward the main table, where

Koch, Mayor Beame,[1] Mayor Lindsay and some university presidents were sitting—stopping to shake hands with John LoCicero and Bob Tierney—the applause grew. It was surprising how much enthusiasm my group was able to generate. By the time I got to the main table and reached out to shake hands with the Mayor, the applause was really quite rousing. At a debate! That hadn't started! All we needed was the *Rocky* theme in the background. I know Ed was unhappy.

Ed won the toss of the coin and chose to let me open so he could close. Seconds after he called and won with "tails," I grabbed the microphone and said, "No wonder he's for casino gambling." The audience enjoyed it. It set a tone immediately. Ed was unhappier.

From there on in, I thought the debate went fairly evenly. I felt he was making telling debater's points on his achievements and that I was suffering because of the superficial disparity between a Lt. Governor's record and the record of a Mayor of the greatest City in the world. He mocked my relationship with Carey in a way that made me suspect he had reason to believe Carey would not embarrass him by contradicting his description. He didn't attack any of my positions—just what he called my failure to have achieved anything. I chose not to dwell on my record because I was scoring on a few twists. I was Willie Pep and doing fairly well at it. I was also able to get a few laughs— which upset him. By the time we were through, received the applause of the assembly, and shook hands, I thought we had a draw.

No one else did. As soon as I stepped off the stage, the press surrounded me. They had spent just a couple of minutes with the Mayor, who had left first while I exchanged some words with Roger Wood[2] on the stage. When I came down, they left the Mayor and rushed to me. Their questions made it clear they thought I had won. "Did you feel you creamed him?" "Isn't this a new you?" "What do you think accounts for the Mayor's poor showing?"

Then my own people—Stern, Irene Mattone, Dodi Hull,[3] a

[1]Abraham Beame was mayor of New York City from 1974 to 1977.
[2]Editor of the New York *Post.*
[3]A staff member and friend.

dozen or more—hugged me, shook my hand, beamed. Everyone on my side thought it was a knockout. I was surprised—pleasantly, but surprised. Matilda thought I did well, but I think her appraisal was closer to my own—a draw.

Over the next half hour, I learned it was the unanimous opinion of the press corps and media teams that it was a decisive victory. Even the waiters voted for me—unanimously—and did it on TV that night for Vic Miles.[4]

After the debate, Pat Caddell, Haddad, Cohen and a team of our friends, including Saul Weprin, Arthur Eve, Denny Farrell, Larry Kerwin,[5] Ray Harding, Jim Featherstonhaugh, Norman Adler and Jan Pierce, sat around planning the rest of the campaign. The judgment has been made to go on TV as soon as possible. I'm a little leery of it, but for the moment I'll go along with it. We tried fashioning 3 or 4 general commercials. Our main hangup is whether to try dealing with my record point by point or in some general way. I'm eager to see what Harvey Cohen comes up with.

However it happened, the campaign has taken a turn because of the debate and the fortuitous appearance of a new Gannett poll showing I've picked up two more points since their last poll, leaving me 8 points behind and actually ahead with most likely voters. I don't believe it, but who knows for sure?

The result of the poll and the debate, I believe, will finally bring down this wall of invulnerability that in many people's minds made Koch a winner despite what I said and the polls actually revealed. One of the newscasters, Roger Sharp, actually admitted flatly that he had been wrong—he said, on-screen last night, that he had thought Koch was a sure winner and now he fully believed Cuomo could be an upset winner. Heady stuff. But as always, when the news is best, the applause the loudest—my throttle slows things down. I have spent hours since the debate trying to figure out how to use the moment well. By circulating our money people, which Stern is doing, increasing our public scheduling, following up on the points made in the debate. Generally, I want to spend the time mak-

[4]A television reporter and commentator.
[5]Laurence J. Kerwin, chairman, Monroe County Democratic Committee.

ing the most of this temporary high. But again, as always, I seem incapable of enjoying it the way people expect me to. In the moments that seem right for exultation, my head turns to analysis.

SATURDAY, JULY 10, 1982

The campaign does not consume all the attention. Margaret's wedding is set for October 10. With typical efficiency she has found the place, made the invitation list, put together her bridal party, ordered gowns, arranged dinner parties so the two families could meet one another, and is setting up house. She has managed her campaign better than we are managing ours. We all pray that Margaret and Bob are right for each other; no one deserves happiness more. If all it takes is hard work, there is no question it will work.

Andrew's personal life is in a respite time. He's finished law school but won't be taking the Bar exam until February. These several months are an assignment and an adventure he couldn't resist—and shouldn't have. It's valuable experience, it's exciting, and it could be very important to him. Surely, it has been to us.

Matilda is enjoying it all. She's a great communicator; more gregarious than I; more attractive and more convincing. Physically, the campaign can be too demanding for her. That happened in 1977. She lost too much weight and got weak. I've instructed the scheduling people to be more careful this time.

Maria and Madeline are working full time in the campaign, and everyone loves them both.

Chris is busying himself in various ways and seems reasonably content. He's so bright that it's not difficult to integrate him into the discussions about the campaign, and that reduces his feeling of remoteness. His big unhappiness is that he may not get the new boat he wants for a year or so more.

More and more it becomes clear how important it is to be strong physically. I'm tired today and wouldn't want to have to debate tomorrow. I'm convinced that the reason I did so well last time was that I had spent three or four days basically resting. I should have done it again this weekend, and certainly must before the first TV debate in August.

MONDAY, JULY 12, 1982

The second debate.[1] Koch was on the attack. And personal. He brought up the Cabin incident—hard. He also attacked me for having no record. His constant repetition of the "no record" theme is effective. He feels that if he repeats it enough it will stick. If it's not answered, it will.

Haddad was surprised because Garth had promised him not to use Cabin, and Haddad feels betrayed. I wish I could say I was surprised.

A foul-up in the procedure put me at a large disadvantage. I lost the coin flip, and Koch chose to go last. That was interpreted to mean that he would speak last on every question—it gave him every last word. That's obviously wrong.

I thought he was effective and I wasn't. I think the Cabin thing hurts because it's used to indicate I have no administrative strength. That may be unfair, but it's the kind of proposition the public understands. Koch is a master at this kind of thing—he will do wonders with "How can he run a big government if he doesn't know who was on his payroll?" The truth is that in the end every system has to depend upon individuals, and if they go wrong, there's little protection. Ask any of the largest corporate chiefs. The real question is whether in choosing the individual you should have known he would go wrong. In Cabin's case there was no way I might have suspected it. But how do I say all this in 20 seconds?

Since this debate was upstate, there was all the radio in the state but only one downstate television camera. That means it won't get the kind of coverage the first debate did.

Altogether—as usual—the implications are largely obscure. Koch is reported to be telling people at City Hall he "killed" me. He'll probably get a lot of people to believe him. There is a discernible "down" feeling in my campaign now, a dramatic

[1] At Grossinger's, the famed resort in the Catskills.

difference from the ecstasy the office felt last week. That's the way this game is played. That's the way life is played. Always we tend to overestimate the importance of episodes. I'm sure that's as true today—when we didn't win—as it was last week when we did.

Tomorrow is another day. Teilhard would tell us that it will be good just because it will come. That is worth remembering, because this business requires us to give up so much of what we'd really like to be.

TUESDAY, JULY 13, 1982

I woke before 5 A.M. No matter how hard I try to focus on the ultimates, the challenges of the moment—what the books used to call the "temporalities"—intrude. My mind feels assaulted by Koch's attacks yesterday and struggles to defend.

There was more than just Cabin and "no record." I thought he made effective points in saying he had put up money to cover senior citizens' day-care centers and that many of the 17,000 units he's built were low- and middle-income. That certainly makes my Reaganomics-in-the-local-garb argument vulnerable if I use housing and cutting senior citizens as examples. On the other hand, he is weak in trying to justify his urging repeal of the capital gains tax on real estate transactions, his philosophical vacillation and his original embrace of Reagan.

For the moment, therefore, I believe this should be my approach:

1. A high-road approach to issues and ideas—"This is what we need to do. I have a plan for jobs, for financing, for education."
2. Part of my plan is helping New York City, which, after all is said and done, still has problems—crime is up, unemployment above the national average, budget still in jeopardy, infrastructure crumbling; subways are in need of repair.
3. I have a different basic philosophy. I believe in traditional Democratic principles. He—at the moment—believes in COLA reduc-

tion,[1] mandatory retirement, no Flynn-Dearie,[2] subminimum wage,[3] taxing the middle class and relieving rich real estate developers.[4]

4. "Can you think of one thing that Koch is speaking up for right now that isn't something a poll would say is politically popular?"

5. We need the whole state—no one knows the whole state better, no one can help the whole state more than Cuomo.

Then I need to answer Cabin and the charge of no record.

THURSDAY, JULY 15, 1982

The Cabin attack is still being discussed by the media. I'm not sure how it strikes people. I suspect some of the media are turned off by it, but more of them regard it as just good, tough politics. I told the carpenters' union[1] in Westchester that I was pleased that Koch was shooting at me because I didn't know of anyone who shoots behind him except in a cowboy movie. It does create the impression that Koch is concerned.

It seems, too, that the *Post* debate has had a much greater impact than the second one. I'm glad of that.

Commercials are now the focus of attention. No one is totally sure of what we want to say. The forces are so complex—swirling —that our creative work has been stymied. I'll take a crack at it myself after tomorrow's debate in Syracuse.

---

[1]The idea of reducing the Cost of Living Adjustment in wages, pensions, etc., to a percentage of the rise in the cost of living.

[2]Legislation sponsored by Senator John E. Flynn and Assemblyman John C. Dearie to offer various kinds of protection to tenants. I favored the bill; Koch did not.

[3]Some, including the mayor, have suggested allowing employers to hire young workers at less than the currently mandated minimum wage. I was—and am—opposed to the proposal as retrogressive.

[4]While the mayor had asked for the repeal of a capital gains tax on profits in real estate transactions of a million dollars or more, he was urging increases in commuter taxes and other measures that would have had considerable impact on middle-class earners.

---

[1]United Brotherhood of Carpenters and Joiners of America.

FRIDAY, JULY 16, 1982

The candidates in both the Republican and Democratic primaries appeared together for the first time yesterday, at the Farm Bureau debate just outside Syracuse. The questions had been given in advance and there was no rebuttal provided for, so the exchange was relatively dull. The Mayor was not comfortable with the material and it made him tentative and flat in his presentation. Lehrman—whom I had not seen campaign before—is light, almost bantering in style. He wore red suspenders, went jacketless, waved, chatted and made bad jokes. Curran is a classy candidate who started too late—or at least that's the way it looks now.

The exchange was devoid of interplay until, in his prepared closing, the Mayor struck his theme. That theme keeps evolving as the campaign progresses. That's because—as I've noted repeatedly—he's never had a clear rationale. Yesterday he even disparaged "ideas and visions" in favor of experience. He's arguing, "Because I was Mayor, I should be Governor. Don't listen to these people who say they have ideas—only executors of ideas should be considered." He dismissed all the ideas as "nothing new." The position is vulnerable, obviously. I responded, "If you're saying *you* should be Governor because you were Mayor, that's like the Captain of the *Titanic* saying he should be Admiral of the fleet. Crime is up . . ." etc., etc. He is formidable, however, because his popularity has so little to do with performance and rationale. There is a gap between the perception that makes him popular to the bulk of voters and the perception of those with a closer look. The problem I face is how to win the game of perceptions when he has 2½ million dollars and I have a million to spend and most people say the race will come down to television.

I'm surprised he's not yet gone on TV, unless he still believes that he has a comfortable lead in the polls and is saving his money for the general election. The basic difference between his polls and mine seems to be that he weighs the Jewish vote more heavily.

In any event, trying to figure out exactly what message to deliver on TV is the challenge now, and I will spend a couple of days looking at Harvey's scripts and writing some of my own.

It must be a message that sticks, that distinguishes me from him in a way that people like—and will remember until September 23.

I must also work toward an event in September that will be attended by both President Carter and Ted Kennedy. I think we can do it if we work hard. I'm sure the President would be willing, and if we can create a context that would make the Senator comfortable—perhaps a memorial to some "traditional" Democrats—Haddad should be able to persuade him to help.[1]

SUNDAY, JULY 18, 1982

It's not easy to keep one's perspective in the kinetic and frenetic life of a campaign. It helps to pause for these diary notes. It's useful to step back from the canvas.

I would guess that I am somewhere around 10% behind Koch right now. That's probably an accurate guess as to the polls. The polls are apt to be off, however. For example, if you assume an intense interest and resulting vote from groups like the disabled, unions and Blacks—that would not be reflected in the polls. In any event, I still believe I have to play catch-up.

The most serious problem for my side is that Koch will have perhaps three times as much money to spend on television.

The only way I can win is by outthinking them or outlucking them. I will try very hard to outthink them, and I will pray that we outluck them.

I have a limitation on my ability to outthink them: we won't switch positions to succeed. That's not morality: it's my belief that unless I have my credibility intact as Governor I will not be able to function efficiently.

How, then, do we proceed?

Roughly, like this:

The Mayor has no good rationale for running other than that he wants to be promoted.

The Mayor's case is simple: "I have successful executive experience; Cuomo doesn't."

[1]We were never able to arrange this: Kennedy remained neutral, and Carter never appeared for me in New York.

Cuomo's position should not be to match him experience for experience. I must beat him by showing I am competent and I am different from him because I am a traditional Democrat, I don't waffle, I have specific ideas and a vision.

That's the case. Here's how we make it.

First we get it down into a kernel:

NO ONE KNOWS THE WHOLE STATE BETTER, NO ONE CAN HELP THE WHOLE STATE MORE. AND HE WILL DO IT ON THE BASIS OF TRADITIONAL DEMOCRATIC PRINCIPLES, WHICH HE HAS CONVERTED INTO SPECIFIC IDEAS THAT ARE TRADITIONAL AND DEMOCRATIC.

The kernel should be the essence of commercials, releases, endorsements.

1. Specifically, we have releases like our Upstate Cabinet,[1] MTA[2] and Police[3] all stressing experience, traditional Democratic principles and concrete proposals. And this week, with the Police Chiefs, I'll emphasize, in addition to everything else, jobs.
2. Endorsements from labor, women, Blacks, disabled, ethnics. Use a visual to demonstrate build-up of coalition.
3. Continue to challenge Koch to debates.
4. Work to deflect his approach by getting my own approach out as a preemptive strike. A print ad to be given out at a press conference is a good idea.

THURSDAY, JULY 22, 1982

It's like a cowboy movie I saw a long time ago. The small band of settlers, led by the single white hat capable of shooting straight and willing to try, resists wave after wave of attack from the black

[1] A collection of upstate elected officials who will ensure that the upstate agenda is respected.

[2] The Metropolitan Transportation Authority, as currently set up, takes dollars from the state, then says it doesn't need to consider the state in spending the money—for example, by buying foreign steel when New York steelworkers are out of work. I proposed that the MTA be abolished.

[3] Congressman Mario Biaggi had proposed a "Superfund," to be created by a payroll tax in New York City, that would pay for more police. I supported it; eventually Koch did, too.

hats and Indians. But with each attack they lose a settler or two and there seems less likelihood they will be able to hold out. It's a matter of numbers.

We have overcome all the obstacles—so far. But it has cost us. We have only $500,000 left for television, and the black hats may have as much as $3 million. Wave after wave they will come. Their commercials will say MMC has no record, until people believe it. They will say Koch saved the City, until people believe it. They will take positions, as though they had positions. And people will believe them. The danger is that it's a matter of numbers.

I don't remember how the movie came out. And I don't know how this will come out. But I expect we will need something new and unpredictable to win, just as the movie would have required a *deus ex machina* to save the settlers. It does not seem likely that their television can do anything but help them. Unless my limited television produces dramatically better results with less exposure (not a likely prospect), it will simply move Koch further ahead. Nor does it seem likely that the campaign—aside from television—can make the big difference. Television will dominate.

It is frustrating not to be able to get the message across because it's a matter of numbers. Of course, I may just be sanctimonious about it all. It may just be that he's better for the position of Governor than I am, and that I'm deluding myself. But I don't believe it. And that makes it frustrating.

And it's harder to keep away the unhappy thoughts. Like the guilt at knowing that Andrew and Matilda and Maria and Madeline are working day and night to win. Along with all of our wonderful friends. Knowing that Margaret has to do the planning for her wedding and Chris has to find ways to occupy himself—without the rest of us, for the most part, although Matilda is doing what she can to help Margaret.

It slows you down.

But not for long. Because you remember it's part of the test, part of the preparation, for getting ready to serve. The fatigue, the discouragements, the unhappiness are all together a precursor of what's to come as Governor. If one can't deal with this, surely it is foolish to think that one could serve as Governor.

How to deal with it, then?

By facing it, admitting it and responding to it by working harder. If the problem is Koch's television, we must find a way to overcome it with ours, and by other means available to us. We must find a way to anticipate what he will say and refute it with an intelligent message that sticks.

What will he say? "I saved the City. Brought back jobs. Started construction. Now I'm needed more in New York State because the power is moving to Albany. I've always been successful; I'll be successful again." What do we say?

Tonight a group of us tried answering the question. We spent about four hours, and the net result was that everyone agreed I should write a 60-second commercial called "Differences" that I've been playing with in my head for a couple of days. There was a lot of teasing about my winding up with the assignment of doing it myself.

SUNDAY, JULY 25, 1982

All day yesterday in Syracuse and Buffalo.

Sometimes I think it's easier to understand Teilhard when you're running 3 or 4 miles. I wish I had more time to do it. I did manage to squeeze in a run today, but it was the first time this week. It's a good feeling. Using the muscles and the will so exhaustingly that it's hard to be distracted. It's "being," dramatically. And between the exhilaration of using myself physically and the rest from tortured thought, it does me as much good as most of the sleep I get—maybe more.

I wrote two more commercials today. Carolyn Walsh, Hank Bersani and Tonio Burgos thought they sounded O.K. Andrew and Haddad have reservations. The visuals will make a great deal of difference, but I think the content is right. One makes the case for my record by assuming it. Instead of trying to prove it bit-of-experience by bit-of-experience, which would get outmatched by Koch, I've simply said that everyone says I have a great record. It's a 10-second show of bravado that may work. Both commercials also describe the differences between us in philosophy and in fidelity to "Democratic" notions. I think I'll go with what I have now—the three women, the crime commercial, the definition and the bio.[1] These will be followed with 10-second snippets, each of which will be headed by the screen quoting the Buffalo *Evening News* saying Cuomo has a flair for "bold and innovative ideas"—giving a different idea each time. Five should be enough.[2]

I'll talk to Cohen directly about these so as to save time. Having to do things by committee has slowed us down too much.

Reports have it that Koch will be repeating three themes in his commercials. "Cuomo has no record"; death penalty; "Cuomo will be a spoiler." All attacks and negative. I think it indicates his addiction to the polls. I'm especially interested in his "spoiler" comments—that probably means he's nervous about being regarded as a "disloyal" Democrat. I therefore should make the most of that in my commercials.

WEDNESDAY, JULY 28, 1982

I spent most of the last couple of days trying to write commercials with Harvey. I'm not satisfied, but we film anyway tomorrow because Koch is already on the air.

Koch is spending a lot of time upstate. Pete Piscatelli has said publicly that they have the "Jewish vote," which predominates down here, so they can afford to concentrate elsewhere. He may be right, but he made a mistake saying it.

When you look at how big the Jewish vote is and assume it's in Koch's corner, it's hard to see how I can win. What I need to do is to remember that extrapolations from statistics in past races are not all that accurate. I'm better off concentrating on the Gannett poll and people like Bob Sullivan who seem to think I have an excellent chance. And I'm still better off concentrating on who I think *should* win.

---

[1]The "three women" commercial featured Matilda, my daughter Margaret and my mother all explaining why I would make a good governor. The "crime commercial" showed the place where Matilda and Christopher had been mugged. "Definition" had me describing the difference between any "true" Democratic philosophy and my opponent's departures from it. The "bio" was a quick description of me as a mediator, secretary of state, lieutenant governor and problem solver.

[2]The "10-second snippets" were never made.

Today is the *Times* debate. Free-swinging, issue-oriented, I suspect. I've prepared for it for a lifetime. All I need to do is remember the points I want to make—my experience, my philosophy, my ideas—and stay cool.

I see today as the official beginning of the last third of the campaign—after the launching and survival of the political test, now the fight for public approval. I have been going at about 80% of capacity. I will move it up now to 90.

Later

The debate was grueling. Koch tried to make it appear that I had changed my mind on abortion, which I never have—it was *Roe v. Wade* that changed the law.[1]

Despite his preparation, he blundered on subjects like the referendum provision of the state constitution—which he seemed to misunderstand—and how pension funds are invested. I'm not sure how much of it was picked up by the print media.

I had lunch with Abe Rosenthal of the *Times* after the debate. He concluded both Koch and I are men of "quality." I said if that's what the voters concluded, I should win, because the only way to keep us both is to vote for me. At the outset of the campaign, I argued with Roger Green that this logic would be the key. Caddell now feels I may be right ultimately, but that it's premature to use the logic until I establish myself as a more identifiable quantity through television. We'll see.

SATURDAY, JULY 31, 1982

A.M.

On the way to Elmira for the American La France parade,[1] then on to Albany.

Enthusiastic meeting in Nassau with volunteers. It's clear that although Koch has the more popular side of most of the issues,

---

[1] By declaring a woman's constitutional right to an abortion under certain circumstances.

---

[1] Part of a two-day celebration of the hundredth anniversary of the American La France Company, manufacturers of fire engines in Elmira, New York.

my side generally raises the commitment level higher. There seems to be more intensity in people who will march for a nuclear freeze or take on the crowd by being against the death penalty. And the unions that are with us are strong. This intensity factor will be important on primary day.

My visit to the St. Rocco's feast[2] was interesting. I wasn't well recognized. Once people knew who I was, I was warmly—although certainly not wildly—received. There is no question that Koch still has the benefit of superior recognition. It will be interesting to see how much difference the TV will make. If I'm lucky, it won't say much new about Koch but will add a favorable impression of MMC that many haven't yet dealt with. On this score I'm troubled by the television spots we've made. I've rewritten every one we did—at least in part. So far we've settled for messages that will say "family," "reasonably tough on crime," "women," "different from Koch," "some newspapers say he's good." We'll decide on Monday which to use.

P.M.

A couple of days ago, Bernie Ryan,[3] in response to a question, told a small class at SUNY at Albany how I had thrown a policeman out of my campaign office in 1977 because he was making allegations concerning Koch's sexual orientation. Dicker got the story and made a front-page item of it. I'd rather the subject had not come up again. We'll never know exactly what impact it will have, but I'm sure Koch will exploit it to pretend he's being "victimized" again. It's the most predictable part of his strategy.

I saw Erastus Corning yesterday in Albany, where he's hospitalized. He spoke more intimately to me than he ever has. I was distressed to see him: forty or so pounds lighter; the purple marks of transfusions in both arms; struggling for breath occasionally—but energetic, almost exuberant. He pointed out that in his entire adulthood he had not had this long a period—now about seven weeks—to think, to adjust his perspective. He had concluded that he had spent too much time reacting to stimuli. He felt he had been so occupied "putting out fires," "dealing

[2]Annual celebration of the saint's feast day, in Sunset Park, Brooklyn.
[3]Guest lecturer, and a volunteer in my campaign.

with situations imposed from outside," that he hadn't done enough of the things he wanted to. He suggested I profit from his experience. It's worth thinking about.

SUNDAY, AUGUST 1, 1982

All day in Orange County, first at the State Fair, then a Democratic picnic and finally a $20 fund-raiser. While it was of dubious political utility, it was a great old-fashioned bit of politicking. I shook a couple of hundred hands and danced and kissed babies. I liked it; I liked the people.

With all of the intense activity, it was still difficult to keep my mind from wrestling with the problem of how to deal with the television campaign. Now that Koch's ads are on and we know what he's saying, we have to make the best judgments possible as to where we should go.

Spoke with Stern tonight. He had seen rushes of the commercials Cohen is making and for the most part he liked them.

MONDAY, AUGUST 2, 1982

In the tired moments, the temptation is to duck. On mornings like this one, after two or three hours of sleep, looking forward to a grilling at the AFL-CIO, being told the polls are worse, every negative is seen out of proportion, every challenge seems more severe, the course longer and more arduous. It's a time for reflection, but even that grows more difficult.

Unless one is careful, this feeling communicates itself, first to those nearest, then to the media and eventually to the world.

So I make a special effort. Teilhard, some quiet thought. Remembering the importance of giving, doing, trying. Remembering vanity and where it's found. Looking forward to privacy. Trying hard not to grow mentally tired.

All of this on the way to the AFL-CIO Executive Committee meeting. I can't afford to lose their endorsement, especially since Koch doesn't expect to win it.

In his presentation, Koch argued his record. He was supremely confident. He said, in effect, that he is going to win the election and they had better be with him—or else! He answered a few questions, then he left. Paul Curran spoke next. Then Cuomo.

I was better than I had been for a while. I took Koch's record apart. The Committee loved it. Later this afternoon I discovered they voted for me with only two dissents—the International Longshoremen's Association and the Operating Engineers. This is a recommendation to the Convention only, but it is a big win.

Frank Barbaro was in. We will cross-endorse,[1] and he will help. Another win.

THURSDAY, AUGUST 5, 1982

I spent 15 hours campaigning in Westchester yesterday. I'm not sure we reached a lot of voters, but we did well with the people we talked to.

I'm more and more convinced that what people want is simple. Before everything else, they want to believe in something uplifting, pure, good. The vacuum I've sensed for years is more obvious to me now than ever. It is frustrating, because I'm afraid it requires more than I can offer, although occasionally we do appear to reach people.

It happened yesterday a couple of times. First in Harrison, alongside the Hudson, at a lovely "heroes and wine" party. An elegant, white-haired, Rockefeller-faced Republican woman said she had come just to hear me speak. She was with her son, who was an artist of some type, and an elderly lady friend of hers. They all appeared to have come out of curiosity. When I told them I hadn't planned to speak but just to shake hands and chat a bit with individuals, they were disappointed and even a little indignant.

I believe they felt they had been misled. So I spoke—without form—about things that are basic, like a nuclear freeze that says only that peace is better than war because life is better than death; about wanting people to have opportunity; about the

---

[1] Frank was running for reelection to the state assembly.

importance of courage—Winston Churchill's quote, "Never give up," and about Momma never giving up. I told them that I was eager to see whether we could go a whole campaign telling the truth as we see it—even about the death penalty—and still win.

When I finally finished, some of the many middle-aged and older Italians, who didn't understand all of what I'd said, were crying. Some hugged—even kissed—me. I was a 50-year-old candidate who became everybody's son.

The elegant lady took the microphone from me at the conclusion of my remarks and uttered a better speech than I had—about having come to be shown and having been shown. She said she was a Republican but would wait until November and then vote for me. She said, "It's nice to be able to vote for somebody who believes in something—even if I don't agree with all of it."

FRIDAY, AUGUST 6, 1982

I spent a day with the elite, the great trainers and owners of our growing horse-racing industry in Saratoga. It's a beautiful track and it was a lovely day.

Bill Levin[1] and Jerry Weiss reported later that the people I met would be willing to make contributions. Jerry expects the campaign to get about $30,000. Who says you can't make money at the track!

SATURDAY, AUGUST 7, 1982

The hay fever season begins. It's annoying. If you take antihistamines, you get groggy; if you don't, you feel worse. It's a small annoyance by itself, but added to other provocations, it can edge you into mistakes.

The Women's Caucus in Manhattan gave the Mayor and me the opportunity to be heard separately. Some "plants" were especially unpleasant, deliberately provocative. If I had been

[1]President of Gold Mills, a New York City textile manufacturer.

better prepared and better rested, I might have handled it better —I was angry and hostile in return. But added to everything else, the three-hour drive down from Saratoga and Albany before my appearance left me vulnerable. The Mayor's police helicopter gives him an edge.

I made a good point that I should have made sooner. By arguing that the "New Federalism" requires him to move to Albany, the Mayor is collaborating with it. My posture is to call on him to attack it, not to acquiesce in it.

I also pointed out that I believed the Mayor's jobs commercial is inaccurate.[1] It's important to rebut the ad because it's an effective one that gets at a core issue in a powerful way. I think Garth made a mistake by making the ad vulnerable.

The rest of the day was with Blacks in Baisley Park, Italians in Brooklyn and the White middle-class of Woodhaven at a concert in the park. They all seem to have one thing in common —their desire for the death penalty. Again, the fragility of my political support is obvious. Dedicated liberals suspect me because I'm a Catholic; the Italians and the other middle-class ethnics are put off by my position on the death penalty.

SUNDAY, AUGUST 8, 1982

One thing is for sure, the difference between reality and the communicated perception is unpredictable. The newspaper stories and TV accounts today were all favorable to me. More than that, Garth replied to my TV criticism of his ad, in the *Daily News*.[1] That's a break, and we will have to make the most of it. I will do what I can to keep the argument alive over the next few days.

---

[1]Koch's commercials claimed that New York City gained jobs for New York City residents. In fact, the increase in jobs was due to an increase in the service sector, and for the most part those employees live outside New York City.

---

[1]Garth responded as follows: "As far as taking credit for these things, if, in fact, something happened in the city that was negative, I am quite sure that Mario would be happy to hang it around the mayor's neck." He also said federal statistics support claims made in the job-gains commercial and said his balanced-budget TV spot noted that Koch "led the fight" to balance the city's books.

I went to the Brighton Beach Baths. I never saw so much burnt skin. All of it oiled and creamed. These people voted against me about 8 to 1 in the last election. Many of them are still fierce on the subject of the death penalty, but I sensed less of the alienation, suspicion and hostility that I experienced in 1977.

Hy Cohen[2] allowed me to speak from the stage. At the conclusion of my remarks, I told the audience that I had passed a card game and asked the four players, "Who's winning?" They told me, "We are all winning!" The audience laughed. I told them, "Don't laugh; there's a game that we can all play and win. This year's election is such a game. Those of you who want Koch can have Koch. Those of you who want Cuomo can have Cuomo. All you have to do is vote for Cuomo for Governor and you get Koch for Mayor." A lot of them laughed again. That's all I wanted to hear.

After Brighton Beach I was with Coretta King and Carl McCall in Coney Island.[3] They were both gracious and I tried to be as well. It produced some good pictures.

After that Andrew and I drove to Lake Hopatcong, where for the first time in a couple of weeks all of us (except Margaret) were in one place at one time. I don't like thinking that this will occur less and less frequently in the future. If only it had occurred more frequently in the past.

MONDAY, AUGUST 9, 1982

I got up at 5 A.M. and wrote a speech on the "New Federalism" by 7. I used it to welcome the Council on State Government to Rye. It went well.

I was feisty in Rochester and spent too much time attacking Koch.

The press still doesn't think I can win.

[2]Owner of Brighton Beach Baths, community leader and my friend.
[3]At a spiritual crusade held by the Coney Island Improvement Association, with the object of getting the community involved in voter registration and community concerns. Mrs. King was the keynote speaker.

Tuesday, August 10, 1982

I was endorsed by Assemblyman Ed Sullivan, Senator Leon
Bogues and Assemblywoman Geraldine Daniels. It's the beginning of a whole wave of Black endorsements. I think they are
coming at just the right time.

Wednesday, August 11, 1982

Gene Spagnoli prepared what I thought was a clever and effective device to attract attention to the inaccuracies in Koch's television commercials—"A Guide to TV Guile." It was
pocket-sized, attractive and punchy. We were lucky—we thought
—to have a good turnout at the press conference, especially from
the TV stations. But last night the 5th person to be executed
since the death penalty was restored in 1976 died in the Virginia
electric chair. Roger Sharp of Channel 7 couldn't resist asking
me about it, and I couldn't resist a long answer. The result was
that our story was replaced by death penalty stories everywhere,
and Gene Spagnoli's good work went down the drain. It was the
kind of impolitic move—allowing myself to be engaged by
Sharp's question—that Koch probably wouldn't have made.

Thursday, August 12, 1982

Denny Farrell set up a meeting with minority lawyers this morning. They were bright, attractive and interested. I enjoyed going
back and forth with them, and I think they enjoyed the exchange,
too.

  This evening I met with a group of Venerables from the Sons
of Italy at the Per Sempre Lodge in Rosedale. It went extremely
well—but then, most of my personal appearances have—this
time.

FRIDAY, AUGUST 13, 1982

All our people thought I had won the debate today at WGBB on Long Island. A poll was taken immediately after the show. The Station Manager later admitted that the Koch people may have known about it and been prepared. We didn't, and weren't. I would never have agreed to the debate if I had known about the poll, since the listeners—in the middle of the day—were Republicans or well-to-do. They said Koch won 59–41, and the station announced it.

That made the rest of the day more difficult, but not intolerable. More and more Koch's conduct indicates to me that he doesn't think he's doing well. I have no way of knowing the truth, but if I had to judge—by his testiness, mostly—I'd say he's not too confident. I don't think he ever expected a real challenge. He was conditioned to believe it would be a coronation.

I finished the day at a Glen Cove rally for Solidarity.[1] Only a couple of hundred people showed up, but I felt very good about being there.

SATURDAY, AUGUST 14, 1982

A good meeting with Al Vann and some of his people. I was comfortable with them and I believe they are beginning to be comfortable with me.

A not-so-good meeting in Harlem. Few people showed up. It was a demonstration of the weakness in much of the Black political organization outside of pockets like Vann's and Arthur Eve's.

Delightful trip in the afternoon to beautiful Dutchess, then Ulster. Up the Palisades. What a delight to see! The mood continued through the Italian American cocktail party of 125 or so Friends. A lot of them were Republicans who can only help in November,[1] and it was physically grueling—but I enjoyed it.

[1] At this affair the Polish American Congress both honored Lech Wałęsa and the banned Polish union movement, Solidarity, and focused attention on the Russians' role in Poland—the Russian delegation to the UN has its residential compound in Glen Cove.

[1] In New York State, there is no crossing of party lines in the primaries. Hence Republicans so inclined could only vote for me in the general election in November.

Late today I was told Koch was releasing a long document attacking me for misstatements. He must be in trouble. But still the press doesn't think I can win.

SUNDAY, AUGUST 15, 1982

I spoke to my mother today. She is generally confused by all of this. She does not like the idea that I make people unhappy with things I say and do, even if I make other people happy at the same time.

She and Poppa never got over the Depression. There are still a lot of people like them in Bensonhurst and Jackson Heights and even living comfortably in Manhasset. People who remember the Depression, who remember villages in Europe where they could barely scratch a living out of the bad soil; people whose grandest personal aspiration would be to have their own roof over their head, a little something to eat when they were older and couldn't raise it for themselves, and money put aside for a decent funeral. All they want for their kids is security—they should be well; they should be safe; they should have a job; they should stay home and make no trouble. Of course she's confused by her son's name appearing everywhere—being contradicted, condemned. Actually, she wishes I had never left the law firm. I knew this from the beginning of my public life. Momma and Poppa were troubled by the idea of my running for office. I was able to console them by saying that it was the only way I could get to be a judge. They would have liked that—14 years in a robe, safe, with a job, and making no trouble.

What a magnificent piece of work she is, Momma. I'll never forget her advice to me in 1977 when she tried to talk me into the death penalty because she was afraid I would lose the election because of it and also because she thought I was wrong on the question. As a matter of fact, Momma and a lot of other people like her were born to believe that an eye for an eye was not an overstatement. She has no difficulty accepting the death penalty. I won't even write down on this page what she suggests for sex criminals.

In 1977 she came to me and told me I better change my opinion. I told her no. We argued about it a bit, then she said,

"You gonna loosa." And I said, I'm afraid unctuously, "I'd
rather lose than sell out on this." She thought about it for a while
and said, "You don't have to loosa. You listen to me! You tell
thema you changea you mind, you wanna the electric chair.
Then, after you win . . ." And here she made an ancient Italian
gesture, flicking the bottom of the chin, with two fingers; throwing out the whole hand, palm open, waving to a whole world,
saying in effect, "After the election, to h——— with them!" From
anybody else I would call it cynical; from Momma, it's the way
she's made it through 80 years of labor and pain.

MONDAY, AUGUST 16, 1982

On the way to Rochester, our flight was nearly an hour late in
taking off. It will throw off the day's schedule and reminds me
of the advantages of wealth—Koch can go to Rochester in a Lear
jet.

It's difficult to believe there are fewer than 6 weeks to go.
We're into the last 40 days. This is the final stage. I would guess
that more decisions will be made by voters from here on in than
have been made so far. There's something intimidating about
knowing that. It means that you cannot take comfort in all that
you've done already. But there's also something hopeful—it
means that, whatever has been done, you still have a chance to
change things.

The only thing I'm sure of is that I don't know how well—or
poorly—we're doing. All sorts of impressions are received by the
people around me. Some of them I share, some of them I don't.
The polls haven't spoken for a few weeks and probably would
be less reliable than usual now, in the summer doldrums, when
people appear to be paying less attention. So it's really impossible
to know. On the other hand, it's necessary to make assumptions
because strategy is based on the effect of action, or at least the
presumed effect.

I am guessing that we are doing better at becoming an acceptable alternative to Koch for those who haven't yet fully made up
their minds. The television—paid and news—has helped. News
exposure is more effective, and although I haven't been covered

the way Koch has been, my appearances—at Brighton Baths, at the Women's Caucus, at the debates—have been mostly helpful. Our commercials have also been well received. They are not sensational, but they appear to have cast me as a sober, responsible, "gubernatorial" presence. The fact that I wrote most of the words has helped create a feeling of authenticity. I've heard that said many times—as recently as this morning, when 2 young people from an ad agency that works for Kodak made the observation in the airport.

The debates, too, have helped. The general tone—for the few who are paying attention—had me appearing issue-oriented and comfortable. Our weakness has been the print media.

A totally unscientific test for how we're doing is the reaction our volunteers are getting on the streets. Madeline, Maria, Matilda all say the same thing—it's much better than '77. Al Gordon and Tony Menna agree.[1] There appears to be little hostility for me and a strong sense that Koch has been disloyal in planning to abandon the City.

Carolyn Walsh and others who are inclined to be issue-oriented feel that I have still not defined myself in terms of issues clearly enough. The problem is, as she sees it, that while I talk constantly about the issues, I haven't been associated with any in an identifiable way for the public at large. She wants me to select 3 or 4 and make them trademarks. She agreed that Reaganomics, Koch's penchant for real estate special interests, jobs and the future might be enough.

I agree that I am not immediately associated with any issue or issues except perhaps the death penalty. That's because I've refused to eliminate a lot of issues which I believe are relevant in order to achieve the kind of focus Carolyn suggests. Should I? I'm not sure. It may be that my scattershot, diverse, constant reference to "all" the issues creates an impression of its own that's good. I know I'm more comfortable that way—I always have been. Even writing the hundreds of briefs I argued as a lawyer, I preferred arguing large numbers of issues to reducing

---

[1] Al and Tony were volunteers who had also been loyal volunteers all through the 1977 campaign and were well equipped to see the differences.

them to the 3 or 4 points a court would find reasonably digest-
ible.

We'll have to make the decision over the next few days, because we need to make more commercials for the next phase.

As usual, Louise Slaughter was terrific. If I had someone like
her everywhere, it would make a big difference. She thinks I was
received well by the ministers.[2]

TUESDAY, AUGUST 17, 1982

I am close to a mistake. The fatigue is manifesting itself. I had
to strain to make my delivery to the WCBS-TV editorial board,
and I tend to overreact. I haven't been able to keep the kind of
schedule I wanted—with time for exercise—and it's showing.

I tried tonight to do some reading for tomorrow's debate but
couldn't rouse myself to do anything more than a superficial
review.

WEDNESDAY, AUGUST 18, 1982

All my people told me I won the debate at the Buffalo *Courier-
Express*—"better on the issues, looked better; he was arrogant."
If they were telling me what they thought was the truth, they
were wrong. I think it was just the reverse. Koch is effective with
his insistence that he has a record and I have none. I have been
troubled by that from the beginning and have found no good
"formula" way to establish what I believe is actually an excellent
record.

In the afternoon I was interviewed on Channel 4 in Buffalo by
Allen Constantini and Marie Rice. Constantini had a question
about Koch people offering to have me run for Mayor and
paying for my campaign. I said friends of Koch had asked me to
run for Mayor—but I said no because it made more sense for me
to be Governor and him to be Mayor. Constantini elaborated

[2]For the speech to the ministers, see pp. 446–48.

that into a charge that they had tried to bribe me! Koch is off the wall. It's one of those things.

I was at the Lockport Police picnic with Mayor Tom Rotondo, and the North Tonawanda Democrats' "Rally" of 75 people or so with Jim Rogers, Chairman of Niagara County. I enjoy being with these small groups, and I'm sure it makes some difference in the vote, although perhaps not enough to justify the visits. I do it mostly because I want very much for people like Rotondo and Rogers to know how grateful I am for their support.

THURSDAY, AUGUST 19, 1982

The *Courier-Express* says in an editorial that Koch won the debate.

A beautiful Chautauqua and Cattaraugus made the middle of this day a joy. Dr. Barone's house and family are memorable.[1] On hills above Chautauqua Lake in a lovely residential part of this county of farms and families and hamlets we knelt at the Statue of St. Jude that Dr. Barone brought back from Italy. It was pure Carrara marble: the Barones' faith seemed just as solid.

FRIDAY, AUGUST 20, 1982

Conjunctivitis has given me, literally, "blood in the eye." I tried to get some rest today after the return from Buffalo, but I had to go to a fund-raiser early this morning, then do interviews with John Mahacek[1] and Art Greenspan before a television half-hour with Gabe Pressman.

This is still the most difficult race to analyze that I've ever been close to. Most of the inside people agree. Caddell says he has to go more on "instinct" than usual. The issues are not sharply defined; the image of Cuomo is still fuzzy. I hear generally about "momentum" and "good feelings," but the sentiments are not

---

[1]Dr. Anthony C. Barone, a physician and Democratic chairman of Chautauqua County, endorsed me early and remained a stalwart supporter throughout.

---

[1]Of the Gannett papers in Rochester, now asssigned to Washington.

measurable. I am dissatisfied with my efforts to define myself and my differences with Koch. The truth is, I have more knowledge of State problems: I think a better capacity to negotiate and a more consistent philosophy. All these things are tough to say and not necessarily persuasive to the lay public even when they are said clearly. On the other hand, Koch is a master of simple and effective communication—like "Mario has no record!" I need to think more about how to handle the communications.

SATURDAY, AUGUST 21, 1982

I went to the dentist this morning. I think he's working for Koch!

Between him and my conjunctivitis and the hay fever, I decided this was a good time to catch up on my reading and writing.

First thing this morning, I thought up a release—a call on Koch to disendorse the Republicans and to take a pledge to serve a full 4 years as Governor. I'm eager to see how it gets received. I need to take the initiative away from Koch on the party loyalty question. With that in mind, I put the emphasis on "principles" instead of party. That may mean a great deal more *after* the primary.

From the beginning I have said that I thought the election would be decided by 2 or 3 unpredictable events. One may have occurred today. Koch suddenly pulled his commercials and went with one showing Cuomo endorsing him in 1981 and Koch saying in effect, "See! I am a strong voice against Reaganomics"; that's what Mario "said in 1981." The commercial finished with a "You were right, Mario, and he'll do the same thing for New York State!"

My first impression is that Koch thinks he is in trouble or he wouldn't be going with this now. No one puts the other guy's name and face on TV, especially when he has lower recognition! Each time Koch has been threatened, he has responded fiercely, as though afraid another punch would put him away. That's what happened after the first debate, when he came back with Cabin.

I have always felt that there is a vulnerability somewhere in the heart of the Koch candidacy—a fragility of rationale which, when attacked, would bring his candidacy down dramatically. I think they sense this, too. Obviously, they are worried about Reaganomics as an attack. They were also stung by my "Thanks, Ed—and we'll work together!" commercial.[1]

I've instructed my people to get it out to the press that we're pleased by the Koch move. It is evidence of his concern. It dignifies "Reaganomics" as an issue. And it allows me to reconcile the two positions by saying, "Cuomo for Governor (Koch said he'd be 'great'); Koch for Mayor (Cuomo says we need his loud voice)."

We'll think hard on it tonight.

SUNDAY, AUGUST 22, 1982

A birthday cake at the Queens Headquarters was the best we could manage for Madeline's 18th birthday. Actually, it's not until tomorrow, but we won't be together then. Andrew was busy at the campaign, Maria was out on the Island and Margaret at work at the hospital. Chris and I and Matilda were there for 20 minutes for so. I couldn't help thinking again how much the family gives up to make this kind of effort.

I spent the whole rest of the day trying to get my eye clear and generally get some rest and exercise. It's extraordinary how quickly people notice signs of fatigue in the candidate. It doesn't win the candidate sympathy; it begets, instead, a lack of confidence and a sense of the candidate failing. Again, it's the perception that counts.

So, too, with Koch's new wave of negative commercials. With five weeks still to go, they should create the perception that he is worried. Garth is trying to offset that by saying that he's 10 to 12 points ahead. I don't believe him, but maybe he can make it happen by saying so. We need to decide how to respond. I prefer to let a few days pass before deciding.

---

[1] In which I pointed out that he had three times said I would make a "great governor."

Monday, August 23, 1982

6:30 A.M. The hours before my world wakes are the ones I enjoy most. A retreat. A time for thought, for reflection, for planning, for measuring. You can feel all the things the crowded day doesn't allow you to feel.

This morning I sat with Ginger[1] on the cold stone of the porch under the great oak tree that stands, like a guard, right up against the front of the house; looked up through the branches to snatches of gray sky growing black. I noticed that I have more difficulty now seeing clearly, even across the street. I used to think it was just a matter of needing some rest or the temporary effect of hay fever. Now it's clear that it's more than that. It's what Teilhard calls part of the "diminishment" against which we struggle but which is inevitable. It's part of growing older and weaker and, finally, surrendering breath for new life. Understanding that, experiencing it, living it—while life ebbs (who knows at what pace)—is the "Divine Milieu."

The rains come suddenly out of the gray sky grown black. Ginger scampers back up against the house under the eave to shelter herself. I feel the rain on my arms and legs and look up, eyes closed, to feel it on my face. Ginger doesn't think of it as good, only as uncomfortable or dangerous. I can see the black sky and know that it is the color of sustenance for the whole world we live in now. I think of the wonder of rain that destroys with floods but also feeds the soil and the people who till it. I think again of the diminishment of death that ends the symphony of experiences, feelings, emotions, acts that make up life, but only to open the way to a new and fuller existence. I think how everything can be seen that way. That there is no evil or pain that does not, somehow, become part of the ultimate working out of things. That what we see as an ugly flaw or scar in the stone of our existence—the death too soon, the pain undeserved, the disappointment, the failure, the shame, the rejection—becomes part of the overall sculpture of our existence. I think of how our existence is molded around the flaw, shaped by it, formed by it, made more beautiful by it, at least for those who learn to see. For

[1]Our dog. A mutt, like me. But prettier.

those who learn to see clearly, as they notice they are losing the power to identify shapes moving across the street from the porch and the huge oak.

TUESDAY, AUGUST 24, 1982

There was a great deal of press on the publication of the campaign contribution list. Koch has taken millions in contributions from people who do business with him in the City. If it weren't for the extraordinary reputation for integrity that he's developed, he would be condemned for accepting them. Indeed, he gave back contributions to realtor Sandy Lindenbaum in 1977, saying he felt it was wrong to take them. Tonight, Gabe Pressman went after Koch and pointed out that he was receiving money from the very developers involved in Lincoln West.[1] Koch said it was legal and that he was going ahead with it. I intend to say the following on Lincoln West:

"The Mayor has raised an important question. He says it is legal for him to receive thousands of dollars from people who are directly involved in a matter, and having received that money, to vote on that same matter (perhaps casting the critical vote). I say that is a question that must be tested. I call upon Mayor Koch to hold off his vote until it can be legally tested. I go further and say, if it is legal, surely we need a new law. And as Governor, I will see that one is adopted."

On the general matter of campaign contributions, I got off what I think are two effective lines. "Koch spent $2 million to lose 35 points.[2] His next million dollars spent should make me a winner." The other was: "If he's gone negative, it must mean he's in trouble. Only in the movies do you shoot at somebody behind you." These are more than just cute: they communicate important messages, and I've discovered much of this process is a matter of quick and memorable communication.

I got some good news today—a happy first.

---

[1] A proposal for a huge real estate development on the west side of Manhattan. It required various approvals from the city of New York.

[2] At the beginning of the campaign some people had said I was thirty-five points behind. Now everyone conceded we were closer.

A reporter and columnist who has credentials and a good reputation actually predicted my victory. Jim Flateau of Ottaway News Service, basically an upstate wire service, said he thought that despite the polls at the moment, I would eventually win. Although not many of the papers who subscribe to Ottaway thought enough of the prediction to print it, the Associated Press thought it was enough of an oddity to deserve a story about the prediction. Marc Humbert of AP wrote it, and it has been carried by papers upstate. I'm sure Marc doesn't believe it, but I do. And it helps. Smart guy, that Flateau!

WEDNESDAY, AUGUST 25, 1982

Heavy rains slowed traffic so badly I was an hour late for a meeting with the N.Y. Board of Rabbis, but Rabbi Hait, Rabbi Kahn and a few others were accommodating enough to wait. The session was a taping of answers to their questions on the race. The transcript will be circulated to some 1,200 Rabbis in the metropolitan area. It should help me. I'm beginning to get the feeling that this time I won't get devastated in the Jewish community the way I was in '77.

One of the most important meetings of the campaign followed the Barbaro endorsement. I had two and a half hours with Bob Hunt, Jim Wieghart and Jack Smee of the *News*. Haddad and Gene Spagnoli were with me. At one point the discussion turned to the future of the newspaper, and Haddad's knowledgeability and insight were impressive. Hunt also seemed to like my "aggressive vision" for the State. They have met with Koch a few times already and I believe they are about to decide on an endorsement. It would be a heavy blow if they went with Koch.

As it would be if the AFL-CIO fails to go with me next week. Koch is going all out against me with the unions. The key is the teachers' union. I see them Friday.

Two fund-raisers tonight with Stern, small ones with Pete and Ethel Chahales in Maspeth and Susan Alter in Brooklyn.[1] If I could meet with everyone who votes in small groups like these,

---

[1] Pete and Ethel are long-time civic and political activists; Susan is a city councilwoman. All are friends of mine.

I would do much better. I keep hearing that I look better and come over better in person. It's too bad, when so much depends on television. I'll never forget the woman in 1977 who told me, "You know, Cuomo, you're not as ugly in person as you are on television." For this we're paying a million dollars!

THURSDAY, AUGUST 26, 1982

It's not yet Labor Day but the gun lap electricity has started already. Things have changed—almost everyone senses that. Now the press is not so sure about predicting Koch's victory. It's now becoming clearer to them that the race can be won by either side. Koch's change of tactics and refusal to show polls has made people feel he thinks he's in trouble. We've heard about a poll Lehrman took that showed a two-point differential in Koch's favor with most-likely voters. That amounts to a dead heat.

I can only guess as to where we are and how to proceed. I think we're within striking distance, and I think what I have to do is slow down Koch's attack on my credibility with his use of my endorsement by answering him in a commercial. But then I have to be affirmative. I have to have solutions to the problems of crime, taxes and the environment.

How about 10-second snippets—let's be positive?

That plus a bio commercial would be enough until the last week, when we should go to the "Cuomo for Governor, Koch for Mayor."

FRIDAY, AUGUST 27, 1982

It seems *Newsday* doesn't intend to cover the campaign, at least not until after Labor Day. Yesterday I had a press conference at which I discussed three issues that were of major concern to their editorial board, and today's story referred to one of the issues— a feasibility study for a proposed ferry route across the Long Island Sound—but didn't even mention my name.

I also spent a delightful hour or so with Bill and Lynn Bianchi at their beautiful home in Bellport.

The rally last night at the Patchogue Knights of Columbus was attended mostly by union people, who responded well to my speech. The speech was more emotional than usual. I am not sure why. It happens sometimes when I am tired or when we get to the basic philosophical issues of the campaign. Both things were true last night: I was tired enough to be loose and I was talking about life and death.

After the rally, I spent two grueling hours in Elmont fighting over the death penalty with a mostly Italian American audience that ranged from fierce to furious on the subject.

We made commercials this morning with representatives of the disabled community. I am not sure how the message will affect the people, but I felt good making the commercials.

At 1 o'clock I had another one of the campaign's important meetings—what will probably be the final sitdown with Shanker, Hobart and Sanders.[1] I said, in effect, that they would have access not because they support me (if they do) but because their access will be useful to me as Governor. I think they won't endorse Koch. I don't know whether they will decide to endorse me. People tell me that they can make the difference if they do.

More commercials this afternoon.

Out of the blue, a handwritten note appeared on my desk from Dino Amoroso[2] saying that an old friend of his had learned that a poll had just gone in to Koch showing that Cuomo was 3% ahead in a statewide sampling of 1,066. I am inclined not to believe it. It's safer not to believe it, although I'd rather have this kind of rumor than a more negative one.

Speaking of negative rumors. Feathers[3] just called to say that the Teachers had made a deal and were going to see that the AFL-CIO voted neutrality. That could really hurt.

And rumors have been circulated—floated, I suspect, by Garth —that Fritz Mondale is looking at Koch as a possible Vice-Presidential candidate for '84. It's a good rumor for their side. It creates all the right psychology. It treats Koch as a winner and a national figure. It also attracts some attention to the fact that

[1] Albert Shanker, Thomas Hobart and Daniel Sanders, of the New York State United Teachers (NYSUT).
[2] A member of the staff.
[3] Jim Featherstonhaugh.

Mondale has not endorsed me despite what I did for him and President Carter in '80 and what Koch did to them. Actually, while I was pleased when the President spoke out so forcefully for me, I didn't expect Fritz to. From his point of view it's too big a risk. His man Jim Johnson is close to Garth, and I'm sure they expect Koch to win. A Koch who doesn't forget those who went against him could be a real problem as Governor of New York for a presidential candidate next year. I'm not surprised that Fritz regards discretion as the better part of valor.

SATURDAY, AUGUST 28, 1982

Things are happening rapidly now. The rumor about the poll changes some things. If it is true that we have moved ahead in the polls, however slightly, it means we must reassess some decisions. One of these is the question of the commercials. Most of them have been tinged with negativism or are outright attacks. I don't like negative commercials and have felt from the beginning that my biggest problem was telling people about me and my record. Whether or not the poll rumor is totally accurate, all the evidence is that Koch is in trouble. He is telling people everywhere that he is 10 points ahead, but that's a Garth ploy, I'm sure. He believes you can create reality by pretending something is reality, and too often he's right. But the reality nevertheless is that Koch is slipping. I believe the appropriate response now is a powerful positive campaign on behalf of Cuomo—Record, Ideas, Endorsements. I talked to Cohen about that at 7 A.M. this morning. He hadn't gotten to bed till 2 A.M. because he was working on the film we shot yesterday, but he was quick to say he had the same feeling about the commercials. He's going to try to work on some positives today. Koch, in the meantime, is going back to strict positive, is my guess. I think he will pull his "Cuomo endorsement" piece—in which he shows me—any day.

A few phone calls served to clarify the situation involving Shanker. Although he didn't tell me, he's meeting with Koch on Monday. He is now planning to have his Teachers abstain at the convention, which will allow us to get ⅔ of the remainder of the vote—and that will be good enough for an endorsement. Later —after it's happened at the AFL-CIO—the Teachers will give their own endorsement for a "double bang." If that's the way it comes out, it will be great.

Ferro called to say that both the *News* and *Courier-Express* in Buffalo would probably endorse Koch because of local pressure from Crangle and Griffin. That will hurt. I called Murray Light at the *News* to see if I could do something with him. He said he was surprised at my "aggressive tone." I told him that he could expect a lot of that from me as Governor. He seemed to like it. I think Murray thinks I'm too "nice." I must get to see him before September 7th, which is about the time he'll think of endorsing.

My eye hasn't cleared yet. It continues to surprise me how many people notice and are disturbed by it. These "signals" are extremely important in the supercharged, hypersensitive campaign atmosphere.

Chris has been away this week. I miss him. I hate the idea that as Governor I won't have all the time I want for him.

SUNDAY, AUGUST 29, 1982

The pressure is on. You can feel it. The newspaper stories and analyses are more plentiful and sharper—and sometimes disappointing. Today's *Times* "Week in Review" continues to indicate Koch is a winner without mentioning the obvious shift in his tactics and the clear evidence that he is slipping badly.

In the *Daily News* and on TV, Koch has turned to an almost vicious attack. He charges "no record" and accuses me of everything that he is doing—he raises Cabin by saying I raise Smith;[1] he brings up the death penalty saying I do; he brings up the New Federalism as a reason for running and then attacks the New Federalism. And while Koch is attacking, he says, "Cuomo is

[1] Peter Smith, a former employee of the Koch administration who was convicted of a felony.

vicious." The approach is distortive and, so far, effective. Mickey Carroll suggests that Koch's use of my '81 endorsement is effective against me. I hope his saying so won't help make it so.

It's a tough business. It's especially difficult to avoid reacting emotionally to what you know are deliberately false charges and believe are pretenses. There is so much you'd like to say in response—but there's usually not the opportunity, and if there is, it's not always covered by the media. It's a real test of belief and of whether under pressure you will forget who and what you are and make the effort nothing more than an exercise in egoism.

TUESDAY, AUGUST 31, 1982

It's a good time to be philosophical. There's no one I trust more than Bob Sullivan when it comes to polling and projections. He tells me it looks as though we're still 10 points behind and it will be difficult to close the gap. As he analyzes the situation from the polls, Koch is well known and well liked by about 40–45% of the voters. The others would like an alternative, but many of them don't know enough about Cuomo to treat him as an acceptable choice. I have a vague image. I've known that for a long time. It's simply a matter of exposure. If you don't get on the 6 o'clock news at night, you're unknown —unless you're Lew Lehrman and can afford to spend 5 million dollars on TV. I had hoped that the campaign would change things, but it appears I simply haven't been able to get enough TV coverage. I've been after Haddad about it for months, but we've not had any real success in creating opportunities. My paid TV has only been on for 3 weeks, and that hasn't done the job yet. Bob feels that if everybody knew me as well as they knew Koch, I would win easily. What's happening, I suspect, is what I feared when Koch's television campaign started. His constant pounding away has built a wall that I've not been able to penetrate.

It's ironic. Last night I spent a couple of hours worrying about how to deal with the hard problems that will face the State next year. The first budget will be a killer. I wondered how long it would take all my friends, like the unions and others who have supported me, to feel let down by my inability to provide them with what they believe they deserve. I thought a lot about how unhappy a role the governor's would be and remembered Lincoln's somber mood on the night he won his last election for President. I asked myself why I was so often devoted to efforts like this one that seem to wear so hard on the psyche.

But now that Sullivan forces me to think about losing—I feel even greater trepidation. Why? Is it pride? The need to serve? The desire to serve? The fear of a whole new life style? The fear of rejection? Just part of the Divine Milieu?

In 20 minutes or so the time for nominating will be past. I'll have to deliver my address to the Convention of the AFL-CIO. I need them badly. Neutrality will be a victory for Koch. I must now function more efficiently than I have been functioning. I'll have to see Sullivan's report as a goad to greater effort. It was not encouraging, but then there are still 20% undecided and a lifetime of days to come. I will remember that and drive harder than I have so far. I'll have to hope that my television and three weeks of concentrated exposure in the period after Labor Day, when people are really paying attention, will make the difference. If I try very hard, I can choose to believe the rumors about the three-point poll in my favor instead of Sullivan's projections.

It's about 9:30 P.M. I'm at the Concord. We won everything that could be won today. No one even imagined the kinds of victories I had. My speech to the convention[1] turned them upside down.

I don't know exactly why. It wasn't as good a speech as I delivered at Syracuse, but it reached those couple of thousand or so delegates. When I left the hall amidst the tumult, there was no doubt as to who the candidate of the AFL-CIO would be if the vote were taken on the spot.

But there was still a lot of politics to be played. All morning, before and after my speech, there were rumors about what the Teachers would do. By themselves they represent 20% of the delegates. In the afternoon we were told Koch had said at City

[1]See pp. 449–54.

Hall that "neutrality" would be a big victory for him. Andrew and Norm Adler were afraid that was a signal that Shanker would fight for neutrality at their 4 P.M. caucus this afternoon. The full vote is scheduled for tomorrow. There was talk about Koch making a deal not to appeal the lifting of the checkoff ban by PERB,[2] which occurred last week.

But then, dramatically, at 5 P.M., the Teachers voted for me. Shanker indicated to the media that N.Y. City Teachers (the UFT) had suggested neutrality, but NYSUT, the state body, overwhelmed them. This victory locks up the convention for me tomorrow and is a big win.

To make it all sweeter, the SEIU (Service Employees International Union), led by Gus Bevona, disendorsed Koch and endorsed me today. A real turnaround.

But through it all, I could not feel the "thrill of victory." The 10-point barrier is at the front of my mind. I'll have to work hard not to let it show.

During the afternoon I met with the Hispanic labor leaders. Frank Marin[3] told me Matilda was "superb" at the Puerto Rican festival on Sunday.[4] She ignored the notes they supplied and spoke in Spanish. Normally, surrogates—even wives of candidates—are not received well. Not so with Matilda, according to Marin. I hear this kind of thing everywhere. Matilda has been the star of the campaign so far as street campaigning goes. And she would be the star as well on TV, if she had the opportunity. She has done this campaign as she does everything—with all her heart, with preparation, with great strength and success. I'd hate to see her be denied the victory—she deserves it. And so do the kids, who have worked just as hard. Christopher has made his contribution by trying not to let us know how lonely he's been at times. I'd hate to see it all go unrewarded . . . for them. I told Madeline that Sunday night when I kissed her good-bye on her way to the College of New Rochelle. She cried.

---

[2]The Public Employment Relations Board had penalized the teachers' union for a violation of the law by denying them their right to take dues directly out of teachers' paychecks. The process is called a checkoff.

[3]A volunteer from the Hispanic community.

[4]An annual celebration of history and culture by the Puerto Rican community of New York City, *La Fiesta Folklorica* involves the most exuberant of Fifth Avenue parades.

WEDNESDAY, SEPTEMBER 1, 1982

8:10 A.M.

It has started out like a lot of days in a campaign. Sleeping only fitfully because there are so many ideas clinging to the walls of your mind. Up at 5 A.M. to make some notes. Back to bed. Up at 6:30 for a call from Dick Starkey.[1] "Radio is saying your speech turned them around. Good story." "Thanks, Dick"—my head still on the pillow. "Anything I should do?" "No." "O.K., talk to you later." Then lying down and thinking through the Apostles' Creed in my mind—the old creed that said, "He descended into hell." Matching it up to Teilhard. Thinking about it because there won't be time the rest of the day.

I look in a mirror that every day shows me more clearly what "diminishment" means.

Andrew in the room at 7:15. I can't help feeling proud when I see him. He's done so well. He drove with me to the airport to get the plane to Rochester for the WOKR-TV debate with Koch. On the way I ask Joe Anastasi if the papers "hurt us." That's always the question. The sensitivity gets to be so bad—especially after an experience like 1977—that you're almost ready to settle for a draw with the press. "Not bad. Koch is jumping on the Marist poll—says it shows he can't lose."[2] Of course it hurts to hear it. Even when you're disposed to deal with it intellectually, it hurts to hear it.

On the private plane[3] alone because I decide it's better to have Andrew stay behind at the Convention to get ready for the acceptance of the endorsement at 1:30. Maybe he can figure out a story line for me to use.

Too tired to prepare for the debate, I have a cup of coffee and write these notes instead.

---

[1]Public information officer in the lieutenant governor's office. I've known him since our days at St. John's College in Brooklyn.

[2]A poll done by the Institute of Public Opinion at Marist College, Poughkeepsie, New York.

[3]A rented four-seater prop job—a far cry from a Lear jet.

Later

I thought the debate went O.K. Koch stunned me by saying during an answer on the death penalty that of course innocent people would die occasionally, but it was good for the "thousands" it would save. He later noted that the Supreme Court said the people have a right to express their "moral indignation." Is that different from revenge?

The middle of the day was a comedy of errors.

The private plane that was to take me back to Sullivan County for the AFL endorsement couldn't land there because of the weather. I had Joe Minnewany of UPI with me. We were talking about the Apostles' Creed and heaven and hell when the plane was suddenly jolted by an air pocket. I think it was an air pocket —I hope it wasn't that He didn't like what we were saying about the Apostles' Creed.

We flew directly to Utica, where I was supposed to attend a fund-raiser. Calls to New York indicated a legal flaw in the committee that was set up. For a while it looked as though I couldn't go to the fund-raiser. A few phone calls back and forth from Jim Feathers straightened that out.

Because we hadn't eaten, I asked the State Trooper to take us down the road for a hamburger. I decided to drive, because I'm fascinated by the handling of the new Reliant K car. We were stopped by an Oriskany policeman, who apparently recognized the car but not the driver. He cautioned me about speed limits. Minnewany couldn't get over it—I had made his column.

After another series of confused phone calls, we finally made it to the fund-raiser at the Twin Ponds. It was a warm crowd of about 250 people, who raised about $10,000. I enjoyed it a great deal, and so did they.

In the meantime, the AFL-CIO had proceeded to their vote without me. It was overwhelmingly in my favor.

It's clear that Koch and Garth will come up with something. They have to. They can't allow the momentum to build against them. It's not unlike a football game: the "Big Mo" has a life—and force—of its own.

THURSDAY, SEPTEMBER 2, 1982

Well, the party's over for me with the *Post*. They published a poll this morning that said Koch is 24 points ahead. That's what happened in '77, when Koch was only 4 points ahead. Looks like an exact replay. It will hurt again, as it did in 1977, because the voters won't know what we know. It's debilitating. It's bound to discourage some contributions and to dishearten many of our supporters.

I'm writing this in the car with Maria and Andrew, on the way to a finance committee meeting. Andrew is coolly analytical about the situation. He's suppressing his anger and is functioning well. Maria is just quiet. Stern called early to say the poll would hurt us badly with money. There is a peculiar "heartiness" about his resignation to the realities of what he calls the *Post*'s "war" against us.

It's hard for me to measure my own feelings. I've always been half prepared for this and indeed predicted it in the pages of this diary some time ago. It still hurts of course. More because we're doing so well otherwise. The question now becomes: how much does this description change the reality? All I can do to fight it is to continue an unrelenting affirmative course and do what I can to shore everyone up.

SATURDAY, SEPTEMBER 4, 1982

At yesterday's WMCA radio debate, moderated by Barry Gray, I thought I did as well as I had at the *Post* debate. Koch was nervous, agitated and overly aggressive. He's either sure he's going to win and doesn't want to be Governor or he's not so sure he's going to win and wants to.

The *Post* poll has hurt us. We need to respond with a poll of our own as soon as possible.

We are simply not getting the best mileage out of events. Koch has had *Playboy*, the dirt scandal,[1] Lincoln West and a number of

---

[1] It was reported that one of the city agencies had paid thousands of dollars for dirt (landfill) it actually already owned.

other bad situations but has paid no price for any of them. He has been well treated in the press and, in addition, his charm shields him.

Koch's TV has had its impact, according to Caddell. Without knowing for sure, he suspects that Koch has picked up a few points. I'm going to lie down for a half-hour and then figure out what the themes should be for the last three weeks of the campaign. I need the rest because my dentist, Dr. Gilmore, worked on me for an hour this morning. I'm still feeling the needles and the pounding.

At about 3 P.M. I spoke with Bob Sullivan. He's completed his targeted survey. It shows me about 10 points behind. Bob says that with only 19 days to go, we're a long shot, but it's "doable." According to the poll, we're losing in the Black community. The upstate people are reacting to Koch's commercials but haven't seen ours. The Italians are weak. Listening to his analysis is like feeling a series of Dr. Gilmore's needles. He underscores all of this by saying that actually I've done a great job to get this close. "Koch is an international phenomenon: it would have been a miracle for you to win; it still would be." Somehow I'm not consoled. Somehow the idea of accepting another defeat, of losing the chance to serve, of losing the chance to repay the effort of so many, leaves me feeling empty. Knowing that I am supposed to feel this way, knowing that is the flaw around which we build the sculpture, is easy intellectually. But only intellectually.

There is another way to look at it. "It's doable." Longer odds have been overcome. Momma and Poppa did. That whole generation of giants did. It's the story of our nation's success. It's the definition of strength. It's the better way. We can win—if we believe we can win and if we work on that belief. That's the speech I've given a hundred times. Now I ought to listen to it. *Avanti!*

SUNDAY, SEPTEMBER 5, 1982

I went to the Feast of Santa Rosalia in Bensonhurst with Matilda and Chris. A sea of beautiful Italian faces. Many of them spoke little English; I would guess most of them were not registered to vote. I was given a heartier reception than I would have received 3 months ago because of the television commercials. Many people are fascinated by the simple fact that they've seen you on TV.

The TV gives status. It can make you a celebrity. With some, there's even a feeling that if you're on TV you're special or important. You can tell just from hearing them say it—"I saw him on TV!" This "celebrity" status, plus the fact that I'm proudly Italian American, assured me a good reception. Of course it wasn't universally good. There were the few who were angry at my rejection of the death penalty and said so. The polls tell me I don't lose much on the death penalty. I don't believe the polls. I'm convinced I lose people who otherwise would vote for me and that many of those who say they vote for me because of the death penalty would have voted for me anyway.

Matilda was excellent. She moves more freely through the crowds than I do. She was better from the stage: she spoke a pretty fair Italian to them, which they loved. And she is, of course, so attractive physically that she makes, altogether, a much better campaigner.

Chris, taller by a head, it seems, since last year, looked lost from time to time. No surprise. He's never been pushed through a crowd of thousands of police and advance men. At one point one of our supporters pulled him over to a booth, where he had a sausage sandwich suffocated in grilled onions and peppers. It was the kind that gives off the incredible aroma that makes the Italian street festival different from all others. That and a double scoop of Italian ice cream, when we sat for coffee and cappuccino, salvaged the evening for him.

What does it mean in votes, this kind of street campaigning in the era of electronics and a five-million-vote election? If it gets you free TV, it's very useful. If not, it's probably little more than a psychological lift for the troops in the field and for the candidate if he is so disposed. For some candidates, on the other hand, it can be difficult. Matilda seems to love it, although she denies that. I don't like it, although they tell me I seem to. I feel somehow dishonest, because I know there should be so much more to convincing people to vote for me as Governor. Even if I am able to get a vote—or a dozen, or a thousand—just by shaking hands, it offends me way down deep that it should be this way. But then, that's almost as true of doing it on television in 28-second bursts—so maybe it's really the whole system that's somehow intellectually offensive. Interesting . . . but academic.

Another unavoidable experience is the looking back. As the time left grows too short to do many things, the tendency is to consider what might have been. This is another part of the experience that is bothersome. We should have done more with the Blacks. I should have moved more aggressively early instead of waiting for the Black leadership. I should have gone into the Black churches more; I do well in that setting, for whatever reason. I should have spent more time working with the Catholics. I haven't even been interviewed by the *Catholic News* or *The Tablet.* I should have done specifically upstate television to build on the strength I started with there. We should have started a lawsuit for the the *Playboy* tapes: I thought the idea distasteful. We should have been more aggressive in describing my record and attacking Koch's. We should have presented my positions on the issues more clearly. We should have used surrogates more intelligently. I should have made more effort to do street campaigning. We should have used Matilda better. The "should haves" go on and on.

Of course we did some things right, too. Andrew has been extraordinary. Whatever else happens, he has established himself. Stern was extremely effective. Haddad gave us early credibility and helped as political liaison to groups I might not have reached as easily without him. Our announcement went well. The convention was a success. We handled the Liberal Party well. I did O.K. in the debates, and thanks to Featherstonhaugh, Pierce and Adler, we managed the politics of the union endorsements well. Our literature operation has been good. Harvey made excellent commercials once we had established our communications. Overall, we have done well in what we would call individual performances. What has been lacking is an overall strategy and someone to steer our ship according to that strategy. I should have used Andrew and Norm Adler more from the beginning—even before Haddad came aboard.

Overall, it has left us where Sullivan said we are—from his night polling at the CWA—a long shot 10 points behind but doable . . . maybe barely doable, but doable. The key is 20%

undecided and the fact that Ed has not gotten above 45% in the last several polls. Yes, it's doable.

Spoke to Fabian. I could hear the "regret" in his voice. He feels, although he won't say it, that it will be "close but no cigar." That's what Garth and Friedman said 12 months ago. Maybe they do know this business.

And maybe we can show them they don't know all they think they know.

Spoke to Ray Harding, who was at Austerlitz. Some good advice and information. He suggests: quick powerful hookups with McCall. More mention of "Democratic" issues. Mention Bellamy's inadequacies as Mayor. Bring Carter. Reach out for Kennedy. He's also concerned about my attitude. He's afraid I will get Koch-Garth in my mind instead of the constituency. He remembers the runoff of '77. It's a good reminder.

Hank Bersani called. Poll in Syracuse: 39—Cuomo, 30— Koch, 30—undecided. I thought it was not good enough. Bersani and Haddad thought it was good because we can get it out today and people won't realize it's just upstate central New York.

Cohen says we have diluted our commercials too much. He wants to go exclusively with the "accomplishments" spot. I said yes to Cohen and thereby made a big decision: we will go with only 2 commercials for this entire week—my answer to Koch's use of my endorsement of '81 and my "accomplishments." Cohen's judgment is good, and I'm comfortable going with it.

LABOR DAY, SEPTEMBER 6, 1982

For three hours I marched with Labor, down 5th Avenue, and waved at them from the reviewing stand on 42nd Street. Andrew and his gang of Labor volunteers had done a wonderful job getting my posters everywhere. Except for the Operating Engineers and a few other contingents, the marching groups all displayed Cuomo posters. Even the operating engineer membership seemed responsive to me. There were no negatives. How much will it mean? Who knows? Who can measure the conversion power of commitment and passion? I know I'd rather have them than not have them. Matilda stood by my side, and I think that was a good idea. She should be with me as much as possible.

I talked about a lot of things to the media. I should have focused more.

For tomorrow I've asked the staff to schedule a press conference on "Death and Taxes." It will give me a chance to get across my life-imprisonment-without-parole position and my disagreement with Koch's plans.[1] I must be careful not to get irresponsible.

I must also stay in shape. This contest could conceivably go to the person who doesn't make a mistake. Koch, under pressure, said he would kill innocent people to deter others. He also said he would raise taxes if he had to. I need to make the most of those two responses.

At about 5:30 in Buffalo

The reports from New York City are excellent. The parade was described on TV as "Cuomo's Parade." There were more signs for Cuomo than there were for Labor. "Live at Five" said this is the first day of the campaign, and people are beginning to make up their minds. I could hardly have asked for a more auspicious start.

I heard a funny story about the parade. One of our people found out from a Koch advance man that Koch was marching with the Firemen. He went to a cop on duty and told him that the Cuomo van was supposed to be in the line of march after the Firemen—and the cop allowed it in the line only a few feet from where Koch was marching. All the way—a huge truck full of Cuomo signs behind and above Koch. It must have driven the Mayor crazy. It also got picked up on television news at 6 P.M.

This evening I was in Buffalo for a picnic lunch with Tom Pisa[2] and the National Education Association people. They gave me $10,000 and a wonderfully warm reception. It hurts me to think that as Governor so many of these supporters will probably be disappointed at what I can do for them.

Before the NEA we picked up endorsements from most of the

---

[1] As an alternative to the death penalty, I proposed life imprisonment without parole; I opposed Koch's plan to raise commuter taxes and his support of the repeal of the real estate surtax.

[2] President of the New York chapter of the National Education Association.

Black elected officials in Buffalo: Arthur Eve, Jim Pitts, Roger Blackwell, Barry Robinson, David Collins and George Arthur. Delmar Mitchell had already endorsed me.

I also met with IUE electrical workers from Westinghouse. Tomorrow they're going to announce they've chosen me over Koch.

TUESDAY, SEPTEMBER 7, 1982

Tonight at Regine's we had what Stern described as a very successful fund-raiser—about $30,000 at $250 a ticket. It saddens me to see the same faces time and time again—the Albaneses, Mattones, Aiellos, John Jerome, Arnie Biegen, Penny Kaniclides, Dick Lieb et al. If for no other reason than to be able to give them a moment of real satisfaction for all their efforts, I'd like to win this thing.

The interviews by press and electronic media indicated that most of them have been convinced by the Koch force that I am anywhere from 12 to 24 points behind. Most of them don't think I'll win. I thought for a while we were winning them over, but it doesn't look like that at the moment.

I took a zap from an unexpected quarter today; Bill Haddad's daughter, Amanda, has been watching me on television. That's good—being viewed is all-important. She says I look like a frog —that's not so good. When was the last time a frog was elected Governor? I used to feel bad when people mistook me for Al D'Amato; now I'll be grateful for it.

WEDNESDAY, SEPTEMBER 8, 1982

As full a day as I've had in the campaign. It started with bad news. Dick Starkey's 7 A.M. call disclosed that the *Democrat and Chronicle* in Rochester had come out against me. I was hit hard by the news, especially since I had expected to get both papers there.

Koch will probably use the *D and C*'s statements to his good advantage. His heavy TV barrage continues. He has left on the air an attack on me claiming the budget for Lt. Governor has

gone up 76% since I've been in office, when they know it is only
34%, which is less than the inflation rate. A petty matter, but
nettlesome. He's also taken his own voice off the air and is
running large numbers of endorsement commercials. The latest
are Geraldine Ferraro and Claude Pepper.[1]

Bill Spencer, President of Citicorp, had a disappointing turnout at his breakfast designed to pull in Republicans who would
like an alternative to Koch. It's clear that the *Post* poll has had
its effect. The Mack brothers,[2] who have been working hard for
us, made it plain that our stock went down considerably only
because of it. It shows how lethal an instrument the front page
of a paper can be. We must get our own poll out no later than
tomorrow. Stern and Andrew agree.

I ran into the poll again in an interview by Gabe Pressman
outside the ballroom at the Sheraton, where I was to address the
SEIU Local 144, Peter Ottley's group. His assumption was that
I was a loser. Having established that in his mind, in the interview he was exploring reasons for my lack of success. His questions all assumed negatives. "Your staff people say your're flat;
you don't use one-liners well. You don't have Koch's charisma.
What do you say to that?" Of course, I didn't tell him on camera
what I'd *like* to say to that!

The talk to 144 was a different thing altogether. They were on
their feet as soon as I walked into the room—cheering and
screaming. The same thing happened later in the day at the
Amalgamated Clothing and Textile Workers' rally with Jack
Sheinkman. Both unions reflect the new complexion of our city's
lower-skilled workers. Black, brown, tan—Hispanics from Central America, Haitians, a sprinkling of new Mediterraneans.

They are passionate, concerned and beautiful. I don't know
how many of them will vote, but if I could get to them all the
way I got to the couple of thousand today, I'm sure I would win
on the 23rd.

For 2½ hours in the middle of the day, I prayed and thought
at the episcopal ordination of Emerson Moore and Joseph

---

[1]U.S. congressman from Florida.
[2]David, Bill and Earle Mack, introduced to me by our mutual friend Rabbi Mowshowitz, were loyal supporters throughout.

O'Keefe as auxiliary bishops. Moore is our metropolitan area's first Black bishop. It comes late, but it is good that it has come. It was a good 2½ hours.

I was concerned about tonight. I had had little sleep. I was tired and edgy. Some irritating discoveries about small lapses by some of my staff made things worse just before I had to leave for the Telephone Building, so by the time I got there I was afraid the Press Club debate—with all the media—would be a disaster. It wasn't. Although I wasn't happy with it, because I thought it was too harsh and prosecutorial, everyone else seemed to think I was a clear winner.

The QCO[3] appearance afterward was an even bigger success. I wasn't there when Koch addressed the 2,000 or so people, but I received a standing ovation. That was no surprise either, considering how hard I've worked with them and how much we have in common.

THURSDAY, SEPTEMBER 9, 1982

Once again the day started with bad news. This time it was the WCBS-TV endorsement of Koch. They called him a "star" and a "leader" without making any substantive points about his record or mine. There are a lot of people doing that.

All the media present at the debate last night thought I had beaten Koch in the debate. Some called it a "knockout." This morning's written accounts were all flat recitations. For whatever reason, they chose not to describe it to the world the way they described it to us.

The day was hectic. A press conference with Marchiselli[1] on toxic wastes at Co-op City was followed by the *Daily News* Editorial Board at 2, the San Gennaro festival[2] and four fund-raisers.

The *Daily News* was a tough go. I disagreed with some of the

---

[3] Queens Citizens' Organization.

[1] State Assemblyman Vincent A. Marchiselli, from the Bronx.
[2] Held every year in September in New York City's Little Italy, a street festival honoring Saint Gennaro, particularly revered in Naples.

editors, who seemed to want to try the subminimum wage and to have lost some ardor for my subway-car industry idea.[3] Wieghart at one point referred to me as an idealogue, which I didn't think was particularly encouraging. I also said that if they were to go forward with an "issues poll," Koch would win it in most categories. Mostly, I was trying to protect myself from the damage that is inevitable in measuring the candidates by the popularity of their positions. It does raise an obvious question— and Sam Roberts articulated it—as to whether a person who disagrees with the "people" on a number of vital questions should be the "leader." I have seen the role of leadership differently, but judging by the sentiment in the room at the *Daily News* today, they don't expect the public to understand that. Most people don't.

I received a standing ovation from about 2,000 retirees at the Civil Service Retired Employees Association and, predictably, at each of the fund-raisers and the Feast, I was warmly—indeed, enthusiastically—received. One of the factors difficult to measure in the polls is the intensity of the support I get from unions and from the people who are with me. I think if we go into the election less than 4 points behind, we'll win because of that intensity.

Bob Sullivan has been tracking. He reported last night that the vote is shifting from Koch to undecided—gradually but perceptibly. He has the difference at only 7 points, with the undecided at 21 points. That has to be a good sign, but I'll give it a few more days before I take it seriously. It seems clear to me that Koch owns 40–47% of the vote, no matter what we do. He also has about 5% "soft" votes. I have 30% hard, 5% soft and a lot of people waiting to be convinced. Mostly, the convincing comes from staying on TV working hard to sound intelligent and prepared.

[3]My proposal that the MTA buy its subway cars from domestic companies, preferably one located in New York, instead of from Kawasaki in Japan and Bombardier in Canada, even if it would cost somewhat more. Before the end of the campaign, the MTA had consummated contracts to buy nearly a billion dollars' worth of cars from foreign manufacturers.

FRIDAY, SEPTEMBER 10, 1982

Another hard blow against us. The *Daily News* goes with Koch. "He's closer to us on the issues."

I told Andrew. It hurts him, but he's tough enough to handle it. Maria was more hurt; she's less tough. But it's all part of the experience.

More and more I see manifest what is perhaps my greatest difficulty. It's not my experience or record or personal ability—despite Koch. None of these things is a real problem. Rather, it's what I believe about government generally, life and death, emphases and objectives. The real question is going to be what the Democrats believe—at least those who vote.

Amsterdam News Editorial Board interview went well. I expect them to endorse me. Local 1199[1] grilled me for an hour and a half. They are involved in all sorts of internecine wheeling, dealing and struggling. I hope practicalities have not overtaken principle. They used to be a "progressive" union that wouldn't for a minute consider endorsing someone who feels the way Koch does on the issues. But this is pragmatism's moment—in a lot of places.

At 10:15 I got to Temple Israel. I fell asleep in the car on the way there and don't even remember the trip! The talk—on Israel and various other topics—was well received. How I wish I could do this with everybody in the state: person to person. It would make a difference.

SATURDAY, SEPTEMBER 11, 1982

Since the campaign condenses so many life experiences down into several months, it's an excellent opportunity for studying and judging reactions. It's especially effective at revealing response to adversity.

My own instincts have grown quite accurate. I sensed—maybe

[1] A union representing hospital workers and other health-care institution employees.

it was actually a judgment—that the *News* was going for Koch. But that hasn't helped rid me of the feeling of disappointment. I had been counting on it as an offset to the *Post* and probably the *Times* as well. If you allow yourself to reflect on the disappointment, it tends even to depress the energy level of your effort or to escalate it to anger. What you need to do is to see it as just another of the obstacles that will make the victory all the sweeter for having overcome them.

That became a little easier to do today because at about 5 P.M., after my presentation to the statewide National Organization of Women (NOW) in Albany, I received their endorsement. I'm the first male to have been endorsed by them, and it might make a pretty good television ad.

Charlie Rangel also endorsed me this morning, and that can be helpful, especially in the Black community, where I need to do well.

The last ten days. Now is the time to pick up speed. I want to finish sprinting!

SUNDAY, SEPTEMBER 12, 1982

The *Daily News* endorsement of Koch said a lot of nice things about me. And it was surrounded by a good story on our poll and a favorable column. That, together with the NOW endorsement, which was played by the media in tandem with the *News* endorsement of Koch, softened the blow considerably, but even so it costs us what would have been a big advantage.

I was able to handle our WNBC debate with Koch without letting my disappointment over the endorsement show. Pressman was the moderator, and he didn't let Koch get away with a lot. Koch was cocky before and after the debate, but not during it. The reactions to the debate were predictable. My supporters loved the idea that I "made him look bad" a couple of times. That may be good for their morale, but I don't think it gets me many votes. His supporters, I'm sure, pointed out that he made me look bad more than once.

What will get me votes with 10 days remaining? Pat Caddell thinks he knows. He was at the house tonight with Andrew. He was excited. He says that analyzing his last poll he's convinced he has figured out the election. Koch has gotten stronger through his 2½ million dollars of television by convincing people he has a good record and therefore can do the job. I have gotten stronger just by being seen and heard. But, to use Pat's words, the election has never become "engaged": We have moved on parallel tracks, with the undecideds breaking in proportion to the decided vote. If we continue going at this rate, Pat feels we will lose by 4 to 6 points. But he thinks we can win if we push some magic buttons. His polls show that a large number of the Koch voters would shift to Cuomo given certain "new understandings." Ironically, the "new understandings" are all points I've been pushing hard without a poll. Here are some of them:

1. Koch has cut policemen, firemen and sanitationmen, but he has added press secretaries and publicists.
2. New subway cars are being made in Japan and Canada instead of here.
3. Koch favors cuts in Social Security benefits.
4. Koch has cut programs to the disabled, closed hospitals and saved money by taking from those least able to afford it.
5. State had to balance City's budget but City still in trouble; Koch let rich real estate developers off the hook and raised income tax for people with incomes between $15,000 and $40,000; Koch has been good to Reagan; crime is up; streets are dirty.

Caddell also agrees that my "Solomon" notion—i.e., "Solve the problem by keeping them both, Cuomo for Governor, Koch for Mayor"—works well.

His numbers indicate that each of these points, once accepted by the Koch voter, produces a high percentage of changeover. The difficulty until now has been that, for all of my effort, the message has not gotten across. Can we do it now? Maybe. If we regear our commercials immediately and use our new concentration of exposure well for the next 10 days. Pat believes if we do it perfectly, we'll win by 3 or 4 points; if we don't, we'll lose by 3 or 4 points.

For me, it's just a matter of tightening and focusing the message I've delivered. "This is an important issue because we're fighting for the soul of the Democratic party. Koch is different with respect to the people he's concerned about and how he would solve problems. He cuts taxes for real estate, increases them for wage earners, etc." Then I have to conclude by saying that the solution is to leave him as Mayor (where philosophy is not as important) and make me Governor. We'll see.

Matilda's away on her upstate trip. Reports are that she's doing well. I'm not surprised.

Chris has been left out. I spent the late evening with him watching a horror movie and then letting him sleep with me.

Jimmy Breslin got married today to Ronnie Eldridge. I wish Matilda and I could have been with them to wish them well.

"And the days dwindle down, to a precious few."

MONDAY, SEPTEMBER 13, 1982

The morning started with an 8:30 meeting of State and City University student representatives at our headquarters. I enjoyed it, although I became a little too professorial in my presentation. I was able to convey the strong commitment I have to public-sector higher education while at the same time warning of the budget constraints.

After that a trip to 35th Street to get Gus Bevona's endorsement on behalf of the State Council of Service Employees International Union. The union represents 150,000 workers—superintendents, cabdrivers, home-care attendants, elevator operators—and hasn't been active before. This year it first endorsed Koch. I was able to turn them around after Koch "disappointed" them. He apparently failed to deliver on a promise they thought he had made to them in an effort to "turn over a new leaf and win union support," as Bevona put it. The endorsement brought with it a contribution and a private indication by Bevona that he would stay with me on the Liberal line even if we didn't succeed in the primary. He was frank enough to tell me he didn't think I would win on the 23rd.

Gus is relatively young, and bright and well educated: he's a

St. Francis College graduate. But he hasn't had much experience with the media. He had arranged for a large turnout of press and electronic media, and only Beth Fallon,[1] Marcia Kramer,[2] Arthur Greenspan and a young lady from a radio station showed up. He was disappointed. I tried to explain that if it weren't this close to the election, even these few might not have shown up.

He was also too open about describing his union's disappointment with Koch. It began to sound as though they had turned around because Koch hadn't delivered on a "deal." I tried to adjust the perspective, but after a few bad experiences with the press I'm sure Gus will learn a little more discretion. He is certainly one of the more capable younger Labor leaders.

After Bevona I was able to get to Brooklyn 20 minutes early for a rally. It was enough time to buy Chris the sneakers he wanted so much. He was delighted when I told him later in the day. Most of all I think he was pleased I remembered. It was the best thing that happened to me all day.

The rally was a success. Our Brooklyn team did a good job. Signs, enthusiasm, music—all the ingredients of an old-fashioned campaign stop. Even the people we didn't produce were surprisingly positive. One of the reporters went to people on the streets trying to find a negative and couldn't. I'm not particularly comfortable with rallies or street campaigns—sometimes they make me feel like hiding. But I'm told this one will be well received by the media. Since we had TV and might wind up with 30 seconds on the 6 o'clock news, I'd have to consider it a success. The best I can do for myself now is get free TV.

In the afternoon Menachem Savidor, the Speaker of the Knesset, paid a courtesy call. It was a pleasant visit and he invited me to Israel, "win or lose" the election. I tried to convey to him that I didn't think the response to the Pope's acceptance of Arafat's request for an audience was handled well. I told him I thought there had to be a more concerted and effective effort to reach the non-Jewish community, and explained how I had asked Garth to work on that for ZOA[3] and some others before Koch decided

---

[1] A *Daily News* columnist, known for her objectivity and her occasional poetic flourishes.
[2] Albany bureau chief, *Daily News.*
[3] Zionist Organization of America.

to run. He was interested, and I expect I'll be hearing from him again.

I appeared briefly at the Lincoln West rally and didn't do well, but at least my opposition to the project was recorded. Unfortunately, most of the opponents of the luxury housing project aren't particularly happy with my suggested alternative for the site either: a rail freight yard and middle-income housing. I had the feeling some of them wouldn't settle for anything except a park!

I finished the night at Temple Beth-El in Rockland, where I was extremely well received. For a half-hour after my speech and the question-and-answer period, I heard people tell me how I had changed their minds. How it hurts to know that if only I could get to them . . .

The WNBC-AP poll was announced. It was 11 points as of a week ago. We pointed out that's where Sullivan was as well and that we're now at 7. A good direction.

Who knows?

Frank Lynn called me with a rumor that Carey is going to endorse Koch. I was taken aback a little, but then felt quickly resigned to it. I'm not sure of what it would mean, practically. I kind of hope he doesn't do it.

I ended the night with another bit of bad news. The *Times-Union* of Rochester came out for Koch. They said nice things about me but were impressed by Koch's "executive" experience.

Tuesday, September 14, 1982

I was able to run for a half-hour this morning. I've come to look forward to these brief respites. I was thinking this morning about how I once described the Lt. Governor's position as having a characteristic that is at once its greatest advantage and its greatest disadvantage. A Lt. Governor has the great consolation of knowing he doesn't have to make the critical decisions and the great frustration of knowing he's not allowed to make the critical decisions. That ambiguity, ambivalence and tension are present even now as I think of the two possibilities here: winning and losing.

This morning was spent in the Hispanic communities of the Bronx. No matter how many times I see it, I am stunned each time by the devastation of some of the neighborhoods—and some of the people. The hulks of buildings—empty window frames looking like a hundred eye sockets, garbage and burned interiors—side by side with populated tenements, people sitting at the windows smoking cigarettes, waving at a politician they don't know and who probably can't help them much. 40% unemployment. Young men everywhere, without jobs or even the hope of jobs. Young women with infants on welfare; welfare as a way of life. Drug addiction; muggings, filth are taken for granted. Resented, despised, cursed, but taken for granted. How utterly we have failed. How much there is to do. How hard it will be for the people who have to do it.

Editorial Board meeting at *El Diario*. I don't know how it went.

The rumors about Carey endorsing Koch grow stronger. Andrew says Harding and Morgado suggest I call the Governor.

WEDNESDAY, SEPTEMBER 15, 1982

Especially at this stage, the debates are probably not decisive events. The one remaining television debate, which will be taped tomorrow for WPIX, will not play until the night before the election and can change a few minds, but that's all.

Still, the debates are taken seriously by the candidates. The press is in attendance, and a real slip will be seized upon in their eternal quest for a "story." Personal characteristics and moods are measured by the media. They find those things more interesting—and easier to communicate—than the issues discussions. And, of course, there is always the personal element—the excitement of the combat, the fear of embarrassment—that makes the debate a draining experience.

But the hardest part of the nontelevised debates is suffering through the written accounts of the actuality. Again yesterday at the *Times*, I was told by most people that it was a good, solid exchange on the issues, "in substance a superior mutual performance." But by evening, when we got reports of what had been written for the next day, it was clear that's not the way it was being described. Instead, they were writing things like "false grins turned into biting invective"; "two angry candidates approach the finish line showing their teeth." I wonder if you ever get used to it.

I spoke with the Governor tonight. I was reluctant to call him because I was sure he was going to endorse Koch, but I did anyway. He gave me the impression that he was going to endorse Koch, but was embarrassed about it. He tried telling me Koch was good for the State, and I reminded him of all the times he had said the opposite. I reminded him of the death penalty and Koch's "inability to deal with numbers," which he had described many times.[1] He made only the weakest responses. He insisted repeatedly that he "wasn't doing this for personal gain." He suggested, vaguely, that he was doing it because I had never asked him and denied that he had ducked David Burke, who had been trying to set up a meeting for me. I can only suppose that his desire to "punish" me for slights—real or imagined—produced his decision.

I feel it in my stomach—it will go away quickly, but I feel it in my stomach. I'm not sure why—there's no real surprise in what he's done, and I don't think it will hurt me . . . but I feel it anyway.

Local 1199, the hospital workers, voted for neutrality. Norman Adler says too many of them were afraid of Koch. The *Post-Standard* in Syracuse endorsed Koch. "They don't like him, but they think he's going to win" says Hank Bersani. The Crown Heights Jewish Community Council voted to endorse me, but then only one of the several Rabbis who were supposed to show up at the Press Conference did. He explained that they had been "pressured" by a suggestion that they might lose grants. Is it true? Who knows? Isn't it a crime if it in fact occurred? Of course. But no one would admit to it if pressed—neither victim nor threatener—if it did occur.

The accumulation of ugly incidents, reversals and disappointments is depressing. But there are good things, too. Tonight's

---

[1] Different leaders have different emphases; some pay more attention to the details of budget making than others. The mayor has often said he prefers not to deal with the specific budget numbers any more than he has to.

fund-raiser at Joe Mattone's North Hills Club was a smash. We collected about $70,000, and the turnout was excellent. Joe and Irene did a great job—as usual.

To highlight the evening, Andrew called from headquarters to say that Gannett was publishing a poll tomorrow that shows Cuomo leading by a substantial margin with most-likely voters! I don't believe the poll, but I rejoice at the news. It was great to see how much joy it brought to the people who were there. How I'd love them to have a victory.

THURSDAY, SEPTEMBER 16, 1982

A burst of excitement. I didn't believe the poll Andrew told me about last night; neither did Sullivan. Sullivan called me today to say that last night there was a strong movement toward Cuomo in his own sampling. It wasn't decisive by any means, but it was clear from his tone that he felt that strong movement had begun in my direction. On the basis of those calls he said he could "almost believe" the Gannett numbers. Caddell concedes there's movement but thinks we're still well behind. Last week he had us about 20 points behind. He thinks we should attack Koch. Sullivan thinks that's a "no-no." I'm inclined to stay positive. I'll have to decide today.

Just heard WCBS radio endorsed MMC this morning. Good news. As is news that the Poughkeepsie *Journal* has endorsed me.

Big press conference involving the Gannett poll and the Carey endorsement of Koch. I tried to toss off the Carey endorsement with some light banter. I said to the press: "I told Carey to lay off those PCBs."[1] I'm told I got away with it. As a matter of fact, some of the press referred to my conference as a "home run." Andrew said that he never saw me as good. All I know is I enjoyed it!

Shanker and other union people are all over the place trying to help. He's pushing in last-minute money, and it looks right

[1] Governor Carey had gotten into trouble once saying he would drink a glass of PCBs (polychlorinated biphenyl, used in industry and a poisonous environmental pollutant) to prove PCB wasn't as dangerous as people had been led to believe.

now as though we're equipped to stay on TV and radio through the 22nd. God Bless Bill Stern!

Everywhere I hear that the union phones are going great for us. Again, who knows?

Tonight's WPIX debate, to be aired Sunday night, was a bore. The format didn't allow us the back-and-forth. I'm convinced that we ought to start campaigns with a "trial" of the issues, in which each candidate would put in everything he had until relevance was exhausted. At the least it would define issues for the campaign. Thirty debates where answers are only 2 minutes long give you 30 times the same 2 minutes. It guarantees repetition and superficiality, and precludes a real education for the public.

So much enthusiasm at the headquarters on 39th Street today because of the poll. I don't get there as much as I'd like, because I'm out campaigning most of the time. In fact, I have mixed feelings about being there, surrounded by the excitement and confusion. There is something terribly vital about it. The workers are, for the most part, volunteers. Executive secretaries, young lawyers, salesclerks, some unemployed youth, senior citizens eager to stay active, two beautiful young women in wheelchairs: they're all there because they want to be. Many of them love it; there's nothing they want more than to be in the war, to fight the good fight. It's thrilling to them, the effort so important that they have no difficulty performing even small chores: getting out a mailing, writing down a thousand names of potential contributors, doing simple research for a half-hour stop by the candidate. For months, they have come in after work to serve as receptionists, go for coffee and sandwiches, answer the phones. Dozens of them, in makeshift offices created by temporary partitions, with boxes of literature everywhere; walls plastered with posters and maps and bulletins; phones ringing over one another —all going at once.

Of course, there weren't as many people in the beginning as there are now, because now we're getting down to the real action. The campaign is now perking. It's in the papers and on television every day. People talk about it at work, on the way to work, at home. Posters go up. TV commercials appear. It's real.

At the heart of it all is Andrew, surrounded by his tigers— Mark, Gary, Royce, Lendino, Burgos, Kris, Jonathan, Maria,

Madeline.[1] So many others. What a beautiful bunch. I'm tempted always to put my arm around them: a hug, a kiss saying how grateful I am, how lucky we are to have them.

But it's not all joy being in the headquarters. I can't see them all at work, see the lines of fatigue under Andrew's eyes, know how they have given a whole huge chunk of their lives for this effort, and not have my stomach do a flip, thinking of what a disappointment it would be to them—how unfair it would be to them—if I lost. I always leave the headquarters convinced I must try harder, and prepared to do it.

Koch doesn't have a headquarters like this one. Not many statewide candidates do anymore. They work out of their con-sultants' offices. The modern campaign is now oriented toward television and radio advertising. The commercial has replaced a million pieces of literature handed out on street corners. The powerful message on the tube and radio has replaced volunteers spreading the word in the streets. Campaigning is done not so much to meet people and convince them to vote for you as to create an "event" for media coverage or to raise money for media. Of course there are the mandatory visits that all candi-dates make—the Feast of San Gennaro, the 100 Black Men, the union meetings. But the modern campaign isn't done from the back of a train or bus or on foot—it's done electronically.

We have television. But ours is more an old-fashioned cam-paign than a modern one. A campaign of bull horns and party hats and street-corner rallies. If we win, it'll be people who made us a winner, not a pen, pad and television tube.

On primary day there will be more people on the streets of this state pulling votes for us than have ever been working on pri-mary day before. I suspect there will be more phone calls and pieces of literature and coffee klatsches and meetings and rallies than ever before. Certainly, there will be more than Koch's money could buy. There isn't enough money anywhere to get people to work the way they're going to. The organizational effort has been relentless, detailed, tough—the mirror of Nor-man Adler, who has worked with Andrew to set it up. Its back-

---

[1]The "tigers"—young supporters who have been with me from the beginning despite the odds, the experts, the past—included my daughters Maria and Madeline.

bone is made up of the unions—their people and their passion. We have the people and the passion. They have the money and the electronic expertise. They'll have to write new analyses if we win. Wouldn't it be great!

FRIDAY, SEPTEMBER 17, 1982

After yesterday's high—I have never been less certain about a possible election outcome than I am this morning. I have been telling everyone who cares, for a year, that I think Sullivan is the most reliable pollster and forecaster available, but now that he is predicting victory I find it difficult to believe him. There are reasons: too many of the polls over the last 2 weeks showed me behind between 12 and 22 points, and most pollsters—Unger, Caddell, WNBC—say we're still far behind; there appears to be general agreement that Gordon Black's[1] weighting may be off, so his favorable poll is suspicious and there is the cumulative weight of the obvious Koch advantages—his popularity, money, ability to campaign, compatibility with the swing to conservatism. No one is better at functioning on an assumed belief of victory than I, but to actually *believe* is something else.

Then, too, maybe I'm just afraid to get committed to the idea. Having suffered through the disappointment of defeat before, I try, instinctively, to prepare for it. Moreover, there are always the problems that victory will bring—another hard campaign and then governing. Governing. With more needs than resources. With a difficult legislature, an unhappy Mayor of the City of New York, a hostile federal government. And with a tendency to feel other people's unhappiness. That's not an attractive prospect. Sometimes I wish the trappings were more attractive to me.

So I resist thinking of winning. More often, I allow myself to think of the occurrence of what most people regarded as inevitable from the beginning, Koch's victory. It's accompanied by quick stomach flips, because losing is still more undesirable than winning.

Most of all, I resist thinking at all, except when I'm going to

[1]Gannett's pollster.

write these notes. In between, I spend all my time functioning.
It pays dividends.

The debate continues over commercials. Sullivan is strongly
against using negatives. Caddell and Cohen want to attack Koch
on Reaganomics and use the other arguments I have been making. I'm inclined against the negatives because I generally don't
like them, and because the problem is still defining Cuomo, not
eroding the favorable image of Koch. But Caddell, who has just
won big in Massachusetts,[2] is so insistent he's right that it gives
me pause. It's a hard choice, like so many others. I will go with
my own instinct and hope for the best.

All the reports on Matilda's upstate trip are raves. She has long
since emerged as the best campaigner on my side. Now she is
elaborating that idea. We'll never know how much she's meant,
but it has to be considerable. I'm curious as to how all this will
affect her. If we win, she will move naturally into the life of a First
Lady. If we don't, then I think she will need much more than she
used to have, to occupy her time.

I'll see Hank Bersani in a few minutes. He's been one of the
real pleasures of the last 7½ years. There are so many good
people I've worked with: Louise Slaughter, Jean,[3] Jack Ferro,
Ellen Conovitz, Tonio Burgos, Pam Broughton, Linda,[4] Mary
(whom I've known longest of all and who has never changed),[5]
Madeline—how I wish I could present them all with a victory.

Flew up to Albany with Paul Curran. He's handling his impossible mission with grace and dignity. What a shame that money
makes such a difference.

The day in Oswego was lovely. It had only limited political
usefulness, although it did give me the opportunity to get my
Rural Platform on the wires. I wanted to make the trip at this
critical point in the campaign as a demonstration that as Governor I would not forget the upstate because it was politically
advantageous to concentrate in the metropolitan areas.

---

[2]Caddell had been pollster and adviser to Michael Dukakis, a liberal Democrat, who
had just been elected governor of Massachusetts.

[3]Jean Angell, Democratic county chairman of Tompkins County, an old and valued
friend.

[4]Linda O'Hare Dumas, a secretary in my Albany office since 1975.

[5]Mary Tragale, née Bavaro, my first secretary in 1958, close to me ever since.

I spent time on the McMahon farm and at the Zappola vegetable-processing and distributing operation. It intensified my appreciation of the significance of our agricultural industry. It was also great fun.

After two editorial board visits I finished the day at John and Charlotte Sullivan's home, where 125 or so paid $25 to come to a fund-raiser. They were a bright, committed group, largely based at SUNY, Oswego. The university people are always interesting to work with.

SATURDAY, SEPTEMBER 18, 1982

Since the Gannett poll, a whole new feeling has taken over the campaign. Most people won't express it, but there is the growing conviction that we're going to win. Over the last couple of days, rumors have come out of the Garth camp that their own polls also show Koch in trouble. Even Andrew—who has the same cautious attitude I have—let himself go today and said he thought we were going to win. Until now the best he would say was he thought we "had a shot."

I felt better about our chances before I heard that the New York *Times* is endorsing the Mayor tomorrow. According to Haddad, the editorial calls him all kinds of names—demagogic, insensitive racially—but then says we need him. Its only criticism of me is that I had to "reach" to attack the rich.

Another setback occurred today when I never got to the Black rally in Harlem where McCall was going to endorse me and I was expected to endorse him. My failure to turn up annoyed some of the Black leaders and Jan Pierce. I wound up telling the *Daily News* on the phone that I endorsed McCall.

I missed the rally because we spent five hours discussing commercials for the last three days of the campaign with Caddell, Haddad, Jerry Weiss and Andrew. Sullivan wasn't there, but I spoke with him and Stern on the phone.

Because I simply would not let them do it, Caddell and Cohen lost their argument that we should go "strong negative" against Koch. Basically, my feeling is that Koch can afford negatives; he doesn't get votes for being "above the battle." On the other hand, I think negatives would cost me votes because they disap-

point expectations of some of the people who prefer me. Moreover, I think the problem I have continues to be that people don't
know enough about me. I don't want to fill that vacuum with
harsh talk about my opponent.

We finally settled on the following: we will show the "accomplishments" spot that tells people what I've done and the "Quadrant" spot that shows four differences with Koch on the issues,[1]
through Sunday night. For the last three days we'll try to make
two new spots tomorrow. One will be a simple statement of what
I believe as a Democrat that makes me different from Koch and
the other a "Solomon" commercial, a reminder that when you
vote for Cuomo you get Koch, too.

I wrote the first spot and everybody liked it, except Sullivan.
I'll think about it some more tonight.

I'm concerned about what Koch's media will do to us. I think
his ticking-clock commercial, which says I have no accomplishments, is a clever and effective attack on what should be my
strength, my experience. When you put that together with all his
endorsements—especially editorially—it's hard to see how we
can sustain any momentum in the last three days. My only chance
is to take him on conceptually and on the issues and to hope my
primary day operation makes a big difference.

One of the hidden factors in the campaign has been the extensive field operation we've put together. Andrew tells me that we
have distributed about three million pieces of literature—that's
his guess—and that there will be two million palm cards out on
primary day. He expects there to be some 8,000 people working
for us on primary day. 2,000 phones are working right now.
None of this gets written about or measured, but it must have
an impact. We don't match Koch with TV coverage, but we do
have an edge in field communication Again, we'll never know
how important it is, because there's no way to measure it.

Flash from upstate (a telegram from Featherstonhaugh):

[1] "Quadrant" because the screen is divided into four sections in the final frames, each
one containing a different individual, making one of the four issues arguments we were
trying to project. The issues were Social Security (Koch had endorsed a reduction in
cost-of-living increases), building subway cars in Canada (I was against it), Koch's virtual
endorsement of Ronald Reagan in 1980, and Koch's giving of tax breaks to rich real
estate developers. The last showed a pregnant woman saying: "Cuomo knows *we* need
the break."

"FIRST LADY'S TOUR TO BE EXTENDED: WELL RECEIVED EVERYWHERE." Matilda is apparently knocking them dead and is going to stretch her stay for a couple of days. I'm not surprised.

SUNDAY, SEPTEMBER 19, 1982

Running through Cunningham Park, the pain growing stronger in my back, the distance seeming longer because of the hay fever and the lack of sleep, I try hard to remember the long view. But the excitement of the moment pushes in to occupy my mind. No matter how I analyze, how I resign myself, the fact remains that no one knows what will happen on Thursday. "It's a horse race" you hear everywhere. And a spin of the wheel, a turning of the card. It's possible, it can happen. So can "bingo!"; the lottery; a gold strike; disaster. All we're sure of—even now—is that you can't be sure.

I've told Andrew to do a large sample today after two days of not polling. It is probably going to be the final, decisive indicator —if there is one. If the trend holds today, we win. If it stops, we lose. If it's uncertain, so will we be. And all of it, at the very best, will only be "probable."

Only four days of campaigning left. It's hard to believe. Four days more for the prediction of Garth and others that I would "step on my own toe"—commit a gaffe—to come true. Four days more during which I need to avoid a blunder, appear confident, cool, in control. Four days more to avoid lying or selling out so that at least we'll know we made an honorable effort. After six months of campaigning, four more days.

I almost lapsed in the "Newsmakers" show.[1] I thought the questions from the panel of reporters were particularly antagonistic—every one of them might have been written by Koch's research staff. I had no trouble dealing with them, except that my annoyance at being denied an opportunity to make my own case showed.

---

[1] A WCBS Sunday morning interview show. A must for local politicians and aficionados.

There was discussion all day in our camp about our poll. Haddad thought it was a mistake to take the sample on a Sunday. I was inclined to agree, so were Norm Adler and Bill Stern. As it developed, we were able to make 300 calls, and Bob Sullivan is convinced that, while the numbers were uncertain, the trend to us continues. Actually, though, the sample doesn't provide the kind of solid indicator I was hoping for.

There was also discussion about the last two commercials. I'm not happy with either of them. One is an attempt at saying "Vote for Cuomo and get Koch, too" and the other, "Cuomo is Different because he believes in Principles." Neither came off well, for a combination of reasons—no time for a script; I looked tired. Throughout the campaign I have failed to capture on film the strongest parts of our presentation. I'm convinced Haddad was right when he said we should have been shooting *cinema vérité* throughout. Maybe for the general election.

Heard a fascinating rumor from a good source today. Apparently Lehrman's people had been convinced to start attacking Koch on the ground that Lehrman's best chance in November would be against Cuomo head to head instead of Koch head to head or a three-way race. Lehrman then ran a negative ad against Koch (it's nice to have the money to pursue whatever strategy strikes you at the moment), but only for one night. As the report goes, Garth was able to kill it by convincing Adam Walinsky that Cuomo would be unbeatable in November if he won the primary, if only because of the momentum he would have. It confirms the uncertainty Garth indicated to a good mutual friend this week when he said, "Cuomo just may win!" David, from your lips to the voters' ears!

MONDAY, SEPTEMBER 20, 1982

Caddell says the movement is vigorous toward us. All groups are moving. He believes we're still 5 or so points behind. He insisted that we go to a tough commercial saying Koch and Reagan go together. I approved mostly because he insisted. He says Garth is in a panic. They are throwing everything they can at us. They have gone back to the Cuomo '81 endorsement of Koch after pulling it off for a couple of days. Caddell says that's more evidence of their confusion.

Caddell suggested I go to the media and get interviewed all day long. I had Maria, who has been working in the press operation, place calls to all the radio stations she could reach trying to get some free time. A "wrapping up" press conference this morning went well. I described the commercial I wrote yesterday and I hope it will get some press.

Nothing stops the speculating. Will Koch's negative barrage focusing on my "lack of accomplishments" and Cabin stop our momentum? Will the soft Koch votes move back to Koch from undecided? Will the undecided decide in the midst of the Jewish holidays to vote ethnically? Will something said at the debate make a difference? Questions with no answers.

All day I have been disturbed by the feeling that we're not doing enough to add momentum to our campaign. I think we should have had a big hit like Carter-Kennedy, but we haven't been able to come up with anything. Koch came up with Carey, but we're not sure that didn't backfire on him.

For a little while tonight we were forced to deal with ultimate truth again. I was with Nick and Arlene D'Arienzo and their family at the wake of Nick's brother, John. Only 45, he died suddenly of a heart attack. How vain is so much of what we concern ourselves about.

TUESDAY, SEPTEMBER 21, 1982

Up at 4 A.M. Called Andrew. Polls last night showed me we're 4 points behind in New York City, 45–41 with 14% still undecided. If it went even on undecided, it would be 52–48. We were hoping for 45% in New York City. The direction is still good —although not dramatic—*if* the polls are right.

Although I had a slight fever the *News* Debate went well today. Koch is forceful, committed to several clear themes which he repeats over and over until they achieve effectiveness. "You have no record," when said a dozen times without response, can be effective. That forces you to make a response, thereby putting

you in a defensive position. In the beginning of the campaign I
didn't answer, trying instead to discuss my themes and make my
points. That gave Koch a big lead. Especially editorial boards
that did not know him were impressed by the voluminous presentation of his achievements and the inability of my campaign
to get across mine. Looking back, I see that all I would have
needed was a good piece on my record of accomplishments. No
one ever did it or even suggested it. The campaign was allowed
to progress with me handling press conferences, debates and
speeches ad hoc, forming policy as we went along. We have
lacked a strategy other than the one developed by my speeches
—insistence on my conceptual purity and his departure from
Democratic orthodoxy. Maybe the more important element was
the overall impression created by my candidacy. As far as I can
tell, we were able to project competence and assurance—the
latest poll has 63% saying that "Cuomo Looks and Acts More
Like a Governor." Just guessing, that has to be a key factor in
the decision-making process.

Rally at 38th Street and 7th Avenue. Good old-fashioned
"microphone in hand," flat-top truck oratory.

WEDNESDAY, SEPTEMBER 22, 1982

10:30 A.M. *plane back from Buffalo*
I spoke with Sullivan early today; he still believes we'll win,
because the trend is continuing. He believes the *Post*'s most
recent poll, which shows Koch winning by 18 or so points, will
cost us a few, but he knows it's not accurate.

On the way to the Buffalo rally this morning, George Wessel
of the local AFL-CIO handed me a slip of paper showing: Cuomo
—5,711; Koch—787; undecided—1,231. I expected to do well
with labor, but not that well. We're also hearing stories about
minor defections. A phone bank in Buffalo pushing for Judge
Thomas Flaherty dropped Koch (it was Koch's bank) and replaced him with Cuomo. Haddad tells me that some phones in
Manhattan have also gone over to Cuomo from Koch. Jack Ferro
and all our other field people report movement toward me. Of

course, they may no longer be capable of objectivity, but the signs are so consistent and so strong that, together with the Sullivan and Caddell polls, it makes it easier to believe in victory. Really? Despite the editorial endorsements; the money; the political organization; the polls . . . really? I can hardly blame them for asking, but you can hardly blame us for wanting to believe.

In the hours left for speculation, I think about how victory or defeat will be interpreted. If I lose, Koch can say that Democrats have chosen his brand of "common sense"—death penalty, cost-of-living decrease, no capital gains tax—over my theory. Or that they have selected his strong record of executive accomplishment over my less-proven abilities. (Garth will be saying, "I told you to run for the Senate, Mario!") In any event, the conceptual lines will probably be sufficiently blurred so that the race will not be deemed to have important national implications. On the other hand, if I win, the inevitable analysis will be—"Dukakis's victory in Massachusetts and Cuomo's in New York point the way to a return to traditional Democratic principles."

Rain forced our coalition rally indoors, but it worked well. The fact is that this coalition—labor, business, homeowners, minorities, the disabled, those who work and those who want to work but can't—is necessary for governing the whole state. I think it's a message worth delivering.

All afternoon at the headquarters. My temperature goes up and down, but the team's mood only goes higher. Everywhere the excitement is apparent. Reports from the field of excellent response to phone banks, volunteers flocking in to headquarters, more people on the street reaching out to say hello and wish us well. At the slightest urging, the whole roomful of volunteers will burst into cheers; labor is as high as it's been in 50 years; the Blacks are getting interested and beginning to move; the rumors are that the Koch people are nervous. Certainly it's easy to get swept away. But always the lawyer's caution monitors the reaction. I'd like to believe it all—but I don't. I tell the world we expect to win by 3 to 5 points. I mean it, but always there is the reservation, the protection against disappointment, the fear that all the good people who have worked so hard will be disappointed.

As the excitement heightens, Andrew becomes more sober and less sanguine. The apple has not fallen far from the tree. He reacts much as I do, but he is so much more talented.

On "Live at Five," the Mayor is subdued and apparently relieved that it's all over. He doesn't intend to appear on the live debate scheduled for 11:30 on Channel 5—"The Last Word." He's explaining that he gave his word to the *Daily News* that their debate would be the last confrontation. The more likely explanation is that he doesn't want to appear in a statewide televised debate because it could help me. Haddad believes that if either the *Post* or the *News* debate had been televised it would have helped me significantly. In any event, after an excellent meal with Joe Mattone and Peter Cella[1] and Bill Haddad at Giordano's, I did "The Last Word" alone.

Now tell me what this means:

In the middle of a hectic meeting Andrew was conducting at the headquarters, a balding, thirtyish, long-haired, flannel-shirted, jeans-wearing derelict type walked into the room with bagpipes and shouted, "Andrew Cuomo!" The meeting stopped. Andrew asked him who he was. He shouted he wanted to play "Amazing Grace" for Mario. They were able to get him out, but he sat in front of the headquarters all last night piping victory songs on his bag. At one point, with his bare hand he smeared a red paint sign saying "Mario Cuomo for Governor" in the middle of the street. In order to protect it, he barricaded both sides of the street—39th from 5th to 6th. When it started drizzling, he covered his car with Cuomo literature. After a full night of playing and singing he was picked up by the police this morning and taken away. He was still playing and shouting, "Mario is with God, he'll win!"

THURSDAY, SEPTEMBER 23, 1982

3:30 A.M.

In 12 to 15 hours we'll know.

The circle is closing. I started on March 16, saying, "When

---

[1] A friend and supporter, another lawyer; they were everywhere.

you vote for Cuomo, you get Koch for Mayor." I dramatized it by saying I'd wear two buttons, one on each lapel, saying "Cuomo for Governor" and "Keep the Mayor mayor." There was some discussion about whether this was too complimentary to the Mayor and ran counter to my criticism of the Mayor's record. I reconciled the positions by arguing not that the Mayor's record was good, but that he hadn't finished his job. Roger Green, the first pollster, Bob Sullivan, Weiss, Andrew and the rest of the team didn't like the approach. But for months I said it was the key. Yesterday David Burke called to say Garth is worried about the 10% who are liable to vote for Cuomo to keep Koch Mayor. He's made a commercial in which Koch literally pleads with those people who think he's been a good Mayor for a chance to go to Albany. I've made one that embodies the idea, using a woman who says she'll vote for Cuomo as Governor expecting to get Koch as Mayor to finish the job he pledged to do when we reelected him in 1981. This is designed to provide a door for those last undecideds. If it works, they can resolve their difficulty by thinking about getting 2 for 1—Cuomo and Koch in a single vote.

Our second commercial for the last two days has me getting above the battle by accusing Koch of ending the campaign with misleading false ads and saying that we think you can "hold on to Democratic Principles and your integrity and still win." We call it "Principles," and it's designed to end the campaign on a high note.

Last week Caddell asked for $200,000 more for a TV and radio campaign. Stern and Andrew got it. I don't know how, but they did. Koch is spending a fortune on Congressional endorsement ads, attacks on Cuomo and pleas not to "punish" him for being a "good Mayor." He'll outspend us, overall, 2 for 1, but not by that much in the last week. And while he's flailing about in what appears to the media to be last-minute desperation (why else would he attack and spend so much money knowing he has to face the Lehrman fortune in November?), he's trying to tell the voting world at large that he's going to win and it's only the margin that's in doubt. He does that by concentrating on his "Cuomo as spoiler on the Liberal line" theme.

This kind of contradiction has been constant for Koch. He says

Cuomo's disloyal to the Democrats and endorses Republicans himself. He says "trust me" as Governor and violates a pledge by running. He says he saved the City but says, "Don't worry about Bellamy, I'll run the City as Governor by sitting on the Financial Control Board." He says Cuomo has no record, but then uses Cuomo's '81 endorsement of him allowing Cuomo to ask why the endorsement was so valuable if Cuomo didn't have a record. And so on . . .

The contradictions occur because Koch never had a strong rationale to begin with. I notice them, and they seem to make him vulnerable. The important and unanswerable question is how the voters see them.

Last night we had a rally in Long Beach. Only about 150 people came, but it was a lively, intelligent, dedicated group. Mostly Jewish, as is Long Beach dominantly, they reminded me of so many groups we've seen over the last 6 months. I was able to get them to their feet at the end by talking about the "soul" of the Democratic Party. After all was said and done, they want to stand for something. They want to believe in something.

It's clear to me that I was right about the death penalty when I said some months ago—only half believing it—that Koch would be forced to back away from it because I would embarrass him with his "politics of death." He hasn't mentioned it in a single commercial. It may still cost me votes, but I don't believe it's the factor everyone thought it would be. At least not in this Democratic primary.

Matilda finished up the evening on her own. She left me at Long Beach and did another meeting. The raves about her continue from everywhere. The only thing that can slow her down as a campaigner is positions on issues that will make her less popular. Right now, however, they don't really hold her accountable on the issues.

I've also heard good things about Maria and Madeline, who have been forced into new roles which they've handled with skill and charm. Margaret, meanwhile, has gone about the business of arranging the wedding with her typical efficiency. This is quite a group of women.

Andrew is near exhaustion. He has a tendency to overwork himself. It's a syndrome I recognize and understand.

Chris gets taller and more mature. He seems to be growing

before my eyes. I'm eager to bring some predictability into his life after the election. I'm not sure whether victory and the prospects of the Governorship frighten him more than defeat and rejection would depress him, but I know victory will work a greater change. Whatever happens, we'll work to see it's good for Chris.

Perhaps sensing defeat—or maybe just to widen their margin of victory as they predicted—the Koch forces have been spreading the rumor that they are concerned about the reaction of non-Jews to the Israeli invasion of Lebanon. The rumor is they believe it will hurt Koch. A second rumor, also clearly from their side, is that some are voting for Cuomo because they love Koch too much to lose him. I think they are doing two things: trying to produce votes in the Jewish community and laying the groundwork to explain his defeat, should that occur.

Another predicted development has been the way the media gave me equal coverage with Koch after Labor Day. I thought in March that Koch's chasing everyone out of the race would prove to be an advantage for me and that in the end a one on one with Koch gave me my best chance for victory. It has. The amount of coverage the media have given me has been fair— occasionally even generous—and it has helped soften his huge advantage in paid commercials.

We never did get to bring President Carter up to campaign. I wanted to on Labor Day, and he couldn't make it. I must ask him to come up for the general election—if I'm on the Democratic line.

I slept a few hours and was awakened by Harvey Cohen's 7 A.M. call wishing me luck. Matilda, Maria, Madeline and I voted at 7:30 and said the appropriate thanks to the photographers gathered to take the traditional polling-place pictures.

Breslin came to the house to do the first column on me he's ever done. He sat at the table and took notes.

A few hours of puttering and phone calls at the house. I received my first phone call from WABC at about 2:30. The caller said—I thought—that Koch was ahead by 7 points in the New York City suburbs and Erie areas in a test of 200 exit votes.

Inconclusive, of course, but I thought the vote was disappointing, and I went through 15 minutes or so of conditioning myself for the worst. I didn't know that our own calculations showed us losing those areas by 15 and still winning overall by 2 points.

A call to Haddad straightened me out, and I went from resignation to confidence, but having been so recently to resignation I braced myself for a return visit.

President Carter called. He said he had been told by Caddell that I could win. He was enthused. He's eager to work in the general election.

Chris came home from school with two friends. Not even a question about the race—right out to the street to throw a football around.

About 4 o'clock I put on a steak. Spagnoli calls. *Daily News* says first exits say the race is very close. Upstate doesn't start voting until 12 noon. Spagnoli is elated. I make this note.

4:45: With the vote not properly reflecting upstate, where presumably I would do better, exit polls show a dead heat.

Gordon Black says Rochester turnout will be largest in history despite rain and fog.

4:55: Sample of 600. More balanced, but not perfectly balanced: Cuomo—50, Koch—48.

Our vote-pulling operation doesn't start until 5 o'clock; we should do better tonight.

Caddell "guesses" MMC will win by 2 points. He reports a Garth aide telling someone in Washington Cuomo will win by one or two points.

According to Haddad, Caddell reports networks saying we're leading slightly. Haddad asked me to start thinking about a speech—as a matter of fact, two speeches, one for winning and one for losing.

If the election had occurred when originally scheduled—September 14—I probably would have been a 10-point loser. The redistricting struggle and consequent delay has given me 10 days more to make my case. It has also created great confusion in districts, which will probably cost both of us votes.[1]

---

[1] Many voters were not timely informed of their proper polling place in the reapportioned districts.

All the TV reporting is cautious. Rumor from Haddad that WNBC has us slightly ahead.

WABC: MMC up 2½ points. Losing suburbs by 10 points. Koch big in Queens and Staten Island, dead even in the rest of the City. Cuomo getting 70% of the upstate. Pat Caddell had suburbs at 10% Koch, 5% in City, and us 2 to 1 upstate. That would have been 4 points for Cuomo. Pat thinks it could come out 4 points ahead.

8:25: WNBC says Cuomo 4 points up. Caddell says we're going to win.

9:10: WABC exits say 5 points, but at 9:25 WCBS says with 3% of the vote in, Koch is ahead 52–48. We set out for the hotel anyway.

By 9:35, in the suite, I was certain we had won, although it would take the TV reports a while to conclude that from actual returns. The early numbers, mostly from the City, showed Koch ahead.

SATURDAY, SEPTEMBER 25, 1982

I waited until now to do the notes on primary night because it reached such a high emotional pitch and was so large in its implications that I needed some time and perspective.

I stayed in our suite at the Halloran House until Koch conceded at about 11:30 P.M. He called me first. He was gracious and, I thought, even relieved.

As soon as he made the announcement our suite exploded, and downstairs in the small ballroom the cheers and screams shook the walls. People who have attended victory celebrations for many years reported they never saw anything like it. Everybody kissed everybody. There were shouts of "I don't believe it!" The cheering went on for 5 minutes. When I made my entrance with Matilda, pandemonium broke loose. The 8-man security detail could hardly keep the crowd from trampling us.

I finally made it to the platform, where Momma and the family were, and tried to read a speech Mary had typed for me minutes before. The crowd didn't want a speech; all they wanted was to cheer. The people who had helped us for 8 years without ever knowing this sweet satisfaction; the White, Black and Brown union people; the Rabbis from Brooklyn; the Disabled; the Businessmen who had gotten rich without forgetting the Democratic Party; and a whole lot of people who love winning.

It was an emotional victory. It said a lot of beautiful things to people who badly want to hear beautiful things. It said: you can tell the truth, stand up to the power brokers and editorial writers and political leaders, and still win. It was Rocky, David, the last-minute field goal by the underdogs.

At three o'clock, when we finally left the hotel, cabdrivers beeped their horns and shouted and gave me the thumbs up. One of them stopped his cab, jumped out and hugged me. The next day, on the way into headquarters, construction workers in the streets, police, young people all congratulated me.

Of course, it's not going to last. But it was a beautiful moment when all the nice thoughts, all the sweet sentiments that a hard life tends to make unrealistic, won. It wasn't Mario Cuomo—most people don't know a whole lot about me—it was the message we were delivering. Even when only vaguely perceived, it's the little guy against the big guy; the underdog against the favorite. It's nuclear freeze and ban the bomb; it's "save the whales" and Peace Corps; it's "us" against "them." And "us" won!

I was grateful that all those who gave so much for my victory finally got something in return. Matilda was ecstatic, as well she should have been; the victory was largely hers. All the kids will never forget it—Andrew, like his sometimes dour old man, immediately hit the "moderate" button when he saw the emotion raging around him. He started thinking, as I did, about the next step, the general election.

All the reports the next day would describe how we won in terms that would make it sound to me and a few others as though we had written the script over the last 6 months: we had been right about a lot of things. That's nice to know, but the question is whether we were really just lucky . . . and whether we can be lucky again.

PART III

The General Election

I was now the Democratic and Liberal candidate for governor. The Democratic candidate for Lieutenant Governor was Al Del Bello, who, after winning with Ed Koch the majority of votes at the convention, had gone on to defeat Carl McCall in the Democratic primary. Thus the Democratic line on the general election ballot would carry Cuomo–Del Bello as a team. There was, however, a complication having to do, not surprisingly, with the Liberal party and their selection as my running mate on their line of Harold Baer, Jr. With two different teams —Cuomo–Del Bello and Cuomo-Baer—on the Democratic and Liberal lines in the general election, the vote totals would be kept separate, and I would lose the benefit of adding the two lines together. Fortunately, Baer decided to accept a pending judicial nomination, and the Liberals designated Del Bello to replace him.

Thus the candidates for governor and lieutenant governor on the Democratic and Liberal lines on the general election ballot were Cuomo and Del Bello. On the Republican, Conservative and Right-to-Life lines, our opponents were Lew Lehrman and Jim Emery.

Lehrman's candidacy proved a point I had been making for some time, as have many others: given a reasonable amount of commitment and energy, money can buy political success—or come very close.

Lehrman is a highly educated, fiercely competitive and wealthy individual who set out, unabashedly, to spend a large part of his personal fortune in order to win the governorship. He had never held elective office, or even run for office before. Indeed, he hadn't even lived in New York State until a few years before he decided to run for governor. He was virtually unknown, with no record of public service. His only published political statements indicated that he believed in the gold standard and supported Reaganomics.

Armed with President Reagan's pollster, Richard Werthlin, and a long-time Republican television consultant, Roger Ailes, steered by Adam Walinsky, and with an unlimited amount of money for advertising, the Lehrman campaign was as simple as it was masterly. Lehrman's anonymity was an advantage. He was a clean slate upon which any image could be drawn through television and radio ads. Deciding what image was easy—just find out what the polls said would sell. The polls indicated that neither the gold standard nor Reaganomics would enhance the image—the public knew little of the former and New York State was suffering severely from the Reagan Recession and budget cuts—so these issues were ignored. Instead, television ads—four or five million dollars' worth to begin—depicted Lehrman as a genial family man who knew how to produce jobs—his successful business career was proof—and stop crime—with capital punishment.

Lehrman's adversary in the Republican primary, Paul Curran, was an attractive, intelligent, knowledgeable attorney. His credentials were excellent, and there seems little question that, given anything like Lehrman's financial support, he would have been the favorite to win the Republican nomination. But he had little money, was overwhelmed by Lehrman's television ads, and as a result lost badly.

By the time Lehrman got to the general election race his image had been created and firmly fixed by his ceaseless television campaign and a big victory over Curran. He was sold as a new face, a successful businessman who could make New York State thrive the way he had made Rite Aid drugstores flourish. He would cut taxes dramatically, slash government services, halt the state funding of abortions for poor women, and reinstate the death penalty.

On the other hand, by the time I arrived at the general election effort, although I had the advantage of the upset victory over

Koch, I had also paid for it dearly. We had no money at the end of the primary, and the candidate and his team were at the edge of exhaustion from what had been a draining primary.

The lack of money kept us off television for more than a week, during which the Lehrman television campaign was pervasive and relentless. That gave him an immediate edge. To make sure he kept it, Lehrman refused to accept any but a very limited number of carefully selected debates. He even refused to appear at the New York *Times* debate—an election institution in New York.

For these and a variety of other reasons—including a sense of anticlimax—the general election wasn't as much fun as the primary.

MONDAY, SEPTEMBER 27, 1982

It's Yom Kippur, a day for reflection, repentance and renewal.
A good day to look back and prepare to move forward.

I cannot describe the impact of our victory. I suspect I don't
feel it as fully as most of those around me. For all my adult life,
a monitoring device has controlled my emotional experiences.
Whether in tragedy or triumph, my psyche seems incapable of
going all the way. There is a balance wheel that drives me back
toward the center. Poppa's death and the stunning victory on
Thursday pushed toward both extremes, but I never quite made
it there.

When the Mayor conceded, I felt first an enormous relief at
finally seeing the efforts of 10,000 friends and family re-
warded. Then I felt—even in the midst of the glorious clamor
—an eagerness to get ready for the next leg of this trip. But all
around me the signs of ecstasy said there was something extraordinary about this victory: the passion of the crowd at the
Halloran House, the cabdrivers stopping their cabs to hail me
—at 3 o'clock in the morning! In the parade on Saturday,[1] jog-
ging Sunday morning, at the TV station for "Newsmakers," I
got signs of victory and broad, happy smiles. I know it can't
last, but it says something about the message we delivered that
is significant—although I probably don't fully understand the
significance.

Step back, again. He had the money, the establishment, the
media, the presumption of victory. We were not supposed to win
—and we did. "And so can you!" is the message. "As did
Momma and Poppa and generations of Giants who preceded us
here." If I could, I would put up posters everywhere saying,
MARIO CUOMO, HE DID IT OUR WAY, because indeed it is an
experience begging to be shared. I was only the convenient
vehicle for the delivery of the message. The message—what it
said and what it implied—is what is beautiful. For as long as it
lasts.

Matilda and the kids do not spend as much time drying up joy

[1]The Steuben Day Parade, the German community's annual event, in honor of Baron
Friedrich von Steuben, Prussian army general under Washington in the American Revolution.

with analysis. Andrew comes closer to my seriousness. He is already troubled about the rest of the campaign, knowing we have to regroup and find a new message with only 5 weeks to go. As soon as I put down my pen, after writing these notes, I'll be talking to him about themes.

Actually, celebration has not gotten in the way of functioning. The first thing we needed to do was bring all Democrats together. The Mayor was not available over the weekend, but as soon as I can, I need to take a picture with him. Carey has to be brought in as an advocate. I've spoken to Stanley Friedman, Manes, Esposito, Baranello and Mellman, Jim Griffin and others who were with Koch. Pete Piscatelli has called and has been helpful already. Organizationally, we'll be O.K.

I've not thought about Lehrman and his positions except superficially; most of my time has been spent finding themes and responses to themes to deal with Koch. In some ways, Koch was easier to handle. From the first day, I understood where I had to go with my argument. I'm not so sure about Lehrman, because I don't know him as well. I haven't even seen his television! I'll spend the rest of this day thinking about it. My first instinct is to concentrate on: my experience; a program of jobs and justice for New York; an attack on Reaganomics.

Much of the day has been spent making "money calls." What a tough business that is—but not nearly as tough now as it was a few months ago. Our major problem now is that we might not have the time to get the money we need.

A good conversation with Felix Rohatyn. I want to draw Lehrman out on economic and fiscal issues. I know his ideas are unrealistic, and if I'm able to highlight that, maybe Felix and other experts will help us respond.

Everywhere we hear the same thing about the primary—it was a victory that "restored our faith"; gave us "confidence"; inspired the little guys. It was "Rocky to the nth power." Some of it has been embarrassing in its generosity, although I understand it is not addressed so much to me as to the message I was delivering. I wish we could keep it alive forever, but we can't. Through November, perhaps, it will stay alive, but if we win, November is followed by "delivery" time. Then will come the beginning of disappointment and, with disappointment, the return of some of the cynicism. That period will last a couple of years, until we're able to move again.

TUESDAY, SEPTEMBER 28, 1982

Ideally, we would have had a chance by now to analyze all of Lehrman's positions and prepare our replies. But between trying to unite the Democrats and raise money, we haven't had the time. I had to make my "Thank you" and "Unity" tour of the upstate with no analysis and no set speech. I had 4 rallies and several press interviews in Buffalo, Rochester, Syracuse and Albany. The trip successfully tied those who had supported Koch back together with my team. Griffin and Crangle, Tom Ryan,[1] Jack Perry and Tom Fink,[2] Lee Alexander and Charlie Welch[3] are now all aboard. One might suspect they would participate reluctantly, but I don't think so—I sense that some of them would have preferred to be with me in the first place if they had believed I had a chance.

My speeches worked well. I argued: the State is not a drugstore; I have experience in running government that money can't buy;[4] our Administration's record is good; Reaganomics is a disaster; I have a program of "Jobs and Justice" that will build on the good of the past. I didn't spell out the program in any detail. I spent a good deal of time trying to make clear that LL is dealing in slogans and shibboleths. I called some of his proposals simplistic.[5] I'm sure the press believes that. I'm not sure to what extent I can get the public to understand, without a fortune like his for television.

The President held a press conference tonight anticipating the 10% unemployment figure that will be announced next week. The public response tomorrow will be significant.

[1] Mayor of Rochester.
[2] A lawyer from Rochester, secretary of the New York State Democratic Executive Committee.
[3] County chairman, Onondaga County.
[4] Harvey Cohen's gem of an idea for a slogan: "Mario Cuomo: Experience Money Can't Buy."
[5] For example, his Laffer-curve version of an "economic plan," which was dozens of pages long but only called for a tax cut. It was "supply side" for New York State.

WEDNESDAY, SEPTEMBER 29, 1982

We received the endorsement of the Police Conference. That will help with the Death Penalty issue.

I just read *Newsweek*. Like most of the post-election analyses, they concluded the story was Koch's loss, not Cuomo's victory. They refuse to believe that anyone but Koch could have beaten Koch.

THURSDAY, SEPTEMBER 30, 1982

I didn't like today. I was quoted as saying I would fire Carey commissioners; I was accused of attacking Reagan personally and of being willing to accept money from real estate developers. Meanwhile Lehrman commercials are pummeling me on TV all night and day. My speeches have gone well, but without time for analysis we're not as focused as I'd like to be. A cold in the head isn't helping.

The unity breakfast with Meade Esposito and the other County leaders went well. As did the AFL-CIO meeting. It's extraordinary how easily we have reconciled the parties who were divided in the primary.

Pat Moynihan set up a meeting in Washington with the Demo cratic delegation. The response was excellent. Virtually all the Congressional representatives had been with Koch, but they attended and were, I think, relieved at how easy it was to embrace my candidacy for November. The presence of Senators Hart, Cranston, Sarbanes and Jackson underscored the fact that the election in New York is being treated as a referendum on Reaganomics.

FRIDAY, OCTOBER 1, 1982

Last night was the State Committee's Unity Dinner—2,000 Democrats from all over the state.

This afternoon was the State Committee meeting. We had let out the word that there were to be no attempts at changing leadership at this point because it would be disruptive. As a result

Baranello was reelected, as were the various County Chairmen and Chairwomen in their respective counties. The time for change is after we win—if we win.

This morning I spent an hour and a half with Stanley Fink. It was an excellent meeting. He pointed out that he had been considering running for Governor and probably would have, were it not for Koch's entry, but he sees no possible competition with me for any office. We share a common outlook on the purpose of government. And he is both intelligent and sensitive. A strong relationship with him—and with Warren Anderson— would be extremely helpful after the election. I'll do what I can to build on this good start.

At the outset of the campaign I suggested a number of times that there would be 2 or 3 unpredictable events that would change the course of the campaign. There were at least that many: the *Playboy* interview; the AFL-CIO rejection of the bid for neutrality; and the 10-day postponement of the primary, which gave me the time I needed after Labor Day. I wonder what the events will be this time.

MONDAY, OCTOBER 4, 1982

6:00 A.M.

I have not yet been engaged with Lehrman. He's ducking us: he'll give us only one or two debates and they're tough because I've increased the level of expectations by my debates with Koch. And Lehrman's money is awesome. I've not been on television since the night before the election. He's on before and after every weather report. I said yesterday there are more Lehrman commercials than there are daytime tragedies on TV. This has allowed him to create the impression that he is taking the initiative on substantive issues, while I have been politicking.

There's another factor. I'm politically "wrong" on such issues as the death penalty. Lehrman has already announced that he's the "real Italian candidate" because of his positions. I was able to deflect that with a cute response in Italian[1] that made it to television, but the issue will be back.

[1] *"Io non credevo"*—I wouldn't have believed it.

. . .

Despite my reservations, people like Phil Friedman and Bob Sullivan think a good poll would show us about even now. Moynihan told me at the Pulaski Day parade[2] yesterday that his weekly poll showed me a solid 5 points ahead of Lehrman. It may be that because we brought down Goliath in the primary some people expect the rest to be easy. It won't be.

We'll know more when Caddell talks to us this afternoon with the results of our first poll.

Last night Matilda and I went to Campbell's Funeral Chapel to say good-bye to Bill Bernbach, who died Thursday night of leukemia. I had spoken to him only last week and was going to meet with him to go over ideas when he got out of the hospital. He never made it. He was a gentle, intelligent, sensitive genius of his profession. I wish he could have lived and functioned longer.

TUESDAY, OCTOBER 5, 1982

To Plattsburgh, Watertown and Utica. Well received by small organized groups. I finally had an opportunity to talk to the Plattsburgh papers about the Indian problem, and I think I made some progress. They appear not to have heard both sides of the story before now.[1]

One of the things I saw in the primary was how one should not take it for granted that the media have any deep knowledge of issues and background. I assumed a familiarity with my record. Events proved that the papers never did know what my record was: that's why Koch's campaign with the editorial boards was so effective. I never even put before them a complete list of accomplishments, in writing. My "visions" piece spoke generally about having done all the things a Governor has to know how to do, but that's too abstract. I should have given them a punch list. I will this time.

[2]Annual parade up Fifth Avenue in honor of Casimir Pulaski, the Polish general who fought and died in the American Revolution.

[1]See p. 224n. When the traditionalist Mohawks moved to the new location, some of the north country residents were displeased, because they found it a burden on their free access to certain hunting and camping lands.

. . .

Only 5 days till the wedding. I'm looking forward to it as a vacation from less important things.

FRIDAY, OCTOBER 8, 1982

My instinct, which told me I was much too negative in yesterday's debate,[1] has been confirmed. While I might have won some debater's points, I appear to have promoted a real sympathy for Lehrman on the part of much of the public. Trying too hard has something to do with the way I reacted, but probably it was more a reaction to the literature Lehrman is distributing. He says I am for coddling criminals, supporting huge welfare increases, and promoting abortion and homosexuality. I was more aggressive than usual in the debate and, I am sure, subconsciously, it was largely in response to his ugly attacks.

All along I've been unhappy that we've not had the chance to prepare for this race as we should. Yesterday was a missed opportunity and maybe even a damaging episode.

There are bits of good news, like a telephone call from Jim Wieghart saying the *Daily News* will endorse me on Sunday. But overall, I feel that the acceptance that made me a winner in the primary has been dissipated by my own conduct.

Today I disagreed with Caddell on a commercial. He wanted to make a purely negative commercial attacking Lehrman on Reaganomics. I still don't like the idea of being negative. Caddell says that's a mistake and I am giving away the election.

Joe Kraft[2] also wrote a piece saying that he thought I could blow it. And today's Gordon Black poll, which shows us even— is it evidence that victory could be slipping away?

Saw the Mayor at 3 o'clock this afternoon with Pete Piscatelli, John LoCicero and Maggie Weiss[3] in his office. I told him that I needed his help now and later, that the state's fiscal

---

[1] Between Lehrman and me, at the Sheraton Centre in New York City, sponsored by the New York *Post*.
[2] Syndicated columnist.
[3] A member of the mayor's staff.

report was going to be very bad[4] and that Lehrman's money was making him very tough. I told him that after November we should be making a big pitch for federal help, especially since I expected the Republicans to be damaged in the election.

I encouraged the Mayor to think of himself as a national voice. I said I thought he had come out of the election stronger because I had used his popularity. He said he was looking forward to working with me. The Mayor said he never looks back, and that everything works for the good. He sounds fine.

SATURDAY, OCTOBER 9, 1982

I told the Mayor yesterday that he was responsible for my "bad" performance against Lehrman because I was ready for Koch but not for a less feisty debater like Lehrman. I'm told I'm paying a big price for having been "ungracious" in the debate.

Lehrman has big advantages—he has all the money in the world and a willingness to say only what is obviously popular. You won't hear him mention the Gold Standard or Reagan unless I push him into it. My difficulty is that we have little time and not enough money to answer all the distortions and empty phrases.

Apparently the targeted mailing he's sent has gone to all the Irish and Italian surnames in the state. It attacks me—viciously —on "traditional values," crime, abortion and homosexuality. It's especially annoying because I won't have the capacity to answer him pamphlet for pamphlet.

On the other hand, I think I'm beginning to sense the vulnerable core of his candidacy. His entire campaign is a series of "plans." Unattached, unchallenged, they sound good. But it's all television talk. In the debate he was not able to defend them. WCBS-TV has called him "E.T." Rohatyn has said his economic plan is "baffling and frightening."

[4]As revealed in the October quarterly report, the state's financial condition was precarious.

SUNDAY, OCTOBER 10, 1982

The wedding of Margaret and Bob. It could not have been more beautiful unless we could have afforded to have all the people we love at the reception. All brides are beautiful—but Margaret set a new standard. And Bob matched her in his handsome elegance. Chris and the girls were splendid. Andrew and I went the whole day without a word of politics. What a pleasure!

MONDAY, OCTOBER 11, 1982

The campaign saw to it that there were hundreds of posters along the route of the Columbus Day parade. I was well received—mostly, I think, because our claque ran up and down the sidelines cheering.

There are so many ways Lehrman's money can hurt you. Now they're making jokes about it. Today I was told that Lehrman is hiring Carey Cadillacs[1] to take his voters to the polls.

Tonight on television a commentator said Lehrman shouldn't worry if he loses his chance to be Governor; he can always buy a state. For some reason I don't laugh as loud as the others: that's what he's trying to do here.

TUESDAY, OCTOBER 12, 1982

A full day. 7:20 with Bill O'Shaughnessy on WVOX in Westchester. Some stops with Al Del Bello, including a successful presentation to SUNY Purchase students in a public editorial board meeting.

Our economic development paper was released. I'm sure it's sounder and more realistic than Lehrman's: I hope that comes across.

---

[1] A limousine service in New York City.

FRIDAY, OCTOBER 15, 1982

I have not been able to recover my strength or the initiative. From all sides I am being told I am too defensive, too negative, not positive enough about my own programs. I continue to score well at personal appearances, but I have lost the "uplifting" note. Despite it all, I suspect I will win. Lehrman is going totally negative.

SATURDAY, OCTOBER 16, 1982

A.M.

Whirlwind tours of Nassau, Suffolk, Buffalo, Rochester, Syracuse have left me with $375,000 more and 4 days of mail and work from the Lt. Governor's office that I'll need to do today. It's just as well that I don't campaign: I need a few hours of reflection.

Generally there appears to be a sense that I am going to win, despite the polls, despite the television. I don't understand why, but there is no mistaking the prevalence of the view, downstate at least. I don't like it, because I don't feel it. If I had to analyze the race at this point, I could easily have Lehrman a winner. So I'm not analyzing it. Instead, I am reacting to events and thrusts from Lehrman's television. Tired, I find the instinct to hit back hard difficult to resist. So I have lapsed back into a mode that's closer to '77 than to the primary this year—at least it's perceived that way.

What I need to do is get back to talking about my vision and hope and belief. I'll work on that today.

And through it all, there intrudes the feeling that I'm going to be Governor and the concern that comes with the knowledge of how hard it will be to do the things we want to do for people. The thought and the feeling awoke me at 2 A.M. and I worked till 5:30. For a while I told myself it was silly to be thinking about the first steps in transition when I wasn't feeling sure about victory, but a voice strong enough not to need a rationale told me to start thinking about governing.

P.M.

I didn't leave the house except to jog. Matilda was out from noon until late and made four stops. I was able to have dinner with Chris: Madeline prepared it. After dinner I fell asleep watching television.

It was the kind of day I probably won't have again for a long time, if we win. It's clear now that the problems will be severe for a couple of years at least. Monday Governor Carey will announce a 600-million-dollar gap in this year's budget—ending March 31, 1983. Next year's will probably be worse, and added to it will be New York City's billion-dollar hole. So the next Governor will be working hard just to keep the State from tragedy, with fewer opportunities to do the "good" things we want to do to help people. If I am the next Governor, I will spend a lot of time explaining to the people to whom we tried to bring hope why we're not able to help them right away. It will be a time of headaches and frustration. It will be a time for looking back and being grateful for a quiet dinner with Chris and being able to fall asleep on a couch watching TV.

MONDAY, OCTOBER 18, 1982

We filed four *cinema vérité* commercials today. I wrote two pieces I like better than the ads we've put on for the last week. My dissatisfaction with the ads is just part of an overall uneasiness I have with the campaign. The two pieces I hope to get out of the filming are one on "ideas"—manufacturing buses for the MTA in New York, the bond issue for rebuilding the State's infrastructure—with the line, "There's a difference between ideas that sound good and ideas that are good and sound," and one on "visions." We'll know tomorrow if there's anything usable.

Harvey made a commercial with Matilda, Chris, Maria and Madeline that he says is great. It's all "traditional values."

Lehrman has been told the polls show me ahead. Apparently reacting to that, he has gone totally negative. The negatives are all issue-related but are to a large extent distortive. He has me "releasing criminals," saying that "there's nothing we can do about crime," and wanting to increase homeowners' taxes. That's on TV. On radio he's doing Cabin. In targeted mailings to Catholics and Jews it's "family values" and the death penalty. Of course we will never know, but I suspect these negative ads will cost me 3 or 4 points and maybe more. I will have to make some kind of answer, but ads that are merely responsive won't win me votes.

That feeling of not being able to direct the tone or subject of the campaign is enhanced by the fact that two of the dominant forces are the national economy and the perception of Carey. Neither of these is something I am responsible for, although I am affected by both. If I try the Reaganomics argument on television, it doesn't work well, because Lehrman has spent millions describing himself without showing his connection to Reaganomics. That makes my "sudden" effort at linkage less believable. And as to Carey, a lot of people will associate me with him because it's easier. That gives Lehrman the "new boy," "new idea," "fresh" image.

The truth is, his ideas are nearly frivolous, he's tied to Reaganomics, and I'm not tied to Carey. But once again, it's not necessarily the truth that counts in elections.

And more disconcerting than the election is the problem of governing. The deficit was announced to be $579 million for 1982–83. Mike Finnerty[1] and Red Miller believe we will need an income tax surcharge to close the deficit. I'm opposed to additional taxes and said so in writing. It's clear already that next year will be a tough one. Fights with the legislature, disappointed constituents, the confusion of organizing, sleepless nights, increasing unpopularity—at least for a while—not enough time for the people I love most.

THURSDAY, OCTOBER 21, 1982

I have had the feeling for some time that our effort in the general election is vulnerable. Lehrman's enormously expensive media barrage on abortion, crime and distortions of the Carey record

---

[1]Carey's secretary at the time. Bob Morgado had resigned on August 31.

is having its effect. The *Times* poll does not show it, professionals
don't see it, but I am certain it's happening.

This afternoon for the first time Sullivan indicated that he
thought I might be right. Our movement has stopped, and I am
probably less than 5 points ahead now. He had me at 7 three days
ago.

I know the thing that hurts me most is that I am not perceived
as "new." The irony is that I have many more new ideas than the
public has heard in a long time.

The fact that many people think of me as "old hat" is compounded by the media's insistence on calling me "liberal." That
confirms in some minds a tie with the '60s and a failed past.

On the other hand, Lehrman, simply by being previously unknown, is attractive to many. His avoidance of debates has
proved a good tactic, because it has allowed him to make his case
unchallenged.

The Liberal Party dinner last night was the largest since Jack
Kennedy, over 2,100 people. I got the feeling that everyone in
the room but me was sure we were going to win. What we need
to do is summon up our last ounces of energy and see if we can
win back the initiative. We have to get Lehrman back to Reaganomics and his "economic plan," which is nothing more than a
Reagan tax cut that would devastate our mental institutions and
schools and everything else the State runs for our people.

The *Post* is back to '77 in their coverage of the news for
Lehrman. I don't know what the motivation is, but they can
hardly have made it plainer that they want to help Lehrman and
hurt me. Their picture selection, placement and headlines are all
disastrous from my point of view.

FRIDAY, OCTOBER 22, 1982

4:30 A.M.

Tired, very tired, feeling the many months of struggle, last
night I went up to the den to make some notes. I was looking
for a pencil, rummaging through some papers in the back of
my desk drawer, where things accumulate for years, when I

turned up one of Poppa's old business cards, the ones we made up for him, that he was so proud of: "Andrea Cuomo, Italian-American Groceries—Fine Imported Products." Poppa never had any occasion to give anyone a calling card, but he loved having them. He put one in a little gold frame on a red-velvet background on the nightstand near his bed. Momma has one of them now, framed like Poppa's, on display in a prominent place in her china closet.

I couldn't help wondering what Poppa would have said if I had told him I was tired or—God forbid—that I was discouraged. Then I thought for a few minutes about how he dealt with hard circumstances. A thousand different pictures flashed through my mind—he was so used to dealing with hard circumstances. Almost everything was hard.

But one scene in particular came sharply into view.

We had just moved into Holliswood from behind the store. We had our own house for the first time; it even had some land around it, even trees—one, in particular, was a great blue spruce that must have been 40 ft. high.

Holliswood was hilly. Our house sat 10 or 15 ft. above the road itself, and the blue spruce stood majestically like a sentinel at the corner of our property, where the street made a turn, bending around our property line.

Less than a week after we moved in there was a terrible storm. We came home from the store that night to find the great blue spruce pulled almost totally out of the ground and flung forward, its mighty nose bent in the asphalt of the street. Frankie and I knew nothing about trees. We could climb poles all day; we were great at fire escapes; we could scale fences with barbed wire at the top—but we knew nothing about trees. When we saw our spruce, defeated, its cheek on the canvas, our hearts sank. But not Poppa's.

Maybe he was 5 ft. 6 if his heels were not worn. Maybe he weighed 155 lbs. if he had had a good meal. Maybe he could see a block away if his glasses were clean. But he was stronger than Frankie and I and Marie and Momma all together.

We stood in the street looking down at the tree. The rain was falling. We waited a couple of minutes figuring things out and then he announced, "O.K., we gonna push 'im up!" "What are

you talking about Poppa? The roots are out of the ground!"
"Shut up, we gonna push 'im up, he's gonna grow again."

We didn't know what to say to him, you couldn't say no to
him; not just because you were his son, but because he was so
sure.

So we followed him into the house and we got what rope there
was and we tied the rope around the tip of the tree that lay in
the asphalt, and he stood up by the house, with me pulling on
the rope and Frankie in the street in the rain, helping to push up
the great blue spruce. In no time at all we had it standing up
straight again!

With the rain still falling, Poppa dug away at the place where
the roots were, making a muddy hole wider and wider as the tree
sank lower and lower toward security. Then we shoveled mud
over the roots and moved boulders to the base of the tree to keep
it in place. Poppa drove stakes in the ground, tied rope from the
trunk to the stakes, and maybe two hours later looked at the
spruce, the crippled spruce made straight by ropes, and said,
"Don't worry, he's gonna grow again."

I looked at the card and wanted to cry. If you were to drive
past the house today you would see the great, straight blue
spruce, maybe 65 ft. tall, pointing straight up to the heavens,
pretending it never had its nose in the asphalt.

I put Poppa's card back in the drawer, closed it with a vengeance. I couldn't wait to get back into the campaign.

P.M.

Actually, despite my "down" feelings, for the last two days there
has been a perceptible difference in the campaign. Energized—
indeed, traumatized—by the revelation that Lehrman had moved
close to us and was about to pass us, Andrew, Caddell, Sullivan
and Haddad had already begun to "push 'im up!" They have
tightened and focused the TV and radio ads, making sure that
they make the points that we want made—Lehrman's attachment
to Reaganomics, my experience, the vulnerability of Lehrman's
economic plan. They have redirected the media team so that it
produces two beepers[1] a day, statewide, delivering the same

[1]Recorded radio messages available to stations that want them.

message. Andrew has sent signals to all the troops, to snap them into a sharper effort. And I intend to start each day with a commitment not to drift but to make specific points: experience; my program for jobs and justice; "Ideas that are good and sound, not ideas that just sound good," listing some of them—Director of Public Safety,[2] Infrastructure Bond Issue, Expenditure Cap, etc.—Reaganomics and Lehrman's illusory plan. In fact, Sullivan's polling results for the last two days have been better. That can't be because of the change in our tactics and execution, because they haven't had a chance to take hold yet. But the coincidence between the change for the better and our tightening up should be good for the campaign's final spirit. We have all the money we need for the final 10 days; there will be 3 joint appearances, our mailings and ads have been prepared, Adler is back from his trip[3] and working, so altogether we appear to be ready to do what we have to do.

There is no question that Lehrman's literature and ads have succeeded in confusing in many people's minds my position on the constitutional question involved in the abortion issue with my personal view of what would be preferable. I saw it at the Al Smith dinner[4] in the coolness with which much of the clergy received me. It made me feel I'd rather be at the Immaculate Conception[5] parish breakfast.

We continue to have good campaign days. The Hudson Valley today, with receptions in Poughkeepsie, Haverstraw and Tarrytown. And money is rolling in. The people who invested in Koch are making new judgments. Ironically, it's probably coming in too late for us to spend it all. I wish we'd had it earlier in this campaign, then we wouldn't have been off the tube for more than a week and Lehrman wouldn't have gotten so much momentum. Yesterday Lehrman filed with the Board of Elections a report showing he has spent 11.8 million dollars. We have raised 3.8,

[2]I proposed establishing a high-level position through which all criminal justice activities in the state could be coordinated.

[3]Norm had promised his wife a trip to Europe, and since he not unnaturally regarded his marriage as even more important than my victory, he went.

[4]Held annually since 1946, the Al Smith Memorial Dinner honors the late governor of New York and unsuccessful candidate for President, a Roman Catholic who did much for the poor and disadvantaged.

[5]My local church in Queens.

and most of it has been spent since the primary for media that haven't been viewed yet. If we win, it will be the first time anyone was so massively outspent on television and radio and mailings, and succeeded. That by itself is a story. To have a surplus, too— and it looks as if we will—would be an even bigger one.

Al Del Bello has proved to be a real help. He is received well everywhere, and if I am intelligent, he will make life considerably easier for me as Governor.

Dinner last night with E. J. Dionne,[6] Art Greenspan and Adam Nagourney.[7] Nice guys.

SATURDAY, OCTOBER 23, 1982

Matilda, from all reports, is wowing them upstate. Her commercial on traditional values has been the best-received commercial we've offered.

Margaret called immediately upon her return from her honeymoon on St. Martin. She sounded great.

Chris is thinking a lot about girls these days. He's 12. He's about 6 years older than I was when I was 12.

More and more people tell me Andrew should be part of my government if I win. More and more I believe that would be a mistake for Andrew, although it would be good for me and for government. I want to see him pass the Bar and do his own thing. He's better equipped than I am in all ways—except experience. I want to see him realize his potential.

Madeline was home. She seems to have adjusted well at the College of New Rochelle; her midterms start next week.

I haven't seen Maria for a few days; even when I'm at the headquarters she's on a different floor.

Mayor Corning has written me a couple of notes from Boston, where he's receiving treatment. I want to get to see him again as soon as possible. I feel guilty about not having been there already.

. . .

[6]A reporter for the New York *Times* who had been promoted to duty as a foreign correspondent.
[7]Political reporter for the *Daily News*.

One thing that is most troublesome and disconcerting is the stream of distortions we're subjected to. Lehrman now has ads on 100% assessment, quotas, abortion and tax increases that are misleading.[1] I've told Andrew and Harvey I want to answer them, if only in a press conference.

The *Daily News* Straw Poll says I'm ahead by 10 points. I don't feel it.

SUNDAY, OCTOBER 24, 1982

The first confrontation since the *Post* debate, with Gabe Pressman on NBC. The consensus was that I did well, although the format didn't allow for any knockouts.

In the afternoon we appeared for a brief joint interview on the David Brinkley network show, "This Week." Again, there was no exchange, which I believe puts me at a disadvantage. Lew is glib on the monetary issue, but I think he is purely academic. He has not made the transition from the textbook to the real world.

I took off the rest of the day and lay around the den with Christopher watching TV. Andrew stopped by to eat. We treasure these infrequent opportunities more and more.

TUESDAY, OCTOBER 26, 1982

6:00 A.M.

Bobbie Burns's lines[1] suggest it would be helpful for us to understand how we are perceived. Maybe so, but I don't like looking at myself on television, because if "others" see what I see, I wouldn't expect them to vote for me. Last night I watched the

---

[1]"100% assessment" refers to a controversial position that all real property should be required to be assessed at its actual full market value (100%). The result would have been to drive up taxes for many homeowners. The ads misrepresented my position as being in favor of the increased taxes for homeowners. Lehrman said I suggested "quotas"; I didn't and don't. The ads made it appear that I, personally, favored unrestricted abortion and tax increases. All the ads appeared to be designed to trigger negative reactions among carefully targeted special-interest groups.

---

[1]"O wad some Pow'r the giftie gie us / To see oursels as others see us!" ("To a Louse").

taped *Daily News* debate. I looked somber, jowly, occasionally angry and humorless. That, I've learned, is what Roger Ailes has told Lehrman my TV image is, and it helps explain why Lehrman has insisted that our only debates be TV appearances. In any event, there will be only one more, on Friday.

My visit to the *Times* editorial board went well. I expect them to endorse me, mostly because they think Lehrman is "unrealistic."

Lehrman may be unrealistic about government, but he is certainly realistically programmed for a political campaign. He is hitting every emotional chord that the polls reveal—death penalty, Carey connection, "liberal." His "debate" yesterday was a series of paragraphs on those points for the cameras. The insiders know what's happening and are mostly derisive of it. But it works, I believe, on much of the voting public in a general election. That, I think, is what explains the heavy undecided vote—still 19%. Sullivan tells me he "likes" the "structure" of the undecided—they're "my" people. I think "my" people should have been with me already. I'm afraid that Lehrman's campaign of negatives and distortions has kept my people from me and will continue to, unless I can rebut his case. I conclude that massive mailings, ads and TV on "traditional values" and "experience" and "jobs" are the antidote. And that's what we'll do.

If I didn't know about the polls and the heavy "undecided," I could easily be fooled into believing I'd win comfortably just from the reception I get "on the streets." Last night 1,500 of our "old friends" came to Antun's to wish us well. What a show they put on—it was wildly enthusiastic. David Garth doesn't tell his candidates about the polls he takes. He arranges to reserve the truth—as his polls reveal it—to himself, so that he can manipulate his candidate into appropriate postures and moods, as he analyzes them. Just putting a candidate in a setting like last night's would have boosted his confidence substantially. But I know the polls, so it doesn't have quite the same effect.

Today we travel to the Southern Tier. We're weak there, but, like the rest of the State, it's a beautiful area to visit.

11:30 P.M.

A grueling day in Binghamton, Elmira, Ithaca and Utica. There was real warmth and enthusiasm. My victory is assumed by most of my upstate supporters. I tried hard to point out how difficult victory would be; how the impact of the negative mailings could not be measured, how Lehrman's overall advantage in TV and radio exposure was difficult to answer—but nothing I say changes the dominant belief that I will win. I spoke too long and without enough focus. It happens when I need rest, but this is no time for rest.

On the Convair we hired for the trip, we had good discussions with Adam Nagourney, Dave Dawson,[2] Mike Oreskes,[3] Art Greenspan, Jack Shanahan[4] and Marcia Kramer. What a difference money makes—we could have gone to Japan on the plane we had today. Money is being thrown at us by people who think we're going to win and think they should have a part of it. This morning we received a $15,000 check from Herb Allen[5] with a note that said, "Mondale made me do it." A few months ago I couldn't get 15 cents, and if I lose on Tuesday, I won't get 15 cents again. I remember Jackie Gleason and his great line: "SIC TRANSIT GLORIA MUNDI!"

THURSDAY, OCTOBER 28, 1982

Dick Starkey called at 6:45 this morning. He called it "breakthrough" day. Normally conservative and cautious, he said that things seemed to be "too good to be true." The *Daily News* straw poll has us at 13 points—up 3 in about 6 days. The *Times* endorsed us. Upstaters were quoted as saying that Lehrman has not roused the Republicans—"there's no 'pit in the stomach' politics coming out of the Lehrman campaign." And everywhere I go—to the women at a midtown Manhattan hotel, Bishop Joe Sullivan and Catholic Charities at 191 Joralemon Street, rallies in Brooklyn, students at Stony Brook, Grumman in Nassau and the unions

[2]Correspondent, Gannett News Service.
[3]Albany bureau chief, New York *Times*.
[4]Reporter, Associated Press.
[5]Officer of Allen & Co., an investment house.

in Melville—victory is in the air, powerfully, pervasively . . . mysteriously. It happens suddenly. In days everything changes without clear reasons why. Observers and analysts point to episodes and events—a poll, a gaffe, a debate—but none of them individually or cumulatively satisfactorily explain it. At some point a decision seems to have been made almost simultaneously —by vast numbers of people at the center of the process. At the moment it is announced, silently, to the rest of the masses, it begins to percolate. It moves quickly. Waiverers snap to. Tentative opinions change. Undecideds commit. Not all, but enough to make the shift obvious and dominant. It happens too quickly to be reported. Too far under the surface to be photographed. But it is unmistakable. It can be felt. It can be seen on the streets. It can be heard in the crowds. That's what's happened.

It creates no euphoria for me. I resist accepting it with all my strength. My lawyer's caution and an instinct that goes back through generations of a family that's never been economically secure say, "Hold on to disbelief," "Take nothing for granted," "Don't expect, don't want, don't believe, because they'll fool you." I think about Ed in the primary and how sure of victory he was a couple of weeks from the end. My intellect tells me the situation is not analogous, but I want reasons to disbelieve, and I find them. It's still true that the effect of Lehrman's millions of pieces of targeted mail is impossible to predict. I point to that publicly. The media ignore my reservations: they believe it's over. They think I'm coy or too cautious. They don't understand another reason for the resistance to accepting the race as over. It would mean accepting the burden of governing. No one— except perhaps the Governor—knows how difficult that will be; how totally it will consume my life; how frustrating and punishing it will be—at least for a while. Of course, I have always known it and I will handle it. But I allow myself now the reluctance, the tentativeness, the unwillingness, because I suspect that in a few days I will not be able to.

Lehrman must think of it as a desperation effort for him. He's going all out with attacks. He's calling us "anti-Semitic." How? Upstate a cartoon of Lehrman is distributed by my people. It shows him carrying a suitcase full of money, departing Pennsylvania on the way to Albany. In the foreground is the Capitol with a sign staked in the lawn saying "Not for Sale." How is this anti-Semitic? The caricature of Lehrman shows his hook nose. John Buckley, his press person, says the nose makes it anti-Semitic. There's only one way to answer that—with humor. My answer, for Andrew: "If they are trying to beat my father by a nose, it can't be done!"

A strange problem has developed. We have more money than we can spend—much more! I told Stern today that I believe we have a moral obligation to tell people we will accept no more contributions.

My neck is sore. My back aches. My voice is gone. It must be that I'm bracing myself for good news.

SATURDAY, OCTOBER 30, 1982

I have reduced the schedule to the bare necessities—a television event a day and "must" shots like the "whole ticket" picture we took today at the Empire State Building.

The rally at Arthur Avenue[1] this morning surprised some of the media. They hadn't expected the intensity of the support from the Italians. I wasn't quite as taken as they were. I recognized most of these people as unassimilated and heavily unregistered. Their enthusiasm is infectious and encouraging—the shouts, the screams, the hugs, the kisses stimulate everyone. But they do not represent an awful lot of voting strength. I go mostly because I love the place and the people.

Even in their exuberance and unabashed admiration, the Italians of Arthur Avenue have not changed their mind about the death penalty. As I left the rally I heard shouts from different parts of the crowd: *"Pena di morte!" "Pena di morte!"* They are especially loud today after the New York *Post* carried a headline: "Cop Killed by Gunman." I can't believe the issue won't hurt me—but I wouldn't even try to guess at how much.

Yesterday the Jewish Community, today the Italians, tomorrow the Hispanics. I tell them all the same thing—we were never

[1]The main shopping street of the area known as Belmont, in the Bronx—home of the Italian American community there.

meant to be a melting pot; we are a mosaic. Our beauty derives from the harmony of our coming together in our differences. I like the message because it's right and it rationalizes what otherwise could become divisive and harmful. In talking today to the Arthur Avenue Italians, I stressed the Blacks and the African culture in my litany of different people. I heard and saw in those beautiful Italian faces no resistance, no grimaces, no anger. That's a wonderfully hopeful sign.

The meeting with the Jewish Community was also encouraging. 700 or so Jewish leaders at the Sheraton Centre. Howard Rubinstein said he's never seen such a cross section come together behind a candidate—especially a non-Jewish one. Jay Goldin preceded me to the platform. He spoke in Hebrew part of the time. At the beginning of my remarks I complained that Jay had stolen my thunder; that I had been working on speaking in the "vernacular" but now he had done it before me. I told them I would try it anyway because I had spent so much time working on it. Then burst into Italian: *"Cari amici giudei, tanti auguri e saluti."* The place broke up. The surprise delighted them, but beyond that they understood what I was saying—"I'm not Jewish. I'm not going to patronize you. I am aware of our differences and I revel in them." It was the mosaic instead of the melting pot again, and I elaborated on it. They received it at least as well as the Italians. I'm convinced that if all I did as Governor was deliver the mosaic speech 100 times, it would be a worthwhile four years.

I made the mistake of watching "Inside Albany" 's taped replay of the last debate between me and Lew. I didn't like my performance. I looked too hard, too negative, at times arrogant. I was trying hard not to reveal my anger at the increasingly distortive campaign he's been running, especially with the mail to selected—they call it "targeted"—groups, but I failed. I'll have to do better tomorrow morning on "Newsmakers."

It is impossible to convince the people around me that the race is not over. The argument now is over the margin of victory. I won't deny the logic of the conclusion: Lehrman has lost his rationale. But still I don't feel it the way I did in the primary. That may be because the primary was more a victory I won by my positions on traditional Democratic principles, my handling of the role of the underdog, my appearances at the Democratic Convention, AFL-CIO convention and the debates. The general election is more controlled by factors beyond both candidates—Reaganomics; Carey; the desire for a new broom; the desire for experience; ethnicity; party registration. These are all things that were in place as soon as the race started. If I win, it will be because these factors produced victory from the beginning, and all I had to do was not to upset the predictable effect they would have.

I continue to be immensely proud of the way the family has performed. Very few times in our political history has anyone been received the way Matilda has. Everywhere she goes in the State, she is considered sincere, intelligent, dynamic and indefatigable. Her emergence over the last few years is a reminder of how much unrealized potential there is in our nation's women. We are only now allowing them to function fully. Matilda's extraordinary success reminds us—or teaches us, as the case may be—that if we can find ways to free them, they will add dramatically to our ability to achieve good things. Maria has performed as well as her mother, although she has received less publicity. I have heard a dozen times about how poised, intelligent and attractive she is as she moves around the Metropolitan area, pinch-hitting for me. Madeline has had less opportunity because she's back at school, but I have heard similar comments about her.

Andrew has been described as the "revelation" of the campaign. He's done it all. Now there is no question in anyone's mind who is running things. I've even stopped reviewing the commercials. I've written only a couple of scripts. I've left the selection and timing of commercials to Andrew, Pat C. and Harvey. Andrew does most of the dealing with the Press, the Unions—with everybody. The people who know him best—some of whom only recently have come to know him, like Sandy Frucher—think he should be Secretary to the Governor. I'm sure he'd be effective, but I am afraid to get him that close. I'd rather see him outside of Government but in touch with it.

I want him to pass the Bar, establish himself as an attorney and as an independent quantity. I don't want to see him limited by me.

And Chris, our prize. He's not troubled as much as he was by the campaign. He's apparently found a distraction—girls. He's "styling" his hair now and has a much more "sophisticated"

demeanor than he did 6 months ago. The campaign has moved
down a notch in his list of attention holders. I think it's been a
good thing. The outcome can affect him seriously, and it's best
he not be too troubled by it now.

Frank and Joan and Marie and Ted have worked very hard. Jan
Pierce tells me Frank has blossomed as a political honcho. It's
beautiful to see him use ability he's always had and didn't get the
full chance to use.[2] Marian and Natasha[3] and the kids have all
helped. And the greatest stalwart of all, the only father I have left
—Charlie Raffa—has been great! "Puncha! Puncha! Puncha!
Fight! Fight! Fight!" His whole life, a series of wars he *must* win.

Altogether, there have probably been few times in our State's
history when a candidate had more to be proud of in his family's
performance than I this year. I hope someone gives them the
credit they deserve.

Indeed, I believe everyone in the campaign has performed
well.

Bill Haddad is tough and strong. From the moment he came
into this campaign—when we "couldn't win"—he has given us
an additional dimension and plausibility.

Bill Stern has worked a miracle. Now it's easy: all he has to
do is count the money as it cascades in. But in the beginning—
when it wasn't easy—he worked with total dedication, high intelligence, great imagination and unbelievable results. To have
finished the primary not only without a debt, but with a large
surplus—in fact, having generated $25,000 in interest by invest-
ing campaign funds—must have set a record. Whoever heard of
a campaign paying income tax, as we will? That must be a big
story. I hope we can keep Bill involved.

Norman Adler should also be in government, if we could find
an appropriate slot. He's talented, well motivated, honest. He
can help people.

Jim Featherstonhaugh is reliable, bright, hard-working and
resourceful. Sometimes I think I'm glad I don't know more about
his resourcefulness, but there's no question that he will be a
success at anything he chooses to do.

---

[2]Since he was the oldest of the children, the burden of the family's hard early days
fell mostly on Frank.

[3]Frank Raffa's wife, Marian, and Natasha Vecchio, my sister Marie's sister-in-law.

Gene Spagnoli continues to be the steady, pleasant, reliable professional. He is universally loved and admired. He has been a rudder and an anchor, as needed.

Jan Pierce has been giving it 100% since he came aboard. He is passionate about his beliefs . . . his likes and dislikes. Sometimes I wish he were less passionate about his dislikes, but that's mostly a matter of style. Carolyn Walsh, Bella Abzug, Herman Badillo, Denny Farrell—all have performed superbly.

Sandy Frucher didn't think we could win in the beginning, but I suspect he always wanted us to. Once he became convinced we could do it, he went all out to help us. His knowledge of government and of campaigning is hard to match.

Harvey Cohen is still unbeaten in political campaigns. The more I become familiar with his extraordinary instinct for what people feel and understand, the more I'm convinced that his failure to lose is no coincidence. He is another guy I would like to have with me in government, but I'm afraid he would have to give up too much.

The office has also worked far beyond the call of duty. It's been especially hard on them because we've been so insistent on not mixing the campaign and State business.

No part of a campaign is more difficult than scheduling. No one takes more abuse from the candidate and the constituencies than the scheduler. No one has ever done it all better than Tonio Burgos. He's been my friend, my ally, my charge. He started life with very little and he has grown into manhood—stable, sensitive, caring and respected. Peter Drago, Mary, Maria Giammarino and Ellen Conovitz have worked with him to make up a great team. Ellen's intelligence and strengths, especially in the Jewish world and the Nassau community, have been incalculably valuable to me.

Now I'm sorry I began writing down names. Every time my pen stops I think of a dozen more—Saul Weprin, Tony Papa, Ricki Rubinstein, Jack Ferro, Louise Slaughter, Toby Dolgoff, Jean Angell, Hank Bersani, the Corning family of Albany—Pat Carey and the young tigers Mark Gordon, Royce Mulholland, Gary Eisenman, Elaine Ryan, Ethan Riegelhaupt. I could go on and on. And I do in my mind.

Altogether they have conducted a campaign that was strategi-

cally sound (if not flawless), well executed, clean and—at moments—beautifully stylish. The *Rocky* theme at the convention,
the placards at the parade, the inevitable pull-out operation—all
contributed to an extraordinary effort, the excellence of which
would not be diminished by a defeat on Tuesday and would only
be confirmed—not established—by victory. When I think about
victory and defeat, as inevitably one must at this stage, the thing
that saddens me most is contemplating the disappointment all
these people will feel if we don't succeed.

Will we? Will we win on Tuesday? My head tells me we will
—not my stomach, my head. By how much? If it weren't for the
death penalty and the targeted mailings aimed at Catholics and
the murder of the policeman, I would say 55–45. Now I will say
7 points, 53.5 to 46.5. This is risky business, this prediction
business. I was dead right the first time—almost. I hate to risk my
streak this way. But we'll see.

The campaign is a series of hundreds of judgments. One that
I've made hasn't been much noticed by the media. Every potential
presidential candidate has asked for the chance to campaign with
me—Mondale, Kennedy, Glenn, Hart, Cranston. Both Frank
Lautenberg[4] in New Jersey and Dukakis in Massachusetts asked
me to come to their states to campaign with them. Haddad wanted
Kennedy. Burgos wanted Glenn. Weiss wanted Mondale. I
wanted to avoid having any of them and to avoid going out of state
to campaign, on the theory that we were best off keeping the focus
on my experience and the state issues—as well as on Reaganomics
—instead of converting this into a dominantly national campaign.
It was a close call. Much could have been added in terms of
publicity and excitement if we had brought in a whole array of
national Democratic stars. It would have given me national prom-
inence. But my instinct told me otherwise. Bob Sullivan agreed
with me. That's usually a pretty good sign. We'll never know if the
judgment was a good one or not. Here again, the impact is not
clearly measurable the day after election day. But if we win, at
least I'll be able to say the decision didn't beat me.

Thinking about judgments, it occurs to me that I've had to
make a lot of judgments here without the benefit of communal

[4]Democratic candidate for U.S. senator in New Jersey. He won without my help.

thinking. I probably couldn't afford to do that as Governor. I know I wouldn't want to. It saved me a lot of time in the campaign—and a lot of aggravation—but it also cost me a great deal because I lost the benefit of input from really bright people like Sullivan, Andrew, Haddad and the others. For example, the themes for the announcement in March were decided upon by me when I wrote the speech. Seven and a half years; a vision for the future; crime as a number one priority. That didn't change much until near the end, when we put more emphasis on Reaganomics and MMC as "The Real Democrat." Even that development was in part the result of my decision, on a daily basis, to emphasize Ed's embracing of candidate Reagan at Gracie Mansion in 1980. We're finishing on a new tack that I've decided on —one that I've kind of articulated my way into—and it hasn't been highlighted by the media yet. It's the notion that even Pres. Reagan has recognized the failure of his program. There is no way to interpret his 100-billion-dollar increase in taxes and signing of the Jobs and Drug bills except as a correction of Reaganomics. But Lehrman refuses to accept that. He says the tax cut should not have been changed, but that the program should have gone forward on the basis of a balanced budget—and that would have meant devastation to the Northeast. It's another message that can't be delivered in 30 seconds. I've been trying to get it across in my daily appearances, but then anything that doesn't lend itself to 30-second presentation doesn't appear to work well in the media.

Sullivan and I agree as to what has worked—and it's frightening. Lehrman's long, expensive television campaign has created some unshakably strong impressions. Eight million dollars bought him an image as a nice guy—a family man.

It was bought in the nonpolitical season, and it worked with many. Sullivan thought the TV image would be discounted once it became clear that Lehrman was running a negative campaign, but that hasn't occurred. One reason probably is that we didn't have the money we needed to match his television in the beginning. The image has proved deeper and tougher to shake than he thought. Sullivan is also disconcerted by the power of the death-penalty syndrome. He's never heard it as loud and as long as this year. He's also a little surprised at the high number of undecideds so late in the campaign. One never knows for sure about these things.

MONDAY, NOVEMBER 1, 1982

An astrologist sent me a horoscope that said I was going to die on election day. I don't know if she meant literally or figuratively. Just in case she means it literally, I think I'll vote early.

TUESDAY, NOVEMBER 2, 1982 (ELECTION NIGHT)

Voting at 7:45. A battery of reporters and cameramen. The general feeling is MMC will win. A lot of investors believe it, too; checks continue to stream in from people who want us to know how much they are for us even if it's too late for the money to be helpful in this campaign. All morning with Ken Auletta and Eli Tieber of the *Post*—the mood is up.

Then at 3 P.M., I learn that WABC has 360 samples—too few to be a statistical sample, and without knowing where they're from—and the vote is dead even! The first news we receive is bad! It summons up every unpleasant possibility. My chest tightens. I hate to tell Andrew, but I must. He's surprised. Both of us remember our own dark instincts. Today I received 4 pieces of Lehrman mail. The vote is said to be bigger than ever. Is it possible his campaign has had the effect I was afraid of? We'll know more at 4 P.M. Can it be that Garth, who predicted 10 points this morning; Caddell, who predicted 10 points this morning; Gordon Black, who picked 7 points this morning; and all the others who had me winning could be made wrong by the turnout or the effect of the targeted mail? It wouldn't seem so. But at this stage it seems easier for me to believe the worst. Why? Why is it so hard for us to believe the best will happen when we're given a choice?

Matilda hears the news. She philosophizes: "We've done the best we can. You're much better qualified. We can't do any more. If you don't win, it's their loss. Moreover, you did it right, Mario. You have nothing to feel bad about."

Haddad calls at 3:50. 960 votes says WCBS, and it's neck and neck. So the trouble deepens. Matilda notes that Reagan coming on "didn't help." She's referring to President Reagan having gone on television to argue that Americans should "stay the course" and give the Republicans a chance.

Now all the suspicions I had seem to take on substance. The last 2 weeks of the campaign were purely reactive. The negative mail was having its impact. The death penalty was hurting more than it ever has. The new-broom syndrome is strong.

I get ready. What are the advantages of losing? "Obscurity." Call it "privacy" and make it a virtue.

Pat Caddell at 4:23. WCBS says it's better than good. WNBC says it's 6 points–Cuomo with some City bias. He says an hour ago he had his stomach in his throat. He feels 9 million pieces of mail have made it closer than he expected. He says he'll have better results soon.

Haddad calls at 4:52. WABC says Cuomo is 2 points ahead and moving up. Its computer is behind the others.

A brief respite for a pleasant discussion with Clive Barnes.[1]

How quickly things change! How chaotic it is now! I'm trying to dictate a speech to Haddad in between receiving calls from WABC, Caddell and others. 5:05, while talking to Haddad, WABC says ⅓ of possible interviews completed, dead even. But City underrepresented. It sounds as though WABC is still behind the others. Another call at 5:07 from Gordon Black to Haddad. Black says we'll win by 6 points on the basis of exit inter views.

Al Del Bello calls at 5:10 to congratulate me, to say he would disregard the polls—he believes our victory will be much bigger.

Mary Tragale, who has been at the Sheraton all afternoon preparing for my arrival, has been watching TV. Exit polls indicate 50% of the people believe Reagan is right. The principal force working against Cuomo is Halloween candy, Tylenol and crime in general.[2] That's all associated with the death penalty.

---

[1] As a drama critic, Barnes had seen the Koch/Cuomo debates as theater—the beginning of a whole new political art form.

[2] Just before the election, on Halloween, there had been several cases of razor blades concealed in trick-or-treat apples; the first week of October, six people in the Chicago area died after taking cyanide-laced Tylenol capsules.

A call from a radio station: "With ⅓ in, analyzed, you're up by 4 points. You're going to win."

It's extraordinary how things change near the end. How much they are subject to last-minute events—things we couldn't have been prepared for. But most of all, I think, the 9 million pieces of mail have hurt. Maybe we should have some kind of screening before materials can be sent.

Fabian Palomino called. Republicans are preparing an order to show cause to seize voting machines, to investigate alleged irregularities. Palomino, as usual, is on top of it. He's surprised it's so close. But it's still early.

Pat Caddell at 6:33. WNBC and WCBS are saying 6 to 8 for Cuomo. WABC *is* behind the others! He says, "Mario, you're going to be Governor!" In 3 hours and 33 minutes, we went from frustration to relief: imminent failure to victory—a stomach that churns to a good glass of red wine. That's one thing about this business—you get more than one lifetime.

WEDNESDAY, NOVEMBER 3, 1982

7:00 A.M. There was *still* a long way to go. For the rest of the long night, the race was neck and neck, all the way to the finish line. By 11:00 it seemed clear to Caddell and Haddad —who were monitoring results and analysts closely—that we would win a slim victory. Lehrman was prepared to concede, but Haddad said the price Adam Walinsky demanded on his behalf was a virtual coronation of Lehrman as the permanent Republican leader of New York State. According to Haddad, Walinsky wanted Lehrman to come to our headquarters at the Sheraton and join with me in a "unity" effort, saying, in effect, that he would continue to serve as the Republican voice. Haddad seemed willing to do it. I wasn't. I didn't want to put Lehrman between Warren Anderson and me; he didn't deserve it. The Lehrman reaction was an angry discussion between Walinsky and Haddad in which Walinsky said that Lehrman would not concede. I decided not to wait.

At about 12:30 A.M., I wrote out the following lines and read them to the jammed headquarters:

We started 7½ months ago.

We were huge underdogs.

We have taken what are regarded as unpopular positions.

We have refused to distort or even use negative arguments that were available to us.

We had a president using the power of his office against us.

We were said to have an unbalanced ticket.

We were criticized for not making complex issues seem simple.

We were criticized for relying on old-fashioned principles.

We were outspent more than 3 to 1.

We were assaulted by 9 million pieces of literature.

AND WE WON!

Because people and the passion of belief are still more important than money.

Because the truth is stronger than 9 million pieces of slick literature.

Because we had Al Del Bello and Matilda and Andrew and Bill Haddad, Bill Stern, Gene Spagnoli, Harvey Cohen and all of you—and the unions, the women, the disabled and all the rest.

We've won a chance to govern.

To bring this whole state together.

To find new programs for jobs and justice.

To find new ways, better ways, stronger ways to protect our people from criminals.

To move federal policy closer to reasonableness and fairness.

To prove that the sons and daughters of immigrants—of simple people who came with nothing and built the greatest state for the greatest nation in the only world we know—can make it a better state still!

We know we can. We know we will.

We thank you all for the opportunity you've given us. And for a victory that will tell people for a generation—that nothing is stronger than the truth when people are willing to fight for it!

The closeness of the race surprised a lot of people. They had been conditioned to believe that it would be a big win. Last night it wasn't. What should have been exultation was more like relief for our team. The uncertainty for much of the night, the way Lehrman behaved, the obviousness of the death penalty impact, all dampened the evening for the insiders. But not for our supporters—they might just as well have won by 20 points. In fact, it looks like the total will be close to 5 points when the paper ballots are all counted—at least that's Fabian's guess. I'm told four out of the last five Democratic Governors—as well as D'Amato, Kennedy (over Nixon) and Nixon (over Humphrey) —won by much less. As for me, I would have settled for a one-vote victory!

PART IV

After the Election

After the election, we thought, fleetingly, about the possibility of taking a week or so "to get away from things," but there was simply too much to do. The state's budget was in deficit, and the MTA needed revenues on an emergency basis. A special session of the legislature was scheduled to deal with these and other matters.

In addition to participating in that session, I had to put together a staff and a cabinet; prepare an inaugural address, a State of the State message and a budget for 1983–84 that would have to deal with a potential budget gap of $1.8 billion.

So with little time out for reveling, we went back to work.

THURSDAY, NOVEMBER 4, 1982

We had our first post-election press conference today. Most of the questions were predictable and most of the answers were as well. At one point, however, I was asked how I would deal with Koch, who it was suspected would try to give me a hard time. Without thinking about it, I said that I had a perfect solution and then I recited Edwin Markham's "Outwitted":

> He drew a circle that shut me out,
> Heretic, rebel, a thing to flout.
> But Love and I had the wit to win:
> We drew a circle that took him in.

Actually, it's a pretty efficient working principle for this business.

FRIDAY, NOVEMBER 5, 1982

I don't believe the impact of being elected has been felt by us yet. If it has been, it's disappointingly insignificant. Things have been hectic; we've scurried from interview to interview, dinner to dinner—but I can't say that I detect any real sense of a new position or role. Maybe it's just that we haven't paused long enough to detect it. Or maybe it's because we haven't really done anything yet.

Even a standing ovation from the Italian Americans at the dinner honoring Prime Minister Spadolini last night didn't move me.

Andrew continues to function beautifully. He's now into his transition role. It's extraordinary how quickly he adapts—how fast he learns. I have always had some of that ability, but not as much as he. He wins everyone's confidence —usually on a first meeting.

Last night I sat with him after the Spadolini dinner for a couple of hours and we talked about the "talent search." Some things are clear. I want to reflect our entire coalition: Women—Blacks —Hispanics—Italians—Disabled—Business People—Unions.

It's important to distinguish my administration from Carey's, so I can't have too many holdovers. It's also important that the transition effort not function as a patronage machine. Above all, I must have the very best available.

Matilda and I did the Gabe Pressman show for Sunday. Matilda was great. She will be the best first lady ever.

I visited Mayor Corning today in Boston's University Hospital. He was emotional about my victory. It was sad to see this great man, bereft of the voice he's used so well for so many years, trying to communicate in a new, artificial, crippled way. I pray he'll be with us at the inauguration.

Bill Hennessy was in. He's willing to be State Chairman, and I will push for it. He's smart, honest, hard-working. He can raise money, help us with the upstaters.

Ned Regan called. He said "congratulations"—and gave me the bad news: New York is going to borrow $350 million out of the short-term pool. The State has not got enough cash flow at the moment. He will borrow from our own funds instead of going to the market.[1] He thinks Finnerty is a good man and thought I should get him.[2]

He also told me New York City's deficit is going to be bigger than anticipated. Big problems ahead.

Regan was very clear that he thought we should have campaign financing.[3] I don't blame him—he's thinking ahead to four years from now.

"New York audits," said Regan, "may hurt you from time to time, but we'll work together." I said I was looking forward to it.

SATURDAY, NOVEMBER 6, 1982

I ran three miles. I've given myself seven days to get back in shape.

I met with Mike Del Giudice. He's interested in serving as

---

[1] There are always some monies around that are not used on a day-to-day basis but are used as reserves against other than daily operating obligations.

[2] I did. He's now budget director.

[3] Financing of campaigns by the state, so that in the future no candidate would have the advantage Lehrman's fortune gave him.

Secretary. We agree on the way the office should be structured. I told him I wanted strong staff people as liaison to the agencies and a strategy that would make this transition the smoothest and fastest in the history of this state. He will get back to me in two days.

Sidney Schwartz came in to offer his services. He is now Deputy Comptroller assigned to the City of New York. I told him I would like him to perform that function for the state expanded by an additional function, which would consist of monitoring all state agencies to improve productivity. This would include audit implementation. An Inspector-General for efficiency instead of corruption.

Bill Eimicke[1] came in. He is bright, dedicated, good at numbers. I'll have Mike talk to him.

Mike Finnerty came in. I told him I would like to have him as Budget Director, asked him to talk to Wayne Diesel at the Comptroller's Office[2] about being a First Deputy. Diesel is first-rate, a Republican, and would give us depth.

I told Tonio to discuss with Al Levine the possibility of closing the 55th Street Governor's office and moving the operation to the World Trade Center; it would be much cheaper.

Mike Finnerty told me that the Governor will be away in Florida from Wednesday, November 10th of this week to Tuesday, November 16th, and then for a full week from November 20th on. That means I will be locked into staying in the State for that period unless I want to turn the State over to the Republicans.

Saturday evening
Dinner with the Breslins. It was a lot of fun, marred only a little by word from the State Police that we had received a death threat. They will assign City police to the house for the time being.

---

[1] Deputy commissioner of housing for the city of New York. He later joined my staff as deputy secretary.
[2] He was deputy comptroller of the Division of Audits.

SUNDAY, NOVEMBER 7, 1982

I ran this morning. On the street in front of the house when I came out there was an old car going back and forth driven by a young man with a beard and mustache. I assumed he was an undercover policeman. As I came off Francis Lewis Boulevard into the area outside of the parking lot of Cunningham Park, the bearded driver came out of the park and passed me again. Now I was sure that it was an undercover policeman.

Later in the afternoon, I mentioned it to John Foley[1] and he assumed it was the Intelligence Division. I decided to check with the 107th Pct. at about 7:30 P.M. and discovered that it was not a policeman after all.

I think it's not such a hot idea to run tomorrow, at least not alone.

TUESDAY, NOVEMBER 9, 1982

I should have taken some time off perhaps, but the problems of the State are so increasingly obvious and insistent that it would be foolish for me to think I could relax now.

A meeting with Felix Rohatyn and Gene Keilin[1] at Lazard Frères dramatized our fiscal problem. Apparently, thanks to the union contract, the City's budget is much farther out of balance potentially than most expected. The contract is well above the inflation rate for 2 years. It is, according to Kaellin and Rohatyn, inexplicably generous. In any event, it leaves the City 200 or 300 million dollars behind in '82–83 and potentially more than a billion behind for '83–84, unless the economy improves. The Mayor has said he will raise taxes and will ask Albany for the authority. He will also have freeze, attrition, probably some layoffs, although the City unions will accept that only as a last resort—and the concomitant service reductions. The Financial Control Board hasn't yet adopted the financial plan. The strategy on the part of the City seems to be to defer all of this to next

---

[1]State policeman assigned to my security detail.

[1]A partner of Felix Rohatyn at Lazard Frères.

spring—my first budget—and have the State make the hard judgments. I'd like to see the issue forced now, so that some of the
bullet biting gets done now. The City situation is only one of our
problems. There's still the MTA to deal with and the State's own
budget, which is in even bigger trouble.

I called the Governor later in the day. He's leaving for Florida
tomorrow for a week, to be followed by a week in Japan. He says
nothing should be said until we see the City's plan. I agree that
forcing the City to adopt a plan is a good strategy, but I want it
to be a plan that carries beyond this year so as to force action
now!

Saul Weprin was in. He doesn't want anything except to stay
close.

David Rubenstein came up from Washington. He had some
good ideas about transition but wants to stay in Washington
himself. He gave us some recommendations and will want to stay
close to us.

Met with Del Giudice. He's ready to come aboard. He'll meet
with Andrew to discuss details tonight.

The rest of the day was spent with paper work.

WEDNESDAY, NOVEMBER 10, 1982

Coffee with Rabbi and Libby Mowshowitz. The Rabbi wants to
help. I'll have Ellen Conovitz study possibilities.

Ray Harding came in to see me to "reinforce our relationship." He wants Dr. Harrington on the transition team, and we'll
put him on.

Governor Tom Kean[1] called. He was pleasant. We talked
briefly about "neutrality," and I agreed to come over to see him
as soon as the dust settles.

This evening, Andrew, Del Giudice and then later Sandy
Frucher were in. We talked until 10:30. Mostly general discussion, but useful. Sandy and Mike know a great deal about the
internal workings of government that is helpful.

Standard & Poor's has dropped the ratings of the State bonds

[1]Newly elected Republican governor of New Jersey.

to A+ from AA. The reason given is the gap in the budget and the legislature's refusal to deal with it. This is not good news. Clearly our first challenge will be to restore some kind of fiscal stability. I have that very much in mind in putting my team together. Del Giudice, Finnerty, Diesel, Eimicke, Schwartz are all strong numbers people and will be perceived that way. I told Mike that when we announce his selection, I'd like to be able to say this: "We've designed a new staff to fit the new Governor's new style. It will be more broad-based. It will be heavily fiscal-oriented. It will be nonpartisan. It will be more than Carey revisited."

The search for women and Blacks and Hispanics continues.

THURSDAY, NOVEMBER 11, 1982

David Rockefeller came in. We're almost back to 1975 and 1976 when it comes to fiscal problems, and we'll need the private sector again.

FRIDAY, NOVEMBER 12, 1982

I must remember Aristotle: in all things moderation. I have so many ideas about personnel, programs, changes in structure, that it's difficult for me to rest. I leave my bed well before the birds start saying "good morning," filled with notions I want to get to immediately. I've fallen into the habit of calling people before they've had their breakfast just to get things started. While I'm showering, concepts race through my mind, and they come so fast and in such numbers that if I don't write them down, I lose them. It's essential that I get my staff around me and set up a regular staff line that can run with these ideas and report back to me reliably. Regular staff meetings will be essential.

In talking with Norman Scott[1] from Kentucky yesterday, something he said struck me as a major concern. He pointed out that for all of Governor John Brown's good intentions when he

[1] A pseudonym.

became Governor, the fiscal problem so overwhelmed him that his term became little more than a struggle to balance the budget without much time to "do good things for people." It would be a tragedy if that were all I could do. I must find ways to do both. My State of the State must contain agendas of help for the disabled, the unemployed, the elderly—even if they don't cost money. My State of the State should include progressive, family- and people-oriented programs that send a signal. Campaign reform is a good one. Advocate for the Disabled is another. Task Force on the Homeless, Director of Public Safety. I must "do more with less"—not just talk about it: I must do it.

Andrew's situation concerns me. He's not happy being away from government. He now wants to put off the Bar exam until May. Perhaps he should have a dollar-a-year position like Kevin Cahill's[2] and go with a firm as well.

Mary Tragale needs help. This will be too much for her. I'll take care of it today.

SATURDAY, NOVEMBER 13, 1982

My most productive day since the election. I stayed home, leaving the house only to put out the garbage. Changing the numbers on the phones has reduced the frequency of the calls. Matilda was out most of the day and so were the kids. As a result I had an excellent opportunity to catch up. I used it. I wrote a speech for the Israel Bonds dinner honoring Morty Bahr on Wednesday; wrote the Director of Public Safety proposal; analyzed a paper on energy; designed a new office, as yet unnamed, that would combine polling, scheduling, speech writing and media—i.e., all the External Affairs of the government—and had good and useful discussions with Moynihan, Burke, Farrell, Marty Steadman,[1] Haddad and others.

Bob Sullivan and I talked about the election as reflected by the

---

[2]Dr. Kevin Cahill, an internationally known physician and a close friend of Governor Carey, served as coordinator of all health-related institutions and policy matters for the Carey administration. He was also a confidant of the Governor and a strong influence even beyond the health area.

[1]Former newspaperman and investigative reporter, now in the public relations business.

poll he's done since November 3. He hasn't analyzed it yet but he feels it's clear that many people have already forgotten exactly why they voted the way they did. The attention span of the voter is even shorter than I thought. That can be a reason for disappointment. It is also a reason for hope: it allows for redemption and renewal. Ask Nixon.

I can't slow my mind down. The more time I'm allowed, the more ideas I produce. Some of them are good ones. My problem is making sure they don't get lost. For that I need a team.

MONDAY, NOVEMBER 15, 1982

A good meeting with Larry Kurlander. I'm filling the role of criminal justice spokesperson and coordinator that we called, in the campaign, Criminal Justice Coordinator. It will be a top cabinet position—spokesperson for the government on criminal justice, negotiator for legislation—and the first time we have effectively drawn together the various parts of government which deal with Criminal Justice. As a former D.A. with a reputation for no-nonsense law enforcement, an articulate, thoughtful spokesperson, an upstater and a loyal friend, Larry seems to fit the role nicely. I'll do some more detail work on shaping up the office, then move it over into the budget, replacing DCJS. It has to be done in such a way that we are not dependent upon the legislature's approval.

I can feel the transition pace accelerating. The resumes are beginning to flood in even as the budget problems mount and the time left shrinks. So far we've been able to keep the printing of rumors to a minimum—thanks largely to Andrew—but the pressure is building. It's also clear that the first few appointments are going to be carefully evaluated for style, substance and implications.

TUESDAY, NOVEMBER 16, 1982

I made an all-out effort today to take hold of the party machinery. I met with Manes, Esposito and Friedman and spoke with Farrell and Mellman, all by 4:30. My message to them was simple. I want Bill Hennessy as State Chairman, as a unifying force. I wanted all of the Democrats, wherever they were in the primary, to agree on the move. They supported it unanimously. The problem now is a mechanical one of notifying enough County Chairmen quickly enough so that when the story breaks, as inevitably it will, too many people are not offended.

Also I want to make sure that Baranello is not too badly damaged by his stepping aside. I asked Hennessy to call him.

Hennessy will work on the convention for '84 and registration as his two priority items.

WEDNESDAY, NOVEMBER 17, 1982

Stayed home during the day. It's extraordinary how much I can do with nothing more than my black book and a telephone. I touched base with Stanley Fink, Bob Strauss[1] and several others on the Hennessy matter, making sure that he would be well received. I've asked Fabian and Jerry Weiss to meet with him this afternoon to show him some of the ropes.

This evening I spoke at the Israel Bonds dinner for Morty Bahr. It was no surprise that the audience was receptive: they were largely the labor people who had supported me. The speech on Israel went well for three reasons: it's an emotional speech; I wrote it myself and, therefore, was familiar with it; and it was typed on cards. There's no question that reading from cards makes the delivery better, and I must remember that for the future.

THURSDAY, NOVEMBER 18, 1982

Pop Raffa has grown more attached to my father's memory as he grows older himself. He was deeply upset the day before the election because Poppa was not around to enjoy it. With that beautiful instinct for the gracious touch that makes you forget occasional disagreements, he arranged to have a mass said for the

---

[1] Former chairman of the Democratic National Committee.

deceased relatives of both our families. It was this morning at St. Gerard's. The priest who said the mass, to a congregation that consisted of Matilda's cousins, Rosario,[1] his wife, Jenny Brand, my mother, Marie and the kids, talked with simple eloquence about the meaning of death. He also talked about the Governor-elect and how, despite "our imperfections," we who are in public office could project standards of conduct and morality which would benefit all the groups we represented. I thought about the millions of pieces of Lehrman campaign literature saying that I don't believe in traditional values, thousands of people who voted against me because of what they thought to be my position on abortion, dozens of pieces of hate mail, and bit my lip.

I talked about this later in the day to Peter Quinn, who I hope will be a speech writer—it's obvious I can't write all the speeches I'll need to give. Quinn is a sensitive, gentle, gifted young man who loves arranging words and singing songs in prose. I told him one of our missions would have to be to reach the religious people. He's eminently well suited to do that. His Irish Catholic New York City heritage has left him with a deep respect—and affection—for his own religious culture. One thing I don't like about him: he runs; he's thin as a rail and in great shape; he'll be a constant assault on my conscience.

Things have been hectic. I make dozens of phone calls a day to candidates, prospective candidates, political leaders and others. I have already designed three new offices for government. Director of Public Safety, Waste Fighting Office and a reconstituted Department of State.

SUNDAY, NOVEMBER 21, 1982

This morning I ran in Cunningham Park. It was beautiful. The bright colors of autumn have faded, but there are still enough maroon and tan and beige and green to make for a pretty picture. The tennis courts and the football field are lively, but the leaves

---

[1] Rosario Cuomo, a cousin of my father's and my godfather at confirmation, now eighty-five years of age. He, his wife, Maria, and his daughters, Jenny Brand and Florence, have all been part of my extended family since I was thirteen.

are dying. They are everywhere underfoot, especially where there are no paths. You have to be careful where you run, for fear that they cover a ditch, or a hole, or a boulder.

Actually, thinking of the leaves as dying is not the best way to see this beauty. It's better to think of it as a passing from one form of life to another, from one beautiful season to another.

Later in the morning, we knelt at mass at the Passionist Monastery Church of the Immaculate Conception. I've heard people say the old parish is dying because the color of the congregation is changing from white to brown and black. It's not dying; it's passing from one color to another, from one wave of immigrants to another, from one beautiful season in the Church's life to another. I prefer to think of it this way. Life is a passing, a change. I am in the midst of one now, but there will be changes beyond this one.

In the midst of preparations for our inauguration, it struck me as inappropriate to have the large and expensive affair that until now we were all taking for granted. To put a few thousand people in the Convention Center even without paying for meals or entertainment would cost somewhere in the vicinity of $70,000. Especially given our fiscal situation, this seems to me too much to justify. After all, the inauguration will be shared only by our friends—people we choose to invite. It seems like a lot of taxpayers' money to spend on ourselves.

Tonio, Pat Hanrahan,[1] Matilda and Madeline were unhappy with me when I mentioned this at home yesterday while they were making plans. They tried arguing, but they hadn't thought about it enough to answer my objections effectively. Matilda believes I am overdoing the "austerity" approach and that an inaugural has historic and spiritual and motivational value. We'll think about it for a few days, but at the moment I'd rather just have as many friends as we can get into the mansion for a buffet and let it go at that.

We're probably farther ahead at this point than any transition in the history of the state. This week I'll be ready to announce two new offices—the Director of Criminal Justice and the Spe-

[1] A volunteer during the campaign, now a member of my staff.

cial Assistant for Management and Productivity. Following that, maybe even before Friday, we'll be able to announce the entire staff. As soon as possible I want to show the outlines of the pattern of my government—excellence, well balanced to show connection to all the numerous elements of the population of this diverse state. Our differences—ethnically, racially, economically and in life style—are a source at once of enrichment and tension. Dealing with those differences intelligently will be crucial.

I want to make this the last week of my concentration on the details of transition. With the main elements in place, I'm determined to leave more of the search to Andrew and his team and concentrate on substance and strategy—our fiscal situation and the State of the State. I must resist the temptation to deal with so much of the detail, but it's not easy. I've spent a lifetime doing things for myself, and that habit has grown quite strong after half a hundred years.

Mayor Koch called yesterday to urge that I help get items important to the City on the Special Sessions agenda. I could tell just from the sound of his voice that we're in bigger trouble than I thought.

At night with Trixie and Dave Burke at their home. They are gentle, easy, intelligent people whom I enjoy being with.

THANKSGIVING DAY, NOVEMBER 25, 1982

The debate has begun over the Special Session. Yesterday Warren Anderson issued a statement attacking both me and Carey for failing to provide solutions before the session. He pointed to himself as the Broome County David against the Goliaths from Brooklyn and Queens who were "wringing their hands" over their City (not *our* City) and "their MTA." Carey responded by saying Warren's tactics were "indefensible and irresponsible."

This won't be easy. Did I ever think it would be?

. . .

I traveled to the Bedford-Stuyvesant area[1] yesterday to Al Vann's people. I said "thank you" for their overwhelming support. I tried to sketch what I believe will have to be our theme. Of course we must balance the budget, but we must not do it by ignoring the needs of the poor and the middle class. If all we did was balance the budget, then it would become the emblem of our failure as a government. This is not just political poetry—it is a real political test. I'm saying in effect that I accept the challenge of doing more with less. It's probably a challenge that will be very hard to meet in the public's mind, but it's the only valid test as I see it.

The appointment process becomes more difficult. Yesterday I heard that one of the people whose name had appeared in the paper as a possible candidate for agency head might be summoned as a witness in a grand jury proceeding. I'll have to put a hold on the name for a while and see if anything develops.

In a letter to me a professor at Nassau Community College suggested how I should place myself on the issues in order to win 4 years from now with a "real coalition," unlike the "false coalition"—the "fragile coming together"—I've now established. He proposed a series of positions that would make me liberal on fiscal and "conservative" issues and conservative on sociocultural issues: for jobs programs, against Medicaid funding for abortions. I wrote an answer this morning. I told him I don't know how it will come out, but I know how I will proceed to make decisions. I will decide matters one by one—issue by issue: I don't know what image will be formed when all the decision dots are connected, but the image will be formed by the decisions; the decisions will not be made by the image we seek to form.

Does that mean I will not have a philosophy? No. It means I won't start with artificial criteria and parameters into which I must force my judgments.

· · ·

[1]In Brooklyn.

Felix Rohatyn has agreed to a dialogue that will be extremely useful. He is bright, informed, and moves in all the power circles in the City. He is especially good strategically. When you find someone who is as strong substantively as Felix, you have to make the most of him.

SUNDAY, NOVEMBER 28, 1982

Yesterday we announced Sidney Schwartz as Assistant to the Governor for Management and Productivity. There is no question that he can help us to save a great deal by improving our management techniques, avoiding duplication, unnecessary functions and even corruption. There's also no hope that the savings will balance our budget. But it seems to me essential that if we are to call for austerity in other branches of the State government and, indeed, on the part of all the people of the State, we'll have to convince them first that we've done what we can with our own budget. I understand the public's cynicism and resentment—especially their resentment. I feel it myself. Being brought up behind the store, seeing Momma and Poppa and a whole neighborhood of people work themselves into early old age, scrimping and saving, living that way ourselves, teach lessons for a lifetime.

My work is paying off. By the end of next week, I may have my entire Cabinet aboard. Kurlander, Schwartz, Del Giudice, Finnerty are all set. I'm just short of selecting Alice Daniel for Counsel. I'm pleased that Alice is willing to serve. She's a first-rate lawyer, professor of law and experienced administrator. She worked as deputy counsel to Jerry Brown in California and first deputy in the Civil Division for Attorney General Ben Civiletti. Fabian will be Special Counsel. The missing piece is a director of communication.

The second-string team is also pretty much in place. I have Tonio for Appointments' Office, Wayne Diesel in Finnerty's office, Hank Dullea[1] and Eimicke with Del Giudice and Betsy

---

[1] Associate vice-chancellor for employee relations and personnel, SUNY; formerly acting president of SUNY, Purchase, and staffer in the Carey administration.

Buechner[2] in the press office. For me, the rest of the staffing now becomes more mechanical, with Andrew and my people presenting me with choices, and I'll be able to spend more of my time on substance. Not that I've neglected substance. I spent a couple of hours yesterday going through the '82–83 Budget Message and I'm now into the reports of the Council on Priorities.[3]

Stanley Fink called me this morning to talk about State finances and the Special Session. It was a good discussion.

WEDNESDAY, DECEMBER 1, 1982

Ted Kennedy called to say that his decision not to run for President had been a hard one. He said he was inclined to go forward, but his family persuaded him otherwise. He's going to "work hard, stay close to people, work for the party."

I took advantage of the opportunity to press him on Regionalism. It's ridiculous to have the Northeastern states fighting over Federal scraps instead of working together for the region as a whole. He seemed pleased that I would be getting together with Dukakis to help revive CONEG.[1]

Pat Moynihan called. Just touching bases.

I worked in the office until 11 P.M.

THURSDAY, DECEMBER 2, 1982

Wherever we go now, the media follow, whether or not something significant is scheduled. They all listened in to the "Sherrye Henry Show" that I did this morning and then followed us to the press conference where I announced Del Giudice, Finnerty and

[2]Public information officer of employee relations, former newspaperwoman with the Gannett chain.
[3]Group set up by Governor Carey to sum up the work of his administration and to describe the challenge that would be faced by the next one.

[1]Council of Northeast Governors of New York, New Jersey, Connecticut, Rhode Island, Pennsylvania, Massachusetts and New Hampshire. The Council was organized in 1977.

Palomino. Mike and Mike will be considered part of the old guard, and some will call this a continuation of the old ways, notwithstanding the fact that three newcomers—Kurlander, Schwartz and Daniel—were announced first. But so what?

The Governor called the leaders to his 55th Street office for a meeting. We met with Stanley first. His basic approach was that we should deal with the City problem and the MTA deficit and leave the State budget until next year. The Governor wants, at the very least, to deal with the 360 million dollars in human services' overburden aid[1] which the legislature has passed but which is not yet funded. He also wants an expenditure cap in place. I argued that you would need the cap and the funding of the overburden in order to ensure that the City would get its financial plan approved by December 15. In answer to Stanley's argument that the overburden was only one of many items that the control board could reject as speculative, I pointed out that the overburden was different because it was a new program. He wasn't convinced, though.

Warren Anderson came in at 2:30. The Governor proposed a cap, furloughs, alcohol, tobacco and video game taxes. At one point, the Governor said that we need 350 million dollars in cash to balance the '82–83 budget.

Warren came in prepared to put me on the mark. He turned to me and said: "How about you, Mario, do you think we need 350 million dollars?" I paused for a couple of seconds and then said: "Do I think we *need* 350 million dollars? Warren, I believe we can *use* it." Laughter erupted immediately. Carey—never without a quick quip—said: "End of first debate."

But on the whole, the atmosphere is adversarial. There are whispered huddles; the sides peel off in caucuses. There's an assumption that the whole negotiation would fail if everybody put all his cards on the table at once. I am not sure, but I think there is more posturing and feinting than needs to be done.

It looks now as if the legislature will deal with the MTA deficit

[1]State aid to localities, especially New York City, to supplement funds for human services in a period when demands were exceeding the amount budgeted and tax income was falling short of expectations (both as a result of the recession).

and save the State's deficit for me next year. The meeting ended
with the agreement that the four conferences[2] would meet on
Monday and report to the Governor on Tuesday morning
whether and to what extent they would be willing to deal with
the Governor's proposals.

FRIDAY, DECEMBER 3, 1982

I officiated at the swearing in of the Uniformed Sanitation Workers' officers this afternoon. Barry Feinstein and Jack Bigel were
surprised I showed up. I think they expected me to be cool to
them because of their support of Koch. I have never seen much
use in such behavior, especially now that we need to bring so
many competing interests together.

After, an interview with various Italian journalists.

At night Matilda and I attended the Don Monti Foundation
dinner for Tita and Joe. We received the warm welcome re-
served for new winners. Every Republican in the place claimed
to have voted for us. I am sure we will never be this popular
again.

SATURDAY, DECEMBER 4, 1982

Home all day. What a pleasure. I wasn't off the phone much,
but it's still easier working at home. I think we scored a coup.
After I had a 20-minute discussion with Tim Russert, he was
ready to say he would come aboard as my "Counselor," a new
title for a new position. He was Moynihan's Chief of Staff, is a
lawyer, and can clearly do much more then just communications.

Editorial comments—the *Times* and "Inside Albany"—said we
are doing well with our appointments. My difficulty is that it's
still taking too much of my time personally.

---

[2]The majority and minority memberships in each house meet separately in what they
call conferences.

SUNDAY, DECEMBER 5, 1982

Up before the alarm. I disposed of all that was in the pile of correspondence and memos that had accumulated over the last few days. It irritates me to know that I have more left undone.

I had sprayed the oven with a cleaning solution last night, and this morning I spent 15 minutes trying to clean off the greasy residue accumulation of a dozen well-done steaks. Boy, that's hard work! So is shining 5 pairs of shoes, especially if you insist on going all through the steps: liquid polish on the edges of the sole; then a thin coat of wax, preferably the soft kind, applied with a cloth. Let dry. Then a rubbing with another cloth. A second coat of wax, this time even on the edge of the sole covering the leather where I had put liquid polish. Another rubbing. Then a brushing. Then a buffing with a cloth—probably the all-wool leftovers from a suit that had been altered.

I look forward to doing it. Cleaning, arranging, working, catching up, making it neat, putting things in order. Never leave the moments totally empty. If I can, I run. If I can't, I'll work. The one great sin—wasting existence. If you're too tired to read or write or think, do something you're not too tired to do. The refrigerator. The leaves. The shoes. Ten calls you should have made last week. Once in a while I think about "why" and what a psychiatrist might say. But then, I'm usually shining the shoes when the question comes up, and I bury it with the fury of my strokes.

Andrew loved the beautiful gold pocket watch his family bought him for his 25th birthday. Engraved on the inside of the front cover was the inscription: "We are proud of you. Even more, we love you. Your family." It was wonderful to be able to do it.

MONDAY, DECEMBER 6, 1982

Met with Fink for two hours. Del Giudice and Ken Shapiro were there. It was a good meeting. I proposed that the Governor demand that the Special Session deal with the State problem before the MTA question is discussed. Stanley was noncommittal.

Peter Quinn called. *He's* getting worried about the State of the State.

Tuesday, December 7, 1982

After preliminary meetings of the Democrats, Warren Anderson joined Governor Carey and the rest of us for a plenary session. There was unanimity among the Democrats: we should take up all three problems—State's current gap, the City's current problems and the MTA's deficit. Warren still wants to do just the MTA.

The Governor is excellent as a debater at these meetings. He is well prepared and almost always keeps his sense of humor. But the problem seems to be that little is achievable by debate. Or, rather, that there's too much debate and not enough genuine discussion.

After the meeting, the press and other media had a crack at each of the leaders. It's important not to make mistakes in these quick, almost spontaneous eruptions, because public statements can have a disproportionate influence on the policy that is eventually made.

And because of the importance of public communication, our ability to get Tim Russert to join us as the last piece of the "Big 5" is a coup. He will be perceived as a prize. He'll not only help us articulate our positions but offer us a good deal substantively, as well.

Manny Gold[1] called me after my appearance at the Senate Minority conference to thank me and to say, "Your performance was great." All I did was show up and tell a couple of jokes. All the conference wanted was the sense that the Governor was aware of their needs and desires.

Ended the day at 10 at the Wellington.

[1] State Senator Emanuel R. Gold of Queens. A democrat; deputy minority leader. Universally respected and my friend.

WEDNESDAY, DECEMBER 8, 1982

The debate over the Special Session is escalating publicly. Today I said that if the Senate would agree to revenues for closing the gap in the State's budget, I would "take the blame" for any tax increases that are passed.

Spoke to Ralph Nader on the phone yesterday. He's very bright and single-minded: he's apparently totally consumed by consumerism. We'll get together later.

The Russert announcement today was anticlimactic. I had let it out prematurely by not being careful.

THURSDAY, DECEMBER 9, 1982

I met for two hours with a combination of the Business Council and the New York Partnership. There was a strong representation from the leadership of both groups. Together they represent the heaviest part of the commercial establishment in the State. David Rockefeller and Walter Fallon, the leaders of the Partnership and Council, respectively, played prominent roles. They presented their entire "agenda" for the year.

I'm still getting the benefit of very low expectations in some quarters. Much of the business community in the room today didn't know much about me. Their guess was that I was probably not well aware of their concerns and, to the extent that I did know them, I was probably not sympathetic.

I think I was able to convince them that I knew their agenda and was reasonable about it—a "progressive pragmatist" in fact. I'm sure that we will disagree on some matters over the next several months, but this was a good start.

I announced Yvonne Scruggs-Leftwich as Commissioner of the Division of Housing and Community Renewal. She's well educated, knowledgeable in the field, experienced, attractive and articulate. She's also Black—and that's what most will emphasize when they write the story tomorrow. Still, the more people like her we are able to appoint, the less will race be regarded as a dominant feature in selection.

Ned Regan circulated a letter yesterday that, in effect, conformed perfectly with my suggestions throughout the campaign that we begin the budget process by quantifying revenues and agreeing on how much can be spent. I issued a statement saying that I was pleased and that we would do it in our first budget.

SATURDAY, DECEMBER 11, 1982

A lesson in public relations: At the moment we have clearly lost the effort to put the State gap on the Special Session agenda. All that's written about is the MTA. Our message was not clear enough; we did not work hard enough to get it out—we didn't even talk to the Editorial Boards. I should have had Russert aboard a few weeks ago. I must find a way by Monday morning to make the point that the MTA should be divorced from the other problems. Or I should find a way to use the Legislature's rejection of our gap-closing suggestions to improve our position after January.

MONDAY, DECEMBER 13, 1982

I drove to Albany to give myself an hour or so with Chris and a couple of hours to do some catch-up reading in the car.

In the early afternoon Mike Finnerty asked me to come down to talk with the Governor before he met with the Democratic Conference. It was clear to me that there was no preconceived detailed strategy. Finnerty told me later that the process doesn't work that way: the Legislators insist on going from moment to moment. I wasn't persuaded. Maybe I'm wrong but it seems to me there is always a place for some planning.

The Governor presented his idea for a mass transit financing package to the Conference. It called for a repeal of the "no pass through" provision of the gross receipt tax on oil companies,[1] assuming that such a repealer would produce a payment by the oil companies of about $200 million of current but contested tax obligations. It's of dubious legality, and Fink and Ohrenstein jumped all over it. They prefer a payroll tax, and were unhappy because the Governor had disagreed publicly with the idea of a payroll tax as soon as they had mentioned it and without talking to them.

There was a great deal of discussion back and forth about the relative merits of the gross receipts and payroll taxes. I suggested the possibility of a sunset provision on the payroll taxes. Stanley pointed out that the business community had already recommended that. Eventually, I summed up the meeting as follows:

1. The Assembly would reject the Governor's attempt to reduce expenditures, an attempt with which I agreed.
2. The Governor would send a message of necessity on the State revenue bill without a cap.
3. The Governor's staff would meet with the staff of the Democratic conferences to work out an MTA bill, probably a payroll tax with a sunset provision.

TUESDAY, DECEMBER 14, 1982

Tom Poster[1] did a story on the Inauguration that said, in effect, I had gone back on my promise to produce a less expensive Inauguration. He's been misinformed. I will have it corrected with a release today.

Cardinal Cooke finally reached me in Albany after several tries. He was gentle in the way he said it, but it was clear that the Cardinal doesn't expect to have to make more than one effort to reach the Governor. We agreed to have breakfast on the

---

[1]In 1980, the state had enacted a tax on the gross receipts of oil companies, which included a "no pass through" clause—a provision preventing the companies from passing the tax on to consumers in the form of higher fuel prices. The oil companies were contesting the provision in court; eventually the question became moot as part of a compromise between the state and the oil companies in June 1983.

[1]Columnist for the *Daily News*.

22nd, when he wants me to talk to some of his friends from the Public Library.[2]

Fred Ohrenstein came over to say he was pleased about my performance to date; that he was looking forward to a good relationship.

John Marchi came in to wish me well. He is a gentle intelligence, soft-spoken and benevolent. I hope I am able to govern with the kind of dignity he has demonstrated for all these years. A pleasant chat with Jim Biggane[3] along with the Marchi visit made me feel that with a little work I could maintain a good relationship with the Republicans.

At the end of the day there was the inevitable flood of press and the spontaneous press conference that almost always threatens to produce more disaster than enlightenment.

WEDNESDAY, DECEMBER 15, 1982

I met with Tim Russert and Mike Del Giudice and asked them to prepare a statement that described our role over the last few weeks. Mostly this has been a time of testing, and the press will write about how well or poorly I did. It seems we are into the "first 100 days" before I'm even sworn in.

Larry Kurlander came in and discussed with us some items for the State of the State. I will go heavy on criminal justice, and he has some good ideas. I'm lucky to have him.

By 9 o'clock at night it was clear that there would not be enough votes for the payroll tax to pass the Senate. After 5 hours of argument, the session adjourned until the morning.

In the meantime, the Screening Commission's selection of nominees for the Court of Appeals vacancy has stirred a controversy. Although there are dozens of well qualified candidates, they chose to send over only four. One of them is Vito Titone.[1]

---

[2]The head of the Catholic Church in New York was also concerned about the secular city; the New York Public Library always needs funds, and he thought I might help.
[3]Long-time member of Warren Anderson's staff.

---

[1]A classmate of mine from St. John's. Justice, Appellate Division, Second Department.

The other 3 are Joe McLoughlin, a former Professor of Law and Federal Judge with one year's experience, Bertram Gelfand, in the Appellate Division only one year, and Richard Simons, a Republican from upstate, whom I reported on favorably in 1978 when Governor Carey had to select a Chief. Informed insiders and others are upset. They believe the Commission has tailored the list and gone beyond its proper role. I think they should have sent me more names and I intend to fight this one a bit.

THURSDAY, DECEMBER 16, 1982

On the floor of the Senate, Warren allowed the payroll tax, which was passed by the Assembly at about 9 o'clock, to be called up. He then offered a sales tax for the MTA's region instead, as an amendment to the payroll bill. The amendment passed on a straight party-line vote.

The Governor called a six-way leaders' meeting for 11:30 at night. Warren insisted on a regional tax. Impasse.

SATURDAY, DECEMBER 18, 1982

Only a week to Christmas, but the mild weather and the frantic transition activity have muted the music. I'll have to scurry around for gifts at the last minute again.

Koch announced the possibility of 6,000 layoffs and 100 million dollars in new taxes in place of anticipated State aid. Apparently, the Financial Control Board wouldn't consider his plan any other way because the State aid is so speculative.

I did a draft of an inaugural address that Mary Tragale and I liked and no one else did. They thought it was too personal and too "immigrant"-oriented.

Gene Spagnoli's going-away party. We retired his Press Secretary tee shirt and title. A great guy—I hate to see him go.

MONDAY, DECEMBER 20, 1982

One of the reasons for keeping these notes is to learn from our experiences.

The publicity on my dispute with the Judicial Selection Commission has not been good. It has me in a struggle for power with the Commission. I didn't handle the matter well. What I need to do is make clear that I am trying to improve the merit process in order to preserve it, since the entire appointive method is up for review. Everywhere the list of names has been regarded, by insiders at least, as not the best possible. We have to portray it as having discredited and threatened the process. I'm arranging a meeting with groups of public-interest types to see if we can sell our position.

And Poster printed a story—an inaccurate story—saying I was going to have an inaugural ball. It happened because Phyllis Cerf Wagner, the new treasurer of the Party, had not been informed of my desires. Communications!!

TUESDAY, DECEMBER 21, 1982

After this evening's meeting, Warren Anderson left saying that the staffs should work together through the night and we should meet again at 10:00 A.M. Tuesday morning.

We Democrats sat around with the Governor until about 2:00 A.M. At that point, I suggested that the next morning we demonstrate a solid front, proposing a compromise now known as the "Norman Levy Plan,"[1] consisting of an increase in sales tax for the counties outside New York City and a payroll tax for New York City, both with a sunset provision after two years, together guaranteeing no fare increase for 1983 at least. I also suggested that the Governor call the Mayor to make sure he would be with us. He did it . . . at about 2:30 A.M. The call produced one of the funniest episodes I can remember.

Fink, Ken Shapiro, Mike Finnerty, Jack McGoldrick, Eric Lane,[2] Fred Ohrenstein and I sat around listening as Governor

[1]Named after the Republican state senator who had suggested the idea.
[2]Fred Ohrenstein's chief of staff.

Carey got Koch on the phone, apparently waking him up. The Governor moved into a machine-gun-like description of the complicated events of the evening. At one point—about 2:45 in the morning—he said to the Mayor: "Now I want you to think all this through and get back to me by 9:00 A.M."

At about the same time, Stanley turned and said something like: "Can you picture it? Ed in a sleeping gown and stocking cap, with a ball on the end of it . . . half asleep. Nine A.M.!"

It struck me as so hilarious: the whole scene—the late hour— the confusion—the disproportion—the absurdity of suggesting to the Mayor that he should think it all through, this entire mess, and have an answer in a few hours. As though he had nothing else to do and all the time in the world to do it. I started laughing. Stanley did, too; so did Shapiro. Even Jack McGoldrick, who hadn't laughed for a full year. Then like kids in a church pew or in the back of a classroom, we tried to muffle our laughter so it wouldn't be heard over the phone. The more we tried, the harder it got. As we sat looking at one another, struggling to suppress the guffaws, we only began to laugh harder. I had to hold my handkerchief over my mouth; it became wet with tears. At one point, Fink had to get up from his chair and bolt from the room. As soon as he got outside he could no longer contain himself and he let out a loud burst of laughter. McGoldrick and Shapiro also fled.

For a few minutes, the laughter was uncontainable and unsuppressible. The fatigue, the unrelenting pressure and a thousand other circumstances produced this odd explosion.

When the Governor finished and hung up the phone, we filed back into the room, wiping our eyes. The Governor, who had contained himself throughout with a seriousness that only added to the incongruity of it all, then also burst out laughing.

It was a silly episode, almost inexplicable, but then, so is a lot of this business. And maybe it was good for us. I especially enjoyed having a good laugh with Hugh—it's been a long time.

I slept an hour and a half, was up at 6:00 A.M. and for some reason was raring to go. Mike Del Giudice was in my office at 9:00 A.M. and told me that the staffs had come up with a surprise —a new proposal by the Republicans; they are talking about a personal income tax surcharge.

This will make things difficult for the Democrats, who usually prefer the income tax to almost any other tax because of its progressive nature and because many of them represent poor and lower-middle-class constituents.

My advice was for us to hang together and stay with the compromise combination of payroll and sales tax. I suggested Carey call Koch again, and he did and was able to get the Mayor to affirm his position in favor of our proposal and to condemn any personal income tax surcharge, which would be a triple tax on New York State.

We had a press conference in the Red Room with the Governor to restate our unified Democratic position. It went well.

At about 5:30 Stanley called me on the hotline to tell me he had just heard that Warren was going into the conference[3] with a personal income tax and sales tax combination, or, alternatively, a personal income tax and fare increase combination. If that's true, both will be easy for the Democrats to reject and, therefore, our united position will remain intact, though we will be no closer to a solution.

Later

It developed that Warren was not able to get the Republicans to agree to the personal income tax. We caucused but weren't able to come up with anything.

At 10:15 P.M., Warren suddenly, surprisingly, called for a corporate franchise tax increase.

At that point, we had lost the initiative. Indeed, it was worse than that. The corporate franchise tax increase will be even tougher than an income tax surcharge for the Democrats to resist. From the beginning the basic difference between the Democrats and Republicans was that the Democrats wanted to tax business and the Republicans the consumer. Now that the Republicans have shifted to a business tax, that really co-opts the Democrats.

The Democrats met at about 11:00 P.M. There seemed a general consensus they would be stuck with the bill. I raised questions about regionalization, how to calculate the allocation

[3]Of Legislative leaders from both houses, then meeting to try and produce an MTA bill that could be passed by both the Democratic assembly (which had passed a statewide payroll tax) and the Republican senate (which had passed a regional sales tax).

and other relatively insubstantial matters, but there was no powerful argument against the approach.

At about 1:00 A.M., we had a press conference to indicate that we would review the proposal and report later on Wednesday after seeing the bill. It's clear we'll have a bill tomorrow and it will be, basically, Warren's bill.

WEDNESDAY, DECEMBER 22, 1982

About 4:00 P.M., we met in the Governor's office. The Assembly staff detected a special exemption for savings banks in the language of the bank bill. Fink demanded it be dropped, and it was. At about 4:30 P.M., Carey was on his way to the N.Y. Financial Control Board to tell them that the subway fare was saved for one year and that, to the extent the City's financial plan depended on saving the fare, the plan was secure as well.

Somewhere around 6:00 P.M., the Senate concluded its business, with me at the podium. Warren and Fred said their goodbyes to me. The members applauded and I walked off the podium for the last time as Lt. Governor, wondering if I would ever be invited back.

And that is that. We have saved the MTA fare for one year. Neither the State's nor the City's financial problems have been dealt with.

I wonder if more might be accomplished if the Governor were, in advance, to draw the legislative leaders into the circle with him, instead of making public announcements of positions that are then inevitably followed by responses (also public) that are predictably negative, not only from the opposition but even, occasionally, from members of his own party. It seems to me executive leadership is often afraid of a conciliatory approach, probably because it is thought to imply weakness. I see it differently. I believe the executive can reach out, share credit—give credit—compromise and still survive as a strong leader. The object of governing is to achieve results, not just to be a loud voice from a balcony or podium. A "strong" voice and righteous remoteness can leave us without results. At any rate, it's worth a try.

THURSDAY, DECEMBER 23, 1982

I ran this morning, about 3 miles. It's the beginning of another "all out" effort to get in shape. It wasn't easy. All parts of my body ached. My back sent its familiar searing signals of age. My legs at one point told me they would cramp as soon as we finished. My chest cavity was a place for discomfort growing into pain. After a couple of miles, the only thing that kept me going was my refusal not to finish—the childish fantasylike experience that makes of the effort a test of life and gives oneself the chance to make it all right, by winning this simple self-created test. I made the test and I would pass it—whatever the momentary price in discomfort and worse.

And I think that's the way it's going to be for the next few years.

Then two hours at *Newsday*; saying too much because I was tired.

The Christmas party came at 4. Mary thought it wasn't a good party. Mary was right. I didn't help. If I'm awake and enjoying myself too much—and I notice it—I'll stop. Life is motion—not joy.

CHRISTMAS DAY, 1982

11:50 P.M.

It began again today. Everything does. Today is birth and renewal, the beginning of hope. For nearly two thousand years people have used the occasion to feel again the beauty of love. Whatever they know or do not know, believe or do not believe, about virgin birth and signs from heaven, everywhere people believe in warmth and caring. They want it; they need it. The strong thrive on giving it; the rest cannot live well without receiving it. We have done what we can to sully it, confuse it, suppress it, abuse it, but it remains the essence of a good and full life. Life is motion—not joy: except for those strong enough to love and those fortunate enough to have them.

I ran again this morning and thought about it. I can use some renewal; the three miles were tough. It's the price I pay for being too good to myself. And it helps remind me of the need for renewal.

So we begin again. The past is gone. Only the future counts, and who knows how much of that we have?

MONDAY, DECEMBER 27, 1982

Up at 5 A.M. I wrote notes for the inaugural address and later in the day dictated it to Mary. I'll edit and finish it tonight.

As Inaugural Day grows closer, I grow uneasy. I don't understand the feeling yet, but I know I am beginning to feel it.

Since I've been in Albany for 8 years, close to the scene, you would think the experience would not be a new one. But there's a world of difference between watching it and living it. I saw that in the leadership meetings during the Special Session. I knew what they were like from having sat through them. They were different when I participated in them, as different as playing the game is from sitting on the bench watching it.

I've seen the oath taken, and it meant little. But now I am about to take it. My name will be written in the *Red Book* and *Blue Book* under the names of 51 other Governors. As long as there's a State of New York—if it lives for a thousand years—it will be true that once I was the highest elected official of the State. Whether I die the next day or fail or am impeached, it will always be true that I was the 52nd Governor of the State of New York.

How far is it from Kings Park and South Jamaica? How far is it from the stickball game in the backyard—in shoes, because sneakers were a luxury preserved for gym class, where they were required?

There will be a tennis court and a swimming pool and guards and servants and more luxury than anyone should have. How far is that from Von Dohlen Park, with free showers, and the Van Wyck pool, which was too expensive at a quarter, and Momma's chicken[1] and Manuel breaking into the back

---

[1] When I was very young—young enough to be forgiven indiscretions—I went to Momma and told her I was hungry. It was Sunday. The store was busy, with everyone but me helping out. Momma had a chicken in the oven. She told me to go and take some. As she describes it today, "He left us the wings!" The next time I was hungry, Momma gave me a big piece of bread.

door of the store in the middle of the night with a hacksaw?[2]

How far is it from Ellis Island and that imaginary interview with Momma?[3]

Q: Where are you from?

A: Salerno.

Q: What do you do?

A: Nothing, I'm going to meet my husband in New Jersey.

Q: What does he do?

A: Nothing, he's looking for work.

Q: What kind of work?

A: Any kind.

Q: But what can he do?

A: Well, he has no skill, he never was educated.

Q: Well, does he have any friends?

A: No.

Q: Any money?

A: No.

Q: How about you?

A: No, we have nothing, no friends, no money, just a baby.

Q: Well, with no friends, no money, what do you expect of this country?

A: Only one thing before I die. I want to see my son the governor of New York State.

They would have locked her up. That's how far it is. They would have said to her, "You've got to be crazy."

How far is it? Not so far that we didn't make the trip. But it's hard to believe that we did. I feel something but I don't understand it yet, the way I am expected to. Maybe later in the week.

THURSDAY, DECEMBER 30, 1982

This morning I began to feel the uneasiness that comes with moving into this new phase of my life. Mostly it was a queasy feeling in the stomach. I began to feel captured: by the problems,

---

[2]Manuel was an emotionally disturbed neighbor who lived in people's basements, gathered junk and did odd jobs to keep himself alive. One night he tried sawing off a padlock on our back door.

[3]This "interview" was recounted during several speeches in the campaign, and a version was published in 1983.

which every day seem more formidable; the almost total loss of privacy, which every day becomes more apparent; and the concern that we will disappoint so many because of our inability to do all we would like to do.

In a way, the best parts of it all I resist. I don't allow myself to think about the ease and pleasure of living in the mansion and being served and treated as though we were important and being regarded as a national figure. I don't, because I don't particularly care for those things personally and because I'm afraid of caring for them, for fear it will hurt too much when we don't have them.

I've already learned how stifling security can be. State troopers 24 hours a day in the house makes you feel as if you're in prison.

The dominant event of the day was the briefing on the budget. Finnerty, Diesel and Del Giudice pointed out a gap of about 2 billion dollars for '83–84. That means we need some form of new revenues and serious cuts in programs. The challenge will be to balance the budget and help people at the same time. Lord knows it's going to be tough.

Carey did a Carey thing today. In his farewell press conference he managed to insult the legislators by calling them small boys; suggested he had faked the fare crisis; and confessed that he had ordered George Dempster to spend money on the "I Love New York" commercials to answer Lehrman's attack on our tax policies. Lehrman has been temporarily resurrected by the flap, and Carey has been made to look a little odd. But this too shall pass.

Harvey Cohen came by. He saw a draft of my speech for the inaugural. He said he didn't like it—it doesn't sound like me— I should go without a speech and just wing it. That's tempting, but I think I'll opt for safety, although I suspect Harvey's right about the speech being flat.

I spent a couple of hours more working on it with Pam Broughton. She made some suggestions, including one that I mention Poppa. I told her I didn't think that would be a good idea—that it was too personal.[1] At about 11 P.M. I quit. Pam went on to work with the inaugural committee, and I took the opportunity to spend some time with Fabian. We ate a hamburger at Barnaby's at about midnight. Frank the bartender sent

[1] When I delivered the speech, I departed from the text and mentioned Poppa despite what I had told Pam.

over a bottle of Asti Spumante and I played "amore"[2] with a guy
at the bar on the way out. I enjoyed it—no troopers, no press,
no speeches, just a good friend, some chatter, some gentle joking
with good people.

FRIDAY, DECEMBER 31, 1982

Moving out of the Lieutenant Governor's office was sad. It's a
beautiful suite—perhaps the handsomest in the Capitol. And,
despite all the problems, it's been a good four years.

Pam Broughton, Greg Sheldon, Tonio, Linda Dumas and dozens of volunteers are working like Trojans on the details of the
Inaugural. Four thousand people are expected for a full range of
events. There are all kinds of pieces to put in place and things
that could go wrong. It's a demanding effort.

The whole family was at the Mansion. They came up on a bus
this afternoon. The old-timers are beside themselves with excitement. Momma, *Compare* Ross and Maria, Matilda's Mom and
Dad. They can hardly believe it. The whole family is thrilled.

At the last minute Judge Burke called from Florida to say that
he couldn't make it. Chief Judge Desmond agreed to swear me in,
in his place. He read me the oath at about 10:15 P.M. at the
Mansion. After that we had about 100 of our friends in for drinks.
I chatted with David and Trixie Burke till about 2:30, then to bed.

SATURDAY, JANUARY 1, 1983

By all the measures normally applied to such things, this Inaugural Day was a huge success. The weather was clear and comfortable, no major snags; the turnout was larger than expected, the
music beautiful, the pageantry impressive and my speech—for all
of my concern—well received.[1] It proved to be a personal and
emotional speech, and that's what works best on such occasions.

---

[2]An old Italian game—like "choosing." Two players throw out simultaneously any
number of fingers from 0 to 5 and guess at the total.

[1]See pp. 455–61.

Chief Judge Desmond described it as the best inauguration he had ever seen, and he has been going to them since Al Smith's —over fifty years.

We had a three-hour receiving line. It was mostly hugs and kisses. Someone commented that "all of Cuomo's affairs are more like family weddings." I think that's a dimension we should try to keep alive—or to create—statewide.

The Mass this morning at Immaculate Conception Cathedral was beautiful. Bishop Hogg, a representative of Archbishop Iakovos, Bishops Hubbard, Mugavero and Sullivan were all present. The homily by Bishop Sullivan talked of the relevance of our mission and the ultimate purpose of government being to improve the conditions of people's lives. That's still true, but it is an increasingly difficult message to sell to the rich and upper middle class. That's the challenge politically. That's the challenge I accepted for myself in today's inaugural address. We'll know before it's over how well we've met it.

SUNDAY, JANUARY 2, 1983

Mass at the Cathedral. We were able to say hello to the organist, Bob Sheehan. He's a fine-looking Irishman with a handsome face, magnificent voice and permanent smile.

In the afternoon, I stood for over two hours to greet more than 3,000 people who came to Open House at the Mansion. I'm told it was the largest turnout ever for an open house.

I met beautiful people from every part of the State, many of them with infants and young children. They stood for as much as an hour and a half outside the Mansion in the cold, just for a quick glimpse of their place. I felt guilty about their discomfort and the little we had to offer them. I would like to do it differently next year. Perhaps we should do it in the spring or summer; at least the chances are the weather would be better.

The Mansion is an extraordinary place. It will take me some time to get used to it: 40 rooms, 6½ acres, 100 years of history. The Governor's suite is lavish. It opens onto an enormous bedroom area with a huge double bed looming up directly in view of the door as though it were designed to boast of the role that rest plays in the Governor's life. This bedroom area has a large fireplace, sofas facing each other in front of it, a breakfast nook and enough room by itself to serve as a barracks.

To the left as you enter the suite is a long study with two desks and the worst kind of bookshelves—the kind that have no books and look as though they never have had. Adjoining that study is a pleasant sunlit anteroom that serves as the breakfast room, with a table, chairs, windows, credenza and sofa, so that I can drink a glass of orange juice without getting bored with the bedroom environment.

The *pièce de résistance* is the bathroom. It has to be seen to be believed. It is immense. One side of it—some 20 feet long—contains a full-length dressing table with mirrored walls, two sinks and special "make-up" mirrors circumscribed by rows of light bulbs like in an old-fashioned actor's dressing room.

There is a large enclosed shower area with twin showers and simulated gold fixtures. I took one look at it and thought it must be a locker room for a small basketball team.

There's a tub like few I have ever seen. It was built into a platform about three feet high. There are three wooden steps that are ascended in order to reach the tub. The faucet is simulated gold, like the shower handles. It is located on the far side of the tub, away from the three steps. There's only 6 inches of a platform around the edge of the sunken tub, so that it's practically impossible to get to the handles unless you do one of two things: crawl around the edge of the tub to the front, slide into the tub, and then turn the water on while sitting in the tub and thereby risking scalding or freezing, or reach over from the outside of the tub platform, over a box of flowers which is built to adjoin the tub, and —if you are 6' 8" or taller—you can then get two fingers around one of the knobs (I think it's the cold one).

One wall adjacent to the tub is about 8' × 7', covered completely by a mirror. The other wall is about 8' × 5'—also covered completely by a mirror. That's so that you can see yourself either freezing or burning to death.

In this area with the shower and tub there's what was built to be a sauna room, fully lined in cedar, with enough room for the small basketball team to do their saunaing simultaneously.

Beyond this area is the dressing area. It has a long vanity with

6 feet or so of mirrors surrounded by the dressing-room bulbs. The clothes area has a room for the small basketball team's uniforms, sneakers, sweatshirts and their parents' overcoats.

In order that I should not be humiliated, I have had to separate my jackets and pants so as to occupy as much space as possible. There's a series of cubicles for storing accessories, underwear, shirts, etc.

Here, to get decent coverage, I have placed one shirt—and in some cases a pair of socks—in each cubicle.

Standing on the floor of the dressing area there are two wooden valets. One of them is the electric valet for pressing your pants. I don't use it because I don't want to put out of work the women they hired for pressing pants.

I am not sure I understand the object of this suite. I don't see how it makes it easier to tell the legislature that we may not be able to find money for the homeless.

If I can't make any changes in the Governor's suite, I know we can make changes in other parts of the Mansion. I've asked Egan[1] to change both the second and third floors. The second floor will be converted from an "all sports" floor to "the family of New York" floor, with representative contributions from all 62 of our counties. The third floor, which is now the so-called "children's area," will become a cartoon alley, with political cartoons and memorabilia.

I worked on the State of the State. I haven't liked it from the first draft, mostly because it's not well organized. That's not the fault of the people who are working on it with me: we should have begun writing it earlier.

At about 8 o'clock I called in Fabian, Alice Daniel, Tim Russert, Andrew, Del Giudice and Kurlander to discuss my selection of a Court of Appeals judge. Initially, I refused to allow them to tell me the conclusion that they had already come to. I had read all the materials and suspected that the decision would be a relatively easy one. After about an hour's examination and cross-examination, I told the group that I had picked an upstate Republican, Justice Richard Simons of the Appellate Division, because of his experience and universally excellent reputation and because he

[1]John Egan, commissioner of the Office of General Services.

had already been selected four different times as "well qualified" by the nominating commission. I then discovered he had been the staff's unanimous choice even before I announced mine.

I called Judge Simons at his home. He was pleased—to put it mildly. Chief Judge Cooke was, too. Stanley Fink was noncommittal—I think he would have preferred a Democrat. Fred Ohrenstein was surprised. I think he expected me to go with the New York *Times* choice, which had been Joe McLoughlin.

MONDAY, JANUARY 3, 1983

It has been a source of immense gratification to see how the family has been nearly overwhelmed by the excitement and significance of the occasion.

I have never seen my Mother or any of the family this way. They are unabashed in their joy. Ten years ago, none of us would ever even have dared to dream that anything like this could happen.

For most of the family it's still not understood. To this moment, I don't believe it's had its full impact on me. Occasionally, I struggle to feel a change, a difference. I tell myself that being Governor is vastly different from not being Governor, and the difference should record itself on my mind and my emotions. Sometimes I even try pretending that I feel the difference, in the hope that I will recognize it as the right feeling and so hold on to it. But the pretense does not last, the feeling doesn't come. I suspect it never will, if it hasn't yet.

But the rest of the family feels something. They are bursting with it, and I love seeing it. I don't care if it doesn't last another five minutes, it has given all of our lives a feature, a dimension, a character that will never disappear, that will always console and that I suspect will grow in the retelling over the passage of the years.

I announced Simons at a press conference this morning. My first. Then I had the privilege and high honor of escorting him to the Court of Appeals. The Chief and the Judges were generous. They are obviously delighted that Simons was selected.

They allowed me to sit on the Bench. I felt better—more pride, more satisfaction—sitting among the robed Judges of this magnificent Court than I did when I took the oath on Saturday.

I worked on the State of the State message for most of the afternoon. It's getting better, but it won't be what I want.

I had Fabian come back to the Mansion with Andrew for dinner. There was much discussion of the old days, all of it about happy times. At one point Fabian called me "Governor"—it stopped me cold.

TUESDAY, JANUARY 4, 1983

Amidst the joy of the occasion, a grim reminder of the other side of things. Shelly Chevlowe[1] is dying.

I last saw Shelly on the night before the election after the "Last Word" TV appearance. He was with his wife, Maxine, the Winklers, Jimmy Breslin and Ronnie. I thought he didn't look well. A month ago he was told he had cancer.

Today I called him in the hospital and got Maxine. She told me how proud she and Shelly were "of what you've accomplished." Shelly was too sick to talk. He's "very, very bad." But he is "trying." Maxine's a nurse and has been through this a thousand times. She was at Rosemary Breslin's bedside for months. She was still a nurse today, talking intelligently, crisply about his condition. But every other paragraph, she was a wife.

Still, she must have said three times, "Please do a good job! It means a lot to us." If I hadn't heard it from Maxine, I would not have thought so grandly about what we have the capacity to achieve in this office. Maxine's words said something that is now inescapably clear to me. There are many people out there who will be deeply affected by our performance, not because it will mean money in their pocket, or a road past their farm, but because they are associated in some way, empathize in some way, share in some way, in what we do. People who know us and love us and fail when we fail and succeed when we succeed. People

---

[1]A friend from Queens whom I first met in 1974 at the inception of my public career. He was a continuing source of good advice. He was a quintessential New Yorker, a chauvinist about his town who would never use the word "chauvinist." A guy who played stickball and listened to Harry James and had a lovely wife and family, and died so young no one could understand it.

who think of us as representing a feature of their own lives.
People who have made a judgment in our favor and want to see
their judgment vindicated. Of all the awesome responsibilities
included under the oath, one of the greatest is not to disappoint
all of the Maxine Chevlowes who will talk about our opportunity
and feel it's important enough to talk about even in the midst of
their own pain.

WEDNESDAY, JANUARY 5, 1983

Since the Inaugural I have received a flood of mail applauding
the speech. Presidential candidates have sent word that they
liked it. The closest I've come to this kind of response is after the
Convention speech in Syracuse.

I think a combination of factors produced it: the setting, the
emotional theme, the Rocky context and the enormous hunger
the people have for something to believe in.

I noticed it early in the campaign and throughout all the ups
and downs. Everyone wants desperately to be able to hold on to
something—some idea, some hope.

But the reaction to the Inaugural created a high level of expec-
tation for the State of the State message, which I delivered today.
I thought it was fair; I would have given it 79–80 at the most.

Actually, it was better received than I expected it to be, but
by no means did the reaction approach the reception given the
Inaugural.

Fabian, Andrew, Lucille[1] and I had dinner at the Mansion with
Ken Auletta.[2] In the midst of the meal, Stanley Fink called from
the Capitol to say that the members had received the message
very well. His own comments to the press were generous. Anderson and the others who commented were not as negative as
they will probably be in a few months.

So the week of excitement, festivity and challenge is over. We
have done much better than we would have dared to expect. As
the guy who fell off the Empire State building said to the people
at the windows of each floor on the way down, "All right so far!"

---

[1]Lucille Falcone, an attorney and a friend of Andrew's
[2]Auletta was working on a profile of me for *The New Yorker*.

FRIDAY, JANUARY 7, 1983

Three hours with Mike Finnerty on the budget this morning. The more one learns about the situation, the more difficult it gets. We have our fingers crossed that the third and fourth year of this term will be better. But all we know for sure is that this year and probably the next one will be fiscal disasters.

Bill vanden Heuvel[1] has sent on a good suggestion for a Service Corps that would be in effect a kind of Vista, a basically volunteer operation designed to do various public chores like delivering surplus foods and working in hospitals and nursing homes. It's no doubt difficult to do as a practical matter, but it would help foster the kind of spirit we're trying hard to generate. We'll go all out to make it work.

SATURDAY, JANUARY 8, 1983

5:30 A.M.
A week ago at this time I was getting ready to be sworn in. In seven days I have been inaugurated, given two major speeches, met personally with record numbers of visitors and legislators, received national publicity on several occasions, appointed a Court of Appeals Judge, sat on the Bench of the Court and begun the hard process of preparing the budget.

There is no doubt we have gotten off fairly well. The Inaugural was an organizational triumph, thanks to Pam and company. The open houses, too, were well thought out and handled. Our dealings with the media have been professionally conducted by Tim. The Court appointment was done smoothly, with perfect attention to all the protocols.

So we have given evidence of being able to organize our government, conduct its business efficiently, make the decisions that have to be made promptly and resolutely.

But perhaps the best-received aspect of the week's effort were the two speeches, particularly the Inaugural. The mail has been constant all week—the word "superb" has been used over and over. My surprise about this continues. Before I gave it, I was

[1]Lawyer, former ambassador, respected political figure since the Kennedy years.

not happy with the speech, probably because it was nothing more than a stringing together of a lot of pieces of speeches I had given over the years. What made the difference was that this time I gave the speech as Governor. That changed its significance; the office gave the words new meaning and importance.

I've tried hard to understand precisely what it was about the speech that people liked most. Some friends said it was the words. I don't think so—they weren't that good. Surely, for those who were in the room, the occasion, the pageantry, the drama all added to the effect. But that doesn't account for the excellent reaction from all those who merely read the speech—like Felix Rohatyn and Walter Mondale.

I think the principal effectiveness was in the ideas—simple ideas that a lot of people feel good about. The idea of "family" appeals because it makes sense. Our interdependence as a society is clear: our need to share and protect; even our need for one another's concern. The reminder of our obligation to the less fortunate also struck home. For a time now we have been trying to forget that obligation—or deny it. It's become fashionable to categorize the needy in terms that suggest—or state—that most of the needy get that way through their own fault. The reminder that some needy are victims and not offenders, that many of us were ourselves once needy or the offspring of people in trouble who received help, has given some people a fresh perspective.

Most of all, I think people want to feel good about themselves and the world. We are often a cynical people, but we don't want to be. We'd prefer to believe, to love, to hope . . . if only for a little bit. I must try hard not to let the harsh realities of the budget dampen this flame.

One thing is clear—whatever I choose to do, whatever judgments will be made on me, my past until January 1, 1983, has become politically irrelevant. Corona, Forest Hills, Secretary of State, Lt. Governor, the Cabin affair, budget savings, successful negotiations—none of them will count. The election and inauguration eclipse all of that. From now on, I'll be measured on what we do as Governor.

Selected Speeches

Sabbath Service at Temple Sholom
Glen Oaks (Queens), February 20, 1981

Rabbi Abramson, Cantor Sussman, Mr. Gerard and Mr. Du-
naisky, members of the congregation:

Thank you so much for inviting me to share your pulpit during
Brotherhood Week, and for honoring my work this much.

I wish I could speak to you today in terms of pure beauty,
happiness, love and sweetness, but I'm afraid I have a harder,
more realistic earthly message.

This evening is designed—in these most comfortable of sur
roundings—to make a point, maybe a number of points, about
the Jewish community, discrimination and the gentile world.
And in that respect I believe I can—because of the circumstances
of my background—be useful.

I was a Shabbos Goy! Now I know that almost every non-
Jewish politician who ever ran for office in New York City, at
some point claims to have been a Shabbos Goy. But I really and
truly was!

I was born and raised in South Jamaica in Queens. It was then
a poor and low-middle-class neighborhood made up of all kinds
of ethnics: Italians, Blacks, Poles, Jews—a classic polyglot mosaic
of the thirties and forties. Immigrants and the sons and daughters
of immigrants from Europe, the East, the South. People who had
come to New York for opportunity but were only just beginning
to find it.

We had an Italian American grocery store on the corner of

150th Street and 97th Avenue, and on the other corner, down
the block, there was an Orthodox synagogue. And between us
were Lanzone the baker, Rubin the roofer and Kaye the tailor.
We lived in rooms behind the store in a building owned by the
Kesslers. The Kesslers taught my mother how to count and she,
in return, taught Mrs. Kessler (and Mrs. Kessler was reluctant to
learn) how to make tomato sauce—à la marinara, without meat.

On Friday nights, when I was thirteen or so, I would go to the
synagogue, turn out the lights, and snuff out the candles in the
candelabras. In return, I would be given some of the challah to
take home. A Shabbos Goy, a gentile, called upon by Jewish
neighbors to do something their ritual wouldn't permit them to
do for themselves.

I'll never forget it, particularly because there was this sweet
confusion that arose from the fact that at the same time I was
serving in my *own* church as an altar boy, lighting candles, cleaning up, attending at the altar of our own worship. So much of it
was the same to my young mind. The Gregorian chant from the
priest was very much like the chanting I heard at the synagogue,
and the incense and candles at St. Monica's Catholic Church on
Sunday gave the altar and the whole chamber an aroma, an aura
—mysterious, strangely but benevolently powerful—that I felt
also in the synagogue on Friday nights. An altar; a congregation
behind; what looked like chalices of gold; brocaded vestments;
solemnity—a Latin I didn't understand and a Hebrew I didn't
understand, both read out of the same kind of huge, handsomely
ornamented scrolls.

There were differences between the Catholic and Jewish ceremonies, of course: there were no nuns, no kneeling, no collection baskets in the synagogue.

And yes, there were other differences between and among us
in those days. We were of different tribes and we were aware of
those differences. But we didn't think so much about them.
Certainly they weren't differences that created hostility. Indeed,
there was a commonality among us, a commonality of need and
concern and striving.

I never tried to understand it in an intellectual way then. It was
simply reality. We just kind of took for granted that we were
more or less the same and that we weren't supposed to hurt one

another and indeed, at times, we even had a responsibility for one another's welfare and preservation. It came naturally.

Yes, we took it for granted until we, the simple people of South Jamaica, were taught by the Second World War that we *couldn't* take it for granted. The monstrous horrors of the Holocaust taught us that there was an evil afoot in the world that we didn't perceive in the hard but gentle life of South Jamaica. We came to understand that, for some of us, even survival was something that had to be fought for—alone, or, if blessed, with the aid of friends.

This was a crushing lesson: the impact reverberates still.

But actually, I had begun to detect the meaning of discrimination a little earlier, when my family moved from South Jamaica to a so-called better neighborhood. I came to learn the implications of difference. I was taken from the sweet naïveté which instinctively accepted superficial discrepancies in color, language and ritual as being irrelevant, into a new condition. I now began to learn that the sophisticated world around me was not as smart or as good as the world we left in South Jamaica. I began to understand that in the "better" neighborhood, people treated differences almost always as dangerous at least, and evil at worst.

I will never forget when we moved into the small house in Holliswood, which was then inhabited mostly by White Anglo-Saxon Protestants—no Blacks, no Jews and no Italians. Certainly no Italians who had once been poor and illiterate, who had come from the Mezzogiorno, the deprived area of Italy.

If you asked her and she trusted you, my mother would tell you the story today of her first meeting with the neighbors in Holliswood. Three distinguished-looking women came down the hill to see her. She was outside sweeping the walk. They were a welcoming team of sorts, but they bore no gifts. She remembers them as *"freddo"*—cold, aloof. And they said to her: "You must be the Italian woman. Well, we want you to know you are welcome here, but please remember to keep the tops on your garbage pails."

It went through her like a knife! It left a scar that she can feel today, more than thirty years later. The insolence, the crudity, the arrogance. All born of an ignorance that permitted those people to believe that if it's different it's inferior, and somehow wrong.

With maturity I came to the sad awareness that this kind of thing was true almost everywhere, that almost everywhere there was this incipient tendency to exclude, to shun the alien, to be afraid, to be jealous. I learned how ugly our history was in its darker chapters, how, generation after generation, each group of immigrants had sought to resist the new group that followed them, even while they were struggling with the group that had come before. I was stunned by the brutality of what the world had done to the Blacks of Africa and how cruelly even this land of freedom had dealt with them.

But the Holocaust taught me and my generation that there was nothing in our history to equal the perfidy, the sickness, the pure evil which that great sin represented. It was not simply an effort to seize territory or to reduce or diminish or abuse or even enslave—it was an effort to annihilate, to exterminate. That effort failed, although not by much. The forces of good—or almost good—won the war. But that did not end the evil.

The depressing truth is that there still are, as it seems there always have been, forces in the Western world committed to the annihilation of the Jew and Jewish culture. There is clearly a pattern of anti-Semitism, and it has a well-organized, deliberately initiated impetus: a program of aggressive anti-Zionism that started in Russia in the early seventies and has been sustained by it since then, an ongoing policy to delegitimize Israel and to make anti-Semitism once again acceptable.

It is a policy which was manifested in the General Assembly in November of 1975 when a resolution was adopted equating Zionism with racism. We saw it four months later when the United Nations Commission on Human Rights, in one of the UN's bizarre ironies, branded Israel as the perpetrator of war crimes.

And worse—we see it again in our own streets. A thousand desecrations: swastikas painted on synagogue doors; the Torah stolen in Brooklyn; cemetery stones toppled. Why? There is in these sins no profit, only an expression of hate.

The ADL's annual survey, made public just a few weeks ago, showed that anti-Semitic incidents were up 200 percent nationwide and 500 percent in New York State. And a great deal of this activity seems to be the work of young people, like the thirteen- and fourteen-year-olds arrested for a cross-burning in Port Washington, or the fifteen-year-old in Albertson.

There are people much wiser and more learned than I who may understand the reasons for and the causes of the existence of this evil. They find partial explanations in history, sociological development, the distribution of wealth and power, even politics. But I confess that I don't understand fully, or adequately, what exactly or why exactly or how exactly this repulsive phenomenon is and functions.

I *do* know that it is as wrong as anything our society suffers from. It is the basic denial of good: hate. And it is worse than the hate of a person, because it's the hate of a people.

I know, too, thank God, that it is not universal and that those of us rational enough to understand its evil have an an obligation to fight it. And I believe the best weapon against this irrationality is rationality and education.

If so much of the ignorance is found in children thirteen to fifteen, shouldn't we be doing more to teach them the consequences and the real significance of their acts? Isn't it a proper role of our educational system, for example, to teach the Holocaust—what it means, what it implies? For a year and a half I have been urging the New York State Department of Education to make the Holocaust a part of the curriculum of every school in the state. I have been asking them to follow the lead of the Catholic Diocese of Rockville Centre, which instituted courses on the Holocaust in its high schools in 1978.

Of course, Holocaust studies would not eliminate the anti-Jewish bias that is still prevalent in too many homes. But it would be a useful, positive move, similar to one the Catholic Church made, belatedly, two decades ago. At its Second Vatican Council, the Catholic Church confessed that it had allowed a negative attitude toward the Jewish people to grow among its members. And in what I believe was a courageous move, the Church began a massive program to rid its books and teachings of those references that could be perceived as putting the Jews in a pejorative light.

It has also reached out to clasp hands with the Jewish community in a series of Catholic-Jewish dialogue groups. The one in this part of the world—the Catholic-Jewish Relations Committee of New York—was and continues to be particularly successful, and I am pleased to have been a charter member.

There have been other efforts at united activity, such as the ADL's excellent initiative in working with the Sons of Italy to help them set up a committee on social justice to root out anti-Italian discrimination. And the ADL spirit can be found in the philanthropic field as well. One of the first groups to come to the aid of the Italian Earthquake victims was the Joint Jewish Distribution Committee, which has raised many thousands of dollars for the 240,000 homeless victims of that calamity.

No, I don't understand anti-Semitism fully and probably never will, but I know that what you are doing here tonight is a good way to combat it. Brotherhood programs help to remind us that anti-Semitism is only one form of a pervasive evil of the spirit that threatens all groups; that none of us can permit it to pass without some form of intelligent reaction. Not only because we are morally obliged to protect the Jewish people as our brothers and sisters, but because in the process we protect ourselves.

The German theologian Martin Niemoeller perhaps best expressed the reality of this self-interest when he wrote these lines about the terror that spread under Hitler: "In Germany, they came first for the Communists, but I was not a Communist, so I did not object; then they came for the Jews, but I was not a Jew, so I did not object; then they came for the trade unionists, but I was not a trade unionist, so I did not object; then they came for the Catholics, but I was not a Catholic, so I did not object. Then they came for me, and there was no one left to object."

That, then, is—I think—the message of this evening: that it behooves all gentiles to become Shabbos Goys in spirit, and by so doing to act in their own self-interest as they come to the assistance of their Jewish brethren.

Yes, now that I have grown older and wiser, I think, in the ways of the world, I have come to understand the existence of the evil of discrimination in its many forms, the need to protect ourselves by forming coalitions and, indeed, the importance of events like this evening's.

But I want to tell you finally, and personally, that—for all of that—I yearn for the old, naïve days of South Jamaica, for Momma, Poppa, the Kesslers, and Rubin the roofer and Kaye the tailor, when we took one another, with all of our accents, colors and religions, for granted. Because I think, looking back, it was God who taught us that sweet ignorance.

Thank you.

New York State Fair Dinner
Syracuse, September 1, 1981

There has always been some rural blood in my veins.

My mother was born and raised on a farm. She and her family and their workers spoke a language different from ours, but their life was the universal life of the people of the land. For her time and place, it was a large operation and a successful one. It included hundreds of acres of crops, vineyards, woods that were worked, sheep, dairy stock—practically the whole gamut.

We love looking at the pictures and hearing Mom tell stories. She was one of five sisters. There were four brothers. They all worked—all with assigned chores: feeding the animals, feeding twenty laborers and hands. First, the animals: milking, shearing. Making barrels—and working at a hundred different food processes.

It was necessary for everyone to contribute, to share, to sacrifice. When one of her sisters was struck by what was probably infantile paralysis, or polio, the others took up her chores. When her brother was allowed to go to the big city to try his hand at business—successfully—everyone enjoyed the benefits. He brought back confections and frivolous things like hats and even costume jewelry. Most of all, he brought back money—money that was badly needed when God's weather didn't work so well! And when he had a reversal and wound up in debt, everyone on the farm worked a little harder—which wasn't easy—to help him pay the debt, because bankruptcy was a concept they didn't understand.

406

The land belonged to everybody—it was give and take, it was their resource and their charge, mutually. Because they understood that, they succeeded.

So, although I myself hadn't lived the rural life, I had, at least, a kind of predisposition to understand it—to relate to it—when I began moving through upstate New York seven years ago.

I've spent a lot of time doing that, especially over the last few years as lieutenant governor, when I have also been head of the Rural Affairs Cabinet and Council. All of us have worked—and worked hard, I believe—to understand the problems and potentials of our non-city areas, and to do something about them.

It's been a good investment of our time. The importance of the rural areas to all the people of New York State is difficult to exaggerate. Even today, more than a quarter of the state is active farm acreage. New York's number one industry is not tourism, or banking, or manufacturing—it's agriculture. The value of agricultural products is over $2 billion annually, and New York farms supply half the food consumed in the state.

This already huge output has, potentially, an even greater role to play. Some futurists have gone so far as to say that the availability of good water and the capacity to produce food will be to the mid-eighties what fuel has been to the period we're just emerging from. Aware of this, we've worked to maximize our potential. Roger Barber[1] has already pointed out to you some of the things we've done in the areas of real estate assessment, disease control, business taxes, direct marketing and a milk producers' fund. But for all the good we've done, there is a great deal more still to be done.

- The rural infrastructure—bridges, roads, dams—is badly in need of repair and renovation.
- Rural housing is scarce. Programs for the needy are few and dwindling in rural areas.
- Government should be doing something about erosion. Today 75,000 acres a year are lost as a result of physical erosion and non-agricultural encroachments. If unchecked, that means a loss of 1.5

[1]Then commissioner of the Department of Agriculture and Markets.

million acres by the year 2000. Seventy-five thousand acres a year are
the equivalent of 6 million bushels of corn and 80 million quarts of
milk—food for hundreds of thousands of people.

- The farms that *are* worked need to be kept safe from contamination.
Hazardous wastes are threatening to destroy our basic resources.
Pesticides are a necessary evil. But failure to impose restrictions on
their use—to be employed discreetly and with a full understanding
of their impact on the farm operation—can pose a greater threat.

- Generally, some regulation of agriculture is necessary, but it must be
kept to the minimum required for safety, health and the overall good
of the community. Bureaucratic regulations tend to breed too freely:
their population must be carefully controlled.

- We need a food supply policy to link more intelligently the production and consumption of the food we're capable of supplying.

- Increasingly, as in every other part of our society, availability of
power becomes a more and more vital element in the rural world.
The rise in energy costs in recent years has been punishing.

And underlying everything is the problem of constantly escalating interest rates generated from Washington. The problem
was created somewhere in the bowels of our economic system
several years ago, but it is already clear that the federal government's new economic plan has done nothing to bring interest
rates down to acceptable levels. It is too early, of course, to tell
whether so-called supply-side economics will work in some pres-
ently unpredictable way to solve the problem. But we all know
that it sure doesn't look that way today. The reality is that we are
confronted by a larger than expected deficit despite deep cuts in
the budget that will deprive us in New York of money we need
for rural roads and bridges and dams and power plants and
hospitals and clinics.

On these federal issues it is useless to argue politically against
what is being done—the political victory last year was too big and
is too fresh. We can suggest some directions. Such as cutting the
deficit by reducing wasteful defense spending instead of slashing
other programs, a move that will only put a greater burden on
state and local governments, which already have excessive demands on their treasuries.

At the state level, however it is clear that we have the political
and governmental capacity in New York to develop and imple-

ment policies that are good for the rural areas while serving ultimately the purposes of the whole state. We've proved it in the things we have already done—though it's also clear, from the considerable agenda of important things we've *failed* to do, that our system is by no means perfect and could stand improvement. Thus, in addition to the areas of need already described, it's worth noting the following:

- We have underscored the need for a policy controlling the supply and uses of water but have so far not been able to achieve even a strong first step in that direction.
- We know we need expenditure controls at the state and local levels, but we have not been able to negotiate them.
- The Medicaid takeover, which most county officials statewide regard as desirable, has gone nowhere.
- Nor have we been able to establish a long-range policy that deals adequately with our highway and transportation needs or, indeed, the other parts of our crumbling infrastructure.

Again, I'm pleased with the things we've done, from tax reductions to more efficient government. But we should be able to do more. We have made progress. We should be able to proceed farther. We have fallen far short of exhausting our own ability to find intelligent solutions to our problems and to implement them.

Why?

I submit to you that one reason is our tendency to overpoliticize issues: to think shortsightedly in terms of our own specific local interests without regard to the concerns of the whole state, which, in the long run, would better serve us all.

We have a diminishing capacity to do the statesmanlike thing. We—all of us, constituents and elected officials who seek to represent us—too often develop a fortress mentality: "It's not good for me or my area immediately, so I'm obliged to oppose it."

I have suggested ways to deal with this problem—devices as simple as having the four legislative leaders, Democrats and Republicans, travel around the state with the Governor so that all five can address all the issues at the same time in one another's presence. In 1978 I was able to persuade public television—

although it took me four months to do it—to put the Governor and the Republican Senate Leader and the Democratic Assembly Speaker on public television statewide to answer questions from all parts of the state, live. We might repeat that.

The special advantage to having the whole state hear leaders *at the same time*, on TV, or having them speak locally in one another's presence, is that it reduces their temptation to say one thing in one part of the state and another thing in another. If you are going to call for a gas tax, you should make sure you mention it in Franklin County and not just in Manhattan. If you are going to demand less money for welfare, make sure you tell the people of the South Bronx and not just the people of Chenango. If you are going to talk about averaging power rates, you should suggest it in St. Lawrence County at the same time you are telling the people of White Plains how beneficial it's going to be to them. Doing it otherwise is not politically astute: it's crude, divisive, unfair and eventually ineffective.

Generally, we need to make a stronger effort at dealing with the hard political issues in a more effective way. We need somehow to get past the upstate-downstate syndrome that fragments so much of our thinking and our policy. We need a broader, more intelligent, less parochial effort at compromise.

Frankly, we need to think and feel more like a family in this state.

I have suggested this kind of thing for a long time. I wrote a piece about it a couple of weeks ago. It got some of the establishment upset because it calls for changes in our present approach to state government, starting with a change in the way the legislative and executive branches work together. I'm afraid it made some waves, and most of us appear to prefer more placid politics.

I said this, in effect:

In recent years, the first step in formulating state policy has been the State of the State message. Usually, the Governor introduces policy on this occasion largely without prior consultation with the legislature or the general public. The announcement is followed by responses from the legislature, predictably negative from the opposition and, in recent years, occasionally negative even from some presumed supporters. Then a struggle ensues, fought mainly on the television screen and in the editorial and political pages of our newspapers.

This process, being highly political, tends to break down into political patterns. Elected officials withdraw into their constituencies. Regional and party differences are emphasized: minority interests, represented by Democrats, against the better-to-do interests, represented by Republicans; upstate users of Niagara River hydropower against downstaters who pay Con Edison too much. The process tends to become more parochial, less transcendent. The confrontational style forces the sides to draw political lines boldly and brings out the instinct to do only what's good for one's own "people," to get them a "piece of the pie."

Last year we paid a big price for this fiefdom complex and eagerness for political combat. The forty-two-day debacle during which we failed to adopt a budget cost us millions of dollars from the state treasury and even more in respect with the public at large.

And this year threatens to be worse!

At the very least, I believe the situation requires that we adopt a new approach. This year the State of the State message should not be written as a first thrust in a political duel, but only after extensive discussions and negotiations with the legislature through its leaders upstate and downstate, Democrats and Republicans, liberals and conservatives.

Solid, consistent, honest talk, in advance of taking positions, can settle many of the main questions. Differences needed to preserve political identity will, of course, remain, but their number can be minimized.

There is no substitute for the ancient and honorable art of negotiated compromise, not of principles but of implements, compromise that comes only after extended, honest, tedious—sometimes excruciating—dealings and exchange. And compromise that operates from the principle that the common good often requires at least a partial sublimating of what appears to be the individual good. Call it "give and take."

Will traveling bipartisan town hall meetings, statewide television and a new approach to negotiation solve all our problems? Of course not. But we know we have to do more than we're doing in order to reach the full potential of our rural communities. And let's face it—we know that—it only makes it more difficult when we're a house divided, politically or otherwise.

Mom always said that as you moved away from the land you moved away from God. That's an interesting theological notion. But whatever its literal accuracy, I think there's something instructive about the way her people lived—working together, suppressing differences to work for a greater good, sharing burdens, rejoicing in strength and successes, as a community. It worked for them. Why not try to make it work for us?

Thank you.

Police Conference of the State of New York
Albany, March 24, 1982

I'm pleased to be here. Peter [Reilly, president] made it sound as though I were doing you a big favor by coming, and I'm not. You do me the favor by having me.

I'm pleased to have this opportunity to talk to you today for a few minutes. The reason I need to start early and get out on time is that the Governor has a meeting at ten o'clock with just the legislative leaders. We have trouble again on the budget—it has not been put together. We're trying desperately hard to avoid the kind of debacle we had last year, when we were forty-two days late—at which time, when asked about a budget not coming in on time for three years in a row and how I felt about that, I said, frankly, "I feel very bad, because it's another symptom of a society that's gone lawless."

We all talk about violent crime and the increase of violent crime; we all know about that. But if you look around, it's happening everywhere. In every part of our society there's a loss of discipline, a lack of respect for authority, for the rule, for the necessity to defer to the rule. And here is a legislature and a whole government assembled in Albany whose principal function legally is to get the budget done on time. And three years in a row we didn't live up to the law, while at the same time we were trying to tell the people of this state that they must. So the budget debacles are a serious problem that goes way beyond the

These remarks were extemporaneous.

$30 million it cost us last year to be late. And that's what we'll be talking about at ten o'clock this morning.

I wish that I could talk to you about libraries and education and economic development and the things I would do with money in this state if I were the governor—if I were the king. All the wonderful things we've not done that we'd want to do.

We have a whole generation of people in wheelchairs who will never live a reasonable existence because we can't figure out how to transport them. We have senior citizens in Clinton County and Essex County literally stealing from free lunches so that they have something to eat at night. We have 14 percent of the population unemployed in Buffalo. We have problems of every kind that we ought to be directing our attention to, and we're distracted by another problem that we have to talk about whether we want to or not.

I don't like saying it, because it's a disgrace that we have to say it, but the biggest problem in this society today, the one that comes before all the others, is the problem of keeping law and order.

Some time ago a fellow—Teddy White—wrote a book, *In Search of History.* He was talking about Chungking in 1939 and the Communists and why it was that communism was so appealing to the Chinese at that time. White said, "It's because the first obligation of government is to keep people safe from one another and from the hordes, from the attackers, and they did that."

We're not doing it in this state. It's never been worse. We talked about it at the last convention. I've talked about it ever since. I've talked about it for seven years, and it gets worse every year.

I've talked about being born and raised in the 103rd Precinct in South Jamaica. You know, that was supposed to be a tough community in those days. Everybody fought. You had gang wars and someone might even stick you with a knife occasionally. But it was nothing like what it is now. The violence is sick, it's deep, it's penetrating, it's irrational, and it's everywhere.

What do we do about it as a society? Well, I'll tell you. I said in my announcement—and again I say it reluctantly because I'd rather not have to deal with this as the first priority—that when I become governor, the first priority for me will be to do everything we possibly can to bring down the grotesque crime rate. And this is a pledge I made to my family and to myself as well as to you. Because crime has struck us the way it has struck everybody.

I'm a lieutenant governor. I have state troopers; I'm protected. I know every cop in New York City, I think—I taught a lot of them. I knew them when they were sergeants, and now they're inspectors. I even knew Sid Cooper, who is in charge of internal security for the New York City Police Department and became chief inspector.

I and my family should be safe in New York City. Yet my daughter got attacked twice by the same guy down the block from our house at four-thirty in the afternoon, in broad daylight. We haven't caught him yet. We have his picture, or we think we have his picture—we have the police artist's rendition. We've got everybody looking for him, but we haven't caught him. At four-thirty in the afternoon both times, down the block from my house, in a "good" community—a beautiful girl, eighteen years old.

Now she'll never be the same, unless God is very, very good to us. And we're on our knees thanking God that she wasn't badly hurt; that she wasn't raped; that nothing worse happened to her; that she didn't get killed. So I feel it—and we feel it— the passion. If my son ever got his hands on this guy—forget my son, if I ever did, I cannot predict how I would behave. I'm not a saint, and I'm not God. And if you stood that person in front of me and said, "There he is," I don't know what I would do.

So I'm not shocked that a whole society that sees this day after day—that sees police mowed down, that sees nuns brutalized, that sees old women raped—should say, "My God, you've got to do something about this. And you've got to make the ultimate response, you've got to give us capital punishment. Give us something tough, if only because we must say to this world, 'We will not live this way anymore!'" I understand that. I understand the feeling. People have had it for a long time in the history of civilization.

But I think we have to do something more basic about crime.

I think one of the problems with that feeling is that politicians have used the death penalty to eclipse more important questions, more important things that need to be done.

I think basically what we have to do—and every penologist will tell you this, and everybody who ever wrote a book on criminology, and everybody who was ever on the street—is this: we've got to convince potential criminals that we're going to catch them, convict them, and can them. And that we're going to do it for sure. They've got to know they're going to pay a price.

The percentage of arrests for crimes committed is down. I don't care what the books say. You ask anybody who will tell you the truth in New York City or in Buffalo—for crimes committed, the percentage of arrests is way down. It has to be. There are a lot of crimes we don't even pursue anymore. Burglary in New York City: who in the heck investigates a burglary in New York City? Who has the police? Who has the forces to investigate burglaries? If you're lucky and the car is going by and you see a guy going through the window, then maybe you'll be able to make the arrest.

We have to catch them; they have to know they're going to get caught. We have to convict them; they have to know they're going to get convicted. And we have to can them; there has to be a place where they pay a price. It's not happening now. Now they know that the chances are we're not going to catch them. And if we do catch them, the chances are they won't get convicted. Twenty-six arrests and no trial—the death penalty is not going to frighten that kid because he knows nothing is going to happen to him.

I talked to an attorney yesterday from South Jamaica, my old community, who told me you bring these kids in to the judge for sentencing and tell them, "Take the stuff out of your pockets. No hash, none of that stuff, because you may go to jail, and if you go to jail, they'll search you and find the stuff." But the kids bring it anyway. Why? Because they're not going to go to jail, and they know it. They go in with the stuff in their pockets and they come out of the damn place with the stuff still in their pockets. And you think you're going to change that by saying "We're going to have the death penalty"?

If they do get convicted, we have to have a place to put them —a prison cell. We have to do something with them when we get them in Auburn for nine years. What do you do with them? Should we teach them some kind of skill, give them some kind of shot, do something about getting them a job when they get out?

Well, these are hard questions. We need more police, number one. And more state troopers. New York City is down about ten thousand police since 1972. Ten thousand fewer police than in 1972. Is the death penalty going to change that?

We need better prosecutorial capacity. We need more judges. We blew nineteen indictments in Brooklyn because there were no court clerks ready—the cop was ready, the witness was ready, the D.A. was ready, and the judge was on time, but they didn't have clerks.

We need prison cells—yet we lost the argument last year for the Prison Bond Issue.[1] For all the people screaming for the death penalty and outraged at violence, when it came time to put some money up for the prisons, they wouldn't do it.

Will more police and judges and clerks and prison cells cost money? Of course they will cost money. But what I'm saying to you is that everything worthwhile costs money, and this has to be the number one priority.

After you agree to spend the money, you have to learn to spend it more intelligently. You have to *manage* the system. You know what we don't have in this state? With all the police we have, local and state troopers, D.A.'s everywhere, prosecutors everywhere, an attorney general's office, the Feds you have to tie into, rehabilitation programs, parole, probation—we have no single place where all of that is coordinated statewide. Does that make sense? I don't think so. We coordinate everything else. We coordinate education. But there's no single place in state government where criminal justice is coordinated.

This year, for the first time, the Governor, in response to that need, has asked Tom Coughlin of Corrections to put together a panel and at least start talking. But there has to be more than talk.

[1] A bond issue of $500 million for prison construction was defeated by the voters in 1981.

There has to be a working, coordinative mechanism. We're just getting started in New York.

Now let me talk about my position on the death penalty. The truth is that I don't believe it works; that I remember this state when we had it; that I don't believe it deters; that I don't believe it protects my daughter or my mother. I believe it is a "copout" and I believe that the politicians have used it for years to keep from answering the real questions, the questions like these: How come we're short some ten thousand police? How come the state troopers are paid so little in this state, where they're supposed to be so important? How come we have run out of prison cells? How come probation and parole are not all that they should be? How did we get here? Politicians don't want to deal with those questions. So they deal with a nice, simple question—the electric chair—and that gets everybody off the hook.

Now, to those of you who want the death penalty, and I assume that's most of you, I want to say at least this: "Look, if you want the death penalty, at least don't let them con you. Insist on cops, insist on prosecutors. Insist! Don't let them buy you cheap." Hey, if I were a policeman, what I would want is a cop to my left and a cop to my right. You ask the fellows in New York City who are ten thousand short or the troopers upstate—in Herkimer County one night, there was one trooper on duty in all of Herkimer County—ask them what they'd like. I think "more police" is an answer they'd give you.

In the end, the people will decide for better or for worse what they want. I hope they will come to agree with me. I hope with all my heart that they will agree with me, because as much as I love and respect you, I think on this issue you're wrong, and I feel that deeply.

That's all that I feel on criminal justice that I can tell you in ten and a half minutes. If you have any questions, now or later, I'd be delighted to address them.

I'll add only this. I intend to stay in this race until the very end. I intend to be governor of this state. When I am, your concerns —what you need, what you are, what you represent—will be very, very important to me. There won't be anything more important. I pledge that to you. And I don't think you've ever heard anybody say about Cuomo that he didn't mean it when he said it—and he didn't live up to his word.

Thank you.

MIDDLE ATLANTIC STATES CORRECTION ASSOCIATION CONFERENCE
SWAN LAKE, NEW YORK, APRIL 18, 1982

Your conference this evening couldn't be more timely.

There have always been lawbreakers: Adam and Eve conspired to bite the apple, and Cain slew Abel; jewels were stolen from Egyptian tombs; and acts of murder, even genocide, have been performed down through the ages. The penchant for evil and violence is forever present in man. But it does vary from time to time in the intensity of its expression in our society. And today, it is particularly intense.

There is, almost everywhere, an apparent increased willingness to ignore and violate principles, rules, regulations. Some of it is sophisticated and elegant, like large-scale tax evasion and commercial bribery. It exists, as well, in the highest political echelons of our society—we have still not closed the book on Watergate.

Some of it is pedestrian and middle-class, like the off-the-books culture that lives by a distorted version of the old principle of occult compensation: the right to beat the tax law because the tax law is unfair to hard-working people, even if that can't be proved in the tax courts. And suburban use of pot and worse is working as an effective repealer of the drug laws.

In small matters, lawlessness is no longer considered disrespectful: smoking on the subways, littering, fare beating, speeding. Red lights are ignored by almost everyone—if it's late enough and no one's around. We allow ourselves now to interpret exceptions to the rules based on our sense of what's practical. There appears to be no consensus of disapproval which discourages the lawlessness.

And it's much worse than all of that. We have also somehow bred a willingness—even, occasionally, a desire—to *hurt.*

Violent crime is on the increase everywhere. People who have lived not much more than a generation can look back and see the difference. People who have not can read the statistics: more property crimes, more homicides. The grim numbers are everywhere reproduced and commented upon.

We don't need the statistics to know: just look around. Look at all of our major cities.

Homes and commercial establishments are guarded by the largest army of unofficial security agents in the history of the United States. People make fortunes selling steel fences and grates that lock storefronts against the nocturnal onslaught. Residences everywhere have several locks on their doors and windows. In New York City there are hardly any newspaper stands anymore. Only an adventurer or a fool walks in the parks at night —if they are not locked to protect against such foolishness. I have said before that in cities the mugger has become the midnight mayor of the metropolis; the streets his jurisdiction; the subways his limousine.

So, it is time that the system undergo a thorough analysis. This process—this analysis—is something which politicians in this state have not often engaged in with respect to our criminal justice system. Indeed, given the undeniable increase in crime, the makers and implementers of our laws—the political and governmental system—have not responded adequately at all. Obviously, we have not created a moral climate that would discourage crime—the statistics tell us that.

And programmatically, the response has been mostly evasion and pandering. We have made *causes célèbres* of narrow approaches and purported solutions that at best are superficial and incidental. We, the political and governmental parts of this society, have, until very recently, pretended to be dealing with the fundamental issue—while actually dealing only with emotional issues that give the appearance of solution without reaching the basic problem.

We have, for example, spent the past few years debating capital punishment. Now, there are many who believe capital punishment would deter homicides. But whatever the merits of that argument, clearly it was wrong to permit the debate on this single issue to replace consideration of the other significant problems in the criminal justice system. By our debate we created the false impression that whether or not we will be able to stop the increase in crime is *simply* a matter of whether we can bring ourselves to the point where every once in a while we can burn a wrongdoer, or hang a wrongdoer or poison him.

Just by having the debate, we, the politicians, took ourselves off the hook. We aligned ourselves with the public indignation and gave the appearance of being deeply involved with the search for solutions, and depicted ourselves as good, tough law-and-order people. And all the while, untouched by the great debate, the criminal justice system continued to deteriorate around us.

A few other cases in point: we argued for gun control—validly —but at the same time we did little else, suggesting that a Sullivan law[1] with new biceps might be all we needed. We excoriated judges as soft unless they met a new public standard of harshness, suggesting thereby that we could deter a generation of felons by telling them that although only a few would get caught, those who were would be treated severely. But the fact is, whatever the individual merit in any of these proposals, we have allowed them to be debated in such a way as to eclipse the more subtle truth.

Of course, it makes the people feel better to think they have tough laws and judges and the ultimate in punishment. But you and I know that apparent toughness is not nearly enough. You and I know that the real truth is more complicated and more difficult to manage politically. Indeed, we know that, in fact, the problem of lawlessness and crime has only a limited relationship to the criminal justice system, even when that system is operating at its very best.

Whether fashionable or not, an appreciation of the truth must start with the recognition that it is not the failure of the law or the criminal justice system that creates crime. Crime starts further

[1]New York State's gun-control law.

back in society, in a basic intent, in basic needs—in basic perversion—in social discontent and poverty and, yes, in racial oppression.

All these things must have something—not everything, but something—to do with crime. It is the continuing obligation of government to seek to deal with these causes: to provide education, the chance to earn one's own bread, the opportunity for development and enhancement . . . a decent life that will help reduce social pathology and the need for gratification that produces violation of the law.

That the violence grows in our society today provides greater reason for studying and dealing with these basic causes. Judge Bazelon put it well: "The real roots of crime are associated with a constellation of suffering so hideous that, as a society, we cannot bear to look it in the face. So we hand our casualties over to a system that will keep them from our sight. And, if we manage through our exertions to keep up with the criminals, to match their frenzy with our own, we pretend to have solved the crime."[2]

And more. Can we deal intelligently with the question of how cheaply criminals dispose of other people's lives nowadays without considering how the governments of a hundred states allow the world to flirt with nuclear catastrophe? I think not.

On the other hand, we must understand that, whatever its limitations, when violence and crime get as bad as they are now —and while we are probing more fundamental causes, trying to solve more fundamental problems—we need to do everything we can to provide quicker protection. We cannot afford to do nothing because we're waiting to find a way to do everything. We can't—while searching out the roots—allow our people to die from the poisoned bitter fruit.

For whatever deterrence and protection it can afford us, we must more fully implement our criminal justice system and we must do it immediately. It is fundamental that if the criminal justice system is to work effectively, it must persuade a potential criminal that there is a good chance he or she will get caught and

[2]Judge David I. Bazelon, senior circuit court judge of the U.S. Court of Appeals, District of Columbia, in a Letter to the Editor, entitled "Our Wrong Answer to Street Crime," published in the New York *Times*, October 19, 1980.

punished. The certainty of apprehension and punishment is more effective than the threat of harsh, but uncertain, and even unlikely, punishment. This is a wisdom so old that to those not willing to pander, it has become the first operating principle. Cesare Beccaria summed it up two centuries ago when he said: "The certainty of punishment, even if it be moderate, will help make a stronger impression than the fear of another which is more terrible but combined with a hope of impunity."

Right now the system isn't working. It doesn't deter because its ineffectiveness is well known and anticipated. The talk on the street is that the chances of being caught, convicted and canned are so small that violent crime is a very good investment. The plain truth is that if we want to have any real impact on violent crime, we must deal with the entire criminal justice system, from apprehension to reintroduction into society of a punished felon.

We need more police. As the Talmud says, if there are no officers to enforce the laws, what power do judges have? In New York City, we have nearly ten thousand fewer police than we did ten years ago. Did we have ten thousand too many ten years ago? The same is true in many of the nation's cities. It is a dramatic embarrassment in our society that in so many cities the people should pray for a band of young minority people in berets and T-shirts to appear in our subways because there are so few men and women in uniform provided by our government.

The police arrests should be good ones, so we will need to educate the police to the law. Since most of the crime is committed by a relatively small percentage of all criminals—and since our resources will always be limited—we must concentrate on career criminals. We must improve the capacity of our prosecutors, who are understaffed and far from financially competitive with the private sector. Plea bargaining and revolving-door justice are obviously encouraged when we give the D.A.'s less than they need to handle cases as they should.

We can speed trials with special parts and major concentration on offenses.

I believe the federal mode for selecting juries is more desirable.[3]

---

[3]In the federal system, the judge does the questioning of potential jurors, not the lawyers for the defense and prosecution.

In many places, as in New York, we need more judges and better court facilities. In some places we ask our judges to preserve the majesty of the law and at the same time we force them to work in hovels.

We need more space for prisoners who require incarceration and for local jails, which hold them while they await ultimate disposition. We should work with intelligent sentencing modes and alternatives to incarceration because for some there are more efficient methods of punishment than expensive incarceration.

We need, I believe, more definite sentencing.

And if we are serious about discouraging recidivism, we have to help find work for those who have been punished and whom we would ask to earn their way in society. We need more programs to enhance the teaching of marketable skills to inmates. We should find other vehicles of reentry into society for discharged prisoners.

Then, after we work separately on each piece of the system, we need to make sure we relate one part to the other. In my state, for a long time, we have failed to have a single central strong coordinative mechanism.

Finally, as we enhance our capacity to condemn and punish, we need simultaneously to reinforce the ability of the accused to be protected from injustice. At times like this, when the fear and indignation of the people are high, we must protect against erosion of the presumption of innocence and the right to a fair trial, the twin guarantees that are the very foundation of our system.

The one thing that is most obvious is that criminal justice is an enormous problem, much too large for an electric chair, a tough new gun law or even an army of relentlessly hard judges. Achieving it will take money and arguments; it will take publicity and discussion; it will require sacrifice and may even cost some careers. But we—you and I—must do what we can because the safety of the people is government's primary obligation. We have failed in that obligation for too long.

Much can be achieved by discarding failed systems and designing new, more productive ones. Inevitably, however, a complete effort would require financing and further expense. Like it or not, we will need to spend, to provide staff and equipment, personnel and buildings. We need to put our money where our lives are.

This won't be easy. The days of wine and roses are behind us —at least for the time being—and austerity has properly become the government standard. But can my state—which could build the Albany Mall and the World Trade Center; find money for convention centers, an international Olympics, and a Carrier Dome—can such a state honestly contend that we cannot find the resources to protect our citizens from violent attack and even death? Can any state?

Well, the political system has the capacity to do a great deal, if it wants to. And what will make it want to is the strong voice of the public demanding it. So far, in most places, the public has asked only for simplistic answers—and that is what it is getting. Someone has to teach them better, and that is you. You have the position, the skill, the understanding, the dedication. You are trained in law and right reason and justice. You are our natural leaders.

You have done much for this society. We need you to do more. We need you to seize the leadership, to speak, to cajole, to argue, to demand that the right thing be done. You should lead the public in demanding of us the politicians not buzzwords and slogans and shibboleths but an intelligent, comprehensive and useful repair and strengthening of the criminal justice system —all the while recognizing that the problems are deeper even than that.

You must help make the right thing the popular thing. I wish you luck in doing so, for all our sakes.

Thank you for the honor of being here.

Saratoga County Democratic Committee Dinner
Saratoga Springs, May 23, 1982

It's always good to be back in Saratoga Springs—the home of horse races, betting, good cheesecake from the Spa Diner, SPAC[1] and, of course, politics.

Being here in the historic Canfield Casino, surrounded by elegance, where "Diamond Jim" Brady once held court and "Bet a Million" Gates secured his fortune, where H. S. Sinclair once parlayed his winnings into bigger oil wells, and where Lillian Russell gave the Gilded Age its name—being here makes me wish these luminaries from the past were here tonight . . . to join my Finance Committee.

Now, I'm not complaining about the efforts of my fund-raisers. Not for a moment. They've just announced that we're well on our way to our second million, and last Sunday the campaign got another boost. The Gannett chain published its recent poll, which showed me trailing my opponent by only ten points. I was thirty points behind forty-five days ago. I'm heartened by that, and I can't help but draw an analogy or two between this campaign and a horse race: some horses are slow at the start, but a good horse comes on strong at the stretch. Some candidates start high in the polls, but can't sustain their lead.

There are many front-runners who get off early and quickly, but most of them fade in the stretch. What we're seeing in this year's political race is a stretch runner who closes fast. In fact,

[1] Saratoga Performing Arts Center.

many betting men and women have begun to "hedge their bets."
We're just about at the turn—and the pace is picking up.

You know, Mayor Corning is my trainer. He's got me on the
track from early morning until late at night. But he's been good
to me. Last week, he gave me 100,000 of his leftover campaign
buttons to distribute in New York City. You remember his
slogan: "Keep the Mayor mayor." That Corning—he's a genius.
And he keeps his promises, too. I asked him to join my ticket.
He said no. I offered to step aside if he would run for governor.
I offered to join his ticket and run for lieutenant governor. He
said no—again—and added, "Look, Mario, I can't do that. When
the people of Albany reelected me last November, I promised
the people that I would serve out my term. I can't run out on
them now; I can't go back on my word." Erastus Corning is some
kind of mayor. I'm glad he's on my side! In this state, Mayor
Corning has come to epitomize the Democratic party. He helps
all of us remember what it is to be a Democrat; he reminds us
that Democrats don't forget the fundamental truths of Franklin
Delano Roosevelt, Harry S. Truman, John Fitzgerald Kennedy,
Al Smith, Herbert Lehman, Averell Harriman, Eleanor Roosevelt, Hugh Leo Carey and, yes, James Earl Carter.

We're a party that remembers the people. All the people.
We're a party that believes in people, serves them, cares about
them. We're the party that proposes solutions to human problems. Remember Social Security, the Peace Corps, the Marshall
Plan, the CCC,[2] Medicaid, Big Mac,[3] student loans, unemployment compensation, the school lunch program? Remember the
thousands of other plans and programs all designed to help people lead more livable lives?

I'm proud to be a Democrat. I've felt honored to serve the
people of this state for seven and one-half years—as secretary of
state and now as lieutenant governor. I have come to understand
the way government works, and it is clear that it rewards involvement and punishes aloofness. Indifference gets nothing.

All of us in this room tonight understand that. This room is
filled with people who have made the right choice—more than

[2]Civilian Conservation Corps.
[3]The Metropolitan Assistance Corporation, set up by the state, under Governor
Carey, in 1975 to issue $3 billion of general obligation bonds to bail out New York City.

once. We might have chosen to be Democrats because we like or admire great Democrats, or it might have been by accident, or by inheritance, or even for expediency's sake. But we chose to *stay* Democrats because there is too little time in life to waste on anything less than the significant, and there is a significant difference between us and the Republicans.

We have emphases and priorities that they don't have, and we believe their emphases are wrong.

We believe there was a difference between Hoover and Roosevelt, Nixon and Kennedy, and Carter and Reagan. If President Reagan has done nothing else, he has made that difference clear. The Republicans have produced an economic plan that helps the rich at the expense of the middle class and the poor. A plan that is generous only to the weapons makers and ammunition manufacturers. A program that punishes workers, students, the disabled, pregnant women, the elderly. I have described it before as operating from a new ethic: God helps those whom God has helped.

The differences are clear.

We are involved in a political campaign for governor, a campaign that will raise a lot of questions—basic questions—about those differences. It's a time to remind the people of New York State that Republicanism—now and in the past—damaged this state, making it the most heavily taxed state in the nation and nearly bankrupted in 1975. We must remind the people how they are threatened by the Reagan brand of Republicanism that has brought us national unemployment, impossible interest rates and a recession hellbent on becoming a depression.

It's a time to remind them that the President's insistence on "fair trade" programs has made it possible for the Metropolitan Transit Authority in New York City to export jobs to Japan and now Canada and import subway cars for the city's mass transit system. New York could not compete with the financial arrangements offered by foreign governments. So our blue-collar workers in places like Buffalo and Hornell and Athens and Brooklyn, and in hundreds of other communities, are unemployed. And plants—once bustling centers of production—have been idled because leaders in Washington, because bureaucrats and authorities in New York City did not have the vision to insist that these subway cars—a billion-dollar industry—could and should be built in this state.

We have less than ten days now to try and reverse this short-sighted decision. The issue is jobs. Jobs for New Yorkers.

When I learned of the plan about one month ago, I began to investigate it. I could not believe that we would seriously consider purchasing subway cars from foreign government-sponsored conglomerates. I was told that no plant or company in New York was capable of doing the work. How did they know? I asked. When no one could tell me, my staff and I began calling around the state. You may remember that I am chairman of both the Rural and Urban Affairs cabinets. I have come to know the resources in New York, and within a few days we had identified five plants in New York capable of doing the work—and they had *never been contacted* by anyone. We put the folks at Hornell's GE plant together with the Budd Company, the only remaining American manufacturer of trains, and they began negotiating. It was too late for the Japanese deal, but we had reason to believe that we could win the contract for 825 more subway cars. Then came the announcement on Tuesday. The deal was going to Canada because the Canadian government had guaranteed the interest rate on a loan at 9½ percent. The best Budd could do —even though their bid was $30,000 less per car than the Canadians'—was 18 percent. And that put the Budd bid at $300 million higher just because of the interest.

This is an outrageous, untenable situation. I have been speaking about it throughout the state. I have been working into the late hours of the night to get them to change their minds, to withdraw their intent, but we have only a few days. I know that we are making some progress because one New York City newspaper, lately known for its efforts to promote the candidacy of its mayor, suggested editorially that I should leave these kinds of deliberations to the power brokers because they know what they're doing. They do. They're sticking it to the blue-collar worker. It should not happen. I am giving you and the people of this great state fair notice. If you elect me, I will be the kind of governor who will do whatever it takes to bring jobs back, to reopen plants, to find a way to continue the work of this adminis-tration—of which I have been a proud part—led by Governor

Hugh Carey. This administration reduced taxes by more than $2.3 billion since 1977—the largest and most effective tax cut in the history of this state. This administration reignited the economy. This administration saved New York City and Yonkers and Utica from bankruptcy.

I know this state. I've spent eight years learning the problems and helping construct solutions to them. I'm a realist. Indeed, I have been accused of being too realistic, but after eight years in this administration, I am not required to be a pessimist.

I believe—honestly and objectively—that continuing this Democratic administration will make this state bigger, stronger and better for all our people, upstater and downstater alike.

I believe this because we are the sons and daughters, grandsons and granddaughters of the people who came before us—those who had larger visions and fewer resources than we now have. But they achieved and accomplished, and they did it grandly. We have inherited their ability to achieve greatly. But it is for you and me—together—to make the decision to do that.

Let us do it, then. Let us win this election. Let us continue to rebuild this state, the way we're supposed to, because we're Democrats.

ORDER OF THE SONS OF ITALY CONVENTION
KIAMESHA LAKE, NEW YORK, JUNE 5, 1982

A young Italian immigrant, at the close of the last century, wrote to his family: "Before I came here, they told me the streets were paved with gold. When I came here, I learned three things. First, the streets were *not* paved with gold. Second, the streets were not paved at all. Third, they expected me to pave them."

I don't think that young immigrant was really disappointed. He, like so many others, had come to this blessed America in search of *"pane e lavoro."* While these words mean, simply, "bread and work," taken together they add up to something more than the sum of the parts. They add up to dignity and pride.

A regular wage and a full plate are, however, only the beginning of life's requirements. Early in this century, thousands of Italian women labored in the firetrap sweatshops of New York City while their men were paving the streets. Their hours were inhumanly long. Conditions were unsafe, unhealthy and degrading. Yet from deep in their Italian souls they found a song to express their demand for dignity: "Give us bread, but give us roses."

And it was a son of Italy, Congressman Fiorello La Guardia, who was the author of the first act of Congress to recognize the dignity of labor in the Norris–La Guardia Act of 1930.

I often speak of our parents as having taught us love. They taught us different kinds of love. They taught us love of God. We are a deeply spiritual people, imbued with a powerful sense of right and wrong. Therefore, we are passionate for justice. And

432

because we believe in a merciful God, we are a compassionate people.

They taught us love of country—*this* country, which bears the name of Amerigo Vespucci. Too few of our children know of Filippo Mazzei, who profoundly influenced his friend Thomas Jefferson with the idea of a democratic republic. But our parents' love of their adopted country was founded on the evidence of their own lives. America afforded them dignity.

They taught us love of family. The love of parents toward their children, and of children toward their parents. And when our parents arrived at the winter of their lives, they needed our love, as we needed theirs. Love eases the ravages of illness. Love breaks through the walls of loneliness. We care about our elders. But, because of the realities of present-day society and economics, we need help in caring *for* them, and we are troubled.

The miracles of modern medicine have prolonged life. In their working years, our elders earned their dignity. But extended years require extended means to preserve that dignity. So, almost fifty years ago, we, as a society, created the means of preserving that dignity. We called it Social Security.

We learned that medical miracles are costly. We learned that the means of prolonging life were beyond the reach of most of our elders. They simply could not afford to stay alive! So we, as a society, created Medicare.

Now we have come upon difficult times. Our national economy is shaken by tremors set off by forces beyond our control. We see the need for rearranging elements of our economy. The problems are enormous and complex, and need to be addressed.

But I am troubled and appalled by measures to solve those problems which lay a heavy burden on our elders. I am repelled by the callousness of assaults on the lifelines of our parents and grandparents. For many unable to work because they have been disabled by injury or illness, the lifeline has been cut entirely. For the rest, their hold on life is being weakened by cutting their access to adequate medical care.

We have made a contract with this generation of elders, and if the terms of that contract need changing for the future, we must find ways to improve it. But first, we must meet our commitment to this generation of our elders.

And if we must, reluctantly, and not without pain, entrust care of our elders to others, we want to know that the conditions are safe and the people caring for them qualified. We want to know that the places to which we have entrusted them are properly inspected and subject to minimum standards of safety and cleanliness. Again, it is our elders who pay the costs of economic upheaval by the removal of federal standards. Thus, greed endangers not only dignity, but life itself. And my Italian heart rebels at this, because we revere our elders.

We love our children. We want them to become adults equipped to make the most of their potential. I applaud the work of the commission on social justice created by our order because of our children. I see the profound effect of the images which parade across the television screen hour after hour, night after night. Overwhelmingly, they show the Italian American in images destructive of dignity and self-esteem. So we determined to expose the absurdity and the ugliness of the stereotypes which populate and pollute prime time in America. And we have told the image makers, "No more!"

Love of our children means concern for their future. The golden key to the future is education. But the cost of higher education in America has risen to dizzying levels, exceeding the immediate means of most American families. Many of our Italian American families face the prospect of sending three and four children through college, often overlapping in time. Children learn the value of education by sharing responsibility for its cost, and there was a time when a student could earn a substantial part of the cost during the summer months and through part-time employment. Now, not only have the costs outraced those capabilities, the jobs have also become scarcer while the applicants have become more numerous. A partial answer was the student loan program. Most of the loans were secured by parents as co-signers. They were a shared responsibility. But these loans are no longer available. The apostles of the new economics, after attacking the aged, have now assaulted the young.

Our parents' acceptance of the necessity of work has given us respect for work. We understand the bond between work and dignity. We have reaped the rewards of work for three generations. Our economic faith is simple. That which promotes opportunity for work is good. That which defeats opportunity is not good. It is not good for us. It is not good for our children. It is not good for our country.

We are not a people given to fads. We cling to our traditions and our values. We tend to be conservative. And when someone comes along calling himself a conservative, we tend to be somewhat attracted to him, and to give him a hearing and a chance at solving the nation's problems.

But what kind of conservatism is this that throws millions of people out of work? What kind of conservatism is this that replaces production lines with unemployment lines? What kind of conservatism is this that prevents young people from learning the value of work because there are no jobs for them? What kind of conservatism is this that actually penalizes work?

My traditional—conservative, if you will—values have guided me in my personal and my public life. Because I love a merciful God, I believe that government must never lose the quality of compassion. Because I love my country, I believe America is ill-served by setting class against class and young against old. Because I love my family, and because I believe in the value of family, I believe we must fulfill our contract with our elders. Because I love my children, I believe we must not defeat the aspirations of the next generation, which is willing to work to fulfill its potential. And because I believe in the fundamental value of dignity through labor, I believe jobs should not be sacrificed on the altar of economic sleight of hand.

All of these are Italian values. You don't have to be Italian to believe in them—but it helps.

Perhaps what drew our grandparents, our parents and some of you in this room to this country is expressed in a line from Dante's *Paradiso*: *"Tu proverai si come al di sale lo pane altrui, e com' è duro calle lo scendere e il salir per l'altrui scale."* "You shall learn that the taste of someone else's bread is salt, and how hard it is to tread a stranger's stair." We came for our own bread and to tread our own stair.

"Pane e lavoro"—bread and work—dignity—and roses, too. Is that not what our Order of the Sons and Daughters of Italy in America is all about?

Your theme, "New Directions for Cities and Villages," reminds me of the story of a knight who returned to his castle one evening in disarray: helmet cockeyed, face bloody, armor dented—even his horse was limping. No one had ever seen such a mess. The king was so concerned that he came out and met him on the drawbridge.

"What hath befallen you, sir knight?" the king asked.

"Oh, sire," said the knight, "it's not an easy thing laboring in your service. I have been robbing, raping and pillaging your enemies east of the Great Mountain, and—"

"Wait a minute," said the king. "I have no enemies east of the Great Mountain."

"Oh?" said the knight. "Well, I think you do now."

Direction *is* important—new or old, east or west. And there has to be a common cause, a common understanding about the direction.

The direction in which we have traditionally looked for help has been up—you at the city and village level looking to us in Albany, and we in Albany looking to Washington. President Reagan proposes a radical change in that direction, a change in the way Americans look at the process of government. The proposal is called the "New Federalism." Given our theme, it is appropriate that we examine the implications of the proposal. The fact is that the New Federalism may well be to the eighties what the New Deal was to the thirties. No one—especially those of us here—should underestimate its revolutionary potential.

One reason that the New Federalism has been underestimated up to now, I believe, is that it has been confused with the President's economic program. That program of so-called Reaganomics can easily be reversed with succeeding elections: taxes raised, defense spending lowered, some programs that had been allowed to die resurrected.

But the New Federalism provides for a permanent change in the relationship between states and municipalities and the national government. Once achieved and institutionalized, it would be difficult to reverse.

President Reagan initially proposed to usher in the New Federalism by having Washington assume the full cost of the Medicaid program, relieving state and local governments of their sizable share. In return, the states would pay wholly for their food stamp program, now fully financed from Washington, and take total responsibility for welfare—whose costs are now borne on a proportional basis in New York State by Washington and Albany. This proposition seems attractive from an administrative point of view: it would tidy things up by eliminating overlapping federal-state jurisdictions.

The Reagan administration no doubt expected an enthusiastic reception for its proposal from governors and mayors, since Medicaid costs to the states and localities keep rising faster than inflation. But a closer look threw some doubt on the bargain. The cost of food stamps and welfare costs will certainly escalate, too, and if a cost-conscious federal government tightens Medicaid elegibility, local hospitals will have to pick up the slack somehow to ensure that the desperately sick are not turned away. It's easy to see how the poor could become pawns in this game of diminishing benefits—a game, the congressional budget office estimates, that would wind up costing the states $1.5 billion a year. And that's only for Phase One of the program.

But the heart of the New Federalism is Phase Two, which involves turning over forty-three federal programs to the states, including those covering such areas as job training, health education, transportation and child welfare. The costs of these transfers are so large that the President has proposed a federal trust fund of $28 billion to be created out of the oil windfall profits tax and federal excise taxes. During the eighties this "turnback aid" would be phased out, however, and by 1991 the states would have to raise the revenue themselves or eliminate some services altogether. This option and the inevitable erosion in programs that would result are the essence of the Reagan Revolution.

In proposing the radical new direction, the New Federalism signals an attempt to reallocate the country's political and social power for the foreseeable future. As such, it reflects both ideology and demography. Since 1945, suburbanization has been the most significant trend in American social and political life. By 1970, the country for the first time in its history had more people in metropolitan areas living outside city limits than within them. The 1980 census figures confirmed this trend, along with a dramatic concomitant decline in city populations. Inevitably, we have seen a steady growth of suburban power in American politics generally and in New York State in particular. The redistricting set in motion by the recent census will reinforce that growth.

The political roots of the New Federalism are to be found in communities like the ones many, if not most, of you represent: communities where property taxes have risen sharply, labor costs increasingly strain the budget, and federal policies are perceived to favor urban populations. By making many programs discretionary and dependent on state and local revenues, the New Federalism will surely increase the financial pinch in urban America.

For the cities, which have benefited from Washington's attention, will now have to compete with suburban interests for shrinking resources. The "War on Poverty," for example, has always been essentially a federal campaign, dependent upon taking money from affluent areas and funneling it into blighted and endangered neighborhoods. Suburban voters have never been happy with these transfers—and opposed them. The New Federalism will institutionalize their opposition.

Supporters of the program argue that in a time of limited resources, allocations ought to be made by those closest to the problems. It would, it is said, be more "democratic" to have states and localities establish priorities for the spending of dwindling revenues.

But suppose those priorities don't include the handicapped or the poor? The New Federalism will place such people at the mercy of state legislatures and unsympathetic suburban representatives. Expensive programs with weak constituencies will almost certainly be pared down; some even eliminated. Municipal governments already saddled with inordinate financial problems will be required to raise new revenues or see traditional services curtailed.

I believe I've made it clear that I don't consider the New Federalism the answer. I think the program poses too great a threat of destabilization and of deepening the division between rich states and poor. But the issue is not what Mario Cuomo thinks of the New Federalism or even what New York State thinks of it. We are one of fifty states that, regardless of whether Democrats or Republicans are in control next January, will be negotiating with Washington to get a bigger share of the federal pie. This negotiation will provide the backdrop for more important decision making that should be going on here in New York. The issue transcends the New Federalism; its resolution will affect the welfare of our localities and our people for years to come.

I'm talking about a new relationship—separate from the New Federalism—a new relationship between Albany and local governments based on cogent solutions to the age-old problems that have plagued us through the years, problems like how best to revise the state revenue-sharing formula. The present system of distributing money to localities on the basis of population is obviously unfair. A village that provides sewers, water and police has much higher expenses and must impose a much heavier tax burden on its citizens than one that provides none or just one of these costly services. We must devise a formula to respond to such variations—with circumstances of legitimate need as well as services part of the equation.

There are many other questions to be raised—those pertaining to the property tax, mandates,[1] the Levittown decision[2] among them—that we have talked about in the past and must resolve in

[1]Laws emanating from one level of government that mandate certain courses of action —such as making the public transit system totally accessible and public education available to the handicapped—at a lower level without providing the funding.
[2]See p. 111.

the near future. As we work toward those resolutions, we will be wise to heed the words of James Madison in establishing our priorities. We must not forget, Madison said, that the supreme object to be pursued in setting the agenda is "the real welfare of the great body of people." That has been our practice in New York State and its localities for more than two hundred years. I'm sure it will continue to be so whatever the future of public policy may bring.

New York State Democratic Convention
Syracuse, June 22, 1982

Chairman Baranello, distinguished officers and leaders of our Democratic party, brothers and sisters of the labor movement, ladies and gentlemen:

I congratulate Ed Koch and all the designees on their victories.

I want to say "thank you." First, to my family, who have always given me more than I earned in loyalty and support. Second, to all of you.

I accept with gratitude and humility the opportunity this convention has provided me to prove to the voters of our party that I should serve as the highest elected official of this great state.

Frankly, I believe that I *will* prove it. And that after our summer struggle we will be joining together again—all of us—in this, our Democratic party, supporting one of the strongest teams of statewide candidates in this state's history.

Matilda and the children and I have enjoyed the convention.

But now I'm looking forward to something I like even better. I'm looking forward to going out of this convention hall to the people. To remind people what we of the Democratic administration led by Governor Hugh Carey have done over the last eight years to bring this state back from the brink of bankruptcy and to point it once again in the right direction. To talk to them about their problems and what we can do to solve them. To talk to them about their opportunities and what we can do to enlarge them. To tell them about my record as secretary of state and lieutenant governor and my ideas for the state's future.

I look forward eagerly to comparing ideas and records with my opponent. I believe that we can make of that process something stimulating and useful to the people of the entire state, instead of something divisive.

With that in mind, I would like to expand on a suggestion that I have made previously. I take this opportunity to suggest a whole new style of campaigning for the next ten weeks. Instead of separate campaigns delivering separate versions of the truth —artificially packaged with prepared scripts, away from the hard comparisons and embarrassing questions—I suggest to my opponent that we campaign in tandem, together, everywhere. A single schedule. A single forum. Answering all questions, revealing all differences, confirming all agreements, giving the people of this state the closest and best look at two candidates they have ever had in the state's political history.

Let's go together to Massena and Niagara Falls and talk about hydropower and whether it's fair to reallocate it to Westchester and New York City.

To Buffalo and Hornell to talk about economic development and unemployment and why we can't build subway cars for New York City in our own great state, instead of in Japan and Canada.

To the farmers of the Southern Tier and central New York to talk about a Rural Development Corporation that will do for the small farmers and businessmen of upstate what the Urban Development Corporation has done for our great cities.

To the capital region and Long Island to talk about what we propose to do to create jobs in the area of high technology.

To Westchester and Rockland and the Hudson Valley to talk about how to control real property taxes by expanding our program of state assumption of local burden.

To New York City to discuss how we in the Carey administration have kept the world's best-known city from bankruptcy, year after year, with the Financial Control Board and Big Mac and annual transfusions of millions of dollars. We should go to New York City to talk about violent crimes in our cities, the terror in our streets, locked doors, gates over windows, and why there are not enough police.

Side by side, we should answer questions from the people on the Staten Island ferry about ferry fares and about subway fares and a selfish spirit that gives capital gains taxes back to rich real estate developers.

I look forward to my opponents' response to this suggestion.

I look forward to something more in this campaign. And that is the chance to define our party in terms of principles and basic beliefs. We want more than a victory in November. We want a victory that is true to things that make us Democrats.

If I have one disappointment at this convention, it is that we did not avail ourselves of the opportunity to tell the world what we stand for and what it is in our programs, plans and philosophy that distinguishes us from the other parties. I regret we did not do that, because unless we stand for something—for something different and for something better—then there is no likelihood of success.

And what is worse, no reason for success. The body of this party will not long survive without its soul.

When we say "we" will oppose the Republicans, who are "we"? What is it that we believe that makes us better? What entitles us to ask the people to allow us to lead them? What gives us the right to have power over peoples' lives?

I think it is this . . . or should be:

We believe that the fundamental purpose of government is to improve the conditions of people's lives. It should provide the talented with an opportunity to use their talent to the fullest. But at the same time it should find the resources to help those who cannot help themselves.

We believe government should tax the people fairly, with those who have received the most contributing to those who have been denied the most.

We believe that a balanced budget that fails to meet the needs of the middle class and poor—the need for work and security and dignity—would be the emblem of hypocrisy.

We believe, despite what some have said, that we have not yet done enough—for the senior citizens of Essex County who are beyond the ability to help themselves; for the people in wheelchairs in Dutchess; for the pregnant women whose nourishment for the life they carry used to be supplied by the WIC[1] program

[1] Women, Infants and Children—a Department of Health program providing nutritious food and nutrition education to eligible individuals in New York State.

in Oneida County; for the unemployed steelworkers in Buffalo, and the millions of others like them who have been denied the opportunity to earn their own bread in this state and in this nation; for the uneducated, for the sick, for the weak.

We believe in a reverence for life. We have always believed in the politics of life, not the politics of death, even when many people are deceived into believing that death is the only remedy.

We proclaim—as loudly as we can—the utter insanity of nuclear proliferation and the need for a nuclear freeze, if only to reaffirm the simple truth that peace is better than war because life is better than death.

We believe in the union movement. We believe in openness by government. We believe in privacy for people and freedom from unnecessary restraints. In the ERA. In the right of free choice.

Altogether, we believe in a government characterized by fairness and reasonableness—a reasonableness that goes beyond labels, that is wiser than naked ideology, that refuses to pander.

We are the party that rejects fear and that offers hope. We are the party that avoids confrontation and encourages conciliation. We are the party that rejects expediency and demonstrates courage.

We should have been the party that attacked Reaganomics in 1980, when it was so popular, instead of waiting until now, when the error of our acquiescence is clear.

We have always been strong enough to use words like "compassion."

We have always been tough enough to tell the truth, even when the polls suggested that many misunderstood the truth. We are supposed to be the party that would never put a poll where our conscience ought to be.

We have always been smart enough to find ways to make our highest aspirations and our most beautiful dreams everyday reality.

That's what my very presence on this platform today represents—the son of immigrants, people who came from deprivation. The second-highest elected official in the greatest state in the greatest nation in the only world we know, presuming to go even higher.

I and my people have had the benefit of every good thing that government—*Democratic* government—could provide: relief from the Depression; education; employment; a chance to work ourselves up through the society with the security of knowing that we would be protected against weakness we could not avoid.

I know about Roosevelt. I know Democratic principles work. They worked for my parents. They worked for me, for you and yours, and for a whole generation of people like us. Those principles made many of us middle-class. They help us to live as middle-class, in comfort, today—with a decent education for our children, with medical care, with security for our old age.

I know Democratic principles can work for today's minorities —*without threatening the middle class.* The way they worked for yesterday's minorities—unless those of us who were at the bottom yesterday forget . . .

What we were.

What we are.

What we are supposed to believe. *Always,* not just when it is convenient.

I pledge I will do everything I can to remember . . . and to remind. As governor—a Democratic governor.

Thank you and God bless you.

BLACK MINISTERS' ASSOCIATION
ROCHESTER, AUGUST 16, 1982

"Beware of Greeks bearing gifts or Whites who claim to understand Blacks." One of New York City's most flamboyant congressmen, Adam Clayton Powell, said that—and he was right.

I wouldn't presume to say that I can put myself in the shoes of people like yourselves or empathize totally with the plight of many of your brothers and sisters. But I think I can come pretty close. I was born, after all, outside the "majority grouping" of Americans—a grouping that looked down upon me and my parents, saw us as different.

Like you, however, we never considered ourselves inferior. My parents indicated to me, as many of yours did to you, that my deliverance would come through education and hard work. It did. And the path I found myself on after college and law school led me eight years ago this summer into politics. Yes, in the summer of 1974 I made my first political speech. I remember I defended a congressman named Ed Koch, who had been accused of betraying the liberal Democratic tradition in a dispute triggered by a decision to build low-income housing in Forest Hills, a middle-class neighborhood in the New York City borough of Queens.

Did I say that was eight years ago? It was a *lifetime* ago. In 1974, New York was a liberal city—more liberal than Rochester, to be sure; but Rochester, after a period of racial problems, had emerged as a city of enlightened moderation. As for the state, in 1974, it was one of the most progressive in the country

446

—a country that had not yet gone conservative. Today, New York City is run by a mayor who ran as a Republican in 1981, that same mayor who helped Reagan win the state in 1980. And we have a federal government firmly in the hands of reactionaries.

And what can we say about Rochester? It's now a moderately conservative town instead of a city of enlightened moderation. More interestingly, its employment picture provides us with a microcosmic look at the national economy and how Blacks are being affected by the slump.

The unemployment rate in the Rochester area is only 5.5 percent—less than half of what it is in Buffalo and about four points under the national average. But Black unemployment in Rochester is 15.9 percent, and joblessness among Black teenagers is 36.7 percent compared to 13.1 percent for White teenagers. Yes, despite its relatively advantageous position in the economy, Rochester reflects precisely the God-helps-those-whom-God-has-helped philosophy that prevails in Washington.

Some people say that the state of the economy and the altering of national attitudes are cyclical in nature, that every eighteen or nineteen years there are swings from liberalism on the one hand to conservatism on the other. The theory is that nothing really works well enough to solve all the problems, and after a while people simply decide to try it the other way, forgetting that the alternative failed before as well.

I believe there's a germ of truth to that, but only a germ. I don't want to go into too much detail now because I came here to discuss, primarily, what is on *your* minds. If you'll bear with me, though, I'll take a few more moments before our discussion to give you a general idea of my philosophy.

I believe, roughly, as follows: The government's basic purpose —even in this free-market society—is to keep people secure and to see that those who need help to live at a decent level are given that help. The government should protect the weak without unnecessarily inhibiting the strong. More than protecting, the government must assure the weak their dignity. This concern for the needy cannot be left to society; it must be public policy to do the right thing.

The Reagan administration obvious feels differently. It says, in effect, "We tried throwing money at the poor; now let's try throwing money at the rich." It espouses a redistribution of wealth, from the poor to the rich, on the assumption that inevitably the lure of additional riches will entice the wealthy into productivity, enhancing investments. A corollary of this so-called trickle-down theory is that all welfare is waste; another is, the less government the better.

In cities like Rochester and New York, we see Reaganomics in local garb everywhere we turn: in the phasing out of social programs, the abandonment of poor neighborhoods, the encouragement of "gentrification" in potentially good neighborhoods and the concomitant expulsion of the poor and lower middle class to clear the way for profitable real estate deals there.

I think, as I said, that there is some validity to the cyclical theory and that the pendulum will eventually come back in what I consider the right direction. But I don't think we should wait for the natural swing. I'm convinced that we should grab hold of that pendulum and not let it drag us. Men of the spirit like yourselves have an obligation to lead that effort—an effort that I intend to assist as governor.

Thank you.

AFL-CIO Convention
Kiamesha Lake, New York, August 31, 1982

Thank you, Ray [Corbett], Howard [Molisani], members of the Executive Council, brothers and sisters.

I come before you this morning to ask you to join me in a very important struggle. When we put aside the campaign clutter, roll away the blue smoke, and take down the barrier and look clearly at the heart of this gubernatorial campaign, we see the struggle over basic beliefs—and it is a very important one, because this is the first battle in the war of 1984, when we will fight for the political soul of this nation.

On the one hand, I think that my candidacy is built on traditional Democratic principles. I believe in those principles. I have always supported them. I am convinced that they work better than the alternatives represented by "trickle down" and "supply side." I believe that they are our best hope for the future. I don't believe in leaving it to the rich to take care of the rest of us. When we tried it in this country fifty years ago and called it "trickle down," we had a depression. Now, Reaganomics has tried it again and called it "supply side," and we have a recession struggling to become a depression. I believe that the Roosevelt correction of our policies in government was a good one. I think that this state's tradition of Al Smith, Herbert Lehman and Averell Harriman that gave us unemployment insurance and a whole array of strong social programs was a good one.

On the other hand, my opponent believes that government has done too much. Specifically, he has said that we have done too much for two groups, the disabled and the working people of the trade unions. And he said it to a national audience in Baltimore only about a year ago. He disagrees with the "right to know" law that allows workers to know that they may be dealing with substances that can hurt or kill them. He opposes Attorney General Abrams's prevailing wage bill, a bill that I supported from the time it was first mentioned. He suggested paying a sub-minimum wage. He wants to reduce the cost-of-living increase for senior citizens on Social Security. He wants to require senior citizens to retire at a fixed age—even if they are capable of working and want to work—because, he suggests, otherwise it is inconvenient for business.

Yesterday, I understand, he told you that he wants jobs at Lincoln West in Manhattan and that I don't. Well, he did not tell you the truth. The truth is that I'm part of an administration that has brought to this state 450,000 jobs in the last five years. The truth is that we can have the same number of jobs and more at Lincoln West, if, instead of building luxury houses out of reach of the people who work for a living because they have to, we build houses for ordinary people—as well as add to the rail freight facilities that would help us with the blue-collar manufacturing jobs we need so badly in this state. And talking about blue-collar jobs, my opponent sent a billion dollars' worth of those jobs to Japan and China. That won't happen when I am governor. And to add insult to injury, as though to mock the union movement, he took the bug off city printing and went to Philadelphia to print the New York City directory.[1]

He has come a long way since he was a congressman, when he had a 90 percent vote record. I've reminded him of that record from time to time, and you know what he has told me in three debates? He disavows that record. He says it was a mistake. He says he didn't realize how foolish he was for adopting those social programs. That record he boasted of here yesterday he has disavowed when it was politically opportune for him to do so— and don't you let him forget it. He has a new philosophy now, and it is compatible with Ronald Reagan's. For he praised Ron-

[1]The directory was printed by a private company in Philadelphia instead of with New York State union labor (a "bug" is a union label).

ald Reagan, ran as a Republican, helped Reagan's party to pay off its debt, and was co-honored with Richard Nixon. This year, this year he talks about loyalty to the Democratic party and then endorses four Republicans in this very race and refuses to disendorse them.

My opponent and I are different. Especially when it comes to you. I don't believe we have done too much for union people or for the disabled. I see the union movements as one of the greatest forces for good in this nation's history. It was less than a lifetime ago that you could work yourself to death in this very state, in a system that would take from those who labored everything it could and give back as little as possible. It was less than a hundred years ago that children worked like slaves, that scores died in burning buildings where working people had been packed in under intolerable conditions. It was less than a hundred years ago that this nation operated largely on the assumption that the rich should get rich at the expense of the working poor, even if it killed the working poor. Government worked to help the rich man by making way for railroads, by providing them with land, by arranging for international trading—but government did very little for the worker. Yesterday we heard a lot about productivity and reindustrialization and trade labor as the stepbrother of Great Britain. But what we don't hear about, what we seem sometimes to be forgetting, are the coal miners who have choked to death to make their owners rich, working women in Southern textile mills who have been treated little better than animals, and the ugly exploitation of New York's sweatshops. We too soon forget the pain and injustice that were casually heaped upon millions of people, people who were destined from birth to struggle for survival, people who lived and died in poverty, working all the while. That was before the organized union movement.

The union movement was nothing more than an expression of basic decency and fairness. It was a movement that said that people who worked for a living because they had to—the people who fill the rows in the shift, who work in the factory, who serve the institutions of commerce and who deliver government services—should not be abused; rather, they should be dealt with fairly. They should be paid a decent wage, should be protected against accidents, should be provided for in their old age because they have earned it. In a more intelligent, fairer society, the union movement would have been unnecessary. But in fact, ever since Adam and Eve, human nature has needed to be coaxed into doing the right thing. And so we needed the union movement and we got it. Thank God for Samuel Gompers, William Green, David Dubinsky, Philip Murray, John L. Lewis, Walter Reuther, A. Philip Randolph and that generation of giants for that union movement. For the people of this state, for the families that have been kept intact, for the fairness and decency the union movement has brought to American society, thanks to all of you. I think it is right to remember how unions have been, but I think it is more than right. I think it is necessary today, because of the challenge that unions face. Let me have a union member describe it for you, a woman, a member of the UAW. She was interviewed on television about six months ago, and this is what she said. These are her words: "We used to be politically active. Then we got good contracts from the unions and we got a winter vacation and even a summer vacation. We got wall-to-wall carpeting and freezers and new cars. Then when new workers come on over the years, we're looking pretty good. We're in the middle class. We don't become politically active anymore with the union or with the government. We believed that Reagan was the guy who would protect what we had. We were wrong. Now we have to start waking up. We didn't get what we have from Reagan. We didn't get it by walking away from the unions or from political fights. We got it from tough unions that fought for what they wanted. Now we've got to wake up. There's a movement afoot in this land not just to knock the unions back. These people want to knock us out. All unions." This is what she said. I tell you, brothers and sisters, I am awake. I know you are, too. And together we can wake up this nation, and I intend to begin to do that in this state as governor.

My administration will come to be known as the administration of jobs and justice. I will work to provide every man and woman in this state with a decent opportunity to earn their own bread in dignity. And those who, because of the imperfections of our system, are not able to work, though they want to, will be treated with the respect and fairness that they're entitled to.

I'll propose an infrastructure bond issue to raise the money we need to rebuild our bridges and our tunnels and our highways. I'll push forward on Westway. I'll continue the work on the Convention Center and Battery Park that was begun by Governor Carey. We'll create centers of high technology around the state, like the ones we put in Rensselaer, to broaden our participation in the exciting prospects of high-tech work. We'll continue to pursue the idea of ICONN-Erie,[2] believing that a state that can build the Erie Canal and the Verrazano Bridge, the Albany Mall and the World Trade Center, need not shrink at this project, which could produce 60,000 jobs just by itself. And I refuse to believe that this great state that has unemployed steelworkers in Buffalo and 13 percent unemployed in Elmira—this great state that makes airplanes, this great state that makes bridges, this great state that makes skyscrapers that threaten the heavens and winds, this great state of the technology of Corning, of GE and of IBM—cannot make its own trains, buses and railroad cars. We have the labor. Lord knows, we have the labor. We have the skills. We have the capital, if we are smart enough to know how to use our pension funds. And we have the need. It was a disgrace and a failure of the worst kind to send those jobs away. And I repeat, it will not happen when I am governor. And so I'll make my administration one of jobs and justice, but I need your help. Not your neutrality. I need your help. The people who discovered this great land didn't do it by being neutral. The people who built our nation didn't do it by being neutral. The people who fought the goons and the greedy and unenlightened government to form your unions didn't do it by being neutral. And you won't survive by being neutral.

You cannot win this fight from the front row. You are going to have to fight as you always have, only harder. You are going to have to be heard. Ronald Reagan, Mayor Koch, the New Right, all ask the same question: what does labor want? We have to tell them clearly. We have to remind them that that's the same question they asked Samuel Gompers nearly a hundred years

[2]Island Complex Offshore New York/New Jersey. The concept is to connect the two states by constructing a deep-water port and island off the shores of New York and New Jersey using dirt from the construction of a larger-capacity canal (Erie) to carry Western coal and grain to Eastern ports and to Europe.

ago. We have to tell them that his answer is our answer, and this is what he said:

> We want more schoolhouses and fewer jails,
> we want more books and fewer arsenals,
> we want more learning and less vice,
> we want more constant work and less crime,
> we want more leisure and less greed,
> we want more justice and less revenge.

And that is what I want! Jobs and justice! That is what we want together. That is what we want together, and that is what we can achieve together, and that is why I need you in this fight with all your heart and all your soul, with all your spirit and all your strength. I want you with me, because when I win, you win! And when you win, we all win!

God bless you all.

Thank you, Chief Judge Desmond.

This is a beautiful celebration—of our state, of our superb system of government and of our extraordinary good fortune. I am grateful that we have been allowed to share it.

Permit me a special word of gratitude to three people:

—to the one most effective instrument of our success, who shares this inauguration with me, Matilda;

—to the man who has led this state for eight years and to whom I owe a special debt for having given me my first opportunity to serve the people of the state of New York, as secretary of state in 1975, Governor Hugh Carey;

—and to an institution among public officials, who cannot be with us physically today, but who has been with me from the beginning of what appeared then to be an improbable pursuit, a man of strength, stature and splendid style, the mayor of the city of Albany, Erastus Corning.

I would be less than honest if I did not admit to some small personal satisfaction at having won two elections—especially since I am all too familiar with what it feels like not to win. But I would be less than intelligent if I didn't recognize that the outcome was not so much a personal vindication as it was the judgment of the people of New York on the body of principles and programs which we advanced as the reason and justification for my candidacy.

Throughout the campaign, I spoke insistently on what we

believe our government must do over the next four years. I hope
the next four years will show that I did not speak idly or cynically.
We will go forward with the program of jobs and justice that I
described in the campaign and that I believe the people of this
state generally regard as a fair appraisal of what we need: a
criminal justice system that is a firmer, surer, more effective
vehicle of deterrence; a new emphasis on high technology,
agribusiness, domestic manufacturing; a responsible approach to
our fiscal difficulties; an infrastructure program that will rebuild
our state's physical strength while we put to work unemployed
New Yorkers; a continuing emphasis on educational excellence;
reformation of our system of regulating utilities; reorganization
of the operating agency for mass transit in the twelve counties
of our metropolitan New York region. We will go forward with
these and the other elements of our program for New York that
I have urged for all of this year.

Part of that program will be our message to Washington. We
will say to our President and the present administration that we
have no intention of using Washington as a scapegoat for all of
our failures and difficulties, or as an excuse for not doing for
ourselves, as a state, everything we can. On the other hand, we
will not allow the national administration to escape responsibility
for its policies. We will continue to point out what we believe
is the massive inequity of the new redistribution of national
wealth—a redistribution that moves our nation's resources from
the vulnerable Northeast and Midwest to the affluent or at least
less troubled parts of the nation. We will point out what we
believe is the cruelty and economic recklessness of the unemployment those policies produce, and the mistake of an excessive
multiplication of nuclear weapons that denies us the resources we
need to put people back to work and to lift others out of wheelchairs.

Because we meant what we said in the campaign, all of these
positions will be part of the flesh and blood—the programs and
policies—of this administration. You will see them described in
detail a few days from now in the State of the State message, and
again in the budget that will be presented to the legislature and
the people of the state.

For now, however, allow me to speak a few words about what
I hope will be the *soul* of this administration.

The philosophy of a government is the pattern revealed by the lines that connect hundreds of decisions government makes on a day-to-day basis. Over the course of our history, these lines have often meandered and formed unclear images. The last few years, however, have raised sharp and profound questions about government's purpose and role. These questions are being discussed at all levels and are operating to affect the policies that touch the lives of our people. In the debate, the Empire State's view of government's ultimate rationale will have special significance.

This is the way I see it: this state has always led the way in demonstrating government's best uses. Overall, it has pursued a course of progressive pragmatism. For more than fifty years, without dramatic deviation—whatever party happened to be in power—New York has proved that government can be a positive source for good. It still can be.

I believe government's basic purpose is to allow those blessed with talent to go as far as they can—on their own merits. But I believe that government also has an obligation to assist those who, for whatever inscrutable reason, have been left out by fate —the homeless, the infirm, the destitute—to help provide those necessary things which, through no fault of their own, they cannot provide for themselves.

Of course, we should have *only* the government we need. But we must insist on *all* the government we need. So, a technically balanced budget that fails to meet the reasonable needs of the middle class and poor would be the emblem of hypocrisy.

It has become popular in some quarters to argue that the principal function of government is to make instruments of war and to clear obstacles from the way of the strong. The rest—it is said—will happen automatically: the cream will rise to the top, whether the cream be well-endowed individuals or fortunate regions of the nation.

"Survival of the fittest" may be a good working description of the process of evolution; but a government of humans should elevate itself to a higher order, one which tries to fill the cruel gaps left by chance or by a wisdom we don't understand.

I would rather have laws written by Rabbi Hillel or Pope John Paul II—than by Darwin. I would rather live in a state that has chipped into the marble face of its Capitol these memorable words of the great Rabbi: "If I am not for myself—who is for me? And if I am for myself alone—what am I?" or heed the words of our great Pope: "Freedom and riches and strength bring responsibility. We cannot leave to the poor and the disadvantaged only the crumbs from the feast. Rather, we must treat the less fortunate as guests."

A society as blessed as ours should be able to find room at the table—shelter for the homeless, work for the idle, care for the elderly and infirm, and hope for the destitute. To demand less of our government or ourselves would be to evade our proper responsibility. At the very least, the government of this generation should be able to do for those who follow us what has been done for us.

And if my election proves anything, it proves how very much the system has been able to do for us.

Like all of us in this room today—and all of us in New York State except our Native American brothers and sisters—I am the offspring of immigrants. My parents came some sixty years ago from another part of the world, driven by deprivation, without funds, education or skills. When my mother arrived at Ellis Island, she was alone and afraid. She carried little more than a suitcase and a piece of paper with the address of her laborer husband who had preceded her here in search of work. She passed through all the small indignities visited on immigrants everywhere, in all ages. She was subjected to the hurried condescension of those who decide if others are good enough to be let in . . . or at least not quite bad enough to be kept out.

Like millions of others, my mother and father were provided with little other than a willingness to spend all their effort in honest toil. They asked only for the opportunity to work and to be protected in those moments when they would not be able to protect themselves. Thanks to a government that was wise enough to help them without stifling them, and strong enough to provide them with an opportunity to earn their own bread, they survived.

They remained a people of modest means. That they were able to build a family and live in dignity and see one of their children go from behind their little grocery store in South Jamaica, where he was born, to occupy the highest seat in the greatest state of the greatest nation in the only world we know is an ineffably beautiful tribute to the magnificence of this American democracy.

This is not a personal story. This is the story of all of us. What our imperfect but peerless system of government did for these two frightened immigrants from Europe, it has done for millions of others in different ways. That experience is a source of pride and gratitude. But it must be more. It must serve as a challenge to all of us, as we face the future.

The achievement of our past imposes upon us the obligation to do as much for those who come after us. It would be a desecration of our history to allow the difficulties of the moment —which pale when compared with those faced by our ancestors —to excuse our obligation to produce government that excels at doing what it is supposed to do.

We need not fear the challenge. Underlying everything I believe about our government is my unshakable conviction that it is good enough to do what must be done—and much more.

For all our present travail—the deficits; the stagnant economy; the hordes of homeless, unemployed and victimized; the loss of spirit and belief—for all of this, I believe we are wise enough to address our deficits without taxing ourselves into bankruptcy, strong enough to reconcile order with justice, brave enough to bring opportunity and hope to those who have neither.

We can—and we will—refuse to settle for survival, and certainly not just survival of the fittest! I believe we can balance our lives and our society even as we manage to balance our books.

We can—if those who today stand on platforms built by our forebears' pain and are warmed by the applause earned by their courage remember who we are and where we came from and what we have been taught. Those who made our history taught us above all things the idea of family. Mutuality. The sharing of benefits and burdens—fairly—for the good of all. It is an idea essential to our success.

And no family that favored its strong children—or that, in the name of evenhandedness, failed to help its vulnerable ones—

would be worthy of the name. And no state, or nation, that chooses to ignore its troubled regions and people, while watching others thrive, can call itself justified.

We must be the family of New York—feeling one another's pain; sharing one another's blessings, reasonably, equitably, honestly, fairly—irrespective of geography or race or political affiliation.

These things I pledge as I begin my term: that I have learned what our forebears had to teach; that if we do not succeed it will not be because we have divided one part of this state from the other or dealt unfairly with any person or region, or forgotten that we are a family. Nor will it be because we have failed to expend all the strength and effort that we might have.

This will be a government as hard-working and realistic as the thousands of families and businesses struggling to survive a national economy more distressed than at any time since the 1930s. I have no illusions about the difficulty of converting these noble aspirations into hard reality. It will be a fierce test of our resolve.

But if the risks we face are great, the resources we command are greater: a rich, good earth; water that ties us together, replenishes us, feeds our capacity to grow; an education system matched by few other states or nations; an intricate, irreplaceable weave of roads and rails; the world's largest banks, financial institutions, communications systems and markets.

And more than all of this, our marvelous people—the offspring of Native Americans, Africans, Europeans, Asians, people from the North and from the South, the children of those who refused to stop reaching, building and believing.

We are the sons and daughters of giants, and because we were born to their greatness, we are required to achieve. We begin to meet that obligation today—all of us together.

So, good people of the Empire State, I ask all of you—whatever your political beliefs, whatever your region, whatever you think of me as an individual—to help me keep the moving and awesome oath I just swore before you and before God.

Pray that we all see New York for the family that it is; that all of us sworn into office today give New York the leadership it deserves; that I might be the state's good servant and God's, too.

And Pop, wherever you are—and I think I know—for all the ceremony and the big house, and the pomp and circumstance, please don't let me forget.

Thank you and Happy New Year to all of us.

SUNDAY SERVICE, ST. JOHN THE DIVINE
NEW YORK CITY, NOVEMBER 27, 1983

As a Catholic, I am particularly honored to be invited here to this magnificent seat of the Protestant Episcopal Church of New York, one of the true architectural jewels of Christendom and one of the great houses of commitment, service and, therefore, worship.

I know that in ritual and theology my church and your church are close. They always have been. Two centuries ago, in fact, Benjamin Franklin described the differences this way: the Roman Church, he said, claims to be "infallible," while the Episcopal thinks of itself as "never in the wrong." Since Vatican II, we've grown even closer. The Archbishop of Canterbury has traveled to Rome to kneel at the tomb of Peter, and the Bishop of Rome has prayed in the mother church of the Episcopal faith. Each has spoken about the respective responsibility of their churches in the schism that divided us some four centuries ago.

Closer indeed. Recently, I spoke with a good friend who is a bishop in my Church. I mentioned the invitation I had to speak here today and asked him about the differences that still divide us. The Bishop thought a moment, then said, "If I'm not mistaken, the Episcopalians still don't have a second collection on Sundays."

But I haven't come here to talk about the ecumenical progress between Catholics and Episcopalians. You've asked me to speak this morning on "The Stewardship of Political Power." Or, as

Dean Morton[1] has written, on the "sacred dimension" that infuses and surrounds every human activity, even politics. This isn't an easy thing for me to do. I'm not a theologian. My grasp of the Bible is probably not much better than that of any ordinary lay person. And while I have a learned and accomplished biblical scholar and homilist on my staff—Rabbi Israel Mowshowitz—he parts theological company with me at the end of what we Christians call the Old Testament.

If, then, I'm to talk honestly and meaningfully about the idea of "stewardship" or "the sacred," it can't be from the perspective of a scholar or an exegete. It must be from my own experience—from the perspective of a person who struggles to be a believer, a person raised in the pre–Vatican II American Church, an immigrant Church of ethnic loyalties and theological certainties that were rarely questioned.

Ours was a Catholicism closer to the peasant roots of its practitioners than to the high intellectual traditions of Catholic theology and philosophy. We perceived the world then as a sort of cosmic basic training course, filled by God with obstacles and traps to weed out the recruits unfit for eventual service in the Heavenly Host. At this, God had been exceedingly successful: the obstacles were everywhere. Our fate on earth was to be "the poor banished children of Eve, mourning and weeping in this vale of tears," until by some combination of luck and grace and good works, we escaped final damnation.

I don't mean to belittle the Church of that time. Indeed, it was not the Church so much as it was we churchgoers. Our faith reflected the collective experience of people who through most of their history had little chance to concern themselves with helping the poor or healing the world's wounds. They *were* the poor. Their poverty and their endless—sometimes losing—struggle to feed themselves and hold their families together had varied little across the centuries.

But what I now understand is that, in those days, in our preoccupation with evil and temptation, we often put guilt before responsibility and we obscured a central part of Christian truth:

[1]The Very Reverend Parks Morton, dean of the Cathedral Church of St. John the Divine. St. John the Divine is the mother church of the Episcopal Diocese of New York.

that God did not intend this world only as a test of our purity but, rather, as an expression of his love. That we are meant to live actively, intensely, totally in this world and, in so doing, to make it better for all whom we can touch, no matter how remotely.

Many of us in the Church had to learn that lesson. The great Jesuit scientist and theologian Teilhard de Chardin was the first to teach us. He reoriented our theology and rewrote its language. His wonderful book *The Divine Milieu,* dedicated to "those who love this world," made negativism a sin.

What an extraordinary reaffirmation of Christian optimism. What a wonderful consolation to those of us who didn't want to think of the world as God's cruel challenge. Teilhard de Chardin glorified the world and everything in it. He said the whole universe—even the pain and imperfection we see—is sacred, every part of it touched and transformed by the Incarnation. Faith, he said, is not a call to escape the world but to embrace it. Creation isn't an elaborate testing ground but an invitation to join in the work of restoration and completion.

All together these exciting new articulations of the world's beauty helped an entire generation of Catholics to realize that salvation consisted of something more than simply escaping the pains of hell. We were challenged to have the faith that Paul speaks of in today's epistle, a faith that "knows what hour it is, how it is full time . . . to wake from sleep."

So for people like me, struggling to believe, my Catholic faith and the understanding it gives me of stewardship aren't a part of my politics. Rather, my politics is, as far as I can make it happen, an extension of this faith and the understanding. There is a paradox here, of course, one I must face daily and one every American who belongs to a religious faith must also face. In fact, it would be impossible to stand here as a Catholic governor—as one elected by Moslems and Sikhs and deists and animists and agnostics and atheists—and talk about politics and Christian stewardship without addressing this paradox.

The paradox was most recently raised in a letter I received on the executive order I issued banning discrimination against homosexuals in state government. The writer attacked what I had written. He took a stand on the executive order that most of us here today would disagree with. Yet the question he raises of religious belief and governmental action is a valid one. And, in one form or another, all of us who mix our faith and our politics—certainly those of us concerned about the stewardship of power—must be ready to answer it. In part, the letter says the following: "Governor Cuomo, you call yourself a Christian, yet how can you claim to be a Christian when you go out of your way to proclaim the right of people to be what is an abomination in the sight of God?"

The answer, I think, drives to the very heart of the question of where private morality ends and public policy begins—how I involve myself in the political life of a world broad enough to include people who don't believe all the things I believe about God and conduct. Am I obliged to seek to legislate my particular morality—in all of its exquisite detail—and if I fail, am I then required to surrender stewardship rather than risk hypocrisy?

The answer, I think, is reflected in the one foundation on which all of us as citizens must try to balance our political and religious commitments—the Constitution. Those who founded this nation knew that you *could* form a government that embodied the particular beliefs and moral taboos of one religion. They knew that choice was available to them. Indeed, at that time there was hardly a government in the world that operated otherwise. Catholic countries reflected Catholic values and did their best to stamp out or contain Protestantism. Protestant countries upheld their own values. Their laws forbade the Mass, and in some places, like the Dutch settlement at Nieuw Amsterdam, the law said that any Catholic priest discovered within its walls was to be hanged, drawn and quartered. And everywhere, as they'd been for centuries, the Jews were persecuted and forced to work and live under whole sets of legal disabilities. That was the world our Constitution was written in.

To secure religious peace, the Constitution demanded toleration. It said no group, not even a majority, has the right to force its religious views on any part of the community. It said that where matters of private morality are involved—belief or actions that don't impinge on other people or deprive them of their rights—the state has no right to intervene.

This neutrality didn't forbid Christians or Jews or Moslems to

be involved in politics. Just the opposite; by destroying the basis
for religious tests, by destroying the basis for making people's
beliefs and private lives a matter of government's concern, it
secured that involvement, ensured it, encouraged it. Our Constitution provides that there are areas the state has no business
intruding in, freedoms that are basic and inalienable. In creating
this common political ground, it created a place where we could
all stand—Episcopalians, Catholics, Jews, atheists—a place where
we could tolerate each other's differences and respect each
other's freedom.

Yet our Constitution isn't simply an invitation to selfishness,
for in it is also embodied a central truth of the Judeo-Christian
tradition—that is, a sense of the common good. It says, as the
Gospel says, that freedom isn't license; that liberty creates responsibility; that if we have been given freedom, it is to encourage us to pursue that common good.

And if the Constitution restricts the powers of the state in
order to save us from the temptation to judge and to persecute
others, it doesn't thereby deny the necessity of the shared commitments—to help one another—shared commitments that are
the basis for justice and mercy and human dignity and therefore
the basis, the most fundamental basis, of any religion that believes in a loving God.

There is, I think, a clear concept of stewardship in the Constitution. And the government it sets up is meant to embody that
stewardship.

I think my religion encourages me to be involved in government because it is very much a part of the world God so loves.
And I think that if I am given the burdens and the opportunities
of stewardship, my principal obligation is to use government not
to impose a universal oath of religious allegiance, or a form of
ritual, or even a life style, but to move us toward the shared
commitments that are basic to all forms of compassionate belief.

Until recently, most Americans accepted this proposition. It
was accepted that government was created among us—by us—
"to promote the general welfare," to protect our water and soil
and air from contamination, to secure decent care for those who
can't care for themselves—the sick, the indigent, the homeless,
the people in wheelchairs—to help people find the dignity of

work. Until recently, our history had been largely one of expanding that concept of stewardship, reaching out to include those once excluded—women, Blacks and other minorities.

But this belief in benevolent stewardship—in the commitment of each to the welfare of all, especially to the least among us—is today increasingly attacked and ridiculed and denied. There is a powerful move toward a new ethic for government, one that says, "God helps those whom God has helped, and if God has left you out, who are we to presume on his will by trying to help you?"

In a country as religious as ours, where over 90 percent of the people express a belief in God and a majority profess attachment to a formal religious faith, it is hard to understand how this denial of the compassionate heart of all the world's great faiths could succeed.

Yet it is succeeding. More money for bombs, less for babies. More help for the rich, more poor than ever.

And the success of this Darwinian view presents us with a choice: either we swim with the tide and accept the notion that the best way to help the unfortunate is to help the fortunate and then hope that personal charity will induce them voluntarily to take care of the rest of us, or we resist. We resist by affirming as our moral and political foundation the idea that we *are* our brother's keeper, all of us, as a people, as a *government*; that our responsibility to our brothers and our sisters is greater than any one of us and that it doesn't end when they are out of the individual reach of our hand or our charity or our love.

This is not a comfortable disposition, believing that as we express ourselves through our government, we have an obligation to love. It can haunt us. It can nag at us in moments of happiness and personal success, disturbing our sleep and giving us that sense of guilt and unworthiness that the modern age is so eager to deny. And it can accuse us—from the faces of the starving and the dispossessed and the wounded, faces that stare back at us from the front page of our newspapers, images from across the world that blink momentarily on our television screens.

I was homeless, it says, and you gave me theories of supply and demand.

I was imprisoned and silenced for justice's sake, and you washed the hands of my torturers.

I asked for bread, and you built the world's most sophisticated nuclear arsenal.

Yet, as people who claim Christ's name—who dare to call ourselves Christians—what choice do we really have but to hear that voice and to answer its challenge?

Teilhard de Chardin in just a few magnificent sentences captured everything I've tried to say here about this challenge of stewardship. Talking about our obligations to involve ourselves in the things of this world, he wrote: "We must try everything for Christ. . . . Jerusalem, lift up your head. Look at the immense crowds of those who build and those who seek. All over the world, men are toiling—in laboratories, in studios, in deserts, in factories—in the vast social crucible. The ferment that is taking place by their instrumentality in art and science and thought is happening for your sake. Open, then, your arms and your heart, like Christ your Lord, and welcome the waters, the flood and the sap of humanity. Accept it, this sap—for without its baptism, you will wither, without desire, like a flower out of water; and tend it, since, without your sun, it will disperse itself wildly in sterile shoots."

And Jesus, answering the question of a lawyer in language to be understood by all, said that the law and the prophets, their wisdom and vision and insight, their teaching about religious obligation and stewardship, were all contained in two commandments: "You shall love the Lord your God with all your heart, and with all your soul, and with all your mind. You shall love your neighbor as yourself."

That is the law, as simply as it can be expressed—for both the stewards and those in their charge, for both the governed and those who govern them, for all who look to Christ's mercy, wherever they might find themselves.

Thank you.

Index